世图版对外汉语教材系列

中高级汉语视听说教程

走进中国百姓生活

刘月华　　刘宪民　　李金玉　编著
Yuehua liu　Xianmin Liu　Jinyu Li

Reality Chinese

A Multi-skill Chinese Course
for Intermediate
and Advanced Students

世界图书出版公司
北京·广州·上海·西安

图书在版编目（CIP）数据

走进百姓生活＝A Spoken Chinese Course for Intermediate and Advanced Students：Reality Chinese/刘月华，刘宪民，李金玉编．
—北京：世界图书出版公司北京公司，2006.8
中高级汉语视听说教程
ISBN 7-5062-8195-3

Ⅰ．走...　　Ⅱ．①刘...　②刘...　③李...　　Ⅲ．汉语-视听说教学-对外汉语教学-教材　Ⅳ．H195.4

中国版本图书馆 CIP 数据核字（2006）第 068333 号

书　　名：走进中国百姓生活——中高级汉语视听说教程
编 著 者：刘月华　刘宪民　李金玉
责任编辑：杨艳慧
装帧设计：春天书装图文设计工作室
图片提供：AI（www. amyimages. com）　何浩（adjust. fotoky. com）　张世涛
出　　版：世界图书出版公司北京公司
发　　行：世界图书出版公司北京公司
　　　　　（北京朝内大街 137 号　邮编　100010　电话　64077922）
销　　售：各地新华书店和外文书店
印　　刷：北京世图印刷厂
开　　本：787×1092 毫米　1/16　印张：31
字　　数：524 千字
版　　次：2006 年 8 月第 1 版　2006 年 8 月第 1 次印刷
ISBN 7-5062-8195-3/H·916　　　　定　　价：180.00 元（含 5 张 DVD）

前　言

　　《中高级汉语视听说教程——走进中国百姓生活》取材于百集电视短剧《咱老百姓》，对象为具有中高级汉语水平的学生。本书可以作辅助教材，也可以作为听说教材独立使用。

　　我们都是在美国从事多年中文教学的教师，深感目前能使学生通过真实鲜活的汉语了解中国现实社会的视听材料十分匮缺。为此我们编了这部教材。

　　《咱老百姓》是一部优秀的百集电视短剧，每集30分钟。中国的电视连续剧很多，但是短剧可谓凤毛麟角。《咱老百姓》反映的是现代中国社会生活的方方面面以及人物百态。大部分故事真实有趣，语言生动活泼。本书从中选取了十个较有代表性的短剧。

　　《咱老百姓》，顾名思义，讲的是普通百姓的故事。剧中人物来自各行各业。本教材所选的电视剧主要反映近年来中国城市的社会生活：工厂工人由面临下岗到下海成为个体户；城市里的钟点工（一种按钟点付钱的家庭服务人员）的工作与生活；服刑人员家属的心态；发生在几个足球迷身边的故事；大学职称评定中出现的良心问题；还有夫妻感情，家庭中的亲情，邻里之间的友情等等。

　　本教材所选短剧大部分题材源于百姓再普通不过的日常生活，因此有很多口语性很强的词语。为了帮助学生理解，我们对此类词语加以注释，给出例句，对用法、使用的场合也进行了一些说明。应该指出，口语性极强的词语，使用场合十分受限制，不能随意乱用，否则会不得体，甚至会闹笑话。这一点在教学过程中，教师应特别向学生说明。《电梯上的故事》反映的是年轻知识分子的生活，《良心问题》反映的是大学教授的事情，这两个短剧成语多，书面语所占的比重也较大，对此我们也都作了较为详细的解释。

　　如何把语言教学与文化教学结合起来，一直是中文教学界重视的问题。我们不主张在初、中级教材中直接讲授中国文化知识。即使在高级阶段，文化知识的内容也不宜过多。但语言是文化的载体，文化渗入于语言材料之中。我们选择的这些短剧都有着深广的文化内涵。对学生来说，陌生、有趣的文化现象随处可见。比如，这些故事反映了中国家庭成员、工作单位的同事，以及社会上不同关系的人之间如何相处，从中可以了解中国人对上述种种人际关系的看法。可以说本教材提供了语言和文化教学相结合的一个新的切入点。

《咱老百姓》每个短剧 30 分钟，长度也比较适合课堂教学。

本教材每课包括课文、生词、注释、语法、练习等五部分。练习中又包括听、说、读、写几个方面。在使用本书时，老师可以根据学习对象与需要对课本的内容决定取舍。

本书教学对象定位于具有中、高级汉语水平的学生，生词基本上选的是汉语水平考试（HSK）词汇大纲丙级以上的词，适量收录了一些丙级以下的词。

本书编者分工如下：刘月华负责全书策划和中文部分（包括"导读"、"注释"、"语法"、"生词解释"，以及练习的定稿）；刘宪民、李金玉分别负责第一、三、四、五、六课和第二、七、八、九、十课的英文部分，以及练习的编写。

美国戴维斯加州大学的储诚志教授用中文教学软件《中文助教》为我们挑选生词，既准确又节省了我们很多时间。世界图书出版公司北京公司在出版这部教材的过程中，帮助我们解决了很多困难，在此我们一并表示感谢。

刘月华　刘宪民　李金玉
2006 年 2 月于美国加州圣地亚哥

PREFACE

This textbook is based on the 100-episode TV series *We Common People* (《咱老百姓》). It is designed for intermediate and advanced Chinese learners. This text can be used as the primary textbook for a listening/speaking course or a supplementary textbook for a comprehensive course.

Having taught Chinese at universities in the United States for many years, we were often frustrated by the fact that our students, after studying the language for several years, still feel awkward communicating with native speakers and still have considerable difficulties understanding Chinese movies and television. They are able to form a sophisticated formal sentence in Chinese, but are often at a complete loss when they encounter a common popular vocabulary or a colloquial expression. They did not have much opportunity to learn practical idiomatic/colloquial expressions. Therefore, we were convinced that there was a great demand for audio—visual teaching materials that can help students learn about current Chinese society through practical, authentic and living language. Hence this textbook.

We Common People is an outstanding TV series consisting of 100 episodes, each of which lasts thirty minutes. There are numerous TV series produced in China, yet *We Common People* is among the few that comprise short and self-contained episodes. Most of the episodes are realistic and appealing, featuring vivacious dialogues. They reflect different aspects of contemporary Chinese society and the lives of various types of people. The ten episodes selected here are among the most representative.

As suggested by the title, *We Common People* tells stories of ordinary people from all walks of life. The ten episodes in this textbook mirror urban life in today's China: the metamorphosis of an unemployed factory worker into a successful business owner; the life and work of an hourly-paid domestic helper; the turbulent emotions of a prisoner's relatives; the story of a group of soccer fans; the sense of guilt of some university professors at the time of their promotion review; the love and affection among family members; and the friendship and compassion between neighbors.

Since the episodes here reflect the most commonplace aspects of everyday life, they involve a significant number of colloquial expressions, for which we provide notes and examples in order to enhance students' understanding. In addition, we also explain the contexts for such expressions in each episode. It should be noted that some colloquial apressions are only applicable in certain situations and must be used when appropriate. If not used in the right context, misunderstanding or awkwardness can frequently occur. Thus, the instructor needs to alert the students to the proper usage of these expressions. In *The Elevator Incident* (《电梯上的故事》), which presents the life of a group of young intellectuals, and *A Matter of Conscience* (《良心问题》), which depicts a number of university professors, the language is more formal with quite a few four-character idioms. Hence, we give more detailed explanations for these two episodes.

How to combine language instruction with culture studies has long been an issue of debate in the Chinese teaching field. We do not advocate teaching Chinese culture directly to beginning and intermediate language learners. Nor do we encourage excessive use of cultural material in the language textbooks for advanced learners. However, language is a carrier of culture, and culture permeates language. The chosen episodes in this textbook contain deep cultural meanings. They demonstrate, for instance, how the Chinese interact with each other in their families, at the workplace, and with people of different social status. This textbook provides a new platform for combining Chinese language teaching with the introduction of Chinese culture. Moreover, thanks to the manageable length of each episode, it is particularly suitable for classroom teaching.

Each chapter of the textbook consists of five components: the main text, vocabulary list, notes, grammar explanations, and exercises in listening, speaking, reading, and writing. The instructor can use the contents selectively based on the students' needs.

Since this textbook is intended for students of the intermediate to advanced levels, the vast majority of the vocabulary is at, or above, the C level of the vocabulary guideline designated for HSK.

The division of labor among the compilers was as follows: Yuehua Liu was the one that initiated the project, wrote the Chinese portions of the book (including those in the introduction, annotations, grammar, and vocabulary explanations), and finalized the exercises; while Xianmin Liu and Jinyu Li were responsible, respectively, for the English portions and exercises in chapters 1, 3, 4, 5, 6 and chapters 2, 7, 8, 9, 10.

We would like to express our utmost gratitude to Professor Chengzhi Chu of the University of California-Davis, who used his newly developed software Chinese TA to help us sift through the texts and pick out new vocabulary in a very accurate and efficient manner. We are also deeply thankful to the very capable editors at the World Publishing Company—Beijing Branch, who patiently and diligently assisted us in overcoming many obstacles in bringing this book into being.

Yuehua Liu, Xianmin Liu, Jinyu Li

San Diego, California

February, 2006

《咱老百姓》主题歌
The Theme Song of *We Common people*

词性及用法缩写表　Abbreviations for Part of Speech

adj.	Adjective	形容词
adv.	Adverb	副词
modal.	Modal verb	能愿动词
conj.	Conjunction	连词
interj.	Interjection	叹词
m.	Measure word	量词
n.	Noun	名词
N.	Noun	专有名词
num.	Numerals	数词
ono.	Onomatopoeia	象声词
part.	Particle	助词
pron.	Pronoun	代词
prep.	Preposition	介词
t.	Time word	时间词
v.	Verb	动词
vc.	Verb plus complement	动补结构
vo.	Verb plus object	动宾结构
col.	Colloquialism	口语用法

目 录

第一课 项 链

The Necklace

导 读：

　　中国实行市场经济以后，一些在国有企业工作的人工资较低，生活不太宽裕。但是因为国有企业的工资是有保障的，所以开始人们还很难下决心辞掉工作。后来，随着国有企业与私营企业收入差距的不断加大，有些人就开始丢掉"铁饭碗"，"下海"经商。他们有的开饭馆，有的卖衣服，有的开出租汽车……出现了大批"个体户"。他们当中不少人的生活因此有了明显改善，甚至有人成为私营企业家。本剧就是写一个"下海"的工人由穷变富的故事。

　　故事中还特别表现了这个家庭中夫妻、母子、婆媳之间的种种感情。

Introduction：

After China adopted the new market economy, some workers in government-owned enterprises saw themselves earning less money and having lower living standards than non-government workers. Because all government employees had a secure job, it was very difficult for them to make up their minds to quit their jobs for better-paid offers in the private sector. As the income of those working in the private sector drastically exceeded that of a government job, some government employees started giving up their "iron rice bowl" (secured job) to become individual businessmen. This is called "the jump into the ocean" (starting your own businesses by taking a risk). Some of these people opened restaurants; others started

clothing stores or became taxi drivers..., Many of them have prospered and raised their living standards; some of them are so successful that they have become entrepreneurs.

The necklace tells such a story of a worker who quit his job at a government-owned factory and opened his own restaurant, and thus became wealthy. As the story unfolds, it depicts the changes of the family's economic status as well as the love and affection among the family members—husband and wife, mother and son, daughter-in-law and mother-in-law.

主要人物（Main Characters）

秀贞	Xiùzhēn	Xiuzhen，a female factory worker
李建强（秀贞的丈夫）	Lǐ Jiànqiáng	Xiuzhen's husband
牛牛（秀贞的儿子）	Niúniu	nickname (Xiuzhen's son)
奶奶（牛牛的奶奶）	nǎinai	Niuniu's grandmother
吴姐（秀贞的同事）	Wú jiě	Sister Wu，Xiuzhen's co-worker
叶子（秀贞的同事）	Yèzi	Xiuzhen's co-worker
小老板	xiǎo lǎobǎn	a shop owner
小吃店经理	xiǎochīdiàn jīnglǐ	a small restaurant owner/manager
女店员	nǚ diànyuán	a saleswoman
东子	Dōngzi	a friend of Xiuzhen's husband

吴　姐：我有金项链。现在叶子**项链**儿丢了，我知道是怎么回事啊？

叶　子：算了、算了。都找着了，别说了。

秀　贞：你凭什么说是我拿的？你拿出**证据**来。你以为你比人们多点儿钱，就可以**随口胡说**？小心我告你**诬陷**罪！

吴　姐：谁说你啦？你**揽**什么**茬**儿[N1]？是不是**心虚**啊？

叶　子：得了、得了。都找到啦，别再说了。

秀　贞：她没凭没据，就说我拿了。这不是**血口喷人**吗？

项链儿	xiàngliànr	n.	necklace
证据	zhèngjù	n.	evidence; proof
随口	suíkǒu	adv.	(speak) thoughtlessly; blurt out (whatever comes into one's head)
胡说	húshuō	v./n.	talk nonsense; nonsense
诬陷	wūxiàn	v.	frame a case against; frame someone
罪	zuì	n.	crime; guilt
揽茬儿	lǎn chár	vo.	take upon oneself
心虚	xīnxū	adj.	lack in self-confidence; have a guilty conscience
血口喷人	xuè kǒu pēn rén		make unfounded and malicious attacks upon sb.；slander

吴　姐：我没说你拿。我说我有金项链儿，我没拿。

秀　贞：那我没有项链儿，就是我拿了？

吴　姐：我可没那么说！

秀　贞：那你还能怎么说呀？这屋里就咱们三个人，你说你这话是什么意思？

吴　姐：没什么意思。

叶　子：行了、行了，该**交班**儿了，赶快走。丢了**饭碗**[N2]，别说我没**提醒**你们俩。

吴　姐：哼，交班儿喽！

秀　贞：牛牛，作业做完了没有？

牛　牛：做完了、做完了。

秀　贞：快点儿，该睡了。牛牛，先把奶奶的洗脚水给**倒**了。

交班儿	jiāobānr	vo.	switch shifts
饭碗	fànwǎn	n.	(col.) job; means of livelihood; rice bowl
提醒	tíxǐng	v.	remind; warn
倒	dào	v.	pour; dump

牛　牛：哎！

秀　贞：妈，将来咱们有了钱呐，一定给您买部**轮椅**，**推**着您**到处**转。

奶　奶：买什么轮椅呀？咱要真有钱了呀，先给咱**孙子**买个新书包、买双新鞋，我看着更高兴。

秀　贞：**亏**不了您孙子[N3]的。

奶　奶：本来我身体不好，够**拖累**你们的了[G1]。别再为[G2]我花钱了。

秀　贞：您说什么呢。快睡了，啊。牛牛……

牛　牛：妈，咱家什么时候有钱啊？

奶　奶：不许问这个。快睡觉吧，啊。牛牛，**刷牙**了没有？

牛　牛：刷了。

秀　贞：好，**乖**孩子。牛牛，明天想吃什么呀？

牛　牛：牛奶饼干。

秀　贞：**噢**，没问题。晚上别**缠**着奶奶讲**故事**啊。

奶　奶：不许看**小人ㄦ书**。快睡了啊。

秀　贞：妈，有事ㄦ叫我啊。

奶　奶：哎。

秀　贞：你说你**娶**了个多么**物美价廉**的老婆，不要吃、不要穿，还把你**伺候**得像个**爷**！你听到我说话没有？

轮椅	lúnyǐ	n.	wheelchair
推	tuī	v.	push
到处	dàochù	adv.	about; everywhere
转	zhuàn	v.	move around
孙子	sūnzi	n.	grandson
亏	kuī	v.	treat unfairly
拖累	tuōlěi	v.	burden; be a burden (to sb.)
刷牙	shuā yá	vo.	brush teeth
乖	guāi	adj.	(of a child) obedient; well-behaved
噢	ō	interj.	(of surprised understanding or awareness) Oh
缠	chán	v.	pester; trouble
故事	gùshi	n.	story
小人ㄦ书	xiǎorénrshū	n.	picture books (for children)
娶	qǔ	v.	marry (a woman); take (a wife)
物美价廉	wù měi jià lián		excellent (goods) at modest prices
老婆	lǎopo	n.	wife; old woman
伺候	cìhou	v.	wait upon sb.; serve
爷	yé	n.	老太爷, master; ancestor

李建强：得，这**隔段时间**呀，就得**表扬**和**自我表扬**一次。你说又没人跟你**抢功**。真是的！说吧，谁又**招**你生气了？

秀　贞：李建强，你说你**对得起**^{G3}我不？跟你八九年了，一件**首饰**也没买给我，让我在**姐妹**面前都抬不起头！

李建强：这……你**戴**那**玩意**儿干吗呀？**俗了吧唧的**^{G4}，俗不俗啊。

秀　贞：你少**甩风凉话**！我就**俗气**，我就好俗气。你得让我俗气得起啊！

李建强：呵，想俗啊？那，给你**出个主意**：买一个**镀金**的，那玩意儿跟真的差不多，物美价廉，你说丢了吧，还不生气。再买一个，没什么钱^{G5}，是不是？

秀　贞：你这**奸商**，你**安的什么心**啊你？你**嫌**我在外面丢的脸还不够啊？你……你还让我去**现眼**？

隔（一）段时间	gé(yí)duàn shíjiān		once in a while
表扬	biǎoyáng	v.	praise
自我表扬	zìwǒ biǎoyáng		自己表扬自己, self-praise
抢功	qiǎng gōng	v.	steal (other's) credit
招	zhāo	v.	provoke sb.
对得起	duì de qǐ	vc.	be fair (to sb.) (as used in this story)
首饰	shǒu·shì①	n.	jewelry
姐妹	jiěmèi	n.	female co-workers (as used in this story); sisters
戴	dài	v.	put on (or wear) sth. on the head, face, arm, etc.
玩意儿	wányìr	n.	(col.) thing
干吗	gànmá		(col.) 干什么, why
俗了吧唧的	sú le bājī de		(see grammar note 4)
甩	shuǎi	v.	toss out (comments)
风凉话	fēngliánghuà	n.	sarcastic remarks
俗气	súqi	adj.	tacky
出主意	chū zhǔyi	vo.	offer an idea or a solution
镀金	dùjīn	adj.	gold-plating; gilding
奸商	jiānshāng	n.	unscrupulous merchant
安的什么心	ān de shénme xīn		What evil intent do you have in mind?
嫌	xián	v.	(col.) 觉得 (as used in this story)
现眼	xiànyǎn	v.	lose face; make a fool of oneself

① 既可读轻声，也可读原调的字，注音时上标调号，注音前再加圆点，下同。

李建强：妈，妈睡了。哎，跟你商量件事儿，你说我们那厂，**半死不活**^{N4}的，**整天**。我要**吊**非得吊死在那儿？我决定不在那儿干了，我自己找点儿事儿。

秀　贞：你能干什么事儿啊？

李建强：哎，我跟你说啊，你说咱们**这片儿**，要买个什么**早点**呀什么东西，得跑大街上**超市**去买，特别不方便。就咱们这片儿，开个小饭馆儿，特别地合适。东子给我**联系**了一家，他**哥们儿**，**门面房**。这个**价钱**呢，开个小饭店儿也合适。你说咱们干不干？

秀　贞：不干！咱家可**赔不起**。你妈治病要钱的，你拿什么做**本钱**？

李建强：嘿，我要有钱，你说咱们干不干？

秀　贞：不干！咱家跟别人家不一样，**折腾**不起。哎，你真有钱呀？

李建强：嘿嘿，你**少来这套**。你这一**温柔**啊，你这肯定就是使**美人儿计**。肯定让我……你这是**诱供**！**得得得**，我告诉你、告诉你。我不是给东子联系上事儿吗^①？人家**成了**，给了我 5000 块钱的**劳务**费。

半死不活	bàn sǐ bù huó		half-dead; more dead than alive
整天	zhěng tiān	adv.	all day long; all the time
吊	diào	v.	hang
这片儿	zhè piànr		this area (即 this neighborhood)
早点	zǎodiǎn	n.	breakfast; morning snack
超市	chāoshì	n.	(超级市场) abbreviation for supermarket
联系	liánxì	v.	make connection with
哥们儿	gēmenr	n.	buddy; guy
门面房	ménmianfáng	n.	a shop on the street (facing the street)
价钱	jià·qián	n.	price
赔不起	péi bu qǐ	vc.	cannot afford to lose money
本钱	běn·qián	n.	principal (used to gain or pursue profit, gamble, etc.)
折腾	zhēteng	v.	spend freely; take financial risks (as used in this context)
少来这套	shǎo lái zhè tào		(col.) stop doing this; drop the act
温柔	wēnróu	adj.	gentle; tender; feminine
美人儿计	měirénr jì	n.	sex-trap; sexual entrapment
诱供	yòu gòng	vo.	trap a person into confession
得得得	dé dé dé		(col.) alright, alright, alright
成了	chéng le		(col.) (sb.) got it! succeed
劳务	láowù	n.	labor and service

① 这个句子应该是："我不是给东子联系事儿吗？"，不应该有结果补语"上"。

秀　　贞：5000? 那你给我买条项链儿! 我要气死我们商场那个吴姐。她狗眼看
人低儿[N5]呀!

李建强：你跟她**较什么劲**呐? 她戴那**没准儿**就是**假的**呢。再说了，这钱买了项
链儿，不成了**死钱**了吗?

秀　　贞：我就知道你心里没我! 你老婆在外面**受了人家的气**，你就那么不当回
事儿啊? 跟你这么多年了，我要过什么呀?

李建强：行行行，不就是项链儿吗? 得得，明天买一条!

秀　　贞：你明知道你就算要买，我也**舍不得**要的，你就不能**痛痛快快**地答应
啊? 死人! **哄哄嘴**不会呀?

李建强：好，哄哄你。答滴滴……回头回头回头。滴滴滴，回头喽……

较劲	jiào jìn	vo.	(col.) compete
没准儿	méizhǔnr		(col.)说不定，perhaps；probably
假的	jiǎde	adj.	fake
死钱	sǐ qián	n.	money that you cannot use for other purposes
受气	shòu qì	vo.	be bullied；suffer wrong
舍不得	shě bu de	vc.	grudge (money)；hate to spend (money)
痛痛快快	tòng tong kuài kuài	adv.	joyfully；delightedly
答应	dāying	v.	agree；comply with
哄嘴	hǒng zuǐ	vo.	say sth. sweet；sweet talk

注释 Notes

1. **"揽什么茬儿"**：意思是"揽什么事"，"揽"的意思是"拉到自己这边"，整个句子的意思是"你为什么把事情（责任）拉到自己身上？"

   "揽什么茬儿" is the same as "揽什么事", meaning "why take the blame?" "揽" literally means to take something upon oneself. The whole sentence says "why would you take the blame for something you didn't do?

2. **"丢了饭碗"**：失去了工作。

   To lose one's job.

3. **"亏"**：意思是"亏待"。"亏不了您孙子"的意思是"不会亏待您孙子。"

   "亏（待）" means to treat someone poorly or unfairly. "亏不了您孙子" means your grandson will be well taken care of.

4. **"半死不活的"**：形容没有生气。

   "哎，我跟你商量件事儿，你说我们那个厂，半死不活的，整天。我要吊非要吊死在那儿？"在这个句子里，"我要吊非要吊死在那儿？"是反问句，意思是：如果我想要上吊，也不应该在那儿吊死，应该换一个地方。整个句子的意思是：

   我跟你商量一件事儿，我们那个厂没有一点发展前途（甚至可能快倒闭了），我应该找一个更好的地方（换一个工作）。

   "Ah, I'd like to discuss something with you. You know, our factory is doing really poorly now. If I stick with it, I'd be going to the dead end with it. (I'd better change my job before it shuts down)."

   "半死不活的" means lack of life or half-dead. In this context, however, it means that the factory is losing money, or doing badly. "我要吊非要吊死在那儿" literally means "If I have to die (by hanging myself), why do I have to do it at this specific place?" By using this expression, Jianqiang is telling his wife that his factory is not making money at all, or worse, is about to shut down, so he must leave his factory and find some opportunities somewhere else.

5. **"狗眼看人低"**：字面意思是"狗眼睛看人时，会把人看得很矮"。比喻低俗

的人或势利小人把别人也看得很低下。

The literal meaning of this expression is that if one viewed others from the position of a dog, he/she then would consider others very low due to his/her own lower perspective. This expression is used to indicate that in the eye of a mean person, there are no noble-minded people in the world. What the speaker is trying to say here is if one looks down upon other people, it is because he/she has a mean or indecent personality.

语法 Grammar Notes

1. **"够……的了"**：**"够"** 在这里的意思是：达到某种程度。**"够……的了"** 的意思是 "这样已经很……，（你不要［再］……"）。

   "够" in the pattern of **"够……的了"** means that a situation (usually expressed by a stative verb) has reached a certain degree or extent. The whole sentence says that "it is... enough, and you don't need to... any more."

   （1）本来我身体不好，够拖累你们的了。别再为我花钱了。

   I have already burdened you enough with my poor health. Please don't spend money on me any more.

   （2）这所学校够有名的了，你不要再换学校了。

   This school is famous enough, don't switch schools any more.

   （3）你的薪水够多的了，不要找老板讨价还价了。

   Your salary is high enough, don't go bargaining with your boss.

2. **"为……"**（介词）：引进动作的受益者。

   "为" is a preposition that is usually followed by a prepositional object. The prepositional phrase means "on someone's behalf", "or for someone's sake".

   （1）别再为我花钱了。

   Don't spend any more money on me.

   （2）你不要为他辩护，他肯定犯了罪。

   Don't try to defend him—he has certainly committed a crime.

   （3）我们都为你担心，怕你回不来了。

   We are all concerned and worried that you cannot make it back home.

3. **"V 不起"**：补语 "不起" 是 "没有时间或经济能力做某事的意思"。

   "V 得起"：补语 "得起" 是 "有时间或经济能力做某事的意思"。

   "V 不起" has the connotation of not being able to afford the time or money to do something.

   "V 得起" means being able to afford the time or money to do something.

   （1）你少甩风凉话！我就俗气，我就好俗气。你得让我俗气得起啊！

   这句话的意思是：你别讽刺我！我就是俗气。我就是喜欢俗气。（虽然

俗气不好，可是）你能让我有钱俗气吗？（你能给我钱让我俗气吗？）

Quit the sarcasm! Yes, I am following the trend, and I like following the trend (even if it is not a good thing). The problem is—whether you can afford to let me do that or not!

(2) 咱家跟别人家不一样，折腾不起。

这句话的意思是：咱们家跟别人家不一样，没有钱折腾。"折腾"在这里的意思是"胡闹"，秀贞指的是李建强不安心在工厂工作，而要冒险做生意。

Our family is not as rich as others, so we don't have money to lose.

"折腾" in this sentence means to mess things up or to make trouble. By using this term, Xiu Zhen expresses her concern about Jianqiang's plan of quitting his job in the factory and taking the risk of starting his own business.

(3) 退了吧，啊？咱家要得起这个吗？

这句话的意思是：退了吧，咱们家有钱要这个吗？

本课还有几个"V 得起"：

The meaning of this sentence is: "Let's return the necklace. We can't really afford it." There are several phrases involving "V 得/不起" in this lesson, which are provided below:

(4) 你说你对得起我不？"Do you think I deserve this treatment?" 这是个反问句，整句的意思是"你对不起我。"这句话中的"对不起"的意思是"对人有愧"。（本剧第三部分有一句："你说，我妈要是出点儿什么事儿，我对得住谁呀我？"这里的"对不住"跟"对不起"意思基本一样。）

The expression "对不起" here means to let down someone, or to fail to meet someone's expectations. The meaning of it is quite similar to "having a guilty conscience towards someone for not treating someone well enough ("对人有愧"). "对不起" here has the same connotation as "对不住", as in the sentence "你说，我妈要是出点儿什么事儿，我对得住谁呀我？" Notice that this "你对得起我不？" is a rhetorical sentence, which can be interpreted as an affirmative sentence with this emphasized tone: 你对不起我!

(5) 跟你八九年了，一件首饰也没买给我，让我在姐妹面前都抬不起头！

I've been married to you for eight to nine years; you haven't even bought me any jewelry. I feel so embarrassed in front of my co-workers/girlfriends.

"抬不起头"在这里的意思是：因为没有钱，买不起项链，在姐妹们面前没有面子。见《心锁》第四部分注释 2。

The expression "抬不起头" means feeling embarrassed or losing face in front of other people since the speaker cannot afford to buy a necklace. (See note 2 in part 4 of《心锁》)

4. **"俗了吧唧的"**：有些形容词后可以加上"吧唧的"，含有不喜欢、厌恶的意思。再如"湿了吧唧的"、"傻了吧唧的"、"穷了吧唧的"、"酸了吧唧的"等等。

"吧唧的" can be attached to some adjectives to mean "pretty ADJ/rather ADJ", with some negative connotation. It is used to express the feeling of dislike or disgust. For example, "湿了吧唧的"（pretty wet），"傻了吧唧的"（pretty silly），"穷了吧唧的"（rather poor），"酸了吧唧的" （rather sour），etc.

5. **"没什么钱"**："没什么钱"意思是"钱很少"。再如：

"没什么钱" means to have very little or hardly any money. For example：

（1）这个商店没什么东西。意思是"这个商店的东西不多/很少。"

This store has hardly anything.

（2）今天公园里没什么人。意思是"公园里人很少。"

There are very few people in the park.

〔没什么 + N（oun）〕means " to have no N or to have hardly any N". "没什么钱" indicates "having little money or hardly any money." "没什么东西" means "hardly anything" or "there is nothing", and "没什么人" means "hardly any people".

练习 Exercises

■ 一、口语练习 Oral Practice

（一）回答问题 Answer the following questions

1. 秀贞跟吴姐因为什么事情吵架？
2. 你认为秀贞该不该为吴姐的话生气？
3. 举例谈一下秀贞家的经济状况。
4. 根据你的理解，秀贞是一位什么样的妇女？请用实例说明。
5. 秀贞家都有什么人？秀贞跟她丈夫李建强的关系怎样？跟她婆婆的关系怎样？请用实例说明。
6. 李建强在哪儿工作？他对他的工作满意吗？
7. 李建强想做什么工作？
8. 秀贞为什么一定要让她丈夫给她买项链？

（二）角色扮演 Role Play

两人一组作对话，一人扮演秀贞，一人扮演秀贞的丈夫。秀贞一定要买一条项链，但丈夫认为秀贞跟别人比很俗气。两人为此争吵起来。争吵的结果如何，由对话双方自己决定。对话中请用以下词语。

Make a dialogue in pairs. One acts as Xiuzhen, and the other one acts as Xiuzhen's husband. Xiuzhen insists on buying a necklace for herself, but her husband thinks that it is tasteless to try to compare herself with others, and try to get what others have. In the argument, both parties try to convince each other. What is the result? The speakers decide. The dialogue should incorporate the items provided below.

1. 抬不起头	2. 受气	3. 俗气	4. 舍不得
5. 要不然	6. 折腾不起	7. 物美价廉	8. 伺候

■ 二、书写练习 Written Exercises

（一）用"Ｖ不起／Ｖ得起"改写下列句子中的画线部分 Replace the under-lined part with "Ｖ不起／Ｖ得起"

1．（在商店）

甲：这件大衣样子不错，你穿一定好看。

乙：<u>我现在没有钱买</u>，等（我）有了钱再说吧！

2．甲：你这辆车都开了好几年了，不想换一辆新的吗？

乙：我最近刚买了一台新电脑，现在<u>没有钱换车</u>。以后再说吧。

3．甲：这两天商店的东西都在打折，咱俩去逛逛街吧！

乙：今天我可<u>没时间陪你</u>，我还得准备下个星期的考试呢！

4．甲：晚上去看足球赛吗？

乙：票那么贵，<u>没有钱（去）看</u>，还是在家看电视吧！

（二）作文 Composition

写一篇 200～300 字的课文大意，至少要用下列词语中的 5 个。

Write a summary of this section containing 200～300 Chinese characters. Your summary must involve at least five of the following items.

1. 抬不起头	2. 受气	3. 俗气	4. 舍不得
5. 要不然	6. 折腾不起	7. 物美价廉	8. 伺候

李建强：哎，谢谢，您给我拿这个。这个多少钱？

女店员：1200。

李建强：这……它怎么能看出是**纯金**的还是镀金的？

女店员：这里卖的**绝对**是纯金的。如果不是……您可以拿去**检测**。如果不是纯金的呢，我们可以**加倍赔偿**您。

李建强：噢，这不用**机器**能看出来吗？

女店员：哟，那我们就**说不准**了。

李建强：40！40 我就要一条。

小老板：40？40 我赔了。

李建强：这不成。我就出 40 块钱，这要不然就算了。

小老板：好了、好了，给你了。唉，先生真能**砍价钱**^{N1}啊！

李建强：**有首饰盒**吗？

小老板：哎，有。不过得**单**买，这个。哎，您看。

李建强：这不行啊。有没有好的？

小老板：有！这个可贵啊，20 一个。

李建强：妈，你**没事**儿吧？

店员	diànyuán	n.	shop assistant
纯金	chúnjīn	n.	pure gold
绝对	juéduì	adv.	absolutely
检测	jiǎncè	v.	test; examine; check up
加倍	jiābèi	adv.	double
赔偿	péicháng	v.	compensate; pay for indemnity
机器	jī·qì	n.	machine
说不准	shuō bu zhǔn	vc.	(col.) unsure; uncertain
砍	kǎn	v.	cut or reduce（price）
首饰盒	shǒushì hé	n.	jewelry box
单	dān	adv.	separately
没事(儿)吧	méi shì(r) ba	(col.)	Are you all right?

奶　奶：没事儿。

李建强：你要热啊，你就开**电扇**，啊。别老舍不得那几个电。

奶　奶：哎，行了。

秀　贞：金项链儿！这么漂亮！给我的吗？

李建强：喜欢吗？

秀　贞：假的吧？

李建强：假的？这别**冤枉**人呀！你看见没有？这盒儿多**精致**啊！一看就**上档次**[N2]。假的？860呢。不，你不愿意要我们**退**了。

秀　贞：怎么样？漂亮吗？

李建强：**开玩笑**！纯金的，这是[G1]。

秀　贞：我是说我戴上之后，我漂亮吗？

李建强：嗨，漂亮漂亮。那是，我喜欢谁呀？

电扇	diànshàn	n.	electric fan
冤枉	yuānwang	v.	treat (someone) unfairly; wrong (someone)
精致	jīngzhì	adj.	exquisite; delicate
上档次	shàng dàngcì		high-quality
退	tuì	v.	return; send back
开玩笑	kāi wánxiào	vo.	make a joke; break a jest

秀　贞：也别说，你**媳妇**儿当年也是这**胡同**里的一**枝**花。哎，真 860 啊？

李建强：这，哪还能骗你呀？这个。

秀　贞：这么贵！哎，没有再便宜点儿的了？哎，**赶明**儿咱们去换条更便宜点儿的。

李建强：得得得，省省吧。这换什么换^{G2}？丢不**丢人**呐？这戴着不挺好的吗？

秀　贞：其实我也不是特别喜欢这东西。我这也就是**好面子**[N3]，我从小儿就是，做什么呀都要比别人**强**，不能比别人差。这面子又有什么用呢？这又不能当衣穿，又不能当饭吃。咱把它退了吧。你说这牛牛学校要做**校服**了，妈**治病**要钱。这……早知道你真买，我**昨**儿就不该说这话。退了吧，啊？你说咱家要得起这个吗？

李建强：你先戴上吧。真是……

秀　贞：不不，我不要，咱不要。把它退了吧。

李建强：这……我**发誓**，我一定让你过上好日子。

李建强：又怎么啦？

秀　贞：我还是穿这件白的吧？白的**配**黄的，**显眼**。你说呢？

李建强：唔……

秀　贞：都没看呢。你快看看嘛！

媳妇(儿)	xífu(r)	n.	(col.) wife; young married woman
胡同	hútòng	n.	lane; alley
枝	zhī	m.	(for flower)
赶明儿	gǎnmíngr	adv.	(col.) 以后，将来 later; later on
丢人	diū rén	vo.	lose face; disgraced
好面子	hàomiànzi	v.	care (too much) about how other people think of oneself
从小儿	cóng xiǎor	adv.	从小的时候，from childhood; as a child
强	qiáng	adj.	better (than); superior (to)
校服	xiàofú	n.	school uniform
治病	zhì bìng	vo.	treat illness
昨儿	zuór	t.	(col.) 昨天，yesterday
发誓	fā shì	vo.	swear; pledge
配	pèi	v.	match; go together (nicely)
显眼	xiǎnyǎn	adj.	conspicuous, showy; eye-catching

李建强：哎哟喂！我这**姑奶奶**[N4]，这都几点了？这是……**折腾**[N5]一宿了。早知道，我就不给你买这个了。

秀　贞：你敢！

李建强：行了，得……你快睡觉吧、睡觉吧。

秀　贞：买了这项链呀，就觉得没衣服配它了。你那**小金库**[N6]里面还有多少钱？

李建强：干吗呀？啊？是不是要买**套装**啊？买完套装是不是觉得鞋不**配套**？买完鞋以后，是不是又觉得**化妆品**不配套？最后，是不是觉得丈夫也不配套了，都得换了？啊？

秀　贞：换就换，谁怕谁呀？

李建强：睡觉吧！谁要你？

姑奶奶	gūnǎinai	n.	a woman hard to please or to deal with (as used in this story); sister of paternal grandfather
折腾	zhēteng	v.	do sth. repeatedly; toss from side to side
一宿	yì xiǔ		(col.) 一夜, one whole night
小金库	xiǎo jīnkù	n.	money secretly put away (as used in this story)
套装	tàozhuāng	n.	suit
配套	pèi tào	vo.	make a complete set
化妆品	huàzhuāngpǐn	n.	makeup; cosmetics

注释 Notes

1. **"砍价"**：**"砍价"** 就是还价，要求卖方减价。

   This expression "砍价" means to bargain, to ask for a lower price from the seller.

2. **"上档次"**：达到较高的档次，可以用于商品、衣服、旅馆等。这里指"戒指"质量好，是比较贵的。

   This expression is used to refer to the quality of merchandize, clothes, hotels, etc. Here the speaker means that the ring is of good quality and has high value.

3. **"好面子"**：也可以说爱面子。

   "好面子", same as "爱面子", suggests that one cares too much about how other people see or think of him/herself.

4. **"姑奶奶"**："姑奶奶"本来指父亲的姑姑，当故意叫一个女人为"姑奶奶"时，意思是"你很厉害，我惹不起你"或"你很麻烦，我对你没有办法"等等，常含有不太满意或讽刺的意味，也可以用于哀求，要求对方做什么或不要做什么。

   "姑奶奶" originally refers to the aunt of one's father. When used in situations like this story, the term implies that the female person one deals with is tough, and the speaker has to succumb to her wishes. It is also possible that the speaker uses this term with someone (could be a female child) who is difficult or troublesome (for the speaker) to handle. This term is often used in a sarcastic way as the speaker is not happy or unsatisfied with the addressee. It can also be used when one begs for help.

5. **"折腾"**：动词，这里的意思是反复重复某一动作、做某事，与本节第一部分意思不同。

   "折腾", a verb. Here it means repeatedly doing the same thing, which is different from the one used in the first segment of this story.

6. **"小金库"**：指一个单位在一般财务以外另外立账的公款。这里秀贞是在问李建强，他手里还有多少钱（没有交给家里）。

The term "小金库" refers to an additional account other than the regular bank account. In this story, Xiuzhen wants to find out how much money Jianqiang has in his "private bank" (the money that he did not bring home).

语法 Grammar Notes

1. **"纯金的，这是"**：这是一种特殊的句子，句子中本来应该在前边的成分出现在句末，这种现象叫"追加"。"纯金的这是。"本来的句子应该是"这是纯金的"。参见《胜负攸关》第三部分注释7。

   This kind of sentence structure（"纯金的这是"）is different from the default sentence that has the word order of〔S V O〕. In this sentence，the element representing the subject，which commonly occurs at the sentence's initial position，appears at the sentence-final position. This phenomenon is called "add-on." The normal word order for "纯金的，这是" should be "这是纯金的。"（Please refer to note 7 in part 3 of《胜负攸关》for more explanation）

   本剧第一部分有一个句子："你说我们那个厂，半死不活的，整天。"也是这种句子，意思是"你说我们那个厂，整天半死不活的。"

   The same type of "add-on" structure occurs in the sentence "你说我们那个厂，半死不活的，整天"（in the first segment of this story），in which "整天" normally goes before the（stative）verb "半死不活的". The element(s) that is/are added represent(s) insignificant information.

2. **"换什么换"**："V/A ＋ 什么 ＋ V/A" 这种格式用来表示说话人不同意对方或别人的想法、看法。课文中有下面这样的句子：

   "得得得，省省吧。这换什么换。丢不丢人呐？这戴着不挺好的吗？"

   这句话的意思是：别说了，你省一点事（力气吧）。（项链）不要换了，如果换的话，多丢人啊。你戴这个项链不是很好吗？

   The pattern〔V（erb）/A（djective）＋什么＋V/A〕is used to express the speaker's disagreement with the addressee or someone else，such as in the following text：

   "Save yourself some trouble，please. Why do you want to exchange（for a cheaper necklace）? Isn't it embarrassing? This one looks good on you，doesn't it?" The sentence can be paraphrased as："Stop talking about this（exchanging for a cheaper necklace）. Just keep this one and save yourself some trouble. It would be really embarrassing to exchange it. It looks really good on you, don't you think so?"

See more examples below:

(1) A：你给我看看，信上写的什么？

　　B：看什么看，这是我男朋友的信。

(2) A：别急，我再吃一点。

　　B：还吃什么吃，已经迟到了。

练习 Exercises

一、口语练习 Oral Practice

（一）回答问题 Answer the following questions

1. 李建强给秀贞买了一条什么样的项链？
2. 他为什么要买这样的项链？
3. 秀贞喜欢不喜欢建强买的这条项链？
4. 秀贞为什么要退掉这条项链？
5. 秀贞说有了项链，她以后还想买什么？
6. 李建强听秀贞说"衣服不配项链"时，他说了些什么？

（二）讨论 Discussion

你认为秀贞俗气不俗气？请举例说明。

二、书写练习 Written Exercises

（一）用下列词语完成句子 Complete the following sentences with the provided items below

A. 拖累	B. 折腾不起	C. 在……抬不起头
D. 好面子	E. 上不起学	

1. 他母亲主动提出要去住养老院，因为她不忍心长期_____他。
2. 她_____，事事都要比别人强。现在丈夫跟她提出离婚，对她的打击非常大。
3. 你让她跟你出国旅行？我看够呛（不行）。她上个月大病一场，这两天刚好，她现在的身体可_____。
4. 在一些偏远地区，有的孩子_____。
5. 他丢了工作以后很少跟朋友联系，可能是因为他觉得_____。

（二）用所给词语完成句子 Complete the following sentences with the provided items below

1. 什么，你还要去买鞋？你的鞋_____，别再买了。（够……的了）

2. 六点半_____，再早我真起不来了。（够……的了）

3. 你的男朋友已经对你_____，你还想让他怎么样？（够……的了）

4. 这个菜已经 _____了，别再放盐了！（够……的了）

（三）用所给词语填空 Fill in the blanks with the provided items

A. 俗气	B. 抬起头来	C. 好面子	D. 甩风凉话
E. 强	F. 差	G. 就	H. 狗眼看人低
I. 受……的气	J. V 得起		

　　建强，我跟你说啊，我也不是一定要戴项链，我这个人从小就_____，事事都要比人_____，不能比人_____。姐妹们都有项链，我没有，让我怎么在人面前_____？现在，叶子姐丢了项链，吴姐不断_____，说她有项链，她没拿，她的意思是说项链是我拿的。我可绝不_____她的_____。我一定得买一条项链，而且要买好的，让她们看看我秀贞_____项链，让她再也不敢 _____了。就为了这个，我宁愿_____！

三

秀　贞：这个多少钱啊？

小　贩：50。

秀　贞：哦。这个呢？

小　贩：这个是20。

奶　奶：你在那儿**琢磨**什么呢？

李建强：哎，我这儿琢磨着呀，给这儿**弄俩板**儿**一钉**，旁边儿呀**装**俩**轱辘**，我给你做一轮椅呀。

奶　奶：咳，别麻烦了。你快来吧，给我**掉个头**吧。

李建强：哎。给你支在哪儿呀？

秀　贞：妈，没事儿吧？

奶　奶：没事儿。挺好的。你回来啦？

秀　贞：建强，我**今**儿**差点**儿买条假项链。假的就是假的，**活**儿特**糙**。比起这条啊，**差远了**。

李建强：你**有毛病**啊？没事儿看什么假项链啊？

小贩	xiǎofàn	n.	peddler; street vendor
琢磨	zuómo	v.	想，ponder; think over
弄	nòng	v.	get; manage to obtain
俩	liǎ		(col.) 两个，two
板儿	bǎnr	n.	board
钉	dìng	v.	hammer a nail into sth. fix sth. to a position
装	zhuāng	v.	install
轱辘	gūlu	n.	wheel
掉头	diào tóu	vo.	turn around
今儿	jīnr	t.	(col.) 今天，today
差（一）点儿	chà (yì)diǎnr	adv.	almost
活儿	huór	n.	(col.) craftsmanship; work
糙	cāo	adj.	rough; coarse
差远了	chà yuǎn le		差多了，much too inferior
有毛病	yǒu máobing		(of a person) crazy; have problems

秀　贞：你懂什么呀？没真的戴假的，那是**寒酸**。有真的戴假的，那是为了安全。丢了也就十来块钱的事儿。这叫会过日子。哎，待会儿帮我把这个**锁好**啊。我去做饭。

李建强：啊、啊。

秀　贞：妈，今儿买了**胡萝卜、扁豆**，想吃什么呀？

奶　奶：吃什么都行。

秀　贞：哎，我去做了啊。

李建强：好，给你这**宝贝**儿**锁上**。

秀　贞：你笑什么呀？

李建强：啊，没有。给你锁上了。

（背景音乐：最近比较烦，比较烦，比较烦，我的头发只剩下从前的一半。每天的工作太……）

李建强：哎，**老板**，**歇**着呐？来来来，抽根儿烟、抽根儿烟。

小吃店经理：哎，抽根儿……

李建强：这一个月不少挣吧？

寒酸	hánsuān	adj.	shabby and miserable；too simple to be respectable
锁好	suǒ hǎo	vc.	lock up safely
胡萝卜	húluóbo	n.	carrot
扁豆	biǎndòu	n.	green beans
宝贝（儿）	bǎobèi(r)	n.	treasure；precious thing
锁上	suǒ shang	vc.	lock up
老板	lǎobǎn	n.	boss；shopkeeper
歇	xiē	v.	(col.) 休息，have a rest；take a break
小吃店（儿）	xiǎochīdiàn(r)	n.	small restaurant

小吃店经理：咳，**瞎忙活**。**刨掉**[N1]这房钱、水钱、电钱，再加上小工的开支，
　　　　　　能剩下几个呀？

李建强：**怎么着**也得**对付**[N2]个几千块钱呀？

小吃店经理：那当然了。多辛苦啊！每天三四点钟起床，12点钟以前没睡
　　　　　　过觉。

　　（画外音：老板，电话。）

小吃店经理：我告诉你，弄好了这一个月**不止**几千块钱。

秀　贞：哎，建强、建强，跟你说，妈**犯病**了。

李建强：啊，在哪儿呢？

秀　贞：哎呀，送医院了。

李建强：哎呀，早说呀，真是。

秀　贞：哎，别急！我跟你说……

李建强：带钱了吗？带钱了吗？

秀　贞：呃，我把**咱俩**的**工资**我都带上了。

李建强：哎呀，那有多少钱哪？现在**押金**得七八千呢。

秀　贞：那要不够，我就打电话给我妈，让她借。

李建强：行了行了。去看看再说吧。哎哟，孩子呢、孩子呢？

秀　贞：哎呀，在小张那儿**管**着呢。你放心吧。

瞎	xiā	adv.	aimlessly
忙活	mánghuo	v.	(col.) busy doing sth.
刨掉	páo diào	vc.	减去，扣掉，exclude; subtract
房钱	fángqián	n.	房租，rent (of house)
水钱	shuǐqián	n.	water fee
小工	xiǎogōng	n.	(temporary) worker/helper
开支	kāizhī	n.	expenses; spending
怎么着	zěnme zhe		(col.)不管怎么样，no matter what
对付	duìfu	v.	得到，manage to make (profit) (as used in this context)
画外音	huà wài yīn		voice outside the picture (screen)
不止	bùzhǐ	adv.	more than; not limited to
犯病	fàn bìng	vo.	have a recurrence of an illness
咱俩	zán liǎ		(col.)咱们两个，two of us
工资	gōngzī	n.	wages; salary
押金	yājīn	n.	deposit
管	guǎn	v.	look after

李建强：你今儿怎么才回来呀你？

秀　贞：我不是**加班**嘛。

李建强：加什么班儿呀？挣不了几个钱。

李建强：你说，这父母啊，把咱们从小**拉扯**[N3]大，咱们没孩子的时候啊，就**体会不到**。现在有了自己的孩子了，能体会到啊，做父母的吧……太辛苦。唉，都说"**娶了媳妇儿忘了娘**"，我啊，真没忘。总想啊，给我妈做点儿什么，总想**报答**报答。哎，这怎么，这总做不了呢？你说，我妈要是**出点儿什么事儿**，我**对得住**谁呀我？我这儿子当的……

秀　贞：你看，开个**小食店**，能赚钱吗？

加班(儿)	jiā bān(r)	vo.	work overtime; work on extra shifts
拉扯	lāche	v.	bring up (a child/children)
体会不到	tǐhuì bú dao	vc.	can not realize or comprehend
娶了媳妇儿忘了娘	qǔ le xífur wàng le niáng		sons tend to forget their mothers once they get married
报答	bàodá	v.	requite; repay with action
出点儿什么事儿	chū dianr shénme shìr		(col.) (if something) goes wrong
对得住	duì de zhù	vc.	对得起，live up to (one's expectation)
小食店(儿)	xiǎoshídiàn(r)	n.	small shop to sell snacks and drinks

注释 Notes

1. **"刨掉"**：意思是"减去"。

   "刨掉这房钱、水钱、电钱，再加上小工的开支，能剩下几个呀?"这句话的意思是：减去水费、电费，再加上给小工（工人）的工钱，赚的钱很少。

   "刨掉" means "减去" (to subtract; to exclude). "Minus the rent, the utility fee, and the payments to the workers, how much do I have left?" The meaning of the sentence is, "Counting out the necessary expenses: the rent, the utility fee, and the workers salaries, I hardly make any money."

2. **"对付"**：意思是勉强做什么，这里的意思是"勉强能赚（……钱）"。"怎么着也得对付个几千块钱呀"：意思是"怎么样也能赚几千块钱呀"。参见《胜负攸关》第一部分注释 6。

   "对付" here means "earn". The meaning of the sentence is, "No matter what, (you) can manage to earn at least several thousand dollars, (I suppose)." (Please refer to note 6 in part 1 of《胜负攸关》)

3. **"拉扯"**："拉扯"有"辛苦抚养"的意思。

   "拉扯" means to take great pains to bring up a child.

练习 Exercises

■ 一、口语练习 Oral Practice

（一）回答问题 Answer the following questions

1. 秀贞为什么去小贩那里询问项链的价格？
2. 秀贞为什么想去买一条假项链？关于戴"真假"项链，她说了几句什么话？
3. 李建强为什么要跟小吃店的老板聊天？
4. 建强的母亲怎么了？
5. 李建强和妻子对母亲好不好？他们孝顺吗？

（二）讨论 Discussion

请讨论建强的性格。你喜欢他吗？为什么？

■ 二、书写练习 Written Exercises

（一）用所给的词语填空 Fill in the blanks with the provided items

A. 才	B. 体会	C. 拉扯	D. 辛苦	E. 报答
F. 开	G. 赚	H. 对得住	I. 为	J. 犯
K. 过	L. 伺候	M. 发誓		

人们都说"不养儿不知父母恩"，现在我 ＿＿＿＿＿ 明白这句话的真实含义。父母把我们从小 ＿＿＿＿＿ 大，多不容易啊！我们没孩子的时候就 ＿＿＿＿＿ 不到。现在有了自己的孩子，才明白做父母的真是太 ＿＿＿＿＿ 了。还有人说"娶了媳妇儿忘了娘"，我啊，真没忘。我妈 ＿＿＿＿＿ 我做的事太多了，我总想着怎么 ＿＿＿＿＿ 我妈。如今，我刚想 ＿＿＿＿＿ 个小店，＿＿＿＿＿ 些钱，孝敬孝敬她老人家。可现在她又病了，你说，我妈要是出点儿什么事儿，我怎么 ＿＿＿＿＿ 我妈呀？我 ＿＿＿＿＿，这次我妈病好了以后，我一定好好 ＿＿＿＿＿ 她，让她 ＿＿＿＿＿ 几天舒服日子。

（二）作文 Composition

请用以下词语描写建强的母亲住院以后建强的心情。

Describe Jian qiang's feelings after his mother was hospitalized，using the items provided below.

| 1. 体会 | 2. 拉扯 | 3. 辛苦 | 4. 报答 | 5. 对不起 | 6. 过 |

【四】

李建强：这……越上越多了啊！

牛　牛：妈，给奶奶**盛**碗早点。

秀　贞：哎，好，我知道了。奶奶想吃点儿什么？

食　客：秀贞，把钱给你**搁**这儿了啊。你说你这儿忙的。**干脆**那班儿别上了，回
　　　　家**踏踏实实**[N1]当**老板娘**多好啊。

秀　贞：您还别说，我还真有那想法。现在干点儿什么呀，不比挣那点儿死工
　　　　资强？

牛　牛：妈，我走啦，你也该上班啦。

秀　贞：哎呀，真是。建强，我得去上班了啊。

秀　贞：牛牛，别做了，**明儿**还上学呢。

盛	chéng	v.	fill (a bowl)
食客	shíkè	n.	restaurant customer
搁	gē	v.	放，put; place
干脆	gāncuì	adv.	simply; just; altogether
踏踏实实	tā ta shī shī	adj.	having peace of mind; free from anxiety
老板娘	lǎobǎnniáng	n.	shopkeeper's wife
明儿	míngr	t.	(col). 明天，tomorrow

牛　牛：写完啦。

奶　奶：你别管我了，都睡去吧，忙了一天**生意**了。

牛　牛：妈，明天早点儿叫我。

秀　贞：好的。妈，有事儿叫我啊。

李建强：哎，别算了，别算了，别算了。

秀　贞：我没算完呢。

李建强：**财迷样儿**[N2]啊。当当……

秀　贞：哪儿来的？你又买了一条？

李建强：去年的今天，还记得吗？我给你买了条项链。你哭了。我当时就对自己说，我发誓，一定要让你过上好日子。

秀　贞：**傻瓜**，过好日子也不一定非要再买一条啊。这得多少钱呀？

李建强：1600 啊。

秀　贞：你说你个**败家**的哟。我们才赚这么一点儿钱，你就这么**糟蹋**。**发票**拿来、发票拿来。

李建强：哎呀，干吗呀？1600 嘛。

秀　贞：1600。你说我说你什么好呢？正好，我**表妹**下个月结婚，这条卖给她，就算少收她 100 块钱，作为**随礼**嘛。

李建强：什么呀，你这合适吗？你这……

秀　贞：这有什么不合适啊？

李建强：这么着，你这个它……不不不……不好。你就戴这个吧，好不好？

秀　贞：哎，我这人还特别**念旧**[N3]，我就喜欢这一条。这是我第一件首饰，你懂什么呀。我得把这个收起来，锁上。我去洗澡了。这天儿也太**闷**了，是不是要下雨了？

生意	shēngyi	n.	买卖, business
财迷样儿	cáimíyàngr	v.	greedy look
傻瓜	shǎguā	n.	fool
败家	bàijiā	v.	spendthrift; wastrel
糟蹋	zāo·tà	v.	waste; ruin
发票	fāpiào	n.	receipt; invoice
表妹	biǎomèi	n.	female cousin（with a different surname）
随礼	suílǐ	n. /vo.	别人办婚事丧事等等时送礼, present given at a wedding or funeral
念旧	niànjiù	adj.	nostalgic
闷	mēn	adj.	stuffy

秀　贞：建强，你看到我的项链了吗？

李建强：啊？你不是戴着洗澡去了吗？

秀　贞：**糟了**，**准**是**冲**到**下水道**去了。

李建强：哎，你别弄了、别弄了。一会儿就下雨了。你……你怎么这么**死心眼**
　　　　呢你？来来，要下雨了、要下雨了。行不行？你听我一回，好不好？

秀　贞：不行！

李建强：你戴我给你买那条新的。这不正好新的买回来，旧的也丢了吗？这是
　　　　天意，**老天爷**让你戴条新的嘛。

秀　贞：**狗屁**天意！**要不是**你又给我买了一条，这条还丢不了呢。

李建强：不就条**链子**吗？

秀　贞：你好大**口气**呀！你发什么财了？800多块钱呐！

李建强：哎呀，这是人重要啊，还是钱重要啊？下这么大雨，你说你找项链，
　　　　这不是**财迷心窍**吗？你快起来、起来、起来。起来！

秀　贞：我不是**心疼**钱。我是心疼那条项链。那是你在我们家最**穷**的时候给我
　　　　买的。我知道，你不说我也知道，你花了那么多钱，心里也**过意不
　　　　去**。快回去吧。

李建强：哎呀，行了，别说了，别说了！那金项链是假的。

秀　贞：假的？

准	zhǔn	adv.	（col.）definitely；certainly
冲	chōng	v.	flush
下水道	xiàshuǐdào	n.	sewer
死心眼（儿）	sǐxīnyǎn(r)	adj.	stubborn
天意	tiānyì	n.	God's will；will of Heaven
老天爷	lǎotiānyé	n.	God；Heavens
狗屁	gǒupì	n.	rubbish；nonsense
要不是	yàobúshi	conj.	（如果不是），if it were not for
链子	liànzi	n.	chain
口气	kǒu·qì	n.	manner of speaking；tone of voice
财迷心窍（儿）	cái mí xīnqiào(r)		mad about money；money grubber
心疼	xīnténg	v.	distressed；love dearly
穷	qióng	adj.	poor
过意不去	guò yì bú qù	vc.	feel very distressed

李建强：对，假的。

秀　贞：你是不想让我找，**骗**我。我不**信**。

李建强：我没骗你。我这次**确实**是没骗你。我骗你啊是一年前骗的你。没错儿，那确实是假的，那就 40 块钱。我买回来就是让你高兴高兴。

秀　贞：你……你敢骗我？你骗我、骗我……

李建强：哎，行了，你听我说。你以为我心里**好受**吗？我也难受啊。我自从给你买了假项链，我就发誓，一定让你过上好日子。我要给你买金项链、金**戒指**、金**耳环**。我要让你在你的姐妹面前抬起头来。我就这么想的！

秀　贞：你啊……

李建强：走吧、走吧……快走吧、快走吧。都**浇**坏了。**擦擦**。来来来。咱们呀，还是回去戴那 1600 的，那是真的。

秀　贞：我这一辈子找着你啊，我真是**有福**了。雨好像小点儿了，要不，我再找找看。

李建强：别找了。下这么大雨，反正不**值**什么钱。

秀　贞：不值钱？不值钱它也是你花了那么大**心思**^{N4}买给我的。不找着我这心里**空落落**^{N5}的。我觉得这假的比那真的还**贵重**。不行，我得再去找找。

李建强：哎，行了行了行了。回来、回来。看你！

李建强：哎，你呀，说实在的，还戴这假的吧。你说的，有了真的戴假的，安全嘛。

秀　贞：不对。平常戴真的。这条假的呀，我要把它好好地放起来。

骗	piàn	v.	deceive; fool
信	xìn	v.	believe
确实	quèshí	adv.	truly; indeed
好受	hǎoshòu	adj.	feel comfortable
戒指	jièzhi	n.	ring
耳环	ěrhuán	n.	earrings
浇	jiāo	v.	get rained on (as used in this context)
擦	cā	v.	wipe
有福	yǒufú	adj.	lucky
值钱	zhíqián	adj.	costly; valuable
心思	xīnsi	n.	thought; thinking
空落落	kōngluòluò	adj.	(see note 5)
贵重	guìzhòng	adj.	valuable; precious

李建强：放起来干吗呀？不能**升值**。

秀　　贞：等咱们儿子结婚的时候我要把它给**儿媳妇**。哎，这也是咱们的传家宝了。

李建强：40块钱的**传家宝**啊？你丢不丢人哪你？回头啊，你传给儿子吧，是不是叫儿子笑我了？

秀　　贞：哎，这有什么好笑话的？让他们也知道，他们的爸爸妈妈是怎么**苦过来**的。

李建强：哟，看不出来，我老婆还挺**深刻**的。

秀　　贞：深刻还让你骗了一年？

李建强：**说明**啊，你丈夫比你更深刻。

秀　　贞：你呀……

升值	shēngzhí	v.	rise in value
儿媳妇（儿）	érxífu(r)	n.	daughter-in-law
传家宝	chuánjiābǎo	n.	family heirloom
苦过来	kǔ guolai	vc.	struggle through difficulties and hardships
深刻	shēnkè	adj.	profound
说明	shuōmíng	v.	show; demonstrate

注释 Notes

1. **"踏踏实实"**：这里"踏踏实实"的意思是"安定、安稳地"。如：

   "踏踏实实" in this story means being free from anxiety or having peace of mind. See more examples below：

   （1）干脆那班儿别上了，回家踏踏实实当老板娘多好啊。

   Just quit your job altogether，and stay home to enjoy your boss's wife's status—free of any worries.

   （2）你踏踏实实地在这儿等，别着急！

   Just wait here，don't worry about it.

   （3）他们都走了好，咱们可以踏踏实实地睡一会儿。

   It's great they have all left，we can have a sound sleep now.

2. **"财迷样儿啊"**："财迷"是指特别喜欢钱的人。"财迷样儿啊"意思是（你看你那个）财迷的样子。

   "财迷" is used to describe those who are greedy for money. "财迷样儿啊" means "Look at how greedy you are."

3. **"念旧"**：意思是不忘以前的物品、朋友、交情等。

   To be nostalgic；to not forget，or to often think of old friends，old times，etc.

4. **"花心思"**：意思是"动脑筋"。"不值钱它也是你花了那么大心思买给我的。"这句话的意思是"虽然那个戒指很便宜，但是也是你动了很多脑筋给我买的。"

   "花心思" means "spend thought on". This sentence says "although the ring is inexpensive，you tried everything you could to buy it for me."

5. **"空落落"**的意思是"空旷而冷清"，可以描写一个地方，也可以描写人的心情。"不找着我心里空落落的"的意思是"如果不找到那个项链儿，我心里会因为少了什么东西而很不舒服。"

   "空落落" usually refers to an empty and lonely state. It is used to describe a place or one's melancholy feelings. In this story it indicates that "if (I) can't find the neck-lace，I would feel really sad because I lost something (very precious to me)."

练习 Exercises

■ 一、口语练习 Oral Practice

（一）回答问题 Answer the following questions

　　1. 李建强开店以后家庭生活有了什么变化？

　　2. 李建强为什么又给秀贞买了一条项链？

　　3. 秀贞为什么要把她的第一条项链收起来？

　　4. 李建强为什么向秀贞承认了他一年前撒的谎？

　　5. 秀贞知道建强对她撒谎以后生气了吗？为什么？

　　6. 秀贞为什么一定要找那条假项链？

　　7. 如果你是秀贞，你会不会因为丈夫对你撒谎而生气？为什么？

（二）角色扮演 Role Play

　　情景：秀贞不小心把那条旧项链掉到下水道里，外边正下着大雨，她一定要出去找项链。为了阻止秀贞出去找项链，建强说出了一年以前的秘密。秀贞听了以后有什么样的反应？她是否原谅了建强？对话的结果由对话双方决定。

　　Situation：Xiuzhen accidentally dropped her old necklace into the sewer. It is raining outside，and Xiuzhen insists on going outside to find the necklace. In order to stop Xiuzhen from going into the rain，Jianqiang confesses to Xiuzhen his secret from a year ago. How does Xiuzhen respond to Jianqiang's confession? Will Xiuzhen forgive Jianqiang? Students are to pair up and act out a dialogue between the couple in which Xiuzhen's response can be decided by students.

■ 二、书写练习 Written Exercises

（一）用所给词语填空 Fill in the blanks with the given items

A. 发誓	B. 心疼	C. 空落落	D. 花了很大心思
E. 确实	F. 死心眼ル		

（有的词语可以用两次）

1. 建强没有骗他妻子，第一条项链_____是假的。

2. 孩子在家时，她总嫌家里乱，现在孩子都离开家上大学了，她又感觉心里_____的。

3. 放假了，学生老师都回家了，校园里_____的。

4. 从上中文课的第一天起，他就_____要学好中文，将来到中国去工作。

5. 他写文章时为了一个词经常要查十几本词典，很多人说他_____，我倒喜欢他这种认真的精神。

6. 刚买的一个手机两天就不见了，真让人生气。我并不是_____钱，而是_____时间，这是我_____挑来的。

（二）作文 Composition

将本电视剧本改写成一个叙事故事。

Write a narrative story based on the movie script.

■ 三、文化方面的讨论 Culture Discussion

"娶了媳妇儿忘了娘"对不对？在中国的传统观念中，有的男人认为母亲比妻子重要。你和你的同胞怎样看这个问题？

There is a Chinese expression that says "sons tend to forget their mothers once they get married." This saying, as you may have figured out, suggests that man is supposed to put his mother before his wife. What do you (or your fellow countrymen) think of this aspect of Chinese culture?

第二课 无端介入

Unwarranted T...

无端介入
VTS_12-1 , 3:00
VTS_13-1 , 6:20
VTS_14_1 , 6:36
VTS_15-1 ~ 5:12

VTS_16-1 27:30
Completed

VTS 17,18,19, 20, Vocab

导 读：

她没有想到突然卷入一场车祸，～～～的男朋友。这起车祸已经成为当地社会～～～～正在寻找她这个唯一的现场证人。可是她如果公开出面做证，指认肇事的车辆、司机，就可能引起丈夫的怀疑，给幸福的家庭蒙上阴影；可是不出面做证，又会使肇事者逍遥法外，让受害者蒙冤，并给其亲人带来莫大的痛苦。她陷于两难之中，到底该怎么办？

Introduction:

She had never thought of being involved in an automobile accident, and, to make things worse, the victim happened to be her former boyfriend. The accident quickly became a highly publicized matter and the officers from the Public Security Bureau were searching for her—the sole witness. If she were to testify in public, pointing out the driver and the vehicle, it would raise the suspicion of her husband and bring a cloud to her happy marriage; but if she were not to come forward, it would let the perpetrator go scot-free and the victim suffer injustice. She is in a dilemma. What should she do?

主要人物 Main Characters

林　慧	Lín Huì	an accountant，female
冯铁民	Féng Tiěmín	husband of Lin Hui
甜　甜	Tiántian	daughter of Lin Hui and Feng Tiemin
童　可	Tóng Kě	victim of the accident
洪　义	Hóng Yì	a police officer
王奶奶	Wáng nǎinai	granny Wang，a volunteer working for the Neighborhood Committee
童　母	Tóng mǔ	mother of Tong Ke

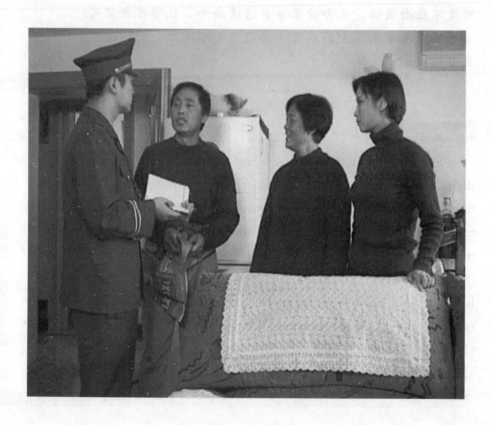

医　　生：快，快，**让**一下，让一让、让一让……

记　　者：好，那你**叙述**一下当天^{G1}的情况好吗？

目击者甲：出来那会儿啊，八点多钟。我那一桶^{G2}**泔水**还没倒完呢，就听见那
　　　　　边"**咚**"的一声^{G3}，车就把那人给撞了。

记　　者：那辆车什么颜色您记得吗？

目击者甲：什么颜色……没看清。那车呀，撞了人以后它就跑了。

目击者乙：我以为自己被撞了。哎哟，声音好大好大呀。当时吧，我想，撞一
　　　　　个人有这么响吗？那车停了一下，**紧接着**吧，"**噌**"地一下就跑了。
　　　　　那人就**落**在那儿。

记　　者：就在那儿吗？

目击者乙：对，就在那儿。

目击者丙：当时**撞**车的时候，我们也没大注意^{N1}。从那边儿来了一个女人，说
　　　　　"撞人了、撞人了"。我一看，真的是撞人了。她这……就一人，急
　　　　　坏了。当时我们看见的时候，**搭把手**^{N2}啊，我们三个人啊，一边儿
　　　　　截车，一边儿搭人。五分钟，也就是五分钟^{N3}，就走了。那女人也
　　　　　跟着上车了。那女人什么**模样**？肯定是女的。

无端	wúduān	adv.	unwarranted; for no reason at all
介入	jièrù	v.	get involved; intervene
让	ràng	v.	yield to
叙述	xùshù	v.	narrate; recount
目击者	mùjīzhě	n.	eyewitness; witness
泔水	gān·shuǐ	n.	slops; dishwater
咚	dōng	ono.	rub-a-dub, rat-a-tat; boom (of a drum)
紧接着	jǐnjiē zhe		immediately; right after
噌	cēng	ono.	describes the sound of certain kind of sudden movement, such as the sudden start of a car or a flock of birds suddenly making flight.
落	luò	v.	fall; toss
丙	bǐng	num.	the third; the third position
撞	zhuàng	v.	strike; run into; bump into
搭把手	dā ba shǒu		to help by lending a hand (to carry or lift things)
截	jié	v.	intercept; stop
模样	múyàng	n.	appearance; looks

记　者：那个……那个车是什么颜色，您记得吗？

目击者丙：那个车吗……我也不能**瞎说**^{N4}。**反正**^{G4}，**肯定**不是白色的，是个深
　　　　　色的。

医　　生：送来的时候呢，病人已经死了。**死者**^{G5}的**腰部**以上的**部位均**^{G6}有**程度**
　　　　　不同的撞伤，**面部伤害尤其严重**。现在还很难**辨认**死者的**身份**。

出租车司机：听说那男的死了，那女的肯定认识。过了一会儿，她说打电话
　　　　　去，她从**包**里**掏出**一个小**本子**，……就走了。就这样，一走就再
　　　　　也没回来。就这样了。

记　者：好，谢谢你啊。

记　者：**警察**同志，**讲述**一下**事故**发生当天的死者的情况好吗？

瞎（说）	xiā (shuō)	adv.	(see note 4)
反正	fǎnzhèng	adv.	(see grammar note 4)
肯定	kěndìng	adv.	definitely; undoubtedly
死者	sǐzhě	n.	the dead; the deceased
腰部	yāobù	n.	腰，waist
部位	bùwèi	n.	position; place; location
均	jūn	adv.	都，(lit.) all; without exception;(see grammar note 6)
程度	chéngdù	n.	level; degree
面部	miànbù	n.	脸，face
伤害	shānghài	v./n.	injure/injury; damage
尤其	yóuqí	adv.	especially; particularly
严重	yánzhòng	adj.	serious; critical
辨认	biànrèn	v.	identify; recognize
身份	shēnfen	n.	identity; status
出租车	chūzūchē	n.	taxi
司机	sījī	n.	driver (of transportation vehicles such as train, automobile, trolley, etc.)
包	bāo	n.	purse; bag
掏出	tāo chu	vc.	draw out; pull out
本子	běnzi	n.	notebook
警察	jǐngchá	n.	police; policeman; cop
讲述	jiǎngshù	v.	tell about; narrate
事故	shìgù	n.	accident; mishap

洪　义：好。被撞死者是**男性**，34 岁左右。穿的是黄色的**衬衣**，**灰色**的长裤。呃，死的时候呢身上没有**身份证**或其他**证件**，只有十几块钱。我们现在不能**确定**这件**案件**的**性质**，不能确定为**交通肇事逃逸**案，当然也不**排除**其他性质的可能。哦，我……就是我们希望当时**在场**那位女**同志**

男性	nánxìng	n.	male; man
衬衣	chènyī	n.	underclothes; shirt
灰色	huīsè	n.	grey; grey color
身份证	shēnfènzhèng	n.	identification card (I.D.)
证件	zhèngjiàn	n.	credentials; papers
确定	quèdìng	v.	sure; certain; definite
案件	ànjiàn	n.	(legal) case
性质	xìngzhì	n.	nature; character
交通	jiāotōng	n.	transportation; traffic
肇事	zhàoshì	v.	cause trouble; create a disturbance
逃逸	táoyì	v.	逃跑, escape; run away; abscond (formal)
排除	páichú	v.	eliminate; rule out; exclude
在场	zàichǎng	v.	be on the scene; be present
同志	tóngzhì	n.	comrade (a customary title used between people in China)

能够出来**协助**警方**破案**，向我们**提供**死者的身份，**包括**肇事**车辆**的**线索**。哦，如果有什么**情况**，请你**拨打**65003474。

协助	xiézhù	v.	assist; help
破案	pò àn	vo.	solve; crack a criminal case; find out the truth of a criminal case
提供	tígōng	v.	provide; supply
包括	bāokuò	v.	include; consist of
车辆	chēliàng	n.	vehicle; automobile
线索	xiànsuǒ	n.	clue; thread; trail
情况	qíngkuàng	n.	information; development
拨打	bōdǎ	v.	dial; call

I saw around you in ... said I've no ... he ... id allow ...
gotten ... Inspection?

注释 Notes

1. **"没大注意"**：意思是"没太注意"。

   "没大注意" means "Didn't pay much attention to. It is the same as "没太注意"。

2. **"搭把手"**：意思是"帮个忙（动手做某件具体的事，比如搬东西、抬人等等）"。

   "搭把手" means "to lend a hand" to help carry or lift something. The sentence：别站那儿看，搭把手啊 means："Don't stand there watching, lend us a hand (to help carry this man)!"

3. **"也就是"**：It's just...；It could only be... 例如：

   (1) 五分钟，也就是五分钟，就走了。那女人也跟着上车了。

   Five minutes, it was just about five minutes, we all left. That woman also got on a bus and left.

   (2) 童可，也就是童可，才能撒出这么个谎来！

   童可，there was no one else but 童可，who could have been able to make up such a lie!

4. **"瞎说"**："瞎"意思类似"胡"、"乱"，口语。如"瞎说"、"瞎写"、"瞎编"、"瞎扯"等。

   "瞎" is similar to "胡"、"乱"，which means "talk groundlessly or irresponsibly；talk rubbish/nonsense". This expression is similar to "乱说"，"胡说"。

   Other verbs which are often used with "瞎" are, for example：

   瞎写　write groundlessly or irresponsibly；write without thinking

   瞎讲　say something groundlessly or irresponsibly

   瞎来　do something without any understanding or plan

   瞎编　to fabricate something

   瞎扯　gabble, prattle, waffle

   (1) 那个车我也没看清楚，不能瞎说。

   I didn't see that car clearly so I can't make an irresponsible comment.

（2）你别瞎来，问清楚了以后再动手也不晚。

Don't screw around with it; you'll have enough time to do it after you've gotten clear instructions.

语法 Grammar Notes

1. "当（dàng）＋ Noun"：

   当天 on that very day

   当时 at the time；then

   当地 in the locality；local

   当场 on the spot

   （1）请你叙述一下病人当天的情况好吗？

   　　Could you please recount the patient's situation on that day?

   （2）当时我并不知道。

   　　I didn't know at the time.

   （3）找个当地人问一下吧，他们比我们熟悉。

   　　Let's ask a local，they know the place better than we do.

   （4）你要是不信，他们就当场表演给你们看。

   　　If you don't believe them，they will show you right on the spot.

2. "桶"：量词。MW for tub；pail；bucket；keg；barrel.

   （1）我那一桶泔水还没倒完呢，就听见那边"咚"的一声，车就把那人给撞了。

   　　I was out pouring dishwater when I heard a loud "bang" and saw someone had been run over by a car.

   （2）垃圾桶在哪儿？

   　　Where is the trash barrel?

3. "声"：动量词。MW，used as Verbal Classifier.

   （1）我那一桶水还没倒完呢，就听见那边"咚"的一声，车就把人给撞了。

   　　I was out pouring dishwater when I heard a loud "bang" and saw someone had been run over by a car.

   （2）邻居的狗刚才叫了几声。

   　　Our neighbor's dog barked a moment ago.

   类似的动量词还有"下"、"眼"、"脚"等等。例如：

   Other verbal classifiers similar to 声 are："下"、"眼"、"脚" etc. e.g.：

(3) 那车停了一下，紧接着吧，"噌"的一下就跑了。

The car stopped for a second, then screeched away.

踢了两脚	kicked sth. /sb. twice
看一眼	take a look; glance at
打了几下	strike/hit (sb. /sth.) a few times
喝了几口	drank a few mouthfuls/sipped some water/tea/beer

4. "反正"：本课"反正"的意思是，在任何条件下结果或结论都不会改变。第一个分句表示任何条件，第二个分句以"反正"开头，表示结果或结论。

"反正" used here to indicate that whatever the conditions, the conclusion remains unchanged. The first clause states the condition and the second beginning with "反正" stresses the conclusion.

(1) 你们谁想去看电影谁去，反正我不去。

Whoever wants to see the movie can go, I'm not going in any case.

第一分句的意思是：无论你们谁去看电影（任何条件），第二个分句表示结果：我都不去。

The first part of the sentence states the condition — i. e. 〔don't care〕 whoever goes to see the movie; the second clause indicates the result：I'm simply not going.

(2) 这次考试好不好没有关系，反正对成绩也没有影响.

It doesn't matter whether I do well or not on this test, it won't affect my grade.

(3) A：昨天有人开我的抽屉了，你知道是谁吗？

Someone opened my draw yesterday. Do you know who did it?

B：不知道，反正不是我。

I don't. Anyway it wasn't me.

5. "者"：助词，用在形容词（短语）或动词（短语）后边，构成表示人的名词。如：记者、学者、老者、领导者、参加者、旁观者、前者、后者。

"者" is an auxiliary word, used after an adjective phrase or a verbal phrase to form a noun which is used to describe a certain kind of person or people. For example："记者" journalist、"学者" scholar、"老者" an elderly、"领导者" leader、"参加者" participant、"旁观者" visitor、"前者" the former、"后者" the latter 。

(1) 被撞死者是男性，34 岁左右。

The person who died in the car crash was a male about the age of thirty-four.

（2）他是一位知名记者。

He is a well-known journalist.

（3）我是您的读者。

I'm a reader of your books.

（4）说者无心，听者有意。

The speaker has no intention to offend; nonetheless, the listener gets offended.

6. "均"：意思是"都"，书面语。

The meaning of "均" is the same as "都", but is often used in written language.

（1）死者腰部以上的部位均有程度不同的撞伤，面部伤害尤其严重。

There were injuries all over his upper body, the most severe was on his face.

（2）学生进出学校均须出示证件。

All the students must show their ID upon entry or exit from the school.

（3）九月之前全部学生均应注册完毕。

All the students must complete registration before September.

（4）五月的亚洲机票均已售出。

Tickets for all the Asian flights in May have been sold out.

练习 Exercises

■ 一、口语练习 Oral Practice

（一）回答问题 Answer the following questions

1. 本剧开始的时候，发生了一件什么事情？
2. 车祸发生的时候，有几个见证人？记者找到了几个？还有一个是男的还是女的？
3. 肇事的汽车是什么颜色的？
4. 被汽车撞的人还活着吗？为什么他的身份很难辨认？
5. 请你说一下被撞死的人的情况。
6. 这次车祸是谁造成的？

（二）角色扮演 Role Play

1. 学生四人一组，饰演记者与三位目击者在事故现场的对话。
   Divide students into groups of four, one plays the reporter and the other three act as the three witnesses.
2. 把学生分成对，一为警察，另一为剧中的那位出租汽车司机，表演他们之间的对话。
   Pair students up, one plays the taxi driver, the other the police officer. The police officer is conducting an interview with the taxi driver who heard all what the witnesses said at the scene.

■ 二、书写练习 Written Exercises

（一）完成句子 Complete the following sentences

1. 你目击了这一撞车事故，请你_____。（当时）
2. 事故发生后，他忙得_____。（一边……一边……）
3. 这次面谈好不好没关系，_____（反正）
4. 撞车后，那车停了一下，_____。（紧接着）
5. 别站着看，_____。（搭）
6. 现在坐飞机所有的行李_____。（均）

（二）填空 Fill in blanks with appropriate words from the script

1. 那辆车是什么颜色的？我没看清楚，也不能_____说。_____，我可以肯定不是白色的，_____个深色的。

2. 送_____的时候，病人_____已经死_____。死_____的腰部以上的部位_____有程度不同的撞伤，面部伤害_____严重。现在还很难辨认死者的_____。

3. 听说那男_____死了，那女的_____认识。_____了一会儿，她说打电话去，她_____包里掏出一个小本子，……就走了。

（三）选择适当的词语填空 Fill in blanks with the most appropriate

A. 可能	B. 性质	C. 包括	D. 协助	E. 左右
F. 提供	G. 者	H. 性	I. 证件	J. 为
K. 一下	L. 场			

　　我现在讲述_____事故发生当天的死_____的情况。被撞死者是男_____，34 岁_____。穿的是黄色的衬衣，灰色的长裤。死的时候身上没有身份证或其他_____，只有十几块钱。我们现在不能确定这件案件的_____，不能确定_____交通肇事逃逸案，当然也不排除其他性质的_____。我们希望当时在_____的那位女同志能够出来_____警方破案，向我们_____死者的身份，_____肇事车辆的线索。

冯铁民：哎，你干吗^{N1}哪？别关哪！

洪　义：这**案子**呀，案子我先**盯**^{N2}三天再说吧。啊，只能这么着（zhāo）^{N3}了。
　　　　行，好**嘞**，再见。啊，这么着了啊。

警察甲：说那事儿呢？

洪　义：啊。还行吧。

警察甲：有线索吗？

洪　义：没什么**正经**电话。除了一**帮**^{G1}**熟人**，多少年不见的都给我打电话。

警察甲：那还不好？

洪　义：嗯，有什么好的^{N4}？

洪　义：喂，喂，喂？

洪　义：喂，您好。**派出所值班**电话。喂。

林　慧：喂？

洪　义：您是看了电视上的报道才打电话的吧？喂，我就是电视上那个警察，
　　　　有什么情况请讲。请你不要害怕。万一有什么事情，警方可以向你提
　　　　供^{N5}**保护**的。喂，喂。哎？

洪　义：62026770。不说也行，就怕你不打电话。

林　慧：哎，今儿^{N6}咱们吃什么呀？

冯铁民：甜甜呀，想吃什么跟爸爸说。

案子	ànzi	n.	legal case
盯	dīng	v.	keep a close watch on; tail
嘞	lei	ono.	indicate a positive and optimistic attitude as in 好嘞,我就去!(All right, I'm going now)! or 雪停了,回家嘞!(It stopped snowing, let's go home)!
正经	zhèngjing	adj.	serious (work-related)
帮	bāng	m.	gang; clique; a group of people (derogatory)
熟人	shúrén	n.	acquaintance; friend
派出所	pàichūsuǒ	n.	local police station
值班	zhí bān	vo.	be on duty(in turn)
保护	bǎohù	v.	care and protect from harm

甜　甜：我喜欢……我爸爸做的我都吃。

林　慧：哎哟，真会说话呀。

洪　义：呃，她叫林慧，是这个**天体**研究所的**会计**。家里条件不错，有个小女儿。她丈夫呢，是她们所里的一个科长。呃，林慧本人也没**前科**[N7]，而且呢，在单位表现还不错。就是头几年[N8]跟她丈夫刚结婚的时候，好像有点**矛盾**。但是后来也**平稳**多了。所以我想，**所长**，面对面地问她一回[G2]，您看行吗？

所　长：问吧。可别**胡问**啊。别问出家庭问题来。

洪　义：哎，好。所长，那我走了。

所　长：哎，好。

林　慧：这是什么？

甜　甜：轮船。

天体	tiāntǐ	n.	celestial body
会计	kuài·jì	n.	accountant；bookkeeper
前科	qiánkē	n.	previous criminal record
矛盾	máodùn	n.	problems；conflicts
平稳	píngwěn	adj.	stable；smooth；calm
所长	suǒzhǎng	n.	head of an institute (head of 派出所 as in this script)
胡（问）	hú(wèn)	adv.	same as "乱（问）" or "瞎（问）"；(see part 1, note 4)

林　慧：这个呢？

甜　甜：火车。

林　慧：这个呢？

甜　甜：太阳。房子。

林　慧：这是什么呀？

甜　甜：嗯，太阳。

林　慧：这个是太阳。这个是什么？

甜　甜：这个啊……这个……

林　慧：铁民——

冯铁民：来了啊。哎哟，王奶奶，你好你好。

王奶奶：你好。冯科长，在家呢[N9]？

冯铁民：哎，在家呢。来来来，进来坐……

王奶奶：哎，好、好。这是派出所的小洪同志。

冯铁民：哎，你好、你好。

王奶奶：我正带着他**挨家挨户**地排查呢。不光是你们家啊，这一片儿全都得查。

冯铁民：哎哟，看您说的。我听见啦，您去对门儿的时候我就听见啦。

林　慧：是……哎！甜甜！

甜　甜：王奶奶——

王奶奶：哎——甜甜，妈妈在家吗？

甜　甜：在，在屋里。

冯铁民：在在在，在里屋。慧儿……

林　慧：您来啦？

王奶奶：哎，在家呐？

林　慧：请里边儿坐吧。来来来……

王奶奶：不坐了、不坐了，两句话问完了就走。

冯铁民：王奶奶，那……你们聊，我锅里煮着东西。

王奶奶：你忙、你忙。小洪同志，这一家就是406。

洪　义：好。

王奶奶：**您画勾**。

林　慧：有事儿啊？

| 挨家挨户 | āi jiā āi hù | | door to door |
| 画勾 | huà gōu | vo. | tick off |

洪　义：啊，是这样。7 号那天晚上有个案子，好像电视上也播了，**牵扯**到一个女**证人**的事儿。**暂且**说"女证人"吧。您是叫……？

王奶奶：林慧。

林　慧：对，我叫林慧。

洪　义：7 号晚上您是在家还是在外面？

林　慧：7 号啊？7 号……7 号是……星期……

洪　义：上星期四，星期四。

林　慧：哦，上周四……周四我在家。

洪　义：您再好好想想，肯定在家吗？

林　慧：在啊，在家。

（冯铁民：甜甜，快过来帮爸爸把豆腐……）

洪　义：有没有什么人能证明啊？

冯铁民：警察同志，这事儿我能证明吗？

洪　义：可以。当然可以了。

冯铁民：可以啊？7 号是上个星期……

洪　义：四！

冯铁民：哦，对，星期四。也不管星期几吧。我爱人呢她是天天晚上在家。她不是搞**出纳**的吗？每天工作都挺累的，下了班还得接孩子。这晚上出门儿的，都是那些**单身白领**和这兼着**肥差**儿的，是吧？你们挺忙啊？

王奶奶：那可不。就连咱老太太也歇不住啊，这是。

洪　义：我记一下啊。406。

冯铁民：对。

洪　义：林慧呢，在家。

冯铁民：啊，没错儿[N10]、没错儿。

洪　义：还有人证明。

牵扯	qiānchě	v.	involve; implicate; drag in
证人	zhèng·rén	n.	witness
暂且	zànqiě	adv.	for the moment; temporarily; for the time being
出纳	chūnà	n.	(of an organization or enterprise) payment and receipt of cash or bills
单身	dānshēn	adj.	unmarried or single person
白领	báilǐng	adj.	white collar (worker)
兼	jiān	v.	do two or more jobs concurrently
肥差儿	féichāir	n.	profitable post or job

注释 Notes

1. **"干吗"**：意思是"干什么"，北方口语。

   A Northern expression meaning："What are you doing now?"

2. **"盯"**："盯"的意思是把视线固定在某一点，这里的意思是"这个案子近三天我会一直注意着"。

   "盯" usually means " to gaze at" or " to stare at"，used in this context to mean "keep a close watch on sb. or sth.

3. **"这么着"**：意思是"这样"。

   "这么着" means "like this" or "So . . .".

4. **"（嗯,）有什么好的？"**：这是一个反问句，意思是"这不好"。

   It's a rhetorical sentence which means："What's good about it?"

5. **"向……提供**（帮助、援助、情报、线索等）"：

   Provide. . . with help/assistance/information/clues/leads etc.

   （1）中国和美国都向伊朗提供赈灾援助。

   Both China and America have provided Iran with disaster relief.

   （2）万一有什么事情警方可以向你提供保护的。

   The police will provide protection to a witness who helps to bring criminals to justice.

   （3）谁向敌人提供了我方的军事情报？

   Who provided the enemy with our military intelligence.

6. **"今ᵣ"**：意思是"今天"。口语。

   "今ᵣ" is the same as "今天"，meaning "today".

7. **"没前科"**：意思是"以前没有犯过罪"。

   "没前科" means someone who has no previous criminal record.

8. **"头几年"**：意思是"一段时间刚开始的几年"或"从现在算以前的几年"。口语。

   "头几年" meaning "in the first few year of . . .".

   （1）就是头几年跟她丈夫刚结婚的时候，好像有点矛盾。

   A few years ago when they just got married, there seemed to be some issues between her and her husband.

（2）公司刚成立的头几年，人少，钱也赚得不多。

In the first few years after the establishment of our company we had fewer employees and the company made little profit.

9. **"在家呢"**:

王奶奶：你好。冯科长，在家呢？

冯铁民：哎，在家呢。来来来，进来坐……

在这个对话中，"在家呢？"也是一种问候方式。就像《风波》第一部分注释1。

王奶奶：Hello, Officer Feng, you are home?

冯铁民：Oh, yes. I'm home, come in and take a seat...

In this dialog, "在家呢？" is merely a kind of greeting, similar to the expression explained in note 1 in part 1 of《风波》.

10. **"没错**儿**"**："错儿"是一个名词，意思是"错误"，口语。剧中冯铁民说"没错儿"，意思是"你说得对。"

"错儿" is a northern colloquial expression for "错误". "没错儿" means："You are quite right!"

语法 Grammar Notes

1. **"帮"**：用于人的量词，有时有一点贬义。

   "帮" is a measure word, used to mean a group of people a gang or a clique. It sometimes carries a derogatory tone.

   （1）除了一帮熟人，多少年不见的都给我打电话。

   Beside a bunch of acquaintances, I also get calls from people who I haven't seen for years.

   （2）这帮年轻人，什么正经事都不干，一天到晚就知道玩。

   This gang of young people idle away all day and never does anything constructive.

2. **"回"**：动量词，用于事情，动作的次数。例如：

   "回" is a verbal classifier. E. g.

   （1）所以我想，所长，面对面地问她一回，您看行吗？

   Therefore, I think we should ask her in person once, what do you think, Chief?

   （2）他来过几回。

   He's been here a few times.

   （3）一回生，二回熟。

   An expression meaning "First time strangers, second time friends"; Experience comes with practice.

练习 Exercises

一、口语练习 Oral Practice

（一）回答问题 Answer the following questions

1. 关于案子里的那个女证人，警察发现什么新情况了吗？

2. 62026770 这个电话号码可能是谁的？那个人为什么给警察打电话又不说话呢？

3. 请你介绍一下林慧的情况（工作，职务，家庭，婚姻）。

4. 冯铁民说发生车祸那天林慧在哪里？

5. 王奶奶是做什么的？有工资吗？小洪是谁？他们为什么晚上到林慧家里来？王奶奶为什么说"我正带着他挨家挨户地排查呢。不光是你们家啊，这一片儿全都得查。"

6. 冯铁民有什么证据能证明发生事故的那天晚上林慧在家吗？

二、书写练习 Written Exercises

（一）选择适当的词语完成下列对话 Complete the following dialogue by filling the blanks with appropriate words or expressions

A. 有什么好的	B. 这么着（zhāo）	C. 干吗
D. 没错儿	E. 别胡问	

1. 甲：_____ 呢？

   乙：打电话呢。有什么事儿？

2. 甲：你日子过得真舒服，每天上班没事儿干！

   乙：_____ ，一个月就这么几个小钱！

3. 甲：我面对面地问他一回，怎么样？

   乙：可_____啊。别问出家庭问题来 。

4. 甲：这案子交给谁呢？

   乙：我先盯三天再说吧。大家都忙，只能 _____ 了 。

5. 甲：我看王奶奶完全相信冯铁民的话了。

乙：_____！

（二）用适当的疑问代词填空 Fill in blanks with appropriate interrogatives

1. 你看到了_____就说_____，不要害怕。

2. 你说的话有没有_____可以证明呢？

3. 你_____天都忙，在家里老也见不到你。

4. 昨晚他_____也没去。一直在家陪孩子看书。

5. 安安稳稳地过日子，比_____都强。

6. 周末想去_____玩玩儿吗？

（三）填空 Fill in blanks with appropriate words

A. 暂且	B. 光	C. 案子	D. 播	E. 牵扯	F. 正

七号那天晚上有个____，好象电视上也____了，____到一个女证人的事儿。____说"女证人"吧。我现在____带着警察挨家挨户地排查呢。不____是你们家啊，这一片儿全都得查。

A. 不管	B. 天天	C. 搞	D. 接	E. 挺

好像是星期四，……_____星期几吧。我爱人她是_____晚上在家。她不是_____出纳的吗？每天工作都_____累的，下了班还得_____孩子。

A. 回	B. 条件	C. 会计	D. 表现	E. 科长
F. 本人	G. 结婚	H. 矛盾	I. 平稳	

她叫林慧，是这个天体研究所的。家里_____不错，有个小女儿。她丈夫呢，是她们所里的一个_____。呃，林慧_____也没前科，而且呢在单位_____还不错。就是头几年跟她丈夫刚_____的时候，好像有点_____。但是后来关系_____多了。我想我们可以面对面地问她一_____，您看行吗？

三

冯铁民：这回可能要赢了。

林　慧：铁民，铁民——

冯铁民：啊？怎么啦^{N1}？

林　慧：那天晚上我出去了。星期四，我不在家。

冯铁民：什么星期四？哦，我记不清楚了。跟他们用**不着**说**实话**，案子最好别
　　　　牵进去。

林　慧：为什么呀？

冯铁民：**本来**^{G1}没什么事儿嘛。一说**倒**^{G2}有事儿了。好！哎哟，差点儿、差点儿。

林　慧：那你说，能有什么事儿啊？

冯铁民：什么什么事儿？你想什么呐？这种**谎撒了就撒了**，无**害**^{G3}。

林　慧：可是我……我……

冯铁民：哎呀，我们现在不是挺好吗？**安安稳稳**地过日子，比什么都强^{N2}，是
　　　　不是，啊？快去睡觉，别冻着了^{N3}。让我看会儿球。

林　慧：看就看呗。

冯铁民：睡觉去吧。

林　慧：看吧……

　　（电视**解说**：好的，扫过了，停，**射门**——）

冯铁民：哎哟，进了进了进了。

女同事：哎，想什么呐？

林　慧：哦。

用不着	yòng bu zháo		there is no need；not necessary
实话	shíhuà	n.	honest words；truth
牵	qiān	v.	involve；pull into；implicate
撒（谎）	sā(huǎng)	v.	说（谎），说（假话）tell a lie；lie
害	hài	n.	harm，意思是"害处"
安安稳稳	ān an wěn wěn	adj.	smooth and steady, e.g. 安安稳稳地过日子 to live a peaceful life
解说	jiěshuō	v./n.	explain (orally)；comment
射门	shè mén	vo.	shoot (at the goal) in soccer, football, etc.
同事	tóngshì		colleague；co-worker

女同事：又想你们家甜甜晚上睡觉尿床的事儿啦？

林　慧：晚上不敢给她喝水。这么大了还尿床。唉，现在的孩子太娇气，就算醒了也不动，非得尿床。

女同事：瞧你把甜甜说的。哎，我听我妈说呀，有个偏方。给她吃两个猪苦胆就好了。回家啊试试去。

林　慧：谢谢你啊。

女同事：喂，你好。哎，在，您稍[N4]等啊。林慧，你电话。

林　慧：谢谢你啊。您好，是我。听出来了。您好。

童　母：林慧，你听我说，你和童可好[N5]了五年，最后没走到一处，主要是我的原因。

林　慧：您跟我说这些干吗呀？

童　母：我很后悔。童可自从你结婚以后，一天一天地走下坡路。这都不说了。他已经五天不见啦。

林　慧：您跟我说那么多干吗[N6]呀？我们已经那么多年没来往了。他不见了您干吗找我呀？

童　母：你听我说，我不光[N7]是给你一个人挂了电话，认识的人我都打了。

林　慧：您别问我了！我不愿意想那些事儿。

童　母：我是担心，不知道他现在去了哪儿了。

林　慧：我告诉您，我不知道！不知道！

童　母：打扰了。最后我借这个机会，算是给你俩的事儿道个歉吧。我很后悔。

尿	niào	v.	urinate; piss; pee
娇气	jiāo·qì	adj.	delicate; squeamish; fragile
偏方	piānfāng	n.	folk prescription
苦胆	kǔdǎn	n.	gall bladder
下坡路	xiàpō lù		downhill path; downhill journey
不见了	bú jiàn le		disappear
道歉	dào qiàn	vo.	apologize

注释 Notes

1. "**怎么啦?**": 意思是 "发生了什么事情?" What's happened? What's up?
   E. g.:
   (1) 冯铁民: 你怎么啦?
      冯铁民, what's happened?

2. "**强**": 意思是 "好"。
   "强" means "better than"。
   (1) 我们现在不是挺好吗? 安安稳稳地过日子, 比什么都强。
      Isn't our situation fine now? Living peacefully is better than anything.
   (2) 他比我强, 足球他都踢了好几年了。
      He is better than I since he has been playing soccer for quite a few years.
   (3) 现在的生活比以前强多了!
      Life now is much better than before!

3. "**别冻着了!**"
   Don't catch cold!

4. "**稍**"(副词): 表示数量不多, 程度不深或时间短暂。
   "稍", an adverb, means "a little", "a bit" or "slightly". It is used to modify monosyllabic verbs, adjectives or localizers, to indicate a moderate degree, a fair amount or a short period of time. See the following examples:
   (1) 请您稍等一下。
      Wait for a second please!
   (2) 这个菜稍咸了点儿。
      This dish is a little too salty.
   (3) 去美国人家做客, 客人稍晚一点到为好。
      Being guests to an American family, it's customary to arrive slightly later than the expected time.

5. "**好(了五年)**": "好" 意思是 "友好", "相好", 可以表示一般好朋友之间的关系, 也可以表示男女朋友之间的关系。此处指的是后者。

"好" in "好（了五年）" means "友好 friendly", "相好 be on intimate terms". It is used to describe a relationship between friends as well as lovers. It's used here to refer to the latter. Examples of using "好" in this context：

(1) 你和童可好了五年，最后没走到一处。

"好", used in this context, means "date". "你和童可好了五年，最后没走到一处" means "You and Tong Ke dated for five years，but did not eventually end up marrying each other."

(2) 甲：他们俩好起来了，你知道吗？

Do you know that the two started dating each other?

乙：我知道。但那是一个星期前的消息了，他们现在已经不好了！

I know. But it is last week's news. They broke up already!

6. "干吗"：在这里是问原因，有"为什么"的意思，常含有责问、不高兴的语气。Why on earth；whatever for，it's different from "你干吗呢" which means "你做什么呢？"

(1) 您跟我说那么多干吗呀？我们已经那么多年没来往了。

Why on earth are you talking to me about all this, we haven't had anything to do with each other for years.

(2) 他不见了您干吗找我呀？

Why did you come to see me about his disappearance?

(3) 问我干吗，我又不知道！

Why do you ask me, how would I know! (polite)

What the hell you ask me for? How could I know! (angry and rude)

7. "光"：意思是"仅仅，只，就"。

"光" is an adverb, meaning "not only"，"not merely"

(1) 你听我说，我不光是给你一个人挂了电话，认识的人我都打了。

Listen to me, you are not the only one I called, I have called everyone I know.

(2) 光学费就得付近3万，还有吃、住和零花钱呢！

Tuition alone will cost nearly ＄30,000 and then there is room, board and pocket money!

语法 Grammar Notes

1. **"本来"（副词）**：意思是"原先、先前"，可以用在主语后，也可以用在主语前。

   "本来" is an adverb. It means "原先 formerly or originally", "先前 before, previously".

   It can be placed before or after the subject in a sentence.

   （1）我们明天本来要去长城，因为下雨，改去中国现代文学馆了。

   We had originally planned to go to the Great Wall tomorrow, but ended up visiting the Chinese Museum of Modern Literature instead because of rain.

   （2）我本来夏天要去中国学中文，因为没有拿到奖学金，就没去。

   Originally I was going to study in China this summer; it didn't happen because I failed to get the scholarship.

   （3）他们本来是好朋友，因为多年不来往，关系越来越疏远了。

   They used to be close friends and became more and more distant due to lack of contact.

2. **"本来……倒……"**："倒"的意思"反而、反倒"，与一般的事实或情理相反。

   "倒" means "反而、反倒". "本来…… 倒……" is used to indicate an opposite outcome, or a situation, contrary to reality or reason.

   （1）本来没有什么问题，一说倒有问题了。

   There had been no problem until you mentioned it!

   （2）本来不觉得有什么病，去医院一检查，现在一天到晚倒觉得不舒服了！

   I had felt fine until the physical; now I somehow don't feel well all the time!

   （3）本来不想吃，一看见这么多好吃的倒觉得饿了。

   I wasn't going to eat, but seeing all the delicious stuff in front of me I felt hungry immediately.

   "倒"前面也可以加上"反"：

(1) 本（来）想省点儿事，你这一帮忙反倒更费事了。

The intention was to simplify things with your help, it turned out we actually brought ourselves more trouble.

(2) 他一直为没有工作发愁，找到工作以后反倒不高兴了。

He had been constantly worried about not having a job, but he's become even unhappy after he found one.

(3) 那年春天中国很多地方出现了"非典"，没想到国民生产总值反倒提高到 8.5％。

SARS was discovered in many areas of China in that spring, but who would have thought that China's GDP increased 8.5％ in that year.

(4) 他职位提升了，薪水反倒减少了。

After promotion, his salary surprisingly dropped.

3. **"无害"**："无"是"没有"的意思，"害"是"坏处"的意思。"这种谎撒了就撒了，无害。"这句话的意思是"既然撒了这种谎，就撒了，（不必觉得内疚），因为没有害处。"

"无" means "没有"，"害" means "坏处". This sentence means "Don't worry about it, this kind of lie is harmless. " It expresses that since a lie has been made, there is no need to feel guilty or bad about it since such a lie is harmless.

4. **中文口语句子常常不用连词**：比如上面这个句子中可以加"既然……就……。"

Note：The conjunction "既然……就……" should have been used in such a sentence（这种谎既然撒了就撒了，无害），but as a common feature in spoken Chinese, it's omitted. See the following sentences.

(1) 那女的，不说就不说吧。

意思是：那个女的，既然不想说，就不说吧，（何必非让她说呢）。

Since that woman did not want to say anything, so be it. (There was no need to force her to speak)

(2) 你没兴趣，不去就不去吧。

意思是：既然你没有兴趣，如果不想去，就不去吧。

Since you are not interested, it's fine if you choose not to go. The sentence implies that since you are not really interested 〔in ...〕, if you don't want to go, you don't have to.

练习 Exercises

一、口语练习 Oral Practice

（一）回答问题 Answer the following questions

1. 冯铁民为什么要证明出事那天晚上林慧在家？他相信自己说的话是真的吗？
2. 他为什么认为这种事情跟警察撒谎无害？
3. 你对冯铁民的态度有什么看法？
4. 林慧在跟办公室的同事说话以前是不是在想女儿甜甜晚上睡觉尿床的事儿？在你看来她大概在想什么？
5. 童母是谁？他为什么给林慧打电话？她为什么说她很后悔，还向林慧道歉？

（二）讨论 Discussion

1. 在冯铁民看来，生活里什么最重要？你同意他的看法吗？
2. 冯铁民和林慧的夫妻关系怎么样？你是怎么知道的？
3. 你觉得林慧对童母的态度怎么样？为什么？

二、书写练习 Written Exercises

（一）填空 Fill in blanks with appropriate words

A. 本来	B. 倒	C. 干吗	D. 进去	E. 就
F. 强	G. 稍	H. 光	I. 一	

1. 去一趟昆明 1500 块不够，_____飞机票就 1000 多，还有吃、住和零花钱呢！
2. 找他_____，他不会帮你的！
3. 他说中文的能力比看书_____。
4. 今天我想跟老师说两句话，所以要_____早一点儿去。
5. _____没有什么事儿，你这么_____说_____有事了。
6. 不愿意帮忙_____不来好了，还撒谎！

7. 跟他们用不着说实话，案子最好别牵扯＿＿＿＿＿＿＿。

（二）完成句子 Complete the following dialogue with the given expressions

1. 甲：你不是说这件事跟你没关系吗？

　　乙：＿＿＿＿＿＿＿＿＿＿＿＿。（本来……倒……）

2. 甲：去了那么多人帮忙，新房布置好了吧？

　　乙：＿＿＿＿＿＿＿＿＿＿＿＿。（本来……倒……）

3. 甲：我们要走了，不然就来不及了。

　　乙：请你＿＿＿＿＿＿＿＿＿＿＿。（稍＋Verb）

4. 甲：要是你们没分手该多好，那样童可也不会出事了。

　　乙：＿＿＿＿＿＿＿＿＿＿＿＿。（干吗）

5. 甲：我对京剧真的没什么兴趣。

　　乙：＿＿＿＿＿＿＿＿＿＿＿＿。（既然……，不＋V就不＋V吧）

6. 甲：这间屋子太小了。

　　乙：＿＿＿＿＿＿＿＿＿＿＿＿。（比……强）

7. 甲：王奶奶和警察洪义是不是只查了林慧一家？

　　乙：＿＿＿＿＿＿＿＿＿＿＿＿。（光）

（三）用下列所给词语写一段你和同学之间的对话，内容是发生在你与中国教授之间的一些事情。对话中要用所给词语。

Write out a dialogue between you and a classmate over something that had happened between you and your Chinese professor. You must use all the words and expressions provided.

1. 本来……因为……就……		2. 本来……，……（反）倒……
3. 干吗	4. 怎么啦？	5. 不 Verb 就不 Verb 吧。
6. 比……强	7. 稍＋Verb	8. 光

四

记　者：喂喂，有**信号**吗？有信号吗？喂，喂？我们可以开始了吗？

洪　义：呃，可以开始了。呃，经过我们的调查，呃，**案情**已经有了**进展**。7号那天的案件呢，基本^{G1}确定为^{G2}交通肇事逃逸案。呃，**车型**呢大概情况是……为**桑塔纳**2000型，蓝色的车。呃，我们希望，肇事司机能够**尽快**^{G3}**投案**。同时也希望……

冯铁民：这不是那天那小警察吗？案子还没破啊？这人业务不行。

洪　义：我们希望肇事司机能尽快投案**自首**。同时也希望……

冯铁民：哼哼，自己没本事^{N1}嘛，劝人家。那女的，肯定不是**局外人**。肯定有见不得人^{N2}的事儿。

林　慧：你怎么知道有见不得人的事儿？

冯铁民：哼，那不**明摆着**的^{N3}吗？那女的知道那男的死了，就跑了，到现在都不敢出来**作证**。

林　慧：甜甜，少喝点儿啊，不然又尿床。

冯铁民：你不能因为怕她尿床就不给喝水呀。

林　慧：甜甜，别画了，妈妈带你去睡觉去。

信号	xìnhào	n.	signal; sign given by light, electric wave, sound, gesture, etc. to convey information or a command.
案情	ànqíng	n.	details of a case
进展	jìnzhǎn	n./v.	new development; making progress
车型	chēxíng	n.	design or model of vehicles
桑塔纳	Sāngtǎnà	N.	Wolks-wagen
尽快	jǐnkuài	adv.	as soon as possible; as quickly as one can
投案	tóu àn	vo.	give oneself up or surrender oneself to the police
自首	zìshǒu	v.	(of a criminal) voluntarily surrender oneself; give oneself up
局外人	júwàirén	n.	outsider
明摆着	míngbǎi zhe		evidently; obvious
作证	zuò zhèng	vo.	testify; give evidence; bear witness

冯铁民：哎，你想看那节目你就看呗。你说那个小警察他也嫩[N4]了点儿啊？那女的，不说就不说吧。我要是碰上这种事儿，我也不说。干吗要说啊。

冯铁民：哎，在里边干吗呢？老半天[N5]的。

林　慧：啊？马桶坏了。

冯铁民：马桶坏了明儿再修呗。你要是怕我忘了的话写个条儿，放那儿提醒我。赶紧睡觉吧，啊。

林　慧：铁民啊，有些话，我当着你说不出来[N6]。几次想说，不知道怎么开口[N7]。那个逃避作证的女人，是我。唉，7 号那天，我对你撒了谎。我没去车站接人。那天，我是接了童可的电话出去的，他要还给我以前来往的书信和照片。这事儿我不知该怎么对你说。见面以后，他问我借 10 万块钱，说欠人家的，不还就过不去了。我说我没有。他说你是出纳，可以先挪用公款。3 年不见，他变成这个样子！我问他要信和照片，他说没带，说了很多话求我。我不知怎么办，就挣开他的手往马路对面跑。他在后面追我的时候被一辆车撞了。童可死了……

甜　甜：爸爸，我要尿尿！

冯铁民：啊，来了啊。

林　慧：……我知道，那一晚的事儿是没法向你解释清楚了……

甜　甜：爸爸，这儿有一封信。

冯铁民：放那儿吧。

嫩	nèn	adj.	inexperienced
马桶	mǎtǒng	n.	night stool; chamber.pot
条儿	tiáor	n.	note; written message
赶紧	gǎnjǐn	adv.	same as 赶快
当(面)	dāng(miàn)		to sb's face; facing sb.; confronting in sb's presence; in front of (someone)
逃避	táobì	v.	run away from; escape
欠	qiàn	v.	owe
挪用	nuóyòng	v.	divert (funds); embezzle; line one's pocket with public funds
公款	gōngkuǎn	n.	public money or fund
挣开	zhèng kai	vc.	struggle to get free
追	zhuī	v.	chase (run) after; pursuing

林　慧：……我安慰自己，童可的死跟我没一点儿关系，我可以把那个晚上的事永远**隐瞒**下去……

冯铁民：甜甜……

甜　甜：哎，我没洗手呢。

林　慧：……我没**把握**说出来，会不会把咱家给**毁**了。我也能想象，你对这事儿的**敏感**。这些天，我过得很**痛苦**。童可的妈来过电话找童可。我无法面对童可那张被撞烂的脸，也不愿意想起老太太着急的样子。想想，只有去说。我可能不会太早回来。如果你看了信不想见我，可以像上次那样把门口的福字**揭**下来。我会……回我妈家住一段^{N8}。

林　慧：您怎么在这儿？

童　母：童可找到了。他被汽车撞死了。我是看了电视去认的。脸烂了。是他……你不用劝我。

林　慧：啊，我……我来找个人。

童　母：那我就不用电话告（诉）你了。有事儿你去忙吧，我坐会儿。

林　慧：不忙……其实那个人找不找，也**无所谓**^{N9}。

洪　义：这位就是死者**家属**。老太太，这是我们所长。

所　长：您坐、您坐……**善后**的事我们会帮您处理。小关，过来一下^{G4}。这是死者家属，善后的事你帮她处理一下。您多**保重**。洪义，我们去见一下肇事司机。

洪　义：好。

隐瞒	yǐnmán	v.	conceal; hide; cover up; hold back the facts from revealing
把握	bǎwò	v.	not sure; not certain
毁	huǐ	v.	ruin; defame
敏感	mǐngǎn	adj.	sensitive; susceptible
痛苦	tòngkǔ	adj.	pain; suffering; agony
烂	làn	v.	broken; badly damaged；（脸烂了）
揭	jiē	v.	remove; peel off
无所谓	wúsuǒwèi		It doesn't matter; it is not important
家属	jiāshǔ	n.	family members;（family）dependants
善后	shànhòu	n.	funeral arrangements; deal with the aftermath
保重	bǎozhòng	v.	take care of oneself

小　关：您还有什么事儿吗？

童　母：让我安静一会儿。回头我找您去。

小　关：好，您坐吧。

林　慧：电梯，电梯等我一下！哎，谢谢……

王奶奶：林慧，你们家信。

林　慧：谢谢您啊。

王奶奶：不客气。

小关	XiǎoGuān	N.	A young man surnamed Guan

"当着你" means "in your presence." "当着你我说不出来" means, "I can't say it in your presence."

2. "开口": 意思是……
几次想告诉你，不知道怎么开口。
Several times I wanted to tell you, but I didn't know how to begin.

3. "歇一歇": 意思是"休息一段时间"。
"歇一歇" means……
……

"无所谓" means "It doesn't matter" and……
那个人挺不使，也无所谓……

注释 Notes

1. **"没本事"**：口语，"没本事"的意思是没有"本领、能力"。

"本事" is the same as "本领" which means "skill"; "ability" or "capability".

"没本事" means "not capable".

这些警察真没本事，都三个月了案子还没破呢！

Those cops are really useless，it's been three months，and they still haven't cracked the case!

2. **"见不得人"**：意思是"不能让人看见或知道"，多因为做了不好的、丢人的事。

"见不得人" means "can not let others see or know", the expression is usually used to describe something shady or shameful that someone has done and tries to hide it.

你怎么知道她有见不得人的事儿？

How do you know she has something shady or shameful to hide from us?

3. **"明摆着"**：意思是"很明显"。"那不明摆着的吗?"意思是"那不是很清楚（明显）吗?"

"明摆着" means "obvious". "那不明摆着的吗?" means "Isn't it obvious?" or " isn't it as clear as daylight?"

4. **"嫩"**：这里的意思是"年轻，没经验"，口语。

"嫩" is a colloquial expression，used here to describe someone who is young and inexperienced.

你说那个小警察他也嫩了点儿呵！

Don't you think that cop is a bit too green?

5. **"老半天的"**：意思是"很长时间"。

"老半天的" means "a long time" or "ages".

在里边干吗呢? 老半天的。

It's been ages，what the hell did you do in there?

6. **"当着你"**：意思是"在你面前"。"当着你我说不出来"意思是"我在你面前说不出来"。

"当着你" means "in your presence." "当着你我说不出来" means "I can't say it in your presence."

7. "开口": 意思是 "说"。

几次想说，不知道怎么开口。

Several times I wanted to tell you, but I didn't know how to begin.

8. "住一段": 意思是 "住一段时间"。

"住一段" means "住一段时间" to live (here) for a while.

9. "无所谓": 意思是 "没关系"。

"无所谓" means "It doesn't matter" and "it is not important".

那个人找不找，也无所谓。

It doesn't matter whether we look for the man or not.

语法 Grammar Notes

1. "基本（上）"：basic，basically
   （1）她基本上同意我们的意见。
       She basically agrees with us.
   （2）那个案子的性质已经基本上定了。
       The nature of that case has been basically decided.

2. "为（wéi）"：意思是"是"，书面语。
   "为" used in written Chinese means the same as "是"（to be）in spoken Chinese.
   7 号那天的案件，基本确定为交通肇事逃逸案。
   The incident that occurred on the 7th has been basically determined to be a hit-and-run case.

3. "尽快（早）"：意思是"尽可能快（早）"。
   "尽快" or "尽早" means "soon" or "as soon as possible". E. g.
   （1）我们希望肇事司机能够尽快投案自首。
       We hope the perpetrator will turn himself in soon.
   （2）这件事情既然已经决定就最好尽快通知他。
       Since a decision has been made，we'd better inform him as soon as possible.

4. "一下"：动词后加"一下"有缓和语气的作用。如本课中的例句：
   "一下" is used after a verb functioning to soften the tone of a sentence. The following use of "一下" is to soften the tone.
   （1）好，那你叙述一下当天的情况好吗？
       So，would you mind describing to us what happened on that day please？
   （2）小关，过来一下。
       Xiao Guan，come over here for a second.
   （3）这是死者家属，善后的事你帮她处理一下。
       This is the family member of the deceased，could you please help her deal with the aftermath of the death.

（4）洪义，我们去见一下肇事司机。

Hong Yi, let's go see the driver who had the accident.

（5）电梯，电梯等我一下！

Elevator, elevator, wait for a second!

练习 Exercises

■ 一、口语练习 Oral Practice

（一）回答问题 Answer the follwing questions

1. 警察洪义在电视上说了些什么？

2. 为什么冯铁民认为那个警察在找的女人一定有什么见不得人的事？

3. 童可为什么想见林慧？他跟林慧有什么关系？

4. 童可为什么对林慧撒谎？它撒了个什么谎？他想叫林慧做什么？

5. 童可是怎么被车撞死的？林慧有责任吗？

6. 如果你是林慧，你会怎么做？

7. 如果你是冯铁民，你会怎样对待这件事？

（二）讨论 Discussion

1. 冯铁民是一个什么样的人？林慧是个坏人吗？为什么？

2. 此剧为何叫"无端介入"？

3. 在你们国家，女证人遇到林慧这种情况，会怎么做？她如果出来作证，对她的家庭会有影响吗？

■ 二、书写练习 Written Exercises

（一）完成句子 Complete the following sentences

1. 看他斯斯文文的样子，想不到竟然＿＿＿＿＿＿＿＿＿＿。（见不得人）

2. 有意见最好＿＿＿＿＿＿＿＿＿。（当面）

3. ＿＿＿＿＿＿＿＿＿，以后还会有机会。（无所谓）

4. ＿＿＿＿＿＿＿＿＿，那个案子都 3 年了还没破呢。（没本事）

5. 你们的看法＿＿＿＿＿＿＿＿＿。（基本上）

（二）填空 Fill in the blanks

A. 嫩	B. 着	C. 得	D. 为	E. 尽	F. 破	G. 者

1. 这些警察真没本事，都 5 个月了案子还没＿＿＿＿呢！

2. 他做过的见不_____人的事儿可多了！

3. 有些话，我当_____你的面说不出来。

4. 你说那个小警察他也_____了点儿啊！

5. 7号那天的案件，基本上确定_____交通肇事逃逸案。

6. 这件事情既然已经决定了就最好_____快通知他。

7. 他是死_____的母亲，善后的事情你帮她处理一下。

（三）补语练习 Exercise on complements

用适当补语填空，每个选项只能用一次。Fill in the blanks with appropriate complements, each word could only be used once.

A. 去	B. 着	C. 烂	D. 上	E. 到	F. 完	G. 开
H. 出	I. 来	G. 住	K. 坏	L. 起	M. 清	N. 来
O. 下去	P. 出来	Q. 下来	R. 进去	S. 不去		

1. 8点多钟我出来倒水，我那一桶泔水还没倒_____呢，就听见那边"咚"的一声，车就把那人给撞了。

2. 那辆车是什么颜色的我没看_____。那车呀，撞了人以后它就跑了。

3. 事故发生以后她四处找人帮忙，急_____了。

4. 过了一会儿，那女的说去打电话，她从包里掏_____一个小本子，……就走了。

5. 她走了以后就再也没回_____。

6. 你可以面对面地问她一回，但是可别胡问啊。别问_____家庭问题。

7. 大家都挺忙的，就连咱老太太也歇不_____啊！

8. 星期四晚上我出_____了，不在家。

9. 跟他们用不_____说实话，案子最好别牵_____。

10. 我要是碰_____这种事儿，我也不说。干吗要说啊。

11. 好几年没见面了，他刚开始说话时，我在电话里没听_____是他。

12. 7号那天晚上有个案子，电视上也播了，牵扯_____一个女证人的事儿。

13. 见面以后，童可问我借10万块钱，说欠人家的，不还就过_____了。我说我没有。他说了很多话求我。我不知怎么办，就挣_____他的手往马路对面跑。他在后面追我的时候被一辆车撞了。

14. 我安慰自己，童可的死跟我没一点儿关系，我可以把那个晚上的事永远隐瞒_____，可是我无法面对童可那张被撞_____的脸，也不愿意想_____老太太着急的样子。

15. 如果你看了信不想见我，可以像上次那样把门口的福字揭_____。

（四）作文 Composition

以林慧的口气给警察写一封匿名信，讲述事故发生的过程及自己的心情。

Write an anonymous letter to the police to describe the accident as well as your emotional state since it happened on Thursday night.

（五）了解中国 Social and Culture Discovery

"街道居委会"是中国城镇居民的一个基层管理组织。剧中的王奶奶就是"街道居委会"的工作人员。请你对这个组织的产生、发展、工作人员及其社会作用做些调查研究。写一个简单的报告。

The Neighborhood Committee is a grass-roots level organization in urban areas of China. Granny Wang is a member of the committee. Please do some research on this organization，its inception，development，its staffing and function. Write out a brief report on your research findings.

第三课 门里门外

Making a Mountain out of a Molehill

导读:

怎样防止小偷进屋子里偷东西呢? 刘伟的妻子听说有一家因为门口放了一双旧男鞋, 小偷就没敢进去。刘伟家也这样做了。热心的刘伟还建议新邻居王娜也这样做, 因为王娜说丈夫出差, 家里只有她一个人, 怕不安全。新婚的王娜没有丈夫的旧鞋, 就借了刘伟的旧鞋放在自己家门口。没想到这双鞋被爱管闲事、爱传闲话的王婶看见了, 由此引起的一场误会, 几乎导致这对新婚夫妇离婚。

Introduction:

What do people do to prevent burglary? Liu Wei's wife heard that one of her neighbors had left a pair of used man's shoes on the front doorstep, which stopped a thief from entering the house. Liu Wei's family followed suit and also suggested the idea to their next-door neighbor, Wang Na, a newly-wed. Wang Na's husband was on a business trip, and kind-hearted Liu Wei thought Wang Na should take some extra precautions. But since newly-wed Wang Na did not have a pair of used man's shoes, Liu Wei loaned her a pair of his own. Unexpectedly, this pair of shoes was spotted by the nosy gossiper, Auntie Wang. This misunderstanding led to a marital crisis that almost brought the newly-weds to the edge of divorce.

主要人物（Main Characters）

刘伟	Liú Wěi	a married young man
刘伟妻	Liú Wěi qī	Liu Wei's wife
王娜	Wáng Nà	a newly-married young woman，Liu Wei's new neighbor
牛俊	Niú Jùn	Wang Na's husband
王婶儿	Wáng shěnr	Aunt Wang（a respectful form of address for an woman of one's mother's age）
老黄	Lǎo Huáng	Old Huang（Aunt Wang's husband）

王　婶：嘿，刘伟。

刘　伟：哟，王婶儿。

王　婶：把车放车棚里去。

刘　伟：啊？

王　婶：现在街道上宣传防盗。

刘　伟：王婶，有您这么一个小……

王　婶：什么？我这小脚侦缉队[N1]？

刘　伟：哎，不是，不是，我是说呀，有您这么一个小区卫士，哎，天天这么一溜达，什么东西也丢不了。

刘　伟：不对呀。

刘伟妻：哎，你在家呢，吓了我一跳。

刘　伟：是啊，在屋里开门，不是我，能是谁呀？

刘伟妻：去放厨房去。

刘　伟：哎。

刘伟妻：哎，那个……放盆里[N2]啊，里面有条鱼。

婶儿	shěnr	n.	本来称叔叔的妻子，也可以称父辈的人的妻子，aunt (uncle's wife); a respectful form of address for an woman of one's parents' age
车棚	chēpéng	n.	awning or shed for bicycles
街道	jiēdào	n.	residential district; neighborhood
宣传	xuānchuán	v.	publicize; promote
防盗	fángdào	vo.	防备强盗，guard against theft; theft-proof
小脚	xiǎojiǎo	n.	bound feet (of women in the old days)
侦缉	zhēnjī	v.	detective
小区	xiǎoqū	n.	residential area; subdivision
卫士	wèishì	n.	guard
溜达	liūdɑ	v.	patrol; stroll
吓(了)一跳	xià (le) yí tiào	v.	be taken aback
盆(儿)	pén(r)	n.	basin; pot

刘　伟：知道了。

刘伟妻：你又在屋里抽烟来着。

刘　伟：啊，**闻出来**了？嗬，要说您这鼻子，比那什么都**灵**。

刘伟妻：你说什么？

刘　伟：哎，不是，我是说比我的鼻子都灵。

刘伟妻：跟你说了，不让你在屋里抽烟，**成心**[N3]哪。

刘　伟：就抽一口，剩下的不（是）在厨房**解决**的吗！

刘伟妻：得了，我看哪，你也改不了。回屋去，给我吧。

刘　伟：哎。

刘伟妻：哎，你**盯**着我干什么，**犯吆挣**[N4]啊。

刘　伟：哎，咱门口那双鞋是怎么回事啊？

刘伟妻：那不是你的吗，我搁的。

刘　伟：我说门口怎么有双鞋呢，**敢情**是我的鞋啊。

刘伟妻：好啊，刘伟，你**小子****居然****怀疑**起我来了。

刘　伟：哎，没有没有没有。

刘伟妻：你还不承认。

刘　伟：不是，我以为呀。

刘伟妻：你以为什么？

刘　伟：我以为咱们家来客人了。

刘伟妻：你也不好好想想，就说咱们家来了什么人，人家把鞋脱在门口，光着脚走啊。

刘　伟：也是，那玩意儿[N5]也**扎得慌**哪。

闻出来	wén chulai	vc.	figure out by smelling; semll out
灵	líng	adj.	clever; sensitive
成心	chéngxīn	adv.	故意,intentionally; on purpose; deliberately
解决	jiějué	v.	finish off (as used in this context);solve
盯	dīng	v.	fix one's eyes on; stare at
犯吆挣	fàn yìzheng	vo.	(col.) (see note 4)
敢情	gǎnqing	adv.	原来,it turns out that ...
小子	xiǎozi	n.	brat; chap
居然	jūrán	adv.	竟,unexpectedly; to one's surprise
怀疑	huáiyí	v.	suspect; question
扎得慌	zhā de huang	vc.	prickly

刘伟妻：哎呀，因为这么点事儿，你就**胡思乱想**，我看哪，这日子没法过。

刘　伟：哎，夫人，夫人，**息怒**，我给您**赔不是**[N6]，**还不成吗**？

刘伟妻：不行。

刘　伟：那，你干吗往门口放双鞋呀？

刘伟妻：听王婶说呀，她爱人他们**单位**的宿舍，**大白天**的呢，让**贼**偷了好几家，其中有一家呀，也没人，可门口就**搁**[N7]了双男鞋，那贼就**愣**[N8]没敢进去。

刘　伟：好主意呀，**敢情**[N9]是双防盗鞋，你怎么早不说呀。

刘伟妻：现在跟你说也不晚呀，可你呢，还敢怀疑我。

刘　伟：没有没有，真不错。哎，我再出一好主意，从今天开始，把我这鞋呀全放在门口那边，然后咱们**出门**之前呀，再把咱们录音机放上，录点**咳嗽吵架摔**东西什么的，然后呢，让声音放个不停。这样屋里老有声，再**胆大**的**毛贼**，他也**休想迈进**咱们家**半步**。

刘伟妻：就你**贫**[N10]。

刘　伟：哎，**乐了**，乐了。以后，哎，我要是再胡思乱想，我就……

胡思乱想	hú sī luàn xiǎng		give way to foolish fancies
息怒	xīnù	v.	停止发怒、别生气,stop being angry（formal）
赔不是	péi búshì	vo.	（col.）apologize（＝道歉）
还不成吗	hái bùchéng ma		还不行吗？Isn't it enough?
单位	dānwèi	n.	unit; work place
大白天（儿）	dà báitiān(r)		bright daylight
贼	zéi	n.	thief
愣	lèng	adv.	（col.）surprisingly（as used in this story）
出门（儿）	chū mén(r)	vo.	go out; be away from home
咳嗽	késou	v.	cough
吵架	chǎo jià	vo.	quarrel; argue vehemently
摔	shuāi	v.	break
胆大	dǎn dà	adj.	bold
毛贼	máozéi	n.	（col.）thief
休想	xiūxiǎng	v.	不要妄想,don't imagine that it's possible
迈进	mài jin	vc.	get in; step in
半步	bàn bù	n.	half a step
贫	pín	adj.	talkative in a witty way
乐了	lè le	v.	（col.）笑了；不生气了,smile, stop being mad

刘　伟：谁呀？

王　娜：您好。

刘　伟：哎，您好。您是？

王　娜：我叫王娜，就住在中间那门。

刘伟妻：是中门的吧，听说你在医院上班呀？

王　娜：是，我是刚搬来的，在**楼道**里我好像见过您。

刘伟妻：见过，见过，你们家的门上还**贴着**喜字儿呢。有事儿呀？

王　娜：可不是嘛，对不起，我得给你们**添点麻烦**了。

刘伟妻：哎，**街里街坊**[N11]的，干吗那么客气。

刘　伟：是。

王　娜：**您瞅我，倒了趟垃圾，门撞上了**，那**钥匙**在屋里头呢。

楼道	lóudào	n.	corridor; hallway
贴着	tiē zhe		posted
（给某人）添麻烦	(gěi mǒu rén) tiān máfan	vo.	trouble (sb.); bother (sb.)
街里街坊	jiē li jiē fāng		(col.) neighbors
瞅	chǒu	v.	(col.) 看，look (at); take a look (at)
倒	dào	v.	dump
趟	tàng	m.	a time; a trip
垃圾	lā·jī	n.	garbage; trash
撞上	zhuàng shang	vc.	locked up; 锁上
钥匙	yàoshi	n.	key

刘　伟：哎哟，赶紧给你爱人打电话。

王　娜：我**爱人**出差了。

王　娜：所以，我想借你们家**改锥**什么的。

刘　伟：干吗呀？

王　娜：我想把门给**撬开**。

刘伟妻：哟，那可不行，让人看见了，你说不清楚啊。

王　娜：这撬自己家门还**犯法**呀？

刘伟妻：来来来，你先别急，坐下，坐下。你呀，可不能撬门，**到时候**出了事儿，**算谁的**呀，再好好想想办法。

王　娜：还有什么办法呀，只能撬门了。

刘伟妻：你家门不是新换的嘛。

王　娜：**可不是**，要不是我着急呢。

刘伟妻：哎，你怎么跑门外头去了。

刘　伟：是啊，现在成了我没钥匙了。王娜，你赶紧回去吧。**幸亏**里面门哪，没用钥匙锁，要不然我都**没招**了，我用东西给你**别开**^{N12}了。

王　娜：真是太感谢您了。

刘　伟：**甭**客气。

刘伟妻：**瞧把你能的**，以后人家要是丢了东西呀，就先找你。

王　娜：大哥大姐可真会开玩笑，我谢你们还来不及呢。

爱人	ài·rén	n.	husband or wife
出差	chū chāi	vo.	go on a business trip
改锥	gǎizhuī	n.	螺丝刀，screwdriver
撬开	qiào kai	vc.	pry open; force open (with a metal stick)
犯法	fàn fǎ	vo.	break the law; violate the law
到时候	dào shíhou		later
算谁的	suàn shuí de		(col.) 谁负责？是谁的责任？who is to blame?
可不是	kě bu shì		(col.) That's true; can't agree (with you) more
幸亏	xìngkuī	adv.	thanks to (that ...)
没招儿	méi zhāor	vo.	(col.)没有办法，helpless
别开	biè kai	vc.	force open (a lock) with a stick
甭	béng	adv.	(col.)不用，need not; no need to (same as 别)
瞧	qiáo	v.	(col.)看，look at
把你能的	bǎ nǐ néng de		(col.) don't boast/show off

刘伟妻：王娜，你爱人老出差，你呀还真得**加点**儿**小心**。

刘　伟：是。

刘伟妻：一个女同志在家。

王　娜：你说那我怎么防啊。我也得上班啊。

刘　伟：这样，你们家门口啊，可以放一双旧鞋。

王　娜：放双旧鞋？

刘　伟：不都那么说嘛，那贼看见门口有鞋呀，肯定屋里有人哪，一进去之后，那也得一**搏**^{N13}呀，是吧，怪^{N14}**费劲**的，**索性**^{G1}他就不进去了。

王　娜：放双鞋不等于说是给贼**预备**的了^{G2}？

刘　伟：哎呀，事儿啊，你得这么想，**顶多**丢双鞋。要是没这双鞋呢，你们家的东西不就等于给贼预备了吗？

王　娜：行，那我回去，找双我不穿的旧鞋给搁上。

刘　伟：不行，不行，要放啊，得放你们家**那口子**的。放你那**高跟**鞋，碰上一个**劫**色不劫财的，你不就**瞎**^{N15}了嘛！

刘伟妻：就你贫。王娜，搁上一双你爱人的旧鞋就行了，我们门口不搁了一双嘛。

王　娜：可我们家牛俊没旧鞋呀，要是放双新鞋，**光**鞋也丢不起呀。

刘　伟：没关系，我们家有。放我的，行吗？

加小心	jiā xiǎoxin	vo.	be careful; be cautious
搏	bó	v.	struggle; fight
费劲	fèi jìn	vo.	labored; with great effort
索性	suǒxìng	adv.	might as well; simply; just
预备	yùbèi	v.	prepare; make ready
顶多	dǐng duō	adv.	at most
那口子	nà kǒuzi	n.	(col.) spouse
高跟（儿）	gāogēn(r)	adj.	high-heeled (shoes)
劫	jié	v.	rob; plunder
瞎	xiā	adj.	(col.) be ruined
光	guāng	adv.	只, only; just

注释 Notes

1. **"小脚侦缉队"**："小脚"指缠足的女人（women with bound feet）。
   改革开放前在城市街道居民中有一种组织，由老年妇女组成。她们在居民区进行巡逻，负责治安，抓坏人。但有时她们也会怀疑好人，甚至探听别人的隐私，影响别人的正常生活。由于她们有些人缠足，所以有人用"小脚侦缉队"称呼她们。这里的"小脚侦缉队"是指喜欢探听别人隐私的老女人，有贬义。

   Before China's economic reform, there were organizations in residential areas or neighborhoods in the cities, consisting of senior/retired women. They patrolled their neighborhoods, maintained safety, and helped report lawbreakers (within their neighborhoods). However, they would sometimes suspect innocent people, or even invade someone's privacy while doing their job. Because some of these elderly women had the experience of having their feet bound (which was a common practice in the old days in China), some people dubbed them "little-footed spies", meaning "old women who love to stick their noses into other people's business."

2. **"放盆里"**：意思就是"放在盆里"，口语中说话快时，"在"常常就被"吃"掉了。

   "放盆里" means to "put (it) in the pot". The preposition "在" ('in') here is omitted, which often happens in everyday speech when people speak fast and casually.

3. **"成心"**：有意、故意（多用于做不好的事）。

   intentionally (usually to do bad things).

4. **"犯呓挣"**：通常说"撒呓挣"，口语，意思是"熟睡时说梦话或有什么动作。"这里说"犯呓挣"，也就是"撒呓挣"，比喻一个人的行为不太正常，好像梦游。

   It is a colloquial expression meaning mumbling or moving in one's sleep. This expression is used here to indicate that someone behaves strangely or abnormally, as if in a dream.

5. **"玩意ㄦ"**："玩意ㄦ"本来有"东西"的意思，在"那玩意ㄦ也扎得慌哪"这句话里，"那玩意儿"是北方人的口头语，没有什么特别的意思。"那玩意儿也扎得慌哪"就是"那（样）也很扎呀"的意思。

The expression "那玩意儿", as a colloquial expression in Northern dialect, does not carry much meaning. In this story "那玩意儿" is similar to "that way", referring to walking without shoes in the sentence "Walking barefoot is pretty prickly."

6. "赔不是"：口语，意思是"赔礼"、"道歉"。

The expression "赔不是" is a colloquial expression, meaning to apologize.

7. "搁"：口语，意思是"放"。

"搁" is a colloquial expression, similar to "放".

There is a pair of man's shoes put in front of the door.

8. "愣"：意思是"竟然"，口语，意思是"与人们的预料不同"。"那贼就愣没敢进去"意思是"没想到那个贼竟没敢进去。"

"Surprisingly, the thief didn't even dare to go in." The meaning of "愣" here is very similar to that of "竟然". It is colloquial expression, meaning surprisingly, or unexpectedly.

9. "敢情"：表示说话人没有料到某种情况会出现，口语。"敢情是防盗鞋呀"，意思是"原来是防盗鞋呀"。

"敢情", a colloquial expression, is very similar to "原来"(it turned out . . .). It suggests that the speaker did not expect a certain situation to happen. "敢情是防盗鞋呀" means "That pair of shoes turned out to be theft-preventive."

10. "贫"：北方口语，意思是"说话太多，令人讨厌"。也说"贫嘴"。（见《良心问题》第一部分注释 7。）

"贫" is a Northern colloquial expression, indicating that someone is talkative to the extent that his/her listeners may feel annoyed. One can also say "贫嘴" (see note 7 in part 1 of 《良心问题》).

11. "街里街坊的"，意思是"我们都是街坊（邻居），关系很近"。类似用法还有"乡里乡亲的"。

"We are all neighbors." This expression "街里街坊的" suggests a close relation between neighbors. There are similar usages such as "乡里乡亲的" (fellow villagers).

12. "别（biè）开"：在"我用东西给你别开了"的句子中，"别开"的意思是用金属或木棍等（把锁）给弄开了。

"别开" means to force open a lock with a stick (metal or wood), as in "I forced open it with an object."

13. **"搏"**：是"搏斗"的意思。"那得一搏呀"的意思是"那也得搏斗、打一阵"。

"搏" is the same as "搏斗" (fighting or struggling). The sentence indicates that even if the thief got in, he would meet serious resistance.

14. **"怪"**：这里是程度副词，意思是"很、非常"，口语。

"怪", as a colloquial expression, is a degree adverb used here to modify an adjective. It means "quite; very."

15. **"瞎"**：北方话，有"糟蹋、损失"的意思。"放你那高跟鞋，碰上一个劫色不劫财的，你不就瞎了吗？"意思是"你门口放一双高跟鞋，如果碰上一个坏人是为了女人而不是为了钱，你就麻烦了"。

The word "瞎" in Northern dialect means "ruined", or "damaged", as in "If you put your high-heeled shoes in front of the door, and the bad guy happens to be going for women instead of money, then you would be in trouble (be ruined)."

语法 Grammar Notes

1. **"索性"**：副词，意思同"干脆"。

   "索性"，an adverb，means might as well，or simply.

   (1) 我们不告诉他病情，他的思想负担很重，不如索性告诉他，也许他能更好地配合医生治疗。

   　　(If) we try to keep him in the dark about his (medical) condition，he would have a heavy weight on his mind (seeing that he does not know what disease he may have). We might as well tell him the truth，so he may be more cooperative with the doctor's suggested treatment.

   (2) 这么晚了，公共汽车已经没有了，你索性住在这里，别回去了。

   　　It's so late，there are no bus schedules still in operation right now. You might as well stay here for tonight.

   (3) 电影 8 点开始，现在已经 8 点半了，索性不去了。

   　　The movie is scheduled to start at 8：00，but now it is already 8：30.（We）might as well not go.

2. **反问句 (Rhetorical sentences)**：

   反问句是汉语表示强调的一种手段。它用反问的语气对一个明显的道理或事实来加以肯定或否定，以便达到加强语气的目的。反问句的特点是：否定形式的反问句加强肯定的语气，肯定形式的反问句加强否定的语气。比如本剧出现的一些反问句：

   The rhetorical sentence is often used in the Chinese language for emphasis. The speaker usually uses a rhetorical sentence to express his/her strong opinion of either affirmation or opposition. The main feature of a rhetorical sentence is that its negative form emphasizes the affirmative sense，whereas its affirmative form emphasizes negative meaning. For example：

   (1) 放双鞋不等于说是给贼预备的了？

   　　这句话的意思是：放双鞋等于说是给贼预备的。

   　　That would be like preparing the shoes for the thief.

   (2) 碰上一个劫色不劫财的，你不就瞎了嘛！

这句话的意思：如果碰上一个劫色而不是劫财的，那你就瞎了。

If you put your high-heeled shoes in front of the door, and the bad guy happens to be going for women instead of money or other valuables, then you would really be in big trouble.

（3）我们门口不搁了一双嘛。

这句话的意思：我们门口搁了一双鞋。

We put one pair (of shoes) outside our door.

（4）你这样做对得起谁？

意思是：你这样做谁都对不起。

You let everyone down by doing this.

练习 Exercises

■ 一、口语练习 Oral Practice

（一）回答问题 Answer the follwing questions
1. 王婶是做什么的？她为什么告诉刘伟自行车应该放在哪儿，街上在宣传防盗？
2. 刘伟的家门外为什么放着一双男鞋？
3. 王娜是谁？她结婚了吗？她家里有几口人？
4. 王娜为什么来刘伟家？
5. 刘伟帮助王娜做了什么事？
6. 刘伟建议王娜做什么？

（二）讨论 Discussion
1. 谈谈刘伟的性格特点。你喜欢刘伟这样的人吗？为什么？
2. 刘伟的家庭关系怎么样？请举例说明。

■ 二、书写练习 Written Exercises

（一）用所给词语改写句子 Rewrite the following sentences with the given items
1. 我有急事找王老师，给他打了三次电话都占线，后来我想去他的办公室更快一点，于是就直接去找他了。（索性）
2. 她为了减肥每天骑自行车上班，可是还觉得运动量不够，最近她改成跑步上班了。（索性）
3. 上班迟到了，他见了老板说："我并不想迟到，我的闹钟坏了。"（成心）
4. A：我还在看书，谁把灯关了？
   B：对不起，我以为房间里没有人了。
   A：是吗？可是我觉得你是故意的。（成心）
5. 刘伟的妻子让刘伟向她道歉，因为刘伟无缘无故地怀疑她。（给……赔不是）
6. 环环拿了陈阿婆的钱，环环的妈妈要求环环向陈阿婆道歉。（给……

赔不是）

7. 真糟糕！我妈妈让我一到学校就给她打电话，可我竟然把这件事忘了。（愣）

8. 他昨天没有来跟我们一起看球赛，后来我才知道他跟女朋友一起吃饭去了。（敢情）

9. 原来她跟丈夫离婚了，难怪她从来不跟别人提她丈夫。（敢情）

10. 这对夫妻离婚以后又有了自己的新家，唯一的女儿谁都不想管，很可怜。（怪……的）

（二）选择适当的词语填空 Fill in the blanks with the appropriate items

A. 刚……就……	B. 偷	C. 愣	D. 敢情
E. 好好的	F. 搁	G. 走	H. 索性
I. 其中	J. 怪	K. 去	L. 放

今天刘伟下班回家，他的妻子告诉他这么一件事：邻居王婶爱人单位的宿舍，大白天的，就让贼_____了好几家。这几家家里都没人，门都锁得_____。但是，有一家，家里也没有人，可是门口_____了一双男鞋，那贼就_____没敢进去。大家都说，这双鞋_____变成了一双防盗鞋。不管当时主人是不是成心把鞋留在门外，但是不在家时把鞋放在门外，倒是个好的主意。有了这双鞋，贼也许就会被吓_____。刘伟的妻子说，"我看，以后我们每天出_____上班的时候，_____也把你的一双旧鞋_____在门外。"

刘　伟：好球！

刘伟妻：你小点儿声。

刘　伟：啊。看球声小了**没劲**[N1]。

刘伟妻：那像你这么喊呀，一会儿呀，谁敲门咱都听不见。

刘　伟：**传**哪。

刘伟妻：你看，说什么来着。

刘伟妻：谁呀。

刘伟妻：王婶。

王　婶：没事儿，我来查**电表**。

刘伟妻：哎。

王　婶：您这干吗呢？

刘　伟：哎哟，王婶，我这看球呢，没工夫招呼您了啊。

王　婶：您看您的。

刘　伟：得了，您忙着。

王　婶：我忙我的。

刘　伟：哎。

王　婶：你说这人也不知是怎么回事儿啊，一看球就和**玩**儿**命**似的，大呼小叫的，有本事，自己踢去呀。您看，**满场子**里跑的没一个中国人，哎这**球有什么看头**啊。

刘　伟：哎，王婶啊，咱中国那球啊，他踢得**不带劲**。您瞧人（家）这球踢得，您看这**队员拿球**，往前……哎，说出来您也不懂啊。

没劲	méijìn	adj.	(col.)没有意思，not interesting；boring
传	chuán	v.	pass
电表	diànbiǎo	n.	meter for measuring electricity；watt-hour meter
玩儿命	wánrmìng	(col.)	exert one's utmost strength
场子	chǎngzi	n.	soccer field (as used in this story)
有看头	yǒu kàntour	vo.	值得看，interesting or exciting to watch
(不)带劲	(bú)dàijìn	adj.	uninteresting；not impressive
队员	duìyuán	n.	team member

王　婶：啧，又添了个新鲜玩意儿啊。

刘伟妻：正**赶上**那**厂家直销**，不是便宜嘛。

王　婶：哟，怪**费电**的。嘿，800**瓦**哪。

刘伟妻：也不怎么费，热个菜哪，也就一两分钟的事儿。

王　婶：我说这**总闸**怎么老跳呢。

刘　伟：哎，王婶。

王　婶：就这么几个字啊，够省电的哎。

刘　伟：哎，王婶，您那儿找什么呢？我们家没**耗子**。

王　婶：谁找耗子呢。我是看看你们那电**插销**的**地**儿安全不安全。

刘　伟：不对吧，我看您这**姿势**像找**地雷**似的。您放心，我们不会为省这几个电钱从外面拉一根线，偷电的事儿啊，我们不干。

赶上	gǎn shang	vc.	be in time for (sth. or event); run into (a situation)
厂家直销	chǎngjiā zhí xiāo		factory direct sale
费电	fèi diàn	vo.	energy-consuming; waste electricity
瓦	wǎ	m.	watt
总闸	zǒng zhá	n.	main switch
耗子	hàozi	n.	mouse; rat
插销	chāxiāo	n.	socket
地儿	dìr	n.	（col.）地方, place
姿势	zīshì	n.	posture; gesture (of the body)
地雷	dìléi	n.	landmine

王　娴：谁说你偷电了，有这么说话的吗？**抽你**[N2]。

刘伟妻：哎，王娴，他这不跟您开玩笑的嘛，您还真认真了？他就这么个人。

王　娴：我要不是看你媳妇的面子，我非跟你**理论理论**[N3]。

刘　伟：好好好，王娴，我这还看球呢。

刘伟妻：来，您呀，再坐会儿。

王　娴：不了，中门王娜那儿，我还没查呢。我敲了她们家几次门了，就是不开门。

刘伟妻：那就是王娜没回来呢。

王　娴：那鞋还在呢。

刘　伟：什么鞋呀？

王　娴：一双男皮鞋。小牛和我们老黄在一个单位工作，小牛不出差了嘛，小牛**前脚**[N4]走，后脚啊，这门就敲不开了。

刘　伟：您没准儿看错了吧，那是防盗鞋吧。

王　娴：那谁知道啊，你别看王娜平时**一本正经**，其实啊，这年轻人，咱说不准。不包括你们俩。

刘伟妻：王娴，那双鞋是……

刘　伟：看球。

王　娴：那我走了啊。

刘　伟：您慢走啊。

刘伟妻：您慢着啊。

王　娴：行了行了，别送了。

刘伟妻：你听见没有啊，这王娴啊，盯上王娜她们家那双鞋了。

刘　伟：哎呀，这王娴啊，人挺好，就是这儿啊，太**复杂**。

刘伟妻：那你干吗不说那双鞋是咱们给的呢？

刘　伟：有些事儿啊，不能让王娴知道太多了，有些话一经过她**传出去**那就变味了。比如啊，你买了一斤包子，等这话**绕回来**啊，你成开包子铺的了。

抽	chōu	v.	（col.）打，slap someone on his/her face
理论	lǐlùn	v.	debate; argue
一本正经	yì běn zhèng jīng		in all seriousness; in dead earnest
复杂	fùzá	adj.	complicated
传出去	chuán chuqu	vc.	（word）get out
绕回来	rào huilai	vc.	turn back to the original place

刘伟妻：那可坏了，王婶看见那双鞋了。

刘　伟：哎呀，看见就看见了呗。不就一双鞋嘛，有什么了不起的，**小题大做**。

刘伟妻：可别**闹出什么误会**来啊。哎，就连你呀还胡思乱想了呢。

刘　伟：又说到我了。

刘伟妻：我不是说你，我是怕呀牛俊**在意**，那王娜又是**眼里不揉沙子**[N5]的人。

刘　伟：那得，明天哪，我把它**收回来**。

刘伟妻：那好意思嘛，就那么一双旧鞋。

刘　伟：哎呀，**就当小偷**给偷了去呗。

刘　伟：哎，进了。

小题大做	xiǎo tí dà zuò		make a fuss over a trifle
闹误会	nào wùhuì	vo.	cause misunderstanding
在意	zàiyì	v.	take notice of; mind; take to heart
揉	róu	v.	rub
沙子	shāzi	n.	sand
眼(睛)里不揉沙子	yǎn(jing)lǐ bù róu shāzi		(refer to note 5)
收回来	shōu huilai	vc.	take back
就当	jiù dāng		就当做，just take it as ...
小偷(儿)	xiǎotōu(r)	n.	petty thief; sneak

注释 Notes

1. **"没劲"**：意思是"没有意思"，北方口语。

   "没劲" here means "not interesting; boring". It is a Northern colloquial expression. "It's not fun to watch a ball game quietly."

2. **"抽你"**：意思是"打你"，一般指打耳光。北京口语。

   "(I will) slap you on your face", a colloquial expression used in the Beijing area.

3. **"理论"**：在这里是动词，意思是"辩论是非"。"我要不是看你媳妇的面子，我非跟你理论理论。"的意思是"如果我不是看在你媳妇的面子上，非跟你辩论清楚谁对谁错不可。"

   The expression "理论理论", used as a verb here, means to debate or to argue with someone (in order to distinguish clearly between right and wrong), as in "If not for your wife, I would have to argue it out with you."

4. **"前脚……后脚……"**：用于两件事紧接着发生。"小牛不（是）出差了嘛，小牛前脚走，后脚啊，这门就敲不开了。"这句话的意思是"小牛出差了，他刚走，他家的门就敲不开了"。

   "前脚……，后脚……" is often used to refer to two events occurring immediately one after another.

   "Xiao Niu is on a business trip, you know. As soon as he left, his door can't be opened —who knows what's going on behind that door?" (indicating that maybe his wife is cheating on him with another man.)

5. **"眼睛里不揉沙子"**：意思是"一个人一点也不容许不合理、不公平、虚假的事情存在。"

   This expression "眼睛里不揉沙子" means that one absolutely does not allow anyone to cheat or hurt him/herself. It can be used to describe a person who cannot stand unfairness or injustice. "Wang Na is a person who does not tolerate any cheating or unfairness on her."

练习 Exercises

■ 一、口语练习 Oral Practice

（一）回答问题 Answer the following questions

1. 王婶为什么来刘伟家？

2. 王婶对刘伟家的什么东西感兴趣？为什么？

3. 王婶注意到王娜家有什么变化？

4. 王婶对王娜的印象如何？

5. 刘伟为什么不想告诉王婶那双鞋是他的？

6. 刘伟的妻子担心什么？

7. 刘伟夫妇最后决定怎么办？

（二）讨论 Discussion

1. 谈谈王婶的性格特点。你喜欢王婶这样的人吗？为什么？请用实例说明。

2. 你怎么理解刘伟的这句话："王婶啊，人挺好，就是这儿啊，太复杂"。

3. 从这个电视剧中，你可以看出中国的邻里关系有什么特点？请举例说明。

（三）角色扮演 Role Play

两人一组对话，一方是刘伟的妻子，她主张告诉王婶，王娜家门外的鞋是刘伟的。另一方是刘伟，他不同意妻子的意见。两个人各有各的理，都试图说服对方。

Make a dialogue in pairs. One party plays Liu Wei's wife who suggests telling Auntie Wang that the shoes outside Wang Na's door belong to Liu Wei; the other party acts as Liu Wei who insists on not telling Auntie Wang anything about the shoes. Both people try to make good points in order to convince the other party.

■ 二、书写练习 Written Exercises

（一）选择题 Circle the answer which most reflects the meaning of the underlined part in the following sentences

1. 王婶，我这看球呢，<u>没工夫招呼您了</u>啊。
   A. 不想跟您说话
   B. 没时间练功夫
   C. 没时间跟您说话
   D. 没招待您

2. 您看，满场子里跑的没一个中国人，<u>哎，这球有什么看头啊</u>。
   A. 看什么球
   B. 这样的球赛没有意思
   C. 没有人看球
   D. 看不到球，只看见很多头

3. 咱中国那球啊，<u>他踢得不带劲</u>。
   A. 运动员踢得不好
   B. 运动员都很累了
   C. 有一个运动员没有力气
   D. 运动员不努力

4. <u>就这么几个字啊</u>，够省电的哎。
   A. 没有用电
   B. 电表上字很少
   C. 电表上没有字
   D. 只用了几度电

5. 谁说你偷电了，<u>有这么说话的吗</u>？
   A. 你怎么说话这样不客气
   B. 你怎么不说话
   C. 你说什么
   D. 你不应该这样说话

6. 他这不跟您开玩笑的嘛，<u>您还真认真了</u>？<u>他就这么个人</u>。
   A. 您是一个认真的人，像他一样
   B. 您要认真听他的玩笑，因为他很喜欢开玩笑
   C. 您是一个很认真的人，他也是这样的人
   D. 您别把他的话当成真的，他就是这样一个喜欢开玩笑的人

7. 小牛不出差了嘛，<u>小牛前脚走，后脚啊，这门就敲不开了</u>。

    A. 小牛刚走，他家的门就坏了

    B. 小牛的脚坏了

    C. 小牛刚走，敲王娜家的门，她就不给开门了（意思是在家里做见不得人的坏事）

    D. 小牛刚走，王娜就把门敲坏了

8. 你别看王娜平时一本正经，<u>其实啊，这年轻人，咱说不准</u>。

    A. 实际上，我们不知道王娜是谁

    B. 实际上，王娜说话我们不能相信

    C. 实际上，年轻人我们都不了解

    D. 实际上，王娜到底是什么样的人，我们不清楚

9. 这王娜啊，人挺好，就是<u>这儿啊，太复杂</u>。

    A. 就是喜欢麻烦别人

    B. 就是总把事情看得太困难

    C. 她的脑子把问题想得太复杂

    D. 就是喜欢问很难的问题

10. 有些事儿啊，不能让王娜知道太多了，<u>有些话一经过她传出去那就变味了</u>。

    A. 有些话不应该让王娜说

    B. 王娜喜欢传话

    C. 有些事情经过王娜一说就跟事实不一样了

    D. 王娜喜欢有味道的东西

11. 王娜又是<u>眼里不揉沙子</u>的人。

    A. 眼睛里有沙子

    B. 不喜欢揉眼睛

    C. 不能忍受眼睛里有沙子

    D. 不能忍受别人欺骗她，或者对她不公正

（二）选择适当的词语填空 Fill in the blanks with the appropriate items

A. 招呼	B. 说不准	C. 小题大做	D. 盯上
E. 前脚……，后脚……	F. 胡思乱想	G. 闹出误会	H. 不带劲
I. 大呼小叫			

    昨天晚上王娜来到刘伟家的时候，刘伟正在看电视里的足球赛，他不但没有_____王娜，而且还一边看电视一边_____的，这让王娜

很不高兴。王婶问刘伟为什么不喜欢看中国球队的比赛，刘伟回答说，中国球队的球踢得_____。后来，王婶又说她以前觉得住在中门的王娜挺不错的，但现在她也_____了，因为她发现王娜的丈夫出差_____走，王娜_____就把一个男的带回家来了。刘伟的妻子问王婶是怎么知道的，王婶说，她看到王娜家的门外有一双男人的鞋。刘伟这才知道王婶敢情是_____他借给王娜的那双"防盗"鞋了。王婶走后，刘伟的妻子让刘伟去找王婶解释一下，免得王婶_____，_____。刘伟说，"别麻烦了，一双'防盗'鞋能有什么问题？你别_____了！"

三

王　婶：您收会儿工吧，那个二秃子他奶奶呀，在那儿给您盯着哪，等着吃完了饭哪，我再去接您去。嘿，牛子，你回来了。

牛　俊：王婶。

王　婶：拿这么多东西。

牛　俊：王婶，我这刚下飞机。

王　婶：王娜没接你呀？

牛　俊：不用，打个的，方便，没什么行李。

王　婶：可是你出这么远的门，你们结婚又没多久，怎么说也应该接接你啊。

牛　俊：我给她打电话了，医院里头值班，**脱不开身**。

王　婶：哎，牛子，你们是不是**闹别扭**了？

牛　俊：瞧您说的，我这老出差，用不着接呀送的[N1]。

王　婶：牛子，你以后，工作再忙，你也得关心你媳妇。

牛　俊：您放心吧，王婶，我们俩好着呢。

王　婶：好好，好就好。哎，晚上到我们家**打牌**去，三缺一[N2]呀。

牛　俊：不是……好嘞。

老　黄：**老伴**儿，**翻**哪。

牛　俊：**对不住**，王婶，我**和**了，卡五魁，龙[N3]。

二秃子	Èrtūzi	N.	a masculine（nick）name
脱不开身	tuō bu kāi shēn		too busy to leave
闹别扭	nào bièniu	vo.	have problems with relationship（as used in this story）
打牌	dǎ pái	vo.	play mahjong or cards
老伴儿	lǎobànr	n.	one's spouse, wife or husband（of an old married couple）
翻	fān	v.	turn over; turn up
对不住	duì bu zhù	vc.	（col.）对不起, sorry（as used in this context）
和	hú	v.	win（term used in mahjong）

王　婶：啧，哎哟，牛子，人家说了，情场上**失意**，到了牌桌上就**得意**[N4]。您
　　　　可倒好，**两头都占**了啊。

牛　俊：瞧您说的，我不就**蒙**上[N5]这两把嘛。

老　黄：牛子，**脑子好使**，在咱们单位**多才多艺**。

王　婶：那是，要不然，像王娜那么个**挑剔**的人能**看上**我们牛子。

牛　俊：您拿我当傻瓜。王婶，我们家王娜，从小让她们家给**惯**的，要是有做
　　　　不到的地方，您还是多说着点儿好。

王　婶：哎哟，我可不能说哟，你媳妇那嘴可厉害了。那回我说她，你别一天
　　　　一身地换，你媳妇一**张口**啊，差点把我**噎**到**墙脚**去[N6]。**人家**说了，您
　　　　和我不是一个**岁数**。

失意	shīyì	adj.	frustrated; disappointed
得意	déyì	adj.	pleased with oneself; proud of oneself
两头（儿）	liǎng tóu(r)	n.	both sides; both aspects
占	zhàn	v.	occupy; take
蒙	mēng	v.	make a wild guess; hit good luck
脑子好使	nǎozi hǎoshǐ		(col.) smart; intelligent
多才多艺	duō cái duō yì	adj.	versatile; talented
挑剔	tiāo·tī	v.	nitpick; hypercritical
看上	kàn shang	vc.	be attracted to
惯	guàn	v.	spoil (a child)
张口	zhāng kǒu	vo.	talk; open one's mouth
噎	yē	v.	choke; choke sb. off
墙脚（儿）	qiángjiǎo(r)	n.	corner
人家	rénjia	pron.	(here refers to 王娜)
岁数	suìshu	n.	年龄，(year of) age

牛　俊：**回头**我说说她。

牛　俊：哎，到庄[N7]了吧，我该回去了。

王　婶：怕你媳妇说你呀。走吧走吧，我今儿也手背[N8]。

牛　俊：王婶，赶明有时间哪，我多跟您打几把大的。

王　婶：好。

牛　俊：今儿还有球呢。

老　黄：别走，就搁[N9]这儿看吧。

牛　俊：不了不了，太晚了。

老　黄：那咱们上那屋看去。

王　婶：牛子，你那个黄**翻毛皮鞋**是哪儿买的？我也想给我们老黄买那么一双。

牛　俊：黄翻毛皮鞋？我哪有那么双鞋呀？

王　婶：年轻轻的，瞧这**记性**。我上个**礼拜**上你们家查电表，那双鞋还在门口放着呢。

牛　俊：上个礼拜，上个礼拜我在**广州**呢。您一定是看错了。

王　婶：你**大婶**是老了，可**眼睛不花**。没错，一双黄翻毛的男皮鞋。哎，就在那门口放着。我敲了半天门，就是没敲开，没人开门。

牛　俊：您说什么？

王　婶：不是都看球了吧？那个刘伟呀，看球就**吆五喝六**[N10]的，连**敲门**都没听见。

牛　俊：没有啊。

王　婶：回去问问你媳妇，哪儿买的，回头告诉我。

牛　俊：黄翻毛皮鞋。

回头	huítóu	adv.	(col.) later
翻毛皮鞋	fānmáo píxié		suede shoes
皮鞋	píxié	n.	leather shoes
记性	jìxing	n.	memory
礼拜	lǐbài	n.	(col.) 星期，week
广州	Guǎngzhōu	N.	Guangzhou (capital of Guangdong Province)
大婶（儿）	dàshěn(r)	n.	aunt (affectionate address for woman about one's mother's age)
眼（睛）不花	yǎn(jing) bù huā		not presbyopic
吆五喝六	yāo wǔ hè liù	vo.	shout aloud
敲门（儿）	qiāo mén(r)	vo.	knock at door

注释 Notes

1. "……的"："我这老出差，用不着接呀送的"：这句话的意思是"我总出差，用不着每次都接送。"

   "……的"：用在描写性句子的末尾，表示一种状态、样子、情况。

   "……的" is used at the end of a descriptive sentence, expressing a state of affair.

   I'm always on the road, so I don't need anyone to greet me and see me off every time.

2. "三缺一"：打麻将（打牌）需要四个人，如果只有三个人，还少一个人，就叫"三缺一"。

   To play mahjong, you need four people. If there are only three people, that is so-called "三缺一".

3. "卡五魁，龙"：中国打麻将的用语。"五魁"是"五万"，"卡"在两张牌中间，比如一个人他有"四万"和"六万"，他就是"卡五魁"；"龙"是赢的人有同花（"万"字、"条"字、"饼"字）的"一二三"、"四五六"、"七八九"三组牌。

   "Five Kui" is a jargon for mahjong, meaning to get stuck between two cards, i. e., "four wan" and "six wan". "Dragon" is to have "one-two-three", "four-five-six" and "seven-eight-nine" three groups of cards of the same suit. The one who has these three groups of cards is the winner.

4. "情场上失意，到了牌桌上就得意"：通常的说法是"情场失意，赌场得意"，意思是"在爱情方面失败的人，在赌博时会赢钱"。

   "情场失意，赌场得意" means "when you break a (love) relationship, you may win money in gambling." This expression indicates that one cannot usually have both.

   "你可倒好，两头都占了啊"，意思是"但是你不同，两方面（情场、赌场）都得意。"

   "(But) you are different, you are lucky with both (your marriage and your gambling)."

5. **"蒙"**：意思是"胡乱猜测"。"我不就蒙（mēng）上这两把吗"，意思是"我赢了这两把不是因为我会打牌，是因为我运气好，是偶然的。"。

The indication of this sentence is：the reason that I won twice was not because I know how to play. It's as though I just hit it (the right card) by accident。"蒙" here means to give a blind guess.

6. **"噎"**：吃东西不能顺畅下咽叫"噎"。说话顶撞人或使人无法把话继续说下去叫用话"噎人"。"噎到墙脚去"：意思是"被噎到墙角去了"，形容被顶撞得很厉害。

"噎" literally means that one cannot swallow smoothly. "噎人" means to talk in a very abrupt and rude manner so that the conversation cannot be carried on. "噎到墙脚去" means one speaks in such a rude way as if he/she chokes someone with words.

7. **"庄"**：是打麻将用语，是打麻将开始时第一个抓牌的人所在的位置。"到庄了吧，我该回去了"的意思是已经打到一个阶段（结束一局）了，所以不再玩儿了，回去了。

"庄" is another jargon used in playing mahjong. It refers to the position of the person who starts to grab the cards at the beginning of the game (indicating that it is the end of one game).

到庄了吧，我该回去了。

It comes to the end of this game，so it's time for me to go home.

8. **"手背"**：意思是赌钱（打牌）时"手气/运气不好，老输钱"。

This expression "手背" means that one had bad luck at gambling，and lost a lot of money，as in "我今天手背，老输钱"（"I had pretty bad luck today，and lost a lot of money"）.

9. **"搁"**（gé）：在"就搁这儿看吧"中，"搁"是"在"的意思，方言。

"搁" here is used as a preposition，similar to "在"。It belongs to Northern dialect.

(You can) just stay and watch the game here.

10. **"吆五喝六"**：是大声喊叫的意思。

"吆五喝六" means to shout and scream.

练习 Exercises

■ **一、口语练习 Oral Practice**

（一）回答问题 Answer the following questions

1. 王娜的丈夫牛俊出差回来时，王娜去机场接他了吗？为什么？

2. 牛俊回来的当天晚上去做什么了？

3. 王婶为什么告诉牛俊"得关心你媳妇"？

4. 牛俊为什么让王婶"说着点儿王娜"？

5. 王婶为什么说"我可不能说……"？

6. 王婶为什么对牛俊提"黄翻毛皮鞋"？

（二）讨论 Discussion

1. 王婶为什么不喜欢王娜？

2. 你周围有没有王婶这样的人？如果有，你怎么跟她相处？

（三）角色扮演 Role Play

两人一组对话，一方是王婶，另一方是牛俊。王婶拐弯抹角地告诉牛俊，他走后王娜做了不可告人的事情。牛俊开始试图为王娜辩护，但最后终于被王婶说服了。对话中要用下面所给词语。

Make a dialogue in pairs. One party plays Auntie Wang and the other acts as Niu Jun. Wang tries to tell Niu what she assumes his wife did after he left in the round-about way. Niu at first tries to defend his wife，but eventually is convinced by Auntie Wang. Please incorporate the following items in the dialogue.

1. 前脚走后脚就 ……了	2. 说不准	3. 门外边
4. 搁	5. 黄翻毛皮鞋	6. ……给惯坏了
7. 怎么说也应该……	8. 挑剔	9. 胡思乱想

■ 二、书写练习 Written Exercises

（一）选择题 Circle the answer which most reflects the meaning of the under-
lined part in the following sentences

1. 那个二秃子他奶奶呀，在那儿<u>给您盯着哪</u>……
   A. 二秃子他奶奶帮您照看着您的工作哪……
   B. 二秃子他奶奶看着您哪……
   C. 有人帮您照顾二秃子他奶奶哪……
   D. 二秃子他奶奶在那儿看见您了……

2. 你们结婚又没多久，<u>怎么说也应该接接你啊</u>。
   A. 你太太不想接你啊
   B. 你太太说她不应该接你啊
   C. 你太太不管有什么事应该接你啊
   D. 你不让你太太接你啊

3. 医院里头值班，<u>脱不开身</u>。
   A. （王娜）不能离开工作
   B. （王娜）没有地方换衣服
   C. （王娜）没有时间换衣服
   D. （王娜）身体不太好

4. 王婶，<u>我又和了</u>。
   A. 我又发烧了
   B. 我又把饭做煳了
   C. 我又输了
   D. 我又赢了

5. 人家说了，情场上失意，到了牌桌上就得意。您可倒好，<u>两头都占
   了啊</u>。
   A. "情场"和"牌桌"上都赢了
   B. 在"情场"和"牌桌"两方面都不顺利
   C. "情场"上输了，但是"牌桌"上赢了
   D. "情场"上赢了，但是"牌桌"上输了

6. <u>我不就蒙上这两把嘛</u>。
   A. 我只不过是今天碰上好运气了，赢了两把
   B. 我只不过是今天运气不好
   C. 我只不过是输了这两次

D. 我只不过才赢了这两次

7. 别走，<u>就搁这儿看</u>吧。

　　A. 就（把东西）放在这儿吧

　　B. 就在这儿吃饭吧

　　C. 就在这儿看电视吧

　　D. 就在这儿聊一会儿天吧

8. <u>你媳妇一张口啊，差点把我噎到墙脚去。</u>

　　A. 你太太一边说话一边把我推到墙脚

　　B. 你太太说话的时候我差一点儿摔倒在墙脚

　　C. 你太太说话的时候（她自己）差一点儿摔倒在墙脚

　　D. 你太太一跟我说话，就叫我说不出话来

9. <u>我今儿也手背。</u>

　　A. 今天我的手有点问题

　　B. 今天我在牌桌上运气很好

　　C. 今天我在牌桌上运气不好

　　D. 今天我在牌桌上手背有点疼

10. 回去问问你媳妇，哪儿买的，<u>回头告诉我</u>。

　　A. 你回头的时候告诉我

　　B. 你等一会儿告诉我

　　C. 我回来的时候你告诉我

　　D. 你现在就告诉我

（二）用所给词语改写句子 Rewrite the following sentences with the words given

　1. 张明非常聪明，而且又爱学习，所以他的成绩一直是我们班的前三名。（脑子好使）

　2. 小王的母亲病了，小王请假回家，走的时候她对同事说："我的工作请你帮我照看点儿。"（盯着）

　3. 我现在在公司工作，一天到晚忙得要死，实在没有办法离开。（脱不开身）

　4. 那所学校对学生的要求很高，不但要学习好，而且还要有体育、文艺等方面的才能。（多才多艺）

　5. 你这两天先别给王娜打电话，她跟丈夫好几天不说话了，你别再去添乱了。（闹别扭）

　6. 他的专业就是计算机，所以对电脑的要求很高。（很挑剔）

四

刘　伟：没传了，好，大脚趟（tāng）出去！走！

刘　伟：哎，**哑巴**球怎么看呢。

　　（王娜：我不是跟你说过了嘛，那是刘大哥给的鞋。

　　牛　俊：刘大哥给你鞋？）

刘　伟：你别动。

刘伟妻：你听你听，王娜她们家吵起来了。

　　（王娜：放在门口防盗。

　　牛　俊：鞋防盗？）

刘　伟：什么呀，人家牛俊刚回来，**两口**ㄦ**热乎**着呢，你起什么**哄**。

　　（王娜：你这人怎么这么不讲道理呀？

　　牛　俊：**我不讲道理**？）

刘　伟：哎，不光是吵，动起手来了。

刘伟妻：我们去劝劝吧。

刘　伟：哎，什么事你就劝劝哪。待会ㄦ再劝出点ㄦ**毛病**来。

刘伟妻：哎，别是跟咱家那双鞋有关系吧？

刘　伟：不会吧。那双鞋我都拿回来了，那会ㄦ啊，牛俊还没回来呢。

　　（王娜：我们可以**协议**离婚，也可以上**法院**。

　　牛　俊：**吓唬**谁啊你，离就离，我还怕你离婚了。）

刘　伟：哎呀，他们俩真急了。

刘伟妻：那你说怎么办呢。

哑巴	yǎba	n./adj.	silent; mute; a mute
两口ㄦ	liǎngkǒur	n.	couple (husband and wife)
热乎	rèhu	adj.	intimate; close (in a relationship)
起哄	qǐ hòng	vo.	stir up trouble
不讲道理	bù jiǎng dàolǐ		unreasonable
毛病	máo·bìng	n.	trouble; problem (as used in this story)
协议	xiéyì	v./n.	reach agreement; agreement
法院	fǎyuàn	n.	court of law; court house
吓唬	xiàhu	v.	吓, frighten; intimidate

刘　伟：没事儿吧，不就一双鞋嘛，闹不出什么**乱子**来。小两口吵架经常的
　　　　事儿，过后不就好了嘛。咱们俩不也吵架吗，是不是？

刘伟妻：要是咱不把那双鞋拿回来就好了。

刘　伟：你怎么**赖**起我来了，我不是为了他们俩好嘛。

刘伟妻：现在人家吵起来了，你再说也说不清楚呀。

刘　伟：哎呀，我说不清楚什么呀。

刘伟妻：得得得，人家的事儿，咱跟着瞎**操**什么**心**呀。

刘　伟：就是。

刘伟妻：王婶，这谁家**搬家**呢？

王　婶：谁家搬家，小牛家，听说要离（婚）了。

刘伟妻：哎，**不至于**呀。

刘　伟：就是呀。那闹出大天去[N1]到底因为什么呀？

王　婶：因为什么？还不是因为小牛子那些日子不在家的那些时候啊，王娜
　　　　哪，老往家**招**（男）人。

刘伟妻：不会吧，我们两家住隔壁，我怎么没看见哪。

王　婶：这事能让你看见？我说呢，那回我上他们家查电表。

刘　伟：哎，等会儿，等会儿，王婶，您是不是说看见门口放那鞋那事儿啊？

王　婶：啊，你说怎么解释？

刘　伟：这事儿，您跟牛俊**叨咕**啦？

王　婶：啊。

刘　伟：都说什么来着？

王　婶：我没说什么呀？我就是说我看见在他们家门口摆着一双男鞋，怎么敲
　　　　门就是没人开。

刘　伟：哎哟，王婶呀，您可添了大乱子啦。那双鞋呀，是我的。

王　婶：你的？

乱子	luànzi	n.	trouble; disturbance
赖	lài	v.	blame; accuse sb. (of doing sth.)
操心	cāo xīn	vo.	worry; concerned
搬家	bān jiā	vo.	move
不至于	bú zhìyú		cannot go so far; unlikely
招	zhāo	v.	beckon; invite
叨咕	dāogu	v.	(col.) 小声（反复）说一件事，talk about; mention about

刘　伟：啊。

刘伟妻：王娜，你们怎么啦？

王　娜：**没意思**。

刘　伟：别呀，就因为那双鞋呀？

刘　伟：就是，你说那双鞋是我的不就完了嘛。

刘伟妻：对呀！

王　娜：我说了。

刘　伟：那他还不信哪？

刘伟妻：谁呀？

王　婶：我。

刘伟妻：王婶啊，来。

王　婶：可**了不得**了，你说这事儿闹得。

刘　伟：哎哟，王婶，别着急，又出什么事儿了？

王　婶：我**今儿个**上王娜她们单位去了，我一了解啊，那天晚上，王娜在她们单位值班，**压根儿** [N2]就没回来。

刘　伟：哎呀，您看看，防贼防贼，防出毛病来了吧。

王　婶：你说这事儿怎么办哪？哎，我看这样，你们两个跟他们谈谈，**趁着**他们还没**办手续**。

刘伟妻：我们说了，说不动啊。

刘　伟：王婶啊，**解铃还须系铃人** [N3]，**说到底**，您得亲自**出面**。

没意思	méi yìsi	adj.	senseless（as used in this story）
了不得	liǎo bu de		（col.）awful; terrible
今儿个	jīnrge		（col.）今天，today
压根儿	yà gēnr	adv.	（col.）从来，根本，at all; simply
趁着	chènzhe	prep.	while; taking advantage of
办手续	bàn shǒuxù	vo.	办离婚手续（as used in this story）
解铃还须系铃人	jiě líng hái xū jì líng rén		the one who tied it can untie it
说到底	shuō dào dǐ		（col.）the bottom-line is ...
出面	chūmiàn	v.	act as a mediator

王　婶：我，我说什么呀，我说那双鞋是你的。小牛子没听清楚，找你来，还没等你说完呢，上去给你两**耳茄子**[N4]，这怎么办呢？

刘　伟：那不成。

王　婶：是啊，这不叫治**聋子没治好治成哑巴了**？

王　婶：你说这事儿闹得，我**好心好意**地让**大家伙**儿管好自己的门，结果闹成这个样子，这怎么话说的。对了，我还是把嘴上弄个**把门**儿的[N5]。真是的。我走了啊。这叫怎么话说的[N6]，真是的。

刘　伟：慢点儿啊。

刘伟妻：您慢点儿啊。

王　婶：甭送。

耳茄子	ěrqiézi	n.	(col.) a slap in the face
聋子	lóngzi	n.	deaf person
聋子没治好治成哑巴了			
	lóngzi méi zhì hǎo zhì chéng yǎbā le		(col.)create a new problem instead of solving the old one
好心好意	hǎo xīn hǎo yì		with all good wishes
大家伙儿	dàjiāhuǒr	n.	(col.) 大家，everyone
把门(儿)的	bǎ mén(r) de		security guard at a gate; gatekeeper

牛　俊：错了。王娜，开门。是我，我回来了。别生气了，我给你道歉。别生气了。

刘伟及刘伟妻：牛俊回来了。

牛　俊：她生气了。

刘伟妻：就这么双鞋，**惹出**这么大事儿。

刘　伟：我也正琢磨着呢。

刘伟妻：你说啊，同样一件事儿，搁在有些人身上，一说就过去了，可搁在有些人身上，它怎么就过不去呢？

刘　伟：我说呀，咱们得**管管**这**闲事**儿。

刘伟妻：怎么管，是劝王娜还是劝牛俊哪？

刘　伟：王娜**自尊心**那么强，**经得住**牛俊那么说嘛。再说啦，一开始你往门口搁鞋那会儿，我不也那什么来着嘛。

刘　伟：我是说呀，小俩口过日子，互相没点**信任**，那还成。

刘伟妻：这种事，这**归**你管吗？

刘　伟：邻居嘛，**好端端**一个家庭，因为这么点儿小事儿就**散**了？

刘伟妻：咱以后啊，也别在门口搁什么防盗鞋了。

刘　伟：对，甭**弄这邪的**了。

惹出	rě chu	vc.	cause (sth. bad) to happen
管	guǎn	v.	interfere (as used in this context)
闲事（儿）	xiánshì(r)	n.	matter that does not concern one; other people's business
自尊心	zìzūnxīn	n.	self-respect; self-esteem
经得住	jīng de zhù	vc.	able to tolerate; can put up with
信任	xìnrèn	n./v.	trust
归	guī	v.	be in sb.'s charge (as used in this context)
好端端	hǎo duānduān	adj.	in perfectly good condition
散	sàn	v.	fall apart
弄邪的	nòng xié de	vo.	do crazy things

注释 Notes

1. **"闹出大天去"**：字面意思是"闹得出了天外面去了"，比喻"闹得很厉害"。

   The expression "闹出大天去" refers to the extremity of the fight.

2. **"压根儿"**：副词。意思同"从来"，一般用于否定句，口语。

   "压根儿" is an adverb，same as "从来" in meaning，used usually in negative sentences. It's used only in spoken Chinese. For example：

   （1）这件事我压根儿不知道！

   　　I knew nothing about it！

   （2）他全忘了，好像压根儿就没有这回事。

   　　He's clearly forgotten all about it，it's as if it had never happened.

3. **"解铃还须系铃人"**，意思是解决某个问题还必须是那个造成该问题的人。

   The person who causes the problem should be the person to solve it.

4. **"耳茄子"**：耳光，也可以说"耳切子（ěr qiē zi）"。a slap on the face.

5. **"把门的"**：意思是"看门的"。"我还是把嘴上弄个把门的"，意思是管住自己的嘴，不乱说话。

   "把门的" usually refers to the gatekeeper or the guard at the entrance who keeps strangers from coming in. This expression means "think first before you say"。"(I have to) watch what I say and not to cause any trouble".

6. **"这叫怎么话说的？"**：意思是"事情怎么会这样？"说话人表示对不该发生的事情感到遗憾、意外。

   "How come things became this way?" This expression indicates that the speaker felt surprised at or was unable to comprehend (the outcome of) a situation.

练习 Exercises

一、口语练习 Oral Practice

（一）回答问题 Answer the following questions

1. 那天晚上刘伟夫妇听到邻居王娜家发生了什么事情？

2. 刘伟夫妇为什么没有去帮忙？

3. 刘伟妻后悔什么？

4. 王娴是怎么知道事情真相的？

5. 王娴后悔了吗？请举例说明。

6. 王娜和牛俊又和好了吗？

7. 刘伟夫妇为什么不去劝王娜和她的丈夫？

8. 刘伟夫妇从这件事中得到了什么启示？

（二）讨论 Discussion

1. 你认为王娜跟她丈夫为什么要离婚？

2. 如果你是王娜，你会怎样？

3. 如果你是牛俊，你会怎样？

二、书写练习 Written Exercises

（一）选择题 Circle the answer which most reflects the meaning of the underlined part in the following sentences.

1. <u>两口儿热乎着</u>呢，你<u>起什么哄</u>！

A. 他们夫妻两人都在发烧，你别去添麻烦

B. 他们夫妻两人正在吵架，你快去劝一劝

C. 他们夫妻两人关系非常好，你不用去瞎说什么

D. 他们夫妻两人关系很不好，你去说也没有用

2. 你怎么<u>赖起我来了</u>，……

A. 你怎么怪起我来了，……

B. 你怎么劝起我来了，……

C. 你为什么让我去解释啊，……

D. 你为什么没让我把那双鞋拿回来啊，……

3. 您可添了大乱子啦！
   A. 您真惹出大麻烦了
   B. 您确实给自己找麻烦了
   C. 您确实把这儿弄乱了
   D. 您确实把事情搞乱了

4. 解铃还须系铃人。
   A. 惹麻烦的人常常会解决麻烦
   B. 惹麻烦的人不能解决麻烦
   C. 谁惹出的麻烦还得由谁去解决
   D. 惹麻烦的人喜欢解决麻烦

5. 聋子没治好治成哑巴了。
   A. 帮助了一个人，但给另一个人惹了麻烦
   B. 给人帮忙没有帮成，反而惹出新的麻烦来
   C. 给人治病，但是没有治好
   D. 给人治病，不但没有治好，反而越治越厉害了

6. 我还是把嘴上弄个把门儿的。
   A. 再也不说话了
   B. 尽量少说话
   C. 去当一个把门儿的
   D. 说话时先想好了再说，不随便乱说了

7. 同样一件事儿，搁在有些人身上，一说就过去了，可搁在有些人身上，它怎么就过不去呢？
   A. 同样是一件事情，有些人说得很清楚，可是有些人就说不清楚
   B. 同样是一件事情，有些人觉得很难做，可是有些人就觉得很容易做
   C. 同样是一件事情，有些人觉得可以不做，可是有些人就非做不可
   D. 同样是一件事情，有些人说清楚了就不再想了，可是有些人为什么就总想，不能忘掉，不能从那里边走出来呢

8. 甭弄这邪的了。
   A. 别做这种违法的事情了
   B. 别做这种不合正常规矩、惹麻烦的事情了
   C. 别做这种不合理的事情了
   D. 别做这种没有用的事情了

（二）用所给词语完成句子 Complete the following sentences with the words given

1. A：我听说小张和小李吵架了，我想去劝劝。

   B：他们夫妻两个人可好了，根本就没吵架，_____。（起哄）

2. 王婶这个人，什么都好，就是说话说得太多，这次差一点儿_____
   _____。我看，_____。（惹出，把嘴上弄个把门儿的）

3. 谁能想到一双鞋竟会_____？（闹出……）

4. 王娜要跟丈夫离婚了，大家都认为_____。（赖）

5. 她身体这么弱，哪儿_____呢！（经得起……）

6. 就是牛俊_____，王娜也不会回来了，她说_____
   _____。（闹出大天，不讲道理）

7. 如果每家都把一双鞋放在门外，那_____，_____。
   （休想）

8. 刘伟真没想到他的那双旧皮鞋_____
   _____。（居然）

9. 昨晚我写完这篇报告，一看表已经是早上 4 点了，我_____
   _____。（索性）

10. 你别看牛俊看起来不太灵，实际上他_____。
    （可）

11. 王婶爱人他们单位的宿舍，大白天的，让贼偷了好几家，_____
    _____。（加小心）

12. 王娜这个人自尊心特别强，从来_____。（添
    麻烦）

（三）用下面所给词语写一篇题目是《这个故事对我们的启示》的作文。

Write a Composition entitled *What the story tells us*, incorporating the items given below.

1. 赖	2. 说不准	3. 小题大做	4. 盯上
5. 胡思乱想	6. 讲道理	7. 添麻烦	8. 闹出乱子
9. 怎么说也应该……	10. 成心	11. 加小心	12. 索性
13. 认真	14. 把嘴上弄个把门儿的		

（四）用所给的词语改写句子 Rewrite the following sentences with the given items

1. 休想：

例句：再胆大的毛贼，他也休想迈进咱们家半步。

我绝对不会同意你这样做，你再会说，也不可能说服我。

2. 居然：

例句：刘伟，你小子居然怀疑起我来了。

他原来是一个工人，没想到现在成了北京的一个名律师。

3. 索性：

例句：交作业的学生寥寥无几（很少），老师索性对全班学生说作业不必交了。

昨晚，我在雨中等了半天公共汽车，最后气得打的回家了。

4. 可……了：

例句：你媳妇那嘴可厉害了。

前天我们去的那家饭馆的菜非常好吃。

因为王婶的话，王娜的丈夫跟王娜差一点儿离婚，王婶后悔极了。

5. 添麻烦：

例句：对不起，我得给你们添点麻烦了。

他不忍心让家里人长期照顾自己，就偷偷去申请进老人院。

6. 加小心：

例句：你呀还真得加点儿小心。

开车时你一定要特别注意，因为车太多，容易出事故。

■ 三、文化方面的讨论 Culture Discussion

1. "王婶，我们家王娜，从小让她们家给惯的，要是有做不到的地方，您还是多说着点儿好。"牛俊说这句话的意思是让王婶批评王娜，这反映出中国人在别人面前不好意思说自己的太太、先生或孩子的优点，相反，常常说他们的缺点。你觉得这样做好不好？你们国家的文化是这样吗？

"Auntie Wang，My wife，Wang Na，was spoiled by her parents. Please don't hesitate to tell her if she does something inappropriate." By saying this, Niu Jun, Wang Na's husband is inviting Auntie Wang to criticize his wife. What Niu Jun did here reflects a typical aspect of Chinese culture：Chinese people usually feel it improper to praise their family, such as their spouse or children. They do not hesitate to criticize their family members,

although what they say usually isn't accurate. They do it to be modest. What do you think of this aspect of Chinese culture? Can you find something similar in your culture?

2. 这个故事中的王婶代表中国老年妇女中的一类人。你在中国遇见过这样的老年妇女吗？你们国家的老年妇女中有这样的人吗？

Auntie Wang represents a category of elderly women in China. Have you ever met such an elderly woman like Auntie Wang in China? How about in your country?

第四课 风 波

A Disturbance

导 读：

　　中国实行改革开放以后，一部分人先富起来了，大多数人都过着低水平生活的平均主义局面被打破。有些生活水平没有明显改善的人，心里开始不平衡。有人认为先富起来的人并不是靠自己的聪明才智，也不是靠自己的劳动。不少人看到别人住大房子，买高级电器，开高档汽车，出入高级饭店，觉得贫富差距悬殊，就发牢骚："虽然现在生活水平提高了，但是心里不如过去踏实。"

　　本剧中的张二，一个不年轻、没有什么技能的人，被先富裕起来的邻居家的变化震撼了。面对巨大的反差，他不仅是发发牢骚，还编造谣言，引起了一场风波，但最后却自食其果。

　　可怜的张二！

Introduction：

After China implemented the opened-door policy and underwent economic reform, some people became wealthy instantly, which overturned the previous situation, in which everyone was equally poor. However, some people, whose living standards did not improve as much, began to feel dissatisfied. They thought that those who became rich did not build up their wealth based on their knowledge or hard work. Having seen the well-off living in big houses, possessing name-brand appliances, owning expensive cars, and eating at high-end restaurants, this group of people realized that the gap between the rich and the poor was widening. They felt that their

status of equality was gone, although the average living standards have been improved. The main character in this story, Zhang Er, a man in his mid-50's, who does not have many skills, was astonished by his neighbors' affluent lifestyle. Facing the difference between his life and his neighbors', Zhang Er did not just complain; he spread a false rumor that caused a big disturbance. However, the person who really suffered the consequences was none other than himself.

Poor Zhang Er!

主要人物（**Main Characters**）

张二（张师傅）　　Zhāng Èr（Zhāng shīfu） a masculine name（Master Zhang, a respectful address of an experienced worker）

张二妻	Zhāng Èr qī	Zhang Er's wife
郝顿	Hǎo Dùn	a masculine name
郝顿妻	Hǎo Dùn qī	Hao Dun's wife
小范	Xiǎo Fàn	a masculine name
小范妻	Xiǎo Fàn qī	Xiao Fan's wife
丽丽	Lìli	first name of Xiao Fan's wife
刘季	Liú Jì	a masculine name

张　二：啊，洗东西[N1]呀？

刘　季：我已经下楼了，我马上就到。啊，张师傅，你回来了，我正要找你呢。

张　二：怎么，找我有事呀？

刘　季：这个月该你家**收电费**了，我把这**单子**和黑**本**儿都放你们家了。

张　二：好的。

刘　季：再见。

张　二：哎，小季呀，怎么？快吃晚饭的时候也出去呀。我说这年头[N2]钱要挣，身体也要注意呀。

刘　季：你这话说得对，这年头挣钱干什么呢？挣钱就是要**消费**，要**享受**。我老婆刚刚打电话来，她和孩子在那儿等我呢。你说这大热天的[G1]，做什么饭呢，出去吃算了。

张　二：你这是有条件，哪儿像我一个人挣钱得填五个人的嘴。

刘　季：张师傅，你也想开了，想吃就吃点儿，想花就花点儿。你说这都什么年代了？嗯？你到现在还喝这种酒？

风波	fēngbō	n.	disturbance; rumpus
收	shōu	v.	collect
电费	diànfèi	n.	cost of electricity; electricity fee
单子	dānzi	n.	list (of items); bill; form
本儿	běnr	n.	本子，notebook
消费	xiāofèi	v.	consume; expend
享受	xiǎngshòu	v./n.	enjoy (life, rights, benefits, etc.)

张　二：啊。

刘　季：这是**散装**的吧？

张　二：嗯。

刘　季：张师傅，你**想不开**，你真的是想不开^{G2}！嗨！

张　二：啊，不想了，想起来让人**伤心**。啊，**老太婆**。

张二妻：回来了。

张　二：饭做好没有？

张二妻：中午有剩饭，一会儿给你热一下就行了。这天热也不想做。

张　二：哎呀，要我说，那今天就别做饭了。咱俩到外面去吃一顿，哈哈。

张二妻：什么，上外面去吃？我说，**老头子**，你今天是不是**捡**到**钱包**了。

张　二：**怎么了**？

张二妻：你口气比**力气**还大呢。就你这点儿**收入**，还^{G3}想下饭馆？能**维持日常**的**开销**就不错了。

张　二：好了好了。哎呀，你呀，一说到花钱就像**割**你身上的**肉**。咱们再^{G4}穷，一个月下一次馆子的钱还有吧？哎呀！

张二妻：哎，你还真**下馆子**呀？

张　二：好了，你放心好了。我哪有钱下馆子呀。每个月工资**奖金**一分钱不留都给你了，（还）下馆子呢？收电费去。

散装	sǎnzhuāng	adj.	unpackaged
想不开	xiǎng bu kāi	vc.	take things too seriously; not able to think through sth.
伤心	shāng xīn	adj.	sad; grieved
老太婆	lǎotàipó	n.	(of old couples) husband's term of address for his wife; my old lady; old woman
老头子	lǎotóuzi	n.	(of old couples) wife's term of address for her husband; my old man; old man
捡	jiǎn	v.	find (something that sb. has lost); pick up
钱包	qiánbāo	n.	purse; wallet
怎么了	zěnme le		Why did you say this? What's up?
力气	lìqi	n.	physical strength
收入	shōurù	n.	income; earnings
维持	wéichí	v.	maintain; support
日常	rìcháng	adj.	daily; day-to-day
开销	kāixiāo	n.	expenses; spending
割	gē	v.	slice with a knife
肉	ròu	n.	flesh
下馆子	xià guǎnzi	vo.	go to a restaurant
奖金	jiǎngjīn	n.	bonus; reward

张二妻：快回来吃饭呀。

郝顿妻：啊，张师傅呀，张师傅您是不是**闻**到我们家酒的**香味**儿了呀？里面坐里面坐呀。

张　二：我我……

郝　顿：别客气嘛。来，喝一杯。来来来来，别走啊。你不来我还想上去找你呢。今天几个朋友来**聚**一聚，来来，坐下喝一杯。这可是**正宗**的人头马，XO呀。

张　二：人头马？人头马我知道，这是**绍兴**酒厂**出产**的一个**新品**种叫人头马。

郝　顿：哎呀，这你就土了。我跟你说，这是**洋酒**，人家外国人喝的，就这一瓶呀，要七八百块钱呢。怎么样，来一杯尝尝。

张　二：是吗？

郝　顿：当然了。来一杯，尝尝，尝尝。

张　二：那这一点儿要几十块钱呢。

郝　顿：**没错**儿，尝尝。

闻	wén	v.	smell
香味（儿）	xiāngwèi(r)	n.	delicious smell
聚	jù	v.	get together
正宗	zhèngzōng	adj.	genuine; orthodox
绍兴	Shàoxīng	N.	shaoxing, a city in Zhejiang Province
出产	chūchǎn	v.	produce; manufacture
新品种	xīn pǐnzhǒng		new product
人头马	Réntóumǎ	N.	Remy Martin (Brand name of French brandy)
土	tǔ	adj.	rustic; unenlightened
洋酒	yángjiǔ	n.	foreign wine or liquor
没错儿	méi cuòr	adj.	对，that's right

张　二：我喝了浪费。

郝　顿：什么浪费不浪费的[N3]，喝吧喝吧，酒我还是管得起的。喝，尝尝味道，怎么样？

张　二：不错，真不错，不错，啊。

郝　顿：哈哈！

张　二：不错，要不一分价钱一分货[N4]！

郝　顿：来来，我再帮你倒上。

张　二：不不。你要是方便的话，先把电费给付了吧。

郝　顿：行行行。

张　二：一共是两百四十——五块？那么多？算错了。

郝　顿：哎，没错没错。你看我们家，电视机，**空调**，**电冰箱**，**微波炉**，这样样都是**进口**的，你说这哪样不用电，是不是？我这个月的电费算是少的了，好了。

张　二：250块钱，找你5块钱。

郝　顿：算了算了。

郝顿妻：好了好了，张师傅，我们都是老邻居了，谁跟谁[N5]呀，您就别太认真啦。这5块钱就别找了。

郝　顿：算了算了。

郝顿妻：您要是吃的话就坐下。

张　二：哦，不不。

郝顿妻：您要是不想吃，那您就忙您的去啊。走吧走吧，那您就忙您的去啊，走好走好。

张　二：待会儿我给你送来。

郝顿妻：不用不用。

小　范：谁呀？

张　二：楼上的。

小　范：张师傅，怎么？

空调	kōngtiáo	n.	air-conditioner
电冰箱	diànbīngxiāng	n.	refrigerator；fridge
微波炉	wēibōlú	n.	microwave
进口	jìnkǒu	v.	import

张　二：收电费。

小　范：哦哦，来来，屋里请，屋里请。来，张师傅，随便坐，我给您倒一
　　　　杯水。

张　二：哟，你们家喝这水了！哦，你们家什么时候换了大的了，啊？

小　范：这个，去年就搬来了。现在还有比这更大的呢。

张　二：哟，这好呀，这家里面就等于看电影呀。

小范妻：张师傅呀，来了，坐呀。

张　二：哎呀，什么时候搬一这大玩意来了？

小范妻：这是我给丽丽买的**钢琴**。

张　二：好啊，这可是个好东西呀，很贵啊。这价钱我知道，没有 1000 至
　　　　少 800。

小范妻：800？我昨天给小范买了一双鞋，500。

张　二：500？

小范妻：还打对折的呢。

张　二：什么？小范，你 500 块买一双鞋，还（是）**打对折**的？

小　范：嗯。

张　二：哎呀，你肯定**受骗**了！你看我这双鞋，哦，我那双鞋在楼上，我那双
　　　　鞋挺好的。50 块钱买两双，你肯定受骗了。

小　范：呵呵，喝水喝水。

张　二：你这人真是……哟，你们家这**游戏机**很漂亮。

小　范：这叫电脑。

张　二：哎，那么多东西，电脑？

小　范：张师傅呀，说起来你也是上海人了，怎么说出来的话跟一个乡下人一
　　　　样？好像什么都没见过似的，是不是？

张　二：我现在就和乡下人差不多，见什么都新鲜。嗯，收电费。

小　范：多少钱？

张　二：168 块。

钢琴	gāngqín	n.	piano
打对折	dǎ duìzhé	vo.	打五折，have 50% discount
受骗	shòu piàn	vo.	be cheated; be deceived
游戏机	yóuxìjī	n.	video game player

注释 Notes

1. "……**洗东西呀？**"：这是在打招呼。中国人常常用说出对方正在做的事的方式来打招呼。

   "……洗东西呀？"：This question is used as a form of greeting. In China，people often greet acquaintances or friends（but not strangers）by asking a question mentioning the current activity at the time of speaking. The question is rhetorical. 再如：

   （1）（看见一个人从家里出来要出去）出去呀？

   （2）（看见一个人正在吃饭）吃饭呢？

   （3）（早饭后）吃了？

2. "**这年头**"：意思是"现在这个时代"，说话人这样说，常含有对现实不太满意的意味。

   "这年头" means "in these days". This expression often suggests that the speaker has some dissatisfaction or negative feelings towards the social reality.

3. "**什么浪费不浪费的**"：这句话的意思是，别说浪费不浪费这样的话。

   "Don't tell me it's a waste of money" or "I don't care whether it's wasting money or not."

4. "**要不一分价钱一分货**"："要不"就是"要不然"。"一分价钱一分货"的意思是东西的价钱和质量是一致的。

   "Otherwise，why did they charge you so much?" "要不" means "要不然". The expression "一分价钱一分货" indicates that the price reflects the quality of the product，that is，products of superior quality are worth more.

5. "**谁跟谁呀**"：表示关系密切，不分彼此。用于亲戚、朋友、同学、邻居等熟人，是一种客套话。常说"咱们谁跟谁呀！""我们都是老邻居了，谁跟谁呀"的意思是"我们都是很多年的邻居了，不必客气。"

   The expression "谁跟谁呀" suggests a close relation between family members，friends or neighbors with whom the speaker enjoys a good relationship， as in "我们都是老邻居了，谁跟谁呀。" ("We've been neighbors for so long，don't bother with the change（money）.") It is often used as a polite expression. One can also say "咱们谁跟谁呀!"

其 in "其们都老老实实了。也地面的。""."We've been thinking for too
long, don't bother with the change (money). ""It is often used as a polite
expression. ["mei" ... long ... see "心锁" grammar 1."]

语法 Grammar Notes

1. **……的**："你说这大热天的，做什么饭呢，出去吃得了。"见《心锁》第三部分语法 1。

   "Why don't you go out for dinner—you don't want to cook on such a hot day. " See《心锁》grammar note 1 in part 3.

2. **补语** verbal complement：

   (1) 想不开 cannot think through (the situation), or take things too seriously

   (2) 管得起 to afford it (the wine, in this lesson)

3. **还**：用于反问，有"不应该"的意思。例如：

   "还" is used in a rhetorical question meaning one shouldn't have asked the question or made such a remark. For example：

   "就你这点收入，还想下饭馆?"意思是："就你这点收入，不应该想下饭馆。"

   "With the small income you make, you want to eat at restaurants?" The speaker really is trying to say that with your low income, you can't afford to eat at restaurants.

   又如：

   (1) 你还说好看，我觉得没有比这件衣服更难看的了。

      How could you say it's pretty? I can't find any piece of clothing that's uglier than this one.

   (2) 天气这么热，你还说舒服。真奇怪！

      It's so hot and yet you still say you are comfortable. How strange!

   (3) 每个月工资奖金一分钱不留都给你了，还（想）下馆子呢？

      I gave all my monthly salary and bonus to you, so where would I find the money to eat out?

4. **"…… 再 ADJ，…… 还/也……"**："再 ADJ"意思是"无论多 ADJ"。

   "再 ADJ" means " no matter how ADJ".

   (1) 咱们再穷，一个月下一次馆子的钱还有吧？

No matter how poor we are，we can at least afford to eat at a restaurant once a month.

（2）你工作再忙，也得去看病！

No matter how busy you are，you still have to go and see a doctor.

（3）他再有钱，我也不会嫁给他。

No matter how rich he is，I will not marry him.

练习 Exercises

■ 一、口语练习 Oral Practice

（一）回答问题 Answer the following questions

1. 张二家的生活水平怎么样？请举例说明。

2. 刘季家有几个人？与张二相比，他家的生活水平高吗？请举例说明。

3. 与张二相比，郝顿家的生活水平高不高？请举例说明。

4. 与张二相比，小范家的生活怎么样？请举例说明。

5. 张二的邻居们怎样看张二？

（二）角色扮演 Pole Play

你的朋友想请你去看一个新电影，可是你不想去，因为你得准备明天的一个重要考试。上次这门考试你就没有考好。你的朋友问你是不是一定要拿 A，你说实际上你能得 B 就很满意了（因为这门课不是你的强项）。对话中要用所给词汇。

Your friend would like to invite you to go and see a new movie，but you don't want to go because you have to study for an important test tomorrow that you scored pretty poorly on last time。Your friend asks if you are aiming at an A，but you say you would be perfectly happy with a B。Try to make a dialogue based on the given situation，using the items provided below：

1. V 好	2. 哪儿有……？	3. 想不开	4. V 不起
5. 是不是	6. 能……就不错了	7. 一……就……	

■ 二、书写练习 Written Exercises

（一）选择适当词语填空 Fill in the blanks with the words given

A. 想不开	B. 一……就……	C. 哪儿	D. 好
E. 来	F. 一下	G. 一会儿	H. 是不是
I. 就……，还……	J. 管得起	K. 能……就不错了	

妻子：回_____了！

丈夫：饭做_____没有？

妻子：中午有剩饭，_____给你热_____就行了。这天热也不想做。

丈夫：今天就别做饭了。咱俩到外面去吃一顿。

妻子：什么，上外面去吃？你今天_____发财了？

丈夫：怎么了？

妻子：_____你这点收入，_____想下饭馆？_____维持日常的开销
_____了。

丈夫：你呀，_____说到花钱_____心疼。别总_____，咱们再
穷，一个月下一次馆子的钱我还是_____的。

妻子：你口气比力气还大呢。哎，去哪儿？你还真去下馆子呀？

丈夫：我_____有钱下馆子呀？我去收电费。

妻子：快回来吃饭呀。

（二）用"就……还……？能……就不错了"改写下列句子 Rewrite the following sentences with "就……还……？能……就不错了"

例：咱们学校的篮球队水平太差，绝对拿不了冠军

→就咱们学校篮球队的水平，还想拿冠军？能进入前五名就不错了！

1. 我现在的薪水，买新车，买一辆旧车

2. 他的 SAT 成绩，上最好的大学，一般的大学

3. 穿这双高跟鞋，跑步，走路

4. 这两瓶啤酒，请五六个人，够两个人喝

5. 这个小教室，坐十二个人，坐七八个人

6. 他的身体，跑步，走路

二

张二妻：干嘛呀，这**副呆头呆脑**的样子。

张　二：刚才，我上他们几家收电费，你**猜**怎么着？哼，他们都比我们好啊，日子都比我们好啊，一个比一个有钱，口气一个比一个大。5块钱不用找了，**显得**他们很有钱似的，还说我像一个乡下人，我又没跟他要饭。

张二妻：你以为别人都像你？实话跟你说吧，我现在都怕别人上咱家来，怕人家来了以后，看见咱家这副**穷搜搜**的样子笑话。怎么会找个这么**窝囊废**的丈夫！

张　二：什么？我窝囊？好，我窝囊。我穷，你去找一个有钱的，找大老板，总经理，坐小**轿车**，住小**洋房**，你走啊，你走啊，你**他妈**走啊！

张二妻：你要死呀你，吓了我一跳，我还以为**地震**了呢。

张　二：地震？我还**巴不得**[N1]来一场地震呢。真要是来了地震，他们这些有钱的比我们更**难受**。地震？哼哼，地震？嗯，嘿嘿，哈哈……

张二妻：这**神经病**。

刘　季：嗨，张师傅。张师傅，我昨天忘了把水费单子给你了，今天还得麻烦你一次。

副	fù	m.	(it is often used for one's appearance, usually in a derogatory sense)
呆头呆脑	dāi tóu dāi nǎo		stupid-looking
猜	cāi	v.	guess
显得	xiǎnde	v.	appear (to be)，seem
穷搜搜	qióng sōusōu	adj.	poor, shabby
窝囊废	wōnangfèi	n.	(a person) good for nothing
轿车	jiàochē	n.	小汽(卧)车，car
洋房	yángfáng	n.	foreign-style house；Western-style house
他妈(的)	tā mā(de)	interj.	(骂人的话) Damn it！
地震	dìzhèn	n.	earthquake
巴不得	bā bu de	vc.	earnestly wish for
难受	nánshòu	v.	feel miserable；feel sad
神经病	shénjīngbìng	n.	(You're) crazy！lunatic

张　二：这算什么？小事**白忙活**了没关系，大事要是**耽搁**了可不得了呀。

刘　季：大事？什么大事？

张　二：你说，我老婆这两天**逼**着我要**装修**房子，我一听我就**着火**[N2]。

刘　季：着什么火？

张　二：这一辈子几十年不装修房子，偏挑这几天装修房子。这几天连**性命**都保不住了，还装修……

刘　季：嗯？张师傅，你可真会开玩笑啊，瞧你这**身子骨**。

张　二：身体好，身体好有啥用呀！这**房顶**要是**塌下来**，身体再好也**照样**压成**肉饼子**。

刘　季：张师傅，您可真会开玩笑啊。

张　二：开玩笑？我跟你开玩笑还是你跟我开玩笑？哎，我说，你真的就是一点都不怕？

刘　季：怕？我怕什么？

张　二：你一点都不知道？

刘　季：我不知道呀。我知道什么呀？哎张师傅，哎张师傅等等，**到底发生**什么事了？张师傅，我真的是不知道啊！到底什么事呀？

张　二：你真的不知道？

刘　季：我真的不知道呀。

张　二：外面**唠唠叨叨**多少天了，要地震了。

刘　季：地震？那，那什么时候呀？

白忙活	bái mánghuo		make efforts in vain
耽搁	dānge	v.	delay; procrastinate
逼	bī	v.	force
装修	zhuāngxiū	v.	fix up; remodel
着火	zháohuǒ	v.	生气，get angry(as used in this context)
性命	xìngmìng	n.	life (of a person)
身子骨	shēnzigǔ	n.	身体，health
房顶	fángdǐng	n.	roof
塌下来	tā xialai	vc.	collapse
照样	zhàoyàng	adv.	as before; in the same way; all the same
肉饼子	ròubǐngzi	n.	肉饼，meat pie
到底	dàodǐ	adv.	after all
发生	fāshēng	v.	happen; take place
唠唠叨叨	láo lao dāo dāo		talk about sth. constantly; chatter

张　二：就最近几天。

刘　季：那，那有几级呢？

张　二：12级呀。

刘　季：啊？12级？这，这哪有12级地震的？

张　二：12级是**台风**，哦对，7级，7级，人家**原话**是这么说的，说有7级左右的大地震，**陪伴**着有12级的台风一起来。

张二妻：哟，老头子啊，这可不是**闹着玩**儿的，你哪儿听来的？

张　二：我早上去**打拳**听人家说的。那个人的儿子呢还是女儿，是地震**局**的，**内部**消息，说，就最近几天，要地震。他们哪，全家都搬到**郊区**去了。

刘　季：真有这事？

台风	táifēng	n.	typhoon
原话	yuán huà	n.	original words
陪伴	péibàn	v.	accompany
闹着玩儿	nào zhe wánr		joke around
打拳	dǎ quán	vo.	practice Taiji(quan)
局	jú	n.	bureau
内部	nèibù	n.	internal
郊区	jiāoqū	n.	suburban district；outskirts

张　二：啊。

小　范：哎，我们几个呢？很**有戏**啊？真的？

小范妻：张师傅啊，进来进来。有事是吧？

张　二：哎，越忙越**添乱**[N3]，昨天来了一回今天还得来，昨天哪，那个老刘把水费单子忘了给我了。

小范妻：小范，钱在我钱包里。

小　范：好好。

小范妻：张师傅啊，您随便坐啊。

张　二：好好好，哎呀，你们家那些大东西，搬起来很不方便哪，啊？可是呢我说，这么贵重的东西，说什么呢也得搬出去**躲**一躲。要是到时等**部队**来**挖**的话，不**压坏**，**刨**都刨坏了。

小　范：刨？还部队给我刨？

张　二：啊，**抢险**队啊？哪次抢险队啊不是**解放军**哪，啊？

小　范：抢险？哎，我不明白。抢什么险啊？

张　二：要闹大地震了。你们都不知道？啊？

小范妻：啊？要大地震？

小　范：谁说的？

张　二：谁说的？我说，你们真的一点都不知道？抢险队都成立了！

小范妻：哎，我说啊，今天咱俩啊，就睡床底下。丽丽啊，就睡在钢琴下面。那呀是**上等木料**做的，**结实**。

有戏	yǒu xì	vo.	(col.)有希望，hopeful (as used in this story)
添乱	tiān luàn	vo.	add trouble to an already chaotic situation
躲	duǒ	v.	seek refuge from (disaster)
部队	bùduì	n.	army; troops
挖	wā	v.	dig
压坏	yā huài	vc.	crush
刨	páo	v.	excavate; unearth
抢险	qiǎng xiǎn	vo.	rush to rescue; rush to an emergency
解放军	Jiěfàngjūn	N.	Chinese People's Liberation Army, PLA men
上等	shàngděng	adj.	superior; of first-class
木料	mùliào	n.	timber; lumber
结实	jiēshi	adj.	sturdy; durable

小　范：嗨，睡那儿有什么用啊？这上面下来的，它能**顶得住**，可**万一**要是脚底下**塌**了呢？还不是一回事哪？

小范妻：早知道这样，咱们**当初**还不如住一楼了。人家一楼，只操上面的心，咱们呀是上下**夹攻**。

小　范：嗯，我看哪，咱们还得多准备点**饮料**、**干粮**。哎，全部进厕所，这儿结实啊，就算是万一给**埋**进去了，也能**坚持**个十天八天的。

小范妻：咱们啊上街再买几把**哨子口琴**，我同学的哥哥啊，**在唐山抢险**过（抢过险），哪儿有**响动**先挖哪儿。哎，咱们，把咱那把**电子琴**也搬进去。

小　范：嗨，我说你想在里边开音乐会？还得先挑值钱的。像这个，电视机，电脑。还那钢琴，全放里头。啊，就这么着。快点！

小范妻：好好好。

郝顿妻：你这是在干什么？

郝　顿：行，这**帽子**还行。戴上这，**保险**多了。

郝顿妻：那我的呢？

郝　顿：我给你弄了一**顶**。

顶得住	dǐng de zhù	vc.	able to sustain
万一	wànyī	adv.	in case; if by any chance
塌	tā	v.	crumple; fall down; cave in
当初	dāngchū	adv.	in the beginning; at first
夹攻	jiāgōng	v.	be caught in a two-way squeeze; attack from both sides
饮料	yǐnliào	n.	beverage; drink
干粮	gān·liáng	n.	staple food
埋	mái	v.	bury; cover up with earth
坚持	jiānchí	v.	sustain
哨子	shàozi	n.	哨儿，whistle
口琴	kǒuqín	n.	mouth organ; harmonica
唐山	Tángshān	N.	Tangshan (a city in Hebei Province)
响动	xiǎngdong	n.	sound of movement
电子琴	diànzǐqín	n.	electronic keyboard
帽子	màozi	n.	hat; cap
保险	bǎoxiǎn	adj. /n.	safe
顶	dǐng	m.	(for hats, caps)

郝顿妻：哎，说不定还**管用**哟。

郝　顿：那当然了。

郝顿妻：这次你倒是想得**蛮周到**的嘛。

郝顿妻：我啊，把家里啊所有的钱啊，都拿出来了。这样，不管发生什么事情，有钱在身边，就不怕。实在不行的话，就住我妈那儿去。

郝　顿：什么？住你妈那儿？你妈住六楼，想坐土飞机啊？

郝顿妻：这你就**外行**了吧？地震的时候，是先塌楼下，**顶层**的房子往下坐，我们就是被埋进去了，先救出来的，还是我们。这样，六楼五楼四楼三楼，**挨着个**地往下挖，你懂不懂啊？

郝　顿：那我也不去，我就是埋也要跟家里的东西埋在一起，那样心里才踏实。

郝顿妻：哼，**要财不要命**！

张二妻：哎呀，都快地震了，你还有心思看电视。你还不来帮我收拾收拾。

张　二：唉，你着急什么呀。这事我自己**有数**[N4]。

张二妻：我跟你说。你以为你是**军烈属**[N5]啊？哦，地震来了会给你**落实个政策**？水火**无情**，地震也一样。**砸**死你张二，第二年还不照样过春节？

张　二：你啊！……

管用	guǎnyòng	adj.	efficacious; helpful
蛮	mán	adv.	(col.) 很, quite; very
周到	zhōudào	adj.	thoughtful; considerate
外行	wàiháng	n.	layman; one that has no knowledge or experience for certain work
顶层	dǐngcéng	n.	top story, top floor
挨个	āi gè	adv.	consecutively
要财不要命	yào cái bú yào mìng		risk (one's) life for money
有数	yǒushù	adj.	certain; knowing how things stand
军烈属	jūnlièshǔ	n.	军人家属和烈士家属 dependant of revolutionary martyr
落实政策	luòshí zhèngcè	vo.	implement policy
无情	wúqíng	adj.	merciless; ruthless
砸	zá	v.	smash; pound

注释 Notes

1. **"巴不得"**：意思是非常希望，但是这个愿望往往很难实现。

   The phrase "巴不得" is used to express a strong wish, which cannot usually be realized, as in "我还巴不得来一场地震呢!" I'd rather have an earthquake now!

2. **"着火"**：这里的意思是"生气"。"我一听就着火"意思是"我一听就生气。"

   "着火" in this case means to get very angry. "I got angry the minute I heard it."

3. **"添乱"**：口语，意思是"在已经很忙的情况下还给增加麻烦"。可以用来说别人，也可以说自己。

   "添乱" is a colloquial expression. It is used to blame someone for "adding more trouble to an already very hectic or chaotic situation." It can also be used to blame oneself.

4. **"有数"**：也说"心里有数"，意思是脑子里清楚某事怎么样或会怎么样。

   "有数" means clear-minded. One can also say "心里有数". This sentence indicates that one is crystal clear about a given situation.

   "我心里有数" means "I know what's really going on behind it (this matter)" or "I know exactly what will be happening (regarding this matter)."

5. **"军烈属"** 包括军属和烈属。

   军属（军人家属）和烈属（烈士家属）在很多方面中国政府是给予照顾的。

   "军烈属" means soldier's dependants and dependants of revolutionary martyrs. These people are entitled to various benefits and financial aids from the government in China. The implied meaning of the sentence "你以为你是军烈属啊?" is "You won't be qualified to get help from the government even if you die."

练习 Exercises

一、口语练习 Oral Practice

（一）回答问题 Answer the following questions

1. 张二收电费回来以后有什么感想？

2. 张二的妻子怎么看张二？

3. 张二的妻子无意中说了一句什么话使张二产生了编造一个故事的想法？

4. 张二编造了什么故事？

5. 张二告诉小范家要发生什么事？

6. 小范家当天晚上准备做什么？

（二）用下面所给词语复述张二收电费回家以后跟他太太说的话 Retell what Zhang Er said to his wife after he came back home，using the items given below

1. 一个比一个	2. 显得……似的	3. 实话跟你说吧
4. 巴不得	5. 真要是	6. A 比 B 更……

二、书写练习 Written Exercises

（一）用所给词语改写句子 Rewrite the following sentences with the given items below

1. 今天天气热死人了，真想马上就能跳进河里洗个冷水澡。（巴不得）

2. 昨天小王的妈妈给他打电话，说他父亲得心脏病住医院了，小王听了非常着急，想马上就飞回北京。（巴不得）

3. 朱莉的父母让她在纽约读大学，这样离家近一点，但她却一定要去加州念书，因为她早就想离父母远远的。（巴不得）

4. 她买东西总是买最贵的，看起来好像很有钱。（显得……似的）

5. 马克来北京以后从来没给家里打过电话，好像一点也不想家。（似的）

6. 李英从宿舍出来，一句话也不说，低着头，眼睛红红的，样子看起来很难过。（显得）

（二）选择适当趋向补语填空，每个词不限于用一次。

Fill in the blanks with the appropriate directional complement，you can use each item more than once.

| A. 起来 | B. 进去 | C. 出去 | D. 下来 |
| E. 回来 | F. 出来 | G. 进来 | |

1. 大家都说我们家那些大东西，搬_____很不方便，可是这么贵重的东西，再不方便也得搬_____躲一躲。要不然，地震一来，就都埋_____了。

2. 这房顶要是塌_____，不管你身体多好，性命都保不住。我劝你还是躲_____住一段时间。

3. 地震这件事可是个天大的事儿，这个消息一旦说_____，想收都收不_____。

4. 地震的时候，是先塌楼下，顶层的房子往下坐，我们住在楼上的，就是被埋_____了，先救_____的，还是我们。

5. 我们好不容易才把这台大电视搬_____，现在又要搬_____。这不是有意折腾人吗？这造谣有地震的人到底是谁？我们非把他找_____不可！

三

张　二：哎，郝顿啊，你这是什么**新型武器**啊？

郝　顿：噢，**防震**床啊，保险公司保过险的，砸死一个**赔**10万哪。

小　范：是不是啊？哎，多少钱一个，这个？

郝　顿：2800，加上**安装费**，3000 **整**。来来来，慢点儿。

张　二：哦，我的天哪！

刘　季：哎，回去准备去啊？

张二妻：哎哎哎，我说老头子啊，天这么晚了你还不睡觉？像**夜游**似的荡什么荡？

张　二：你看看，邻居们，都**慌张**成这个样子，我心里头不好受啊！

张二妻：这是**土地爷**[N1]安排的，你有什么好难受的？这跟你有什么关系？

张　二：怎么没关系啊？我老实告诉你啊，地震这消息，是我**胡编**出来的，根本就没那么回事。

张二妻：什么？你？不会的不会的，你瞎说什么呀？

张　二：是真的，我老实告诉你吧，我，我主要看他们过得比我们强，都比我们有钱，心里不好受。我本想跟他们开个玩笑，没想到，这玩笑，开大了！

新型	xīnxíng	adj.	new type; new kind
武器	wǔqì	n.	weapon
防震	fángzhèn	adj.	earthquake-proof
赔	péi	v.	compensate
10万	shíwàn	num.	one-hundred thousand
安装费	ānzhuāngfèi	n.	installation fee
整	zhěng	adv.	exactly; no less no more (of money)
夜游	yèyóu	v.	a person who is up and about at night; sleep walker
荡	dàng	v.	walk around (as used in this story); swing
慌张	huāngzhāng	adj.	flurried; helter-skelter
土地爷	tǔdìyé	N.	The Earth God
胡编	hú biān	v.	create nonsense; spin yarns

张二妻：啊？你要死了你？你，你怎么能做出这种**缺德**事？

张　二：**哎呀哎**……

郝　顿：哎，这还要吗？

郝顿妻：要要要。

郝　顿：什么都要！

郝顿妻：谁啊？进来！

郝　顿：哟？是你啊！来来来，进来。

郝顿妻：张师傅，我们正忙着，您就随便坐吧，啊。

张　二：我，我，我想问你们一个事。

郝　顿：哎，你怎么了？什么事？快说呀，啊？

张　二：我，我想问的是，你那个，防震床啊……

郝　顿：防震床怎么啦？你也想买一个，啊？

张　二：能不能，**退货**？

郝顿妻：退货？我们费劲巴拉的[N2]，**好不容易**搬回来，退货干什么啊？

郝　顿：退什么货呢？

张　二：唉，它是因为……我对不住你们哪。

郝　顿：怎么了？

张　二：这个地震哪，其实没那么回事。完全是我瞎说的。

郝　顿：你？

张　二：我看你们，费那么大劲儿，心里不好受。真的。

郝　顿：啊哈哈哈，张二啊张二，你可真会开玩笑啊，那唐山大地震，也是你开玩笑**瞎编**的？

张　二：啊不，唐山地震不是我编的。可是这次地震确实是我瞎说的嘛。

郝顿妻：张师傅啊，你要有空啊，你就赶紧回家收拾东西去。这么大的事，楼上楼下，大街上，都**嚷**成一片了。怎么会是你编的呢？

张　二：是我编的。

缺德	quē dé	vo.	mean；wicked
哎呀	āiya	interj.	
退货	tuì huò	vo.	return merchandize
好不容易	hǎo bu róngyì	adv.	with a lot of efforts or difficulty；after all the trouble
瞎编	xiā biān		make up（wild stories）
嚷	rǎng	v.	talk aloud，shout and scream

郝　顿：哎，我说张二啊，你是不是心里害怕，吓**糊涂**了？
张　二：哦不不，这回，确实是我瞎编的，你怎么会不相信呢？
郝　顿：好了好了，张师傅。你就别再跟我添乱了，好吧？你回去忙你的去吧。啊？要地震了，你忙你的去吧。
张　二：你听我说……
郝　顿：对不起啊……
张　二：你听我说啊……
郝　顿：噢，好了好了好了。
张　二：哎，你这人……
郝　顿：好了好了好了。唉，我说这个张二，准是脑子吓出毛病了。

张　二：完全是我瞎编的嘛。
小　范：哎呀呀，你看，这。
刘　季：不可能啊，你看这么大的事，这绝对是**无风不起浪**[N3]啊。怎么会是瞎编的呢？
张　二：跟你说怎么说不明白，我跟你说了多少遍，是我瞎编的瞎编的。
小　范：大家都知道……
大　家：就是……
小范妻：哎，不可能不可能。今天的报纸，报纸看了没有？全是防震知识。
大　家：对啊。
小范妻：**报社**就不知道，登这个赔钱，登广告赚钱啊？那是上面的**命令**。
张　二：唉，你们可以打电话到地震局去问嘛。
小　范：哎，你别说啊，我还真打了。他们说啊，没有。
张　二：这不得了。这不得了。啊？这不得了。啊？啊？
小　范：可是我后来一想啊，**眼下市人大政协会议**正在**召开**，这现在需要的是

糊涂	hútu	adj.	muddled; confused
无风不起浪	wú fēng bù qǐ làng		there is no smoke without fire
报社	bàoshè	n.	news press, newspaper office
命令	mìnglìng	n.	order; command
眼下	yǎnxià	t.	现在，right now; currently
人大	Rén Dà	N.	the National People's Congress
政协	Zhèng Xié	N.	Chinese People's Political Consultative Conference(CPPCC)
会议	huìyì	n.	meeting; conference
召开	zhàokāi	v.	be in session (of a meeting); convene

安定啊。你这个时候**放风**出去说，有 8 级地震。那还不**乱套**了。

小范妻：对对对对。你们发现没有？这两天马路上的车啊，**跑得特别快**。尤其是小轿车。那些**有钱有势**的人啊，也怕地震。

小　范：现在你相信了没有？人家都说了。不是你编的吧？

张　二：不可能啊？

小　范：怎么不可能呢？

张　二：哎呀，就我这张**臭**嘴，干嘛要说地震呢？地震地震，这下好了，真的**震**了。以后不**吉利**的话不能瞎说。

张二妻：哎呀我说，你就别**叨叨**了。你得想办法**熬**过今天晚上。

安定	āndìng	adj.	stable; peaceful
放风	fàng fēng	vo.	spread news or rumors
乱套	luàn tào	vo.	turn things upside down
（有钱）有势	(yǒu qián)yǒu shì		(people) with (money and) power
臭	chòu	adj.	smelly; stinky
震	zhèn	v.	quake; shake
吉利	jílì	adj.	auspicious; lucky
叨叨	dāodao	v.	chatter
熬	áo	v.	endure; put up with

张　二：哦，对了，我准备了一根**绳子**啊。你啊，要是地震一来呀，你啊，抓
　　　　着这个绳子，往下**滑**。千万要，这时候要**冷静**啊，越是这个时候，越
　　　　要冷静，懂吗？不要不抓着绳子下去……

张二妻：哎呀，知道了知道了。到时候啊，你可得**麻利**点，噢？

张　二：地震了地震了！地震了……哎哟……

刘　季：张师傅……

张　二：你看你这么……

刘　季：没事吧？

张　二：没事，没事。

刘　季：那就好。

郝　顿：我说，张师傅，问题不大吧？

张　二：问题不大。两根**骨头**啊，**断**了一根半。

郝　顿：你们说这事闹的。

刘　季：张师傅，你算**命大**。您要是头先**着地**，这后果……谁敢想啊。

郝　顿：可不是嘛。

小　范：张师傅，你啊，就好好养着，这伤**筋**动骨一百天[N4]，过了这劲儿就好
　　　　了。这不，我看报纸上都登出来了。根本就没有地震。是有人**造谣**。

小范妻：是谁啊你说这么缺德？真**可恶**。

郝　顿：就是啊。

绳子	shéngzi	n.	rope
滑	huá	v.	slide
冷静	lěngjìng	adj.	sober；cool-headed
麻利	máli	adj.	fast；quick；agile
骨头	gǔtou	n.	bone
断	duàn	v.	broken
命大	mìng dà		extremely lucky(in a very dangerous situation)
着地	zháo dì	vo.	land；touch down
后果	hòuguǒ	n.	最后的结果(多用于不好的情况)，consequence；aftermath (usu. in a negative sense)
筋	jīn	n.	tendon；sinew
造谣	zào yáo	vo.	cook up a story；spread a rumor
可恶	kěwù	adj.	hateful；abominable；obnoxious

张　二：哎，会不会，就是我造的谣，啊？

郝　顿：啊不是你，你哪有那个**势力**啊？

郝顿妻：就是嘛，你也跟我们一样，是**谣言**的**传播**者和**受害**者。刘　季：对，这最**可恨**的，最可恨的就是第一个造谣的。

郝顿妻：对对对，要是**查出来**是谁干的，非把他**抓起来**不可。

张　二：抓起来？太**便宜**他了[N5]，应该把他，**枪毙**他。枪毙。

大　家：对对对对，没错，该枪毙。

张二妻：枪毙？！

张　二：枪毙！枪毙！枪毙！

势力	shì·lì	n.	power; influence
谣言	yáoyán	n.	rumor
传播	chuánbō	v.	spread (information, news, etc.)
受害者	shòuhàizhě	n.	victim(s)
可恨	kěhèn	adj.	hateful; abominable
查出来	chá chulai	vc.	find out
抓起来	zhuā qilai	vc.	arrest
便宜	piányi	adj.	(col.) be too lenient with sb. let sb. off too easily
枪毙	qiāngbì	v.	execute a death sentence; execute by shooting

注释 Notes

1. "**土地爷**"：管土地的神仙。The Earth God。

2. "**费劲巴拉的**"："巴拉"用在某些形容词性的词语后，只增加程度，不增加什么特别的意思。"我们费劲巴拉的，好不容易搬回来。"意思是"我们很费劲地好不容易搬回来。"

   The expression "巴拉", attached to certain adjectives, suggests some degree modifying the described state. It also adds some colloquialism. "我们费劲巴拉的，好不容易搬回来" means we spent so much effort moving it here (home).

3. "**无风不起浪**"：意思是"事情的发生是有原因的，不是无缘无故的"。

   "无风不起浪" means that there is no smoke without fire. This sentence suggests that everything has a cause to it. "There must be some ground for it (the news a-bout the earthquake)."

4. "**伤筋动骨一百天**"："这伤筋动骨一百天，过了这劲儿就好了。"这是中国人的一种看法，意思是如果筋和骨头受了伤，至少要一百天才能恢复。"过了这个劲儿"意思是"过了骨头受伤这个状态"。

   There is a Chinese saying/belief that says if one has a broken bone or strained muscle, it will take him/her at least one hundred days to recover. "过了这个劲儿" means after the painful period (one will feel better.)

5. "**便宜他了**"：意思是"使他得到了便宜，得到了好处。此处指他（罪犯）受到的惩罚还不够大。"

   "便宜他了", as used in this context, means "the penalty is too light for him" or "it (the punishment)'s too lenient for him."

练习 Exercises

一、口语练习 Oral Practice

（一）回答问题 Answer the following questions

1. 郝顿家为地震做了什么准备？
2. 张二发现大家真的为地震做准备的时候，他怎么想？他很高兴吗？
3. 张二的妻子知道了事实真相以后说了什么？
4. 当张二告诉郝顿事实真相时，郝顿相信不相信张二的话？
5. 小范相信张二的话吗？
6. 小范的妻子说什么？
7. 张二的邻居们为什么不相信地震局说"没有地震"的话？
8. 张二后悔自己做了什么事？为什么？现在他相信有地震吗？
9. 张二这天夜里做了什么？
10. 张二的邻居们为什么不相信张二是第一个造谣的人？
11. 你认为张二通过这件事会不会吸取教训？为什么？

（二）用所给词语叙述张二这个人的特点 Talk about Zhang Er's personality using the items given below

1. A 比 B 强	2. 不好受	3. 巴不得	4. 显得 …… 似的
5. 开玩笑	6. 造谣	7. 可恨	8. 本来……没想到……
9. 有钱有势	10. 越……越……		

二、书写练习 Written Exercises

（一）选择适当的词语填空 Choose the appropriate items to fill in each blank

A. 没想到……	B. 瞎编	C. 收	D. 过得强
E. 不好受	F. 到	G. 叨叨	H. 一……就……
I. 玩笑	J. 大	K. 回	L. 收拾
M. 好不容易	N. 相信	O. 巴不得	P. 反而

地震这消息，完全是张二造的谣言。张二去他的邻居家_____电费

的时候，看到邻居的日子都比他家＿＿＿＿＿，他心里很＿＿＿＿＿，回＿＿＿＿家，妻子＿＿＿＿他，他心里＿＿＿＿＿生气＿＿＿＿想跟大家开个＿＿＿＿，＿＿＿＿这个玩笑开＿＿＿＿了。当张二认识到事情的严重性去找他的邻居们解释的时候，没有一个人愿意＿＿＿＿张二的话，他们＿＿＿＿认为张二在瞎说。这些人＿＿＿＿才把东西都＿＿＿＿好，把防震床买＿＿＿＿家，现在好像他们倒＿＿＿＿有个地震了。

（二）用所给词语改写句子 Rewrite the sentences with the given items

1. 郝顿和他妻子昨天费了很大的力气才把家里所有的东西都收起来，今天就接到市地震局的通知说地震的消息是有人造谣。（好不容易）

2. 小王越想越生气，他花了很大力气写完的学期论文存（to save）在电脑里竟然找不到了。（好不容易）

3. 他们做了很多努力把他请来讲学，没想到他来了以后就病了。（好不容易）

4. 开始的时候他只想跟女朋友开个小玩笑，后来才知道这个玩笑开得太大了，他的女朋友因此跟他分手了。（本来……，没想到……）

5. 开始的时候他只想学一年的汉语，谁都没有预料到他一直学了 10 年，成为今天的"中国通"。（本来……，没想到……）

6. 开始的时候张二想骗别人，但没有料到把自己骗了，而且差一点摔死。（本来……，没想到……）

（三）作文 Composition

1. 看了这个故事以后你有什么想法？你怎么看张二这样的人？写一篇 400 字左右的观后感。

   What did you learn from this story? What do you think of Zhang Er? Write a reflection of the movie with about 400 characters.

2. 根据本剧写一篇 400 字左右的叙述文

   Write a narrative based on the TV story with about 400 characters.

三、文化方面的讨论 Culture Discussion

在你们国家，有贫富差距吗？如果有差别，一些穷人是否也像张二那样心理不平衡？

In your country, is there a gap between the rich and the poor? If yes, does it cause any social problems? Have your seen or heard about someone who is so physiologically unbalanced that he/she behaves like Zhang Er?

第五课 心 锁

Locked-up Secret

导 读：

家里的亲人犯了罪，应该怎么面对邻里和子女？为了面子，对邻里隐瞒，为了不使孩子在别人面前抬不起头而对孩子隐瞒，是不是长久之计？本剧就是讲一个犯罪服刑人员的妻子，谎称进了监狱的丈夫是去日本工作了，同时也把自己的心向孩子、向周围的人紧紧地锁了起来。结果事与愿违。最后，热情、真诚的邻居们帮助她打开了心锁，解除了她的痛苦，教育了她，同时也教育了她的孩子。

Introduction:

How would one face his/her neighbors and children if a family member committed a crime? Should one try to hide it from one's neighbors to save face and hide it from one's child so that the child does not feel inferior to other children? Is this a long-term solution? This story is about the wife of a lawbreaker, who locked up her secret and hence, her heart, from her child and her neighbors. She covered up the fact that her husband was in a reform camp by saying that he was working in Japan. However, this made the situation worse. Eventually, her warm-hearted and sincere neighbors helped her open her heart and relieve her agony. This experience also taught her and her daughter a valuable lesson.

主要人物（Main Characters）

许淑芬	Xǔ Shūfēn	a feminine name
环环（许淑芬的女儿）	Huánhuan	a feminine name (Xu Shufen's daughter)
陈阿婆	Chén āpó	grandma (respectful address of an elderly woman); grandma
王老师	wáng lǎoshī	Teacher Wang
搬家工	bānjiāgōng	mover
邻居	línjū	neighbor
同学 1	tóngxué yī	classmate A
同学 2	tóngxué èr	classmate B

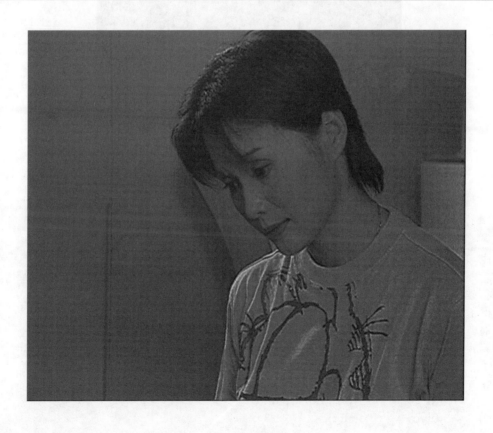

许淑芬：哎，师傅，快，快上啊，哎，好。小心一点儿，噢。

搬家工：哎，哎，**夹住**那个**绳**儿……哎，哎……

陈阿婆：哎哎哎，**当心**当心哪。哎哟，可**不得了**，**闯祸**了。王老师，王老师
　　　　哎，你下来帮帮忙喽。

王老师：陈阿婆，怎么回事儿？

陈阿婆：你**涵养**倒[G1] 蛮好[N1] 的嘛。你看着哦，这**柜子卡住**了，叫你帮忙**拉**。

王老师：哦，噢，我来，我去，来，哎，我来帮忙。

许淑芬：啊？

陈阿婆：**哎哟**，搬家师傅都走啦？你看连口水都没喝。

夹住	jiā zhù	vc.	hold（with a clamp-like device）
绳儿	shéngr	n.	rope
当心	dāngxīn	v.	注意，watch out；look out；careful
不得了	bù déliǎo		terrible；horrible；desperately serious
闯祸	chuǎng huò	vo.	cause a big trouble
涵养	hányǎng	n.	self-restraint；ability to control oneself；virtue of patience
柜子	guìzi	n.	cupboard；cabinet
卡住	qiǎ zhù	vc.	be blocked；be held back；be stuck
拉	lā	v.	pull；draw
哎哟	āiyō	interj.	

许淑芬：哎，他们公司是有**规定**的，在**客户**家里不**抽烟**、不喝茶的。

陈阿婆：就^{G2}你们**娘**儿**俩**搬过来住啊？

许淑芬：哎，对对对，是我们娘俩儿。

陈阿婆：啊。

许淑芬：嗯，她的爸爸在国外呢。

陈阿婆：哎哟，赚大**钞票**去了。哎哟，好**福气**，好福气！现在呀，哎，谁家有人在国外就是好事嘞。哎，他到哪个国家啊？

许淑芬：噢，对，在日本，日本吧。

陈阿婆：噢，到日本，**哟**，倒是你们娘俩儿要辛苦些喽。家里哪没个男人，哟，总有些**难处**的。不过呢，搬进九号就好了。我陈家阿婆就会**照应**你们，**尽管**放心好了。今天我们家啊，包**馄饨**，**荠菜**的，呵呵。

许淑芬：啊，唔。

陈阿婆：我待会儿给你们送过来好了。

许淑芬：哎呀，阿婆，阿婆，不麻烦了，你看我们麻烦了你们那么多，等她爸爸回来以后一定好好谢谢你们，尤其谢谢阿婆。

陈阿婆：哎，哟，哟，瞎说瞎说，用不着，用不着这样啊。哎哟，有什么事儿尽管找我好了啊。

许淑芬：哎，阿婆走好啊。

陈阿婆：噢。

许淑芬：环环，你站在门口干吗？进来呀，赶快把你的**玩具**拿出来。快帮妈妈做些事，噢。妈妈都累死了，哎哟。

规定	guīdìng	n.	rules and regulations
客户	kèhù	n.	client; customer
抽烟	chōu yān	vo.	smoke (a cigarette)
娘儿俩	niángr liǎ		mother and child
钞票	chāopiào	n.	钱，money
福气	fúqi	n.	good luck
哟	yō	interj.	
难处	nánchu	n.	difficulty
照应	zhàoying	v.	look after; take care of
尽管	jǐnguǎn	adv.	unhesitatingly (as used in this story)
馄饨	húntun	n.	wonton (a kind of dumpling)
荠菜	jìcài	n.	a kind of Chinese vegetable
玩具	wánjù	n.	toy

环　环：不好不好，这地方一点儿都不好。

许淑芬：环环啊，怎么了？你看看，人家周围邻居对我们多热情，多好啊。

环　环：就是不好！妈妈，你干吗要搬到这地方来住呢？我们**原先**的房子多好，我还有一个自己的房间。现在做什么事都和人挤在一起，做饭在一起，连上厕所都和人挤在一起！

许淑芬：行了行了，啧，你这孩子，你别再**胡闹**了，行吗？

环　环：我不愿意到这里来，我不要这里！

许淑芬：环环！真是的。环环，妈妈告诉你，啊，家里的事**由妈妈做主**，还轮不到你呢。我搬个家，我搬个家容易吗？啊？里里外外，**坛坛罐罐**，都我一个人来弄，你还尽给我添乱你。这个家，我不想要了！嗯，唔，真是的。

陈阿婆：环环妈妈，你在干什么呀？

许淑芬：啊？哎，我在弄**信箱**，啊。

陈阿婆：哎哟，我们九号有一个**公用**信箱了。

许淑芬：哎咳。

陈阿婆：再说，一天两次，送信送报纸，我都看见，你用不着**单独**装一个。你看，装在这儿多难看呐。哎呀，我们九号啊，可是**诚信里**的**文明**楼哎。

许淑芬：噢，阿婆，那这样吧，我把它往边上钉一点儿，行了吧？

陈阿婆：哎，那也不好看。哎呀，用不着的嘞。

许淑芬：哎呀，阿婆啊，其实我也不想**搞什么特殊**，环环爸爸从国外来封信确实挺不容易的。我想，还是自己家里装个单独的信箱，我好^{G3}放心一些嘛。

原先	yuánxiān	adv.	从前，former; previous
胡闹	húnào	v.	cause trouble
由……做主	yóu……zuòzhǔ		decided by someone; someone has the final say
坛坛罐罐	tán tán guàn guàn		jars & pots; kitchenware
信箱	xìnxiāng	n.	mailbox
公用	gōngyòng	adj.	public; for public use
单独	dāndú	adv.	individually; alone; solely
诚信里	Chéngxìn Lǐ	N.	name of the neighborhood
文明	wénmíng	adj.	civilized
搞特殊	gǎo tèshū	vo.	ask for privileges

陈阿婆：这有什么不放心的？我们九号啊，一年**四季**，送信啊、报纸，从来没少过。哎，王老师，你说是吧？

王老师：哦，怎么了？

陈阿婆：哟，环环妈妈刚搬来，要单独装个信箱，你说**用得着**吧？

王老师：哦，阿婆啊，环环妈妈要钉个信箱，你就让她钉吧，家里有人在国外嘛，信是很重要的。哎，当然，以前是没有丢过信和报纸，那也不能**保证**今后就不会丢啊。哎，再说，环环妈有个单独信箱呢，您**老人家**也**省得**每天为几封信**牵肠挂肚**N2了。哦，阿婆帮我拿着。我来帮你钉。

许淑芬：哦，谢谢啊。

陈阿婆：哟哟哟，看不出，王老师蛮会做**和事佬**N3的嘛。

王老师：哎，阿婆，不就是个信箱嘛。

四季	sìjì	n.	four seasons
用得着	yòng de zháo		需要，有用；necessary
保证	bǎozhèng	v.	guarantee
老人家	lǎorenjia	n.	(an respectful form of address for an old person)
省得	shěngde	conj.	免得，avoid (extra efforts/trouble)；save (trouble)
牵肠挂肚	qiān cháng guà dù		feel deep anxiety about
和事佬	héshìlǎo	n.	peace maker, esp. one who is more concerned with stopping the bickering than setting the issue

注释 Notes

1. **"蛮好"**："蛮"意思是"很"，上海一带口语。

   "蛮" means "很", from the Shanghai dialect.

2. **"牵肠挂肚"**：形容对某人或某事非常惦念，很不放心。

   "牵肠挂肚" means over-concerned (usually about someone's well-being or some situation).

3. **"和事佬"**：指调解争端时没有原则的人。

   This term refers to someone who does not stick to principles in mediating a conflict or a dispute.

语法 Grammar Notes

1. **"倒"**：语气副词，表示与一般情理相反。可参见《无端介入》第三部分语法注释 1 "本来"。

   "倒" is an adverb. It is used to indicate that the situation is contradictory to the common sense. Please refer to the grammar note 1 of "本来" in the third segment of 《无端介入》.

   (1) 你涵养倒蛮好的嘛。

   这句话的意思是"一般人遇到这样的事会很着急，没有想到你一点也不着急，涵养这么好"。

   You have such good self-control（never allowing yourself to be provoked）.

   This sentence indicates："Unlike how most people would react in this situation，you are surprisingly calm and self-controlled."

   (2) 听说最近要地震，别人都急死了，你倒好像一点都不害怕似的。

   There are rumors that an earthquake will take place in the near future. Everyone else is in panic. Amazingly，you behave like you are not afraid at all.

   (3) 这次考试我一点都没有准备，成绩倒最好。

   I was totally unprepared for this test. Surprisingly，I got the best grade.

2. **"就"**：副词，用在名词、代词前，意思是"只有"。

   "就"，as an adverb, occurs before a noun or a pronoun meaning "only".

   (1) 就你们娘俩ㄦ搬过来住啊？

   Only you and your child moved here?

   (2) 我们班就三个外国学生。

   There are only three foreign students in our class.

   (3) 昨天就你没来，别人都来了。

   You were the only person who was absent yesterday. Everyone else came.

3. **"好"**：助动词，用在后一个分句，表示目的，意思接近"以便"，但是位于主语后，而"以便"位于主语前。

"好", as an auxiliary or helping verb, occurs in the second clause (of a complex sentence) expressing the purpose of the action (described in the first clause). This meaning of "好" is very close to "以便" ("so that"). However, "好" follows the subject (if any), whereas "以便" precedes the subject.

(1) 我想，还是自己家里装个单独的信箱，我好放心一些嘛。

这句话的意思是"为了放心一些，自己家单独装一个信箱"。

I would like to have a personal mailbox so that I could feel more comfortable (or so that I could put my heart at ease).

(2) 你告诉我你的航班号，我好去接你。

Tell me your flight number so that I can go pick you up.

(3) 你把房间打扫干净，他们回来好住。

You need to clean up this room so that they can stay here when they come back.

练习 Exercises

■ 一、口语练习 Oral Practice

（一）回答问题 Answer the following questions

1. 许淑芬家有几口人？

2. 跟她以前住的地方比，许淑芬的新家怎么样？

3. 许淑芬的邻居怎么样？举两个例子说明。

4. 环环为什么不喜欢她的新家？

5. 许淑芬说她为什么一定要单独用一个信箱？

6. 陈阿婆为什么一定建议许淑芬用公用信箱？

7. 陈阿婆为什么说王老师是"和事佬"？

（二）讨论 Discussion

谈谈陈阿婆的性格特点。你喜欢陈阿婆这样的人吗？为什么？讨论时要用下面所给词语。

1. 愿意	2. 热情	3. 牵肠挂肚	4. 添乱	5. 帮……做事
6. 麻烦	7.（有）难处		8. 连……都……	

■ 二、书写练习 Written Exercises

（一）用所给词语改写句子 Rewrite the following sentences with the given items

1. 昨天我去看了一场电影，整个电影院里只有五六个人。（就）

2. 住在这儿的人都用公用信箱，只有许淑芬想单独装一个私人信箱。（就）

3. 我的朋友都在北京工作，只有王平一个人去深圳了。（就）

4. 环环一直盼望着搬家，现在她真的搬进了新家，却不高兴了。（倒）

5. 前两天一直下雨，天气还特别热，今天是个大晴天，天气却凉快了。（倒）

6. 陈阿婆本来想给邻居帮个忙，没想到却给他们添乱了。（倒）

7. 把你的电话号码告诉我，我可以给你打电话。（好）

8. 我们应该现在就把功课做完,这样下午就可以逛街了。(好)

9. 你最好每天给父母打个电话,这样可以让他们放心。(好)

(二)选择适当的词汇填空 Fill in the blanks with the appropriate items given below

A. 添乱	B. 愿意	C. 热情	D. 连……都	E. 难处
F. 牵肠挂肚	G. 倒	H. 帮忙	I. 麻烦	J. 所有人

许淑芬带着女儿搬进了新家。周围的邻居都很_____,很_____帮忙。星期天上午,大家一起动手把大大小小的家具一下子都搬进房间,摆好了,走时_____一口水_____没喝。但是许淑芬并没有显得十分高兴,因为最让她_____的信箱问题还没有解决。在这座楼里,大家合用一个公用信箱。_____的信件都放在这个信箱里,然后由退休在家的陈阿婆把信件送到每个人家里。许淑芬想自己装一个信箱,但陈阿婆说,她不怕_____,可以帮助大家发信、收信,没有必要自己装信箱。许淑芬心中的_____跟谁也不能说。她知道陈阿婆是想_____,但是现在_____变成给自己_____了,真没有办法!

邻　居：哎，回来了？

许淑芬：啊，出去啊？

邻　居：哎。

许淑芬：哦。

陈阿婆：环环妈妈。

许淑芬：哟，阿婆。

陈阿婆：哎，**邮递员**来过了。在你们信箱里**塞**了东西，哎，你快点儿去看看，说不定啊，是环环爸爸从日本来信喽。

许淑芬：是吗？

陈阿婆：哎。哎？你快去开呀，东西我来替你拿着。

许淑芬：哎，阿婆啊，我的钥匙啊，在楼上呢。

陈阿婆：哎哟，以后啊，你把钥匙交给我好了，我肯定替你**保管**好。

许淑芬：噢，不不不，阿婆，怎么好一直麻烦您呢？

陈阿婆：哎哟，这有什么麻烦的。

许淑芬：哎，哎，阿婆啊，你看，我和环环搬来以后，您帮了我们家不少忙，今天环环爸爸从日本**托人**回来，带回来些礼物。这是小意思^{N1}，送给你们家孙子，啊。

陈阿婆：哎，哎，不要不要。

许淑芬：哎，这些是些好看的**零食**。我想啊，环环爸爸回来以后，一定会好好谢谢您的。

陈阿婆：啊，不，日本东西又**吃不来**的。

许淑芬：阿婆，你要是不收，我心里会不安的，拿着拿着，啊，拿着。

邮递员	yóudìyuán	n.	mail carrier; postman
塞	sāi	v.	stuff
保管	bǎoguǎn	v.	take care of；store；keep
托人	tuō rén	vo.	ask someone (to do sth.)
零食	língshí	n.	snacks
吃不来	chī bu lái	vc.	(col.)吃不惯，not used to eating(sth.)

陈阿婆：噢，好吧，我先收下。哎，你以后不许这样了，就这一回！

许淑芬：哦，我知道了，我先上楼噢。

陈阿婆：哎，谢谢，谢谢，真是的，哎哟，到底是**外国货**啊，**包装**袋漂亮噢，
哎哟……

许淑芬：王老师。

王老师：哦，进来。

许淑芬：哎，王老师啊。

王老师：啊，环环妈，找我有事啊？

许淑芬：嗯，你现在不忙吧？

王老师：哦，不忙，来，屋里坐吧。

许淑芬：哦，好好好。

王老师：哎，进去啊，哎。

许淑芬：你进。哦，王老师在写信？

王老师：今天收到我爱人来信。

许淑芬：噢。

王老师：正给她回信呢。

| 外国货 | wàiguóhuò | n. | foreign products |
| 包装 | bāozhuāng | n./v. | pack; packing; packaging |

许淑芬：噢，是嘛，那我就**打搅**了。这条烟和这瓶酒啊，是环环爸爸托人从国外带回来的。我**特意**给你带上来，送给你。

王老师：哎呀，哎，你看，这怎么行呢？

许淑芬：哦，不，你一定要收下。王老师，我们搬来以后，你对我们帮助很大，这份情不还，我心里也过意不去。再说了，这也是环环爸爸的一份**心意**，你就收下吧。

王老师：都是邻居啊，相互帮助是应该的啊，再说啊，我不喝酒不抽烟的，你还是拿回去吧。

许淑芬：不不，请你一定收下，其实，我还有事求你呢。

王老师：嗯，噢，坐下慢慢说。

许淑芬：好，

王老师：嗯，哎，什么事儿？

许淑芬：哎呀，最近我们环环考试成绩很不理想，她爸爸在的时候啊，成绩还是比较稳定的。可是我的工作每天**起早贪黑**[N2]的，我有点儿顾不上她。嗯，我知道，你是**重点学校**的老师，要请你抽出一些时间来帮她补**补课**。

王老师：哎，这没问题啊，那孩子的学习没人关心、**督促**啊，那是不行的。哎，这样吧，你让环环每天吃过晚饭的时候，到我这儿来，我给她补一小时的课。

许淑芬：王老师，那太好了。这样，等环环爸爸从国外回来，我们一定要好好谢谢你。

王老师：提这就**见外**[N3]了啊，反正我晚上一个人在家也没什么事儿。你今晚让环环过来吧。

许淑芬：嗯，噢，王老师，你给爱人写信，她在外地工作么？

打搅	dǎjiǎo	v.	disturb; bother
特意	tèyì	adv.	特别，especially; for a special purpose
心意	xīnyì	n.	kindly feelings; regard
起早贪黑	qǐ zǎo tān hēi		work from dawn to dusk
重点学校	zhòngdiǎn xuéxiào		key school
补课	bǔ kè	vo.	tutor; redo sth. not well done
督促	dūcù	v.	supervise and urge
见外	jiànwài	v.	behave too politely (like a stranger)

王老师：哎，是的，她在**白毛岭劳改农场**当**教导员**。

许淑芬：白毛岭？

环　环：爸爸从日本带东西回来了？这可是第一回啊！你把爸爸带来的东西都
　　　　送人了，怎么不给我留一份哪？

许淑芬：怎么这么不**懂事**哪？欠了邻居的情[N4]总是要还吧。

环　环：同学们都知道，我爸爸在日本，可我一样从爸爸那儿来的东西都没
　　　　有。我们班王莹莹的爸爸也在日本，她从**铅笔盒**、书包，到穿的，全
　　　　都是她爸爸从日本带来的。同学们都笑话我了。

许淑芬：日本东西有什么好的？真**没出息**！

环　环：妈妈，吃的、穿的，我都不要，让爸爸在国外给我买一套《**灌篮高
　　　　手**》**漫画**集吧。王莹莹都有，可好看了，同学们都**羡慕**死了。

许淑芬：环环，说你小你也不小了吧？你应该知道，你应该知道，你爸爸在国
　　　　外挣钱也是不容易的。你今天跟妈妈要那个，明天要这个，哪有那么
　　　　多钱啊，啊？

环　环：我不能让王莹莹在同学们面前说，环环的爸爸在日本，却连一套《灌
　　　　篮高手》都没有。他们说我老是**骗人**，老是**撒谎**。

许淑芬：环环，来，坐下。这个月，咱们家的水电费，妈妈还不知道在哪儿
　　　　呢。妈妈每天工作十几个小时，累不累？生了病，妈妈也不敢**请假**，
　　　　这是为了什么？是不是为了这个家？你说你要这么贵的书，妈妈怎么
　　　　买得起呢？你应该听话了吧。

白毛岭	Báimáo Lǐng	N.	Baimao Ridge
劳改农场	láogǎi nóngchǎng		labor camp where criminals get reformed through labor
教导员	jiàodǎoyuán	n.	political instructor
懂事	dǒngshì	adj.	(usu. of a child) sensible; thoughtful
铅笔盒	qiānbǐ hé	n.	pencil box
没出息	méi chūxi	adj.	good-for-nothing
《灌篮高手》	Guànlán Gāoshǒu	N.	name of a set of cartoon books
漫画	mànhuà	n.	cartoon; caricature
王莹莹	Wáng Yíngying	N.	a feminine name
羡慕	xiànmù	v.	admire; envy
骗人	piàn rén	vo.	deceive people; defraud others
撒谎	sā huǎng	vo.	tell lies
请假	qǐng jià	vo.	ask for leave

环　环：爸爸为什么要去日本？爸爸去日本对我们家有什么好？现在我们家什么都没有了，连水费都付不起了。我要爸爸回来，我要他回来和你去给我买书。

许淑芬：这孩子怎么那么不懂事了？不许喊，哎！

环　环：我不读书了，你帮我买，我不读书了。

许淑芬：哎，你怎么这样啊，你！哎！

环　环：我不读书了，你给我买书！我要爸爸回来。

许淑芬：这孩子，我怎么跟你说呢，啊，看我今天非打你一顿不可，气死我了，气死了，气死了，气死了，气死了……

环　环：我要爸爸回来，我要爸爸回来，我要爸爸回来……

陈阿婆：哎呀，环环妈妈哎，不要打了，孩子小，要吓坏的。环环妈妈哎，有什么事儿不给我说哎。你开开门啊！

环　环：我不读书了，我要爸爸回家……

王老师：阿婆阿婆，阿婆阿婆，阿婆，环环妈心里有事儿，她要打孩子就让她打几下吧。

许淑芬：你咋这么不懂事呀，你，这孩子，妈妈把你养大容易吗？

陈阿婆：这，这……

王老师：等气消了，我去跟她谈。

陈阿婆：王老师，你替我劝劝她，我们九号啊是文明楼啊，不准许打孩子的。

王老师：啊，知道知道，哎，哎，你先回去吧，啊。

陈阿婆：劝劝她啊。

王老师：哎，哎好。

咋	zǎ	pron.	（col.）怎么，为什么，how，why
消气（气消）	xiāo qì（qì xiāo）	vo.	cool off (one's anger)
准许	zhǔnxǔ	av.	permit; allow
劝	quàn	v.	persuade; advise; urge

注释 Notes

1. **"小意思"**：很小，微不足道。送礼时可以用来表示客气，意思是我送的礼物很小，只是表示我的一点心意。

   "小意思" literally means "petty, nothing big or significant". It is commonly used when people give presents to others, as in "This is just a little token of my appreciation." By using this expression, the speaker is trying to be humble (or modest) and respectful.

2. **"起早贪黑"**：字面意思是"每天很早就起来，很晚才睡觉"。形容"非常忙"。

   The literal meaning of this expression is to get up early, and go to bed late. It is used to indicate that someone is really busy.

3. **"见外"**：意思是"把关系比较近的朋友等当做外人看"。

   "见外" means to act as an outsider or a stranger towards a close friend or family member.

4. **"欠……情"**：一个人在较大的事情上帮助了谁，谁就欠了那个人的人情。

   The expression "欠人情" means if someone did you a big favor, then you owe that person a favor.

练习 Exercises

■ 一、口语练习 Oral Practice

（一）回答问题 Answer the following questions

1. 许淑芬为什么说她的钥匙在楼上呢？
2. 许淑芬的丈夫真的从日本带东西回来了吗？
3. 许淑芬为什么送给王老师礼物？
4. 王老师的爱人在哪儿工作？
5. 环环希望爸爸给她买什么？为什么？
6. 环环为什么想让爸爸从日本回来？

（二）讨论 Discussion

1. 你觉得许淑芬的邻居怎么样？
2. 中国的邻里关系跟你们国家的邻里关系一样吗？如果有不同，为什么？你个人认为哪种邻里关系更好？

■ 二、书写练习 Written Exercises

选择恰当词语填空 Choose the appropriate item to fill in each blank in the three passages below

（一）第一张便条

1. 放	2. 只好	3. 不下	4. 是	5. 一……就……
6. 过	7. 替	8. 见外	9. 不管	

环环妈：

　　今天邮递员来了，在你的信箱里＿＿＿＿＿＿＿了一封信和一些东西，有一个包塞＿＿＿＿＿＿＿＿＿，他＿＿＿＿＿＿＿给了我，让我交给你。我想这些东西一定＿＿＿＿＿＿＿环环的爸爸从日本寄来的。请你＿＿＿＿＿＿＿回来＿＿＿＿＿＿＿来我家取这些东西。以后你可以把钥匙交给我，这样，＿＿＿＿＿＿＿＿你有信还是包裹，我都可以替你收下。钥匙，我肯定会＿＿＿＿＿＿＿＿＿你保管好。我们是邻居，都是一家人，千万不要_____。

陈阿婆

（二）第二张便条：

1. 取	2. 千万	3. 老	4. 才	5. 自从
6. 把	7. 忙	8. 到	9. 一些	10. 留下
11. 收				

陈阿婆：

　　我来_____东西的时候你不在家，陈阿伯_____东西给我了，谢谢你为我_____信件和包裹，_____麻烦你，真不好意思。_____我和环环搬来以后，你们帮了我们家很多_____，真不知道怎么感谢你们_____好。今天收_____的东西是环环爸爸从日本寄来的_____糖和小食品，我给你_____一包，送给你的孙子。这是我的一点心意，你_____要收下。

许淑芬

（三）第三张便条：

1. 比较	2. 理想	3. 督促	4. 起早贪黑	5. 紧
6. 好	7. 抽出	8. 合适	9. 有经验	10. 给

王老师：

　　最近环环考试成绩很不_____，她爸爸在的时候，成绩还是_____稳定的。可是现在我一个人带她，工作很忙，每天_____，没有时间_____她学习。我知道，你是重点学校的老师，教孩子很_____；当然我也知道你的时间也很_____，每天要备很多课。我想请你_____一些时间给环环补课，不知道行不行。如果你同意教环环，请你回来以后_____我打一个电话，我们_____商量一个_____的时间。谢谢你。

许淑芬

三

陈阿婆：哎哟，不得了了，不得了了，我钱丢了呀，我钱没有了啊。

邻　居：阿婆，阿婆，你别着急，**怎么回事**啊？

陈阿婆：哎，真是**出鬼**了。我今天一早买菜回来哟，**明明**钱包里还有不少钱呢，我**随手**往**篮子**里一放，**一眨眼工夫**，没了呀。

邻　居：哎呀，好好想想吧。

王老师：哎，阿婆，您怎么回事啊？

邻　居：哎，王老师，阿婆钱包里的钱被别人给**偷走**了，就剩一个空钱包。

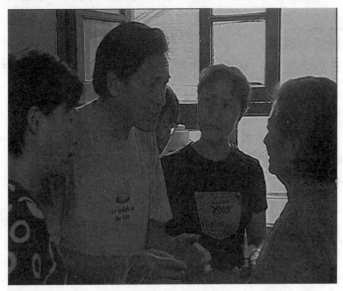

怎么回事	zěnme huí shì		What's the matter? What's happened?
出鬼了	chū guǐ le		（col.）How strange!
一早	yì zǎo		early in the morning
明明	míngmíng	adv.	obviously; undoubtedly
随手	suíshǒu	adv.	conveniently; without extra trouble
篮子	lánzi	n.	basket
一眨眼	yì zhǎ yǎn		（col.）非常短的时间内，in the blink of an eye; in a very short time
工夫	gōngfu	n.	时间，period of time
偷走	tōu zǒu	vc.	steal

王老师：是吗？

邻　　居：哎。

王老师：阿婆啊，你别急啊，你再好好想想，是不是买了别的什么把钱花了？

邻　　居：对，是啊。

陈阿婆：没有没有呀，我记得**清清楚楚**，今天早上拿了 100 块钱到小**菜场**，买了一条**鲈鱼**19 块，一斤**干豆**一块八，还有两毛钱**葱**，四毛钱**豆奶**，还有几毛钱**辣椒**。哎，我一点儿都不糊涂哎，明明钱包里还剩 70 多块，你们看，现在，就剩几个**硬币**了，唉，没有了。

许淑芬：阿婆，哎。

王老师：哎，环环妈。

许淑芬：哎。

王老师：双休日还上班啊？

许淑芬：**双休日**店里更忙。阿婆，你帮我**照看**一下环环好吗？中午饭我已经安排好了，你照顾一下啊。

陈阿婆：哎。

王老师：没事儿，你放心好了。

邻　　居：你去吧。

许淑芬：谢谢你们！

环　　环：你们看，这是我爸爸从日本寄来的。

环环同学：给我看看，给我看看嘛。

环　　环：不给嘛。

同学 1：环环，你这套根本不**齐**。

清清楚楚	qīng qing chu chu	adj.	crystal clear
菜场	càichǎng	n.	菜市场，supermarket
鲈鱼	lúyú	n.	perch
干豆	gāndòu	n.	dried beans or peas
葱	cōng	n.	green onion; scallion
豆奶	dòunǎi	n.	豆浆，soy milk
辣椒	làjiāo	n.	hot pepper; chili
硬币	yìngbì	n.	coin (of money)
双休日	shuāngxiūrì	n.	two-day weekend
照看	zhàokàn	v.	look after; attend to
齐	qí	adj.	complete (of a set of books, furniture, etc.)

同学 2：莹莹那儿她有 12 本呢，莹莹那套才全。

环　环：我爸爸说了，等我这次考完试，他就在日本替我买全！

同学 3：那也要看你考几分啊，还 60 分 70 分的^{G1}，你爸爸才不会替你买呢。

同学 1：环环，你先借我一本吧。

环　环：嗯，好吧，先借给你一本，可不许弄坏了，不许躺在床上看，还不许……

陈阿婆：环环，回来吃饭了。

环　环：我不说了，我要回去吃饭了。

陈阿婆：哎呀，你妈妈都下班了，还不回来。

环　环：来了来了。

环环同学：**小气鬼**，哼，**小气鬼**……

王老师：环环，这不是**形容词**哎。

环　环：嗯？哦，对。

王老师：哎，你看看啊，这地方也不对。

邮递员：收报纸哎，九号王家收报纸啊。

王老师：哦，来了。环环，我交**报费**去了啊，自己好好多看看，多动**动脑子**。
　　　　谢谢啊。**咦**？环环，环环。

许淑芬：哟，王老师。

王老师：环环妈才下班啊？

许淑芬：哎。

王老师：你，你不忙着做饭^{G2}吧？

许淑芬：王老师有事儿？

王老师：哎，我……我，我想找你说几句话。

许淑芬：环环，你跟妈妈说实话，是不是拿了别人的东西了？你现在跟妈妈说
　　　　实话，妈妈还可以**原谅**你！否则！否则，我打断你的腿！

小气鬼	xiǎoqìguǐ	n.	miser
形容词	xíngróngcí	n.	adjective
报费	bàofèi	n.	newspaper fee
动脑子	dòng nǎozi	vo.	think about it; use (your) head
咦	yí	interj.	
原谅	yuánliàng	v.	forgive; pardon

环　环：妈妈，我真的没有。

许淑芬：跪下！你现在变得越来越**犟**了。你给我**跪**下！你还不想跪啊？你跪
　　　　下！**胆子**越来越大了。你说，是不是拿了王老师家的钱？说呀！

环　环：妈妈，我想买一套《灌篮高手》，我不能让同学们笑话我，我不能让
　　　　同学们笑话我爸爸。

许淑芬：这么说，你是真的拿了别人的钱了？你胆子也太大了你，你怎么做出
　　　　这样的事情呢你？我今天我打死你，我打死你，我打死你，我今天就
　　　　不活了，你个臭孩子。你还敢跑你。

环　环：妈妈，妈妈，别打我，妈妈。

许淑芬：你真的让我伤心透了你，臭孩子，你过来！

环　环：妈妈，别打我，妈妈！

许淑芬：你给我说，你还拿了别人什么东西？你快说呀你！你这孩子。

环　环：我还拿了陈家阿婆钱包里的钱。

许淑芬：环环啊，你怎么会变成这个样子呢？啊？好吧，是妈妈没给你吃饱，
　　　　没给你穿暖吗？我们家是不**富裕**，是吃的、穿的是不如别人，可是妈
　　　　妈赚的这些辛苦钱一直在**满足**你，对不对？对不对？不行，你今天一
　　　　定要给妈妈说清楚你这是为什么，你讲，你说！

环　环：我想，我，我想拿王老师钱包里的钱还给陈家阿婆。

许淑芬：好，为什么？这是为什么？

环　环：妈妈，爸爸到底是不是在日本啊？我们为什么没有收到过他的来信、
　　　　他的电话和他寄来的东西？爸爸到底是不是在日本呀？爸爸是不是不
　　　　要我们了？妈妈，呜……（哭声）

许淑芬：哎！

犟	jiàng	adj.	stubborn
跪	guì	v.	kneel
胆子	dǎnzi	n.	guts; nerve
富裕	fùyù	adj.	well-to-do; rich
满足	mǎnzú	v.	satisfy

语法 Grammar Notes

1. **"……的"**：用在描写性句子的末尾，表示一种状态、样子、情况。见《风波》第一部分语法1。

   "……的" is used at the end of a descriptive sentence, expressing a state of affair. See《风波》grammar note 1 in part 1.

   （1）还 60 分 70 分的，你爸爸才不会替你买呢。

   这句话的意思是"（你）如果还是像现在这样考 60 分 70 分（这种状态），你爸爸不会给你买"。

   The meaning of this sentence is "If you still make 60's and 70's, of course your father won't buy them (those books) for you."

   （2）可是我的工作每天起早贪黑的，我有点儿顾不上她。（本剧第二部分）

   However, since I leave early for work and come back late everyday, I don't have much time to take care of her and watch over her study.

   （3）哎，都是些家长里短的，你可以看。（本剧第四部分）

   Oh, it's all about petty family affairs, I don't mind your reading it (the letter).

   （4）她这个人说话总是啰里啰唆的。

   She is always garrulous.

2. **"忙着做饭"**（adj＋着＋v）：这种结构第二部分表示原因。

   "忙着做饭 A" means busy with cooking. In this structure〔形容词＋着＋动词〕the verb phrase expresses the cause (of being busy in this case).

   （1）你不忙着做饭吧？

   这句话的意思是"你现在不是因为要做饭而很忙吧？"

   You're not busy cooking, are you?

   The meaning of this sentence is "You're not busy with cooking, are you?"

   （2）我最近正忙着写毕业论文，所以没有给你打电话。

   I'm very busy now because I'm working on my thesis. Therefore, I didn't call you.

（3）我昨天去他家的时候，他正忙着整理东西准备搬家。

When I went to his house yesterday, he was very busy because he was preparing to move.

练习 Exercises

■ 一、口语练习 Oral Practice

（一）回答问题 Answer the follwing questions

1. 环环拿了陈阿婆多少钱？
2. 她用陈阿婆的钱买什么了？
3. 环环为什么拿王老师的钱？
4. 环环为什么一定要买《灌篮高手》？
5. 环环为什么会有这么多问题？

（二）讨论 Discussion

1. 你认为环环的变化是什么原因引起的？为什么？
2. 你认为环环妈妈教育孩子的方法有什么问题？请举例说明。

■ 二、书写练习 Written Exercises

（一）选择题 Circle the answer which most reflects the meaning of the under-lined part in the following sentences

1. 我今天一早买菜回来，<u>明明</u>把钱包放在桌子上了，怎么一下子就找不到了？
   A. 一个叫明明的孩子
   B. 明天
   C. 记得清清楚楚
   D. 说得清清楚楚

2. 孩子们刚才还在这儿玩儿，<u>一眨眼工夫</u>就都不见了。
   A. 用眼睛一看
   B. 没有时间
   C. 没有想到
   D. 在很短时间内

3. 你看，这套课本根本<u>不齐</u>，所以我们没有办法用。
   A. 不全

B. 不好

C. 不新

D. 不合适

4. 你最好还是别找他借钱吧，他可是个有名的**小气鬼**。

    A. 自私的人

    B. 靠不住的人

    C. 舍不得花钱的人

    D. 爱找麻烦的人

5. 我们别再去说服小王了。他这个人**很犟**，一旦决心要做一件事，不管谁劝他，他也听不进去。

    A. 很有责任感

    B. 很认真

    C. 很不容易听取别人意见

    D. 很独立

6. 那个电影啊，**没意思透了**，我们只看了一半就出来了。

    A. 没意思极了

    B. 有点儿没意思

    C. 蛮没意思的

    D. 挺没意思的

7. 简直是**出鬼了**！钥匙，一进门我就放在这儿了，现在怎么找都找不到了。

    A. 太可怕了

    B. 太奇怪了

    C. 太有意思了

    D. 太气人了

8. 请**随手**关门。

    A. 很容易地一伸手

    B. 特地

    C. 方便

    D. 随便

四

许淑芬：王老师！

王老师：啊，我在这儿。环环妈，有事啊？

许淑芬：嗯，王老师，我没**管教**好自己的孩子，这孩子怎么搞的，会做出^{G1}这么没出息的事情！我们家里也不缺钱花啊，你看她爸爸还经常给我们寄些钱来。咳，怎么会做这种事呢?！王老师，这是环环拿的你的钱，我现在还给你。到明天，我让环环自己来给你**赔礼**道歉。啊，那我就不打扰了，你拿着。

王老师：哎，你别走。哎，环环妈啊，孩子做错了事儿，靠打是解决不了问题的呀。唔，我们做**家长**的，该看看问题出在什么地方。你看多好的孩子，怎么做这样的事呢？

许淑芬：我，我也不知道。不打扰了。

王老师：哎，环环妈，你等一下。哎，我想给你看一封信，是我爱人寄来的。哎，问题是不是出在这上面？哎，都是些**家长里短**^{N1}的，你可以看。

许淑芬：这都是我们家里的事儿。王老师，我们家这些不**体面**的事，我说实话，我不想让人知道，我不想！

王老师：环环妈，我不是**故意**要**为难**你的，我爱人是白毛岭劳改农场的教导员，她是**偶然**发现环环爸爸给家里写信的地址也是诚信里九号，她这……这才知道你们搬这儿来住了。你看，她的信上特意**关照**我，要好好照顾你们母女俩。

管教	guǎnjiào	v.	discipline; control and teach
赔礼	péi lǐ	vo.	apologize
家长	jiāzhǎng	n.	通常为学生的父母，或其他法定监护人，usually parent(s), or legal guardian
家长里短	jiā cháng lǐ duǎn		domestic trivia
体面	tǐmiàn	adj.	decent; respectable
故意	gùyì	adv.	intentionally; deliberately; on purpose
为难	wéinán	v. /adj.	make sb. feel embarrassed; make things difficult for sb.
偶然	ǒurán	adv.	accidentally; unexpectedly; occasionally
关照	guānzhào	v.	tell

许淑芬：事情到了现在，我想，**瞒**也是瞒不下去。可是，你说，我发生了这些事情，我……我也不知道，我这是为了什么？

王老师：环环妈，你，坐下慢慢说吧。我觉得啊，你还是应该找机会把一切都告诉环环。

许淑芬：我是不希望她小小**年纪**在别人面前抬不起头来[N2]，我希望我的孩子和别的孩子一样，健康、快乐地成长。我不能把她爸爸的事儿告诉她，我不能对她说，可是这又是……这又有什么办法？我就是没有**勇气**。王老师，你也看见了，我来了以后，安了这么大的一个信箱，还弄了一把**锁**，可最后，还是什么都包不住。

王老师：就是这把大锁，把你的心给**锁住**[G1]了，而且锁得很**沉重**啊。我知道，你呢，一心想在家里做个好母亲，在社会上做个体面的女人。可是，你知道这样做的后果吗？

许淑芬：我真是的，我害了自己，也害了孩子。

王老师：环环妈啊，不管怎样啊，**往后**的日子要过得轻松，那**坦诚**就是一**剂良药**，对**左邻右舍**要坦诚，对孩子也一样。我们不给孩子做个**榜样**，怎么要求她做个诚实的人呢？你说是不是啊？

许淑芬：王老师，谢谢！

陈阿婆：这个呢，给环环爸爸带去。

许淑芬：阿婆，别客气，我……

邻居们：拿着，拿着，啊，拿着吧，拿着吧。

瞒	mán	v.	hide the truth from; conceal from
年纪	niánjì	n.	age
勇气	yǒngqì	n.	courage
锁	suǒ	n./v.	lock
锁住	suǒ zhù	vc.	lock up
沉重	chénzhòng	adj.	heavy
往后	wǎnghòu	t.	以后，from now on; later on
坦诚	tǎnchéng	adj.	frank and sincere
剂	jì	m.	dose (of medicine)
良药	liángyào	n.	effective drug
左邻右舍	zuǒ lín yòu shè	n.	neighbor (same as"邻居")
榜样	bǎngyàng	n.	example; role model

陈阿婆：要他好好**改造**，争取早点儿回来，环环呢，我们呢，会好好照顾她
　　　　的，放心吧。

邻　居：环环妈，你就放心地去吧，啊，环环有我们照顾呢，啊。

王老师：把诚信里九号的事呀，跟她爸爸好好说说。

许淑芬：王老师，我会说的。我想，我会把最近发生的事情**原原本本**都告诉他。

陈阿婆：走吧，一路上自己当心点儿，啊。

许淑芬：哎，好的。

邻　居：可要小心啊。

许淑芬：哎，对了，等等，你们等我一下啊。

邻　居：哎，环环妈。

王老师：怎么？

许淑芬：阿婆，我把它交给你。王老师，谢谢你啊！我走了。再见！

王老师：哎。

环　环：妈妈，妈妈，妈妈。

许淑芬：环环，不哭，环环！

环　环：妈妈，你告诉爸爸，我会等他回来的。我会好好读书，考上中学，要
　　　　他放心。

许淑芬：环环，妈妈知道环环是个好孩子。环环，妈妈走了，妈妈要走了。回
　　　　去，阿婆带你，啊，听妈妈话。

环　环：不要嘛，不要嘛，妈，妈妈！

许淑芬：再见，环环。

环　环：妈妈，妈妈再见，妈妈再见。

邻　居：再见。

| 改造 | gǎizào | v. | reform; remold |
| 原原本本 | yuán yuán běn běn | adv. | exactly as it is |

185

注释 Notes

1. **"家长里短"**：意思是"（谈）关于家里的一些小事情。"

   "家长里短" refers to chitchat about petty family affairs.

2. **"抬不起头来"**：意思是"因为某种原因在别人面前觉得没有面子，很不好意思。"

   To feel ashamed or embarrassed in front of others due to a certain reason/reasons.

〇〇〇〇〇〇〇〇〇〇〇〇〇〇

语法 Grammar Notes

补语：本课出现很多口语中常见的补语。

Complement：There are quite a few colloquial expressions involving complements in this lesson.

(1) 死

    A. 表示程度：如，我累死了，热死了，冷死了，气死了，麻烦死了，高兴死了，美死了。

        "死"，as an adverb of degree，(literally means to die) is often used to express a state of the extreme. For example，我累死了 means "I'm extremely exhausted."

        ①热死了。   Extremely hot.

        ②冷死了。   Extremely cold.

        ③气死了。   Extremely angry.

        ④麻烦死了。   Extremely irritating.

        ⑤高兴死了。   Extremely happy.

        ⑥美死了。   Extremely pleased.

    B. 表示"死亡"。如：他把爸爸气死了（爸爸真的死了）。

        "His father died of being angry with him." In this case，the complement "死" is used in its literal sense.

(2) 下

    ①收下（礼物）。   To accept (a present).

    ②买下一所房子。   To purchase a house.

    ③租下一个公寓。   To rent an apartment.

    ④存下很多钱。   To save a lot of money.

(3) 出

    ①抽出时间。   To take time out (of a busy schedule).

    ②看不出来王老师蛮会做事的。

        (I) didn't realize that Teacher Wang is pretty good at dealing with different situations.

③空出一个房间。　To evacuate a room.

④听不出是谁的声音。　Cannot tell whose voice it is.

⑤吃不出是用什么菜做的。（One）cannot tell what vegetables were put in the dish.

（4）起

①（这么贵的书怎么）买得起。

（How can I）afford to buy（such an expensive book）?

②（连税都）付不起。　Cannot even pay the tax.

③这个音乐会的票太贵了，我听不起。

The ticket for the concert is too expensive，I cannot afford it.

④这个学校的学费他交不起。（见《项链》第一部分语法注释3。）

He cannot afford to pay the tuition for this school.

（Refer to grammar note 3 in part one of《项链》）

（5）着

①用不着（单独装信箱）。　Do not need to（have a separate mailbox）.

②找不着。　Cannot find.

③借不着。　Not available to borrow.

④买不着。　Not available to buy.

（6）坏

A.（把书）弄坏了。　To damage or ruin（the book）.

B. 表示程度　To indicate degree of a state.

①热坏了。　Terribly hot.

②气坏了。　Terribly angry.

③累坏了。　Extremely tired.

④急坏了。　Terribly worried.

（7）走

①（钱被）偷走了。　（The money was）stolen away.

②把她赶走了。　（Someone）chased her away.

③那本书他拿走了。　He took the book away.

（8）好

A. 动作完成并为下一步做好准备　Action after the completion of an action

①（中午饭已经）安排好了（孩子中午可以吃）。

The lunch is already arranged and ready for the kids.

②衣服做好了。　The clothes are done and ready (to pick up).

③考试准备好了。　The test is ready.

④飞机票买好了。　The airplane ticket is paid and ready (to go).

B. 表示结果

①（我没管教）好（自己的孩子）。I didn't discipline my kids well.

②这个老师教不好学生。The teacher cannot teach students well.

（9）全（齐全）　Complete (as a whole set).

①（把书）买全。　To buy a complete collection.

②今天我们班的学生没来全。Today not everyone in our class came.

（10）断

①打断你的腿。　To beat and break your leg.

②把风筝的线拉断了。(Someone) pulled and broke the thread of the kite.

③电话挂断了。　The phone call was cut off.

（11）饱

（我）吃饱了。　I'm full (with food) now.

（12）暖

①（你）穿暖了。　(You) wear warm clothes.

②把房间烧暖了。　Heat up the room.

（13）清楚

①（把事情）说清楚。　Explain this matter clearly.

②听不清楚。　(One) cannot hear clearly.

③看清楚了。　(One) saw clearly.

④写清楚。　Write clearly.

⑤记不清楚。　(One) cannot remember clearly.

（14）给

①（把钱）还给（王阿婆）。Return (the money to Granny Wang).

②把书寄给姐姐，把作业交给老师。

　　Mail the book（s）to your sister, and hand in the homework to the teacher.

（15）透

表示程度，常用在具有消极意义的词后。"透" is used to indicate the extreme degree, often with a negative connotation.

①（她）伤心透了。She is extremely miserable.

②这个人坏透了。This person is really evil.

③事情糟透了。The situation is extremely bad.

④我伤透了脑筋。I'm really frustrated.

（16）下去

表示继续的意义："下去" when following a verb，means to go on doing something.

①（事情）瞒不下去了。 Cannot cover（this matter）any more.

②说下去。Keep talking.

③我在这里还要住下去。I'll keep on living here.

④天气再热下去，我就受不了了。

    If the weather keeps on getting warmer，I won't be able to stand it any more.

（17）住

①（把信箱）锁住了。Lock up the mailbox.

②生词太多，我记不住。

    There are too many new words，and I cannot remember them.

③（纸）包不住（火）。Paper cannot hold fire.

④这个盖子太小，盖不住杯子。

    This cover is too small，and it won't fit the glass.

⑤这个地方藏不住人。This place cannot hide anyone.

（18）不来：意思是：不习惯做某事。

"Verb ＋ 不来" means not being accustomed to doing something.

①吃不来（日本食品）。Unused to eating Japanese food.

②这件事我做不来。I'm not accustomed to doing this.

③山东话我说不来。I'm not accustomed to speaking Shandong dialect.

下面几个是熟语性的。The following items are some idiomatic expressions：

（19）说不定（环环的爸爸来信了）：意思是 "有可能" probably。

①明年说不定我会去中国。

    I may go to China next year.

②他说不定今天不来了。

    He is probably not coming today.

（20）（我心里）过意不去：意思是由于欠别人的情而心里感到不安。

"My conscience won't let me." One feels uncomfortable because she/he received a favor from someone（often the addressee）.

①让你照顾我的孩子这么多天，我很过意不去。

I feel so much indebted to you since you have taken care of my kids for many days.

②你大老远来我家，连顿饭都不吃，我真过意不去。

You came all the way to visit me without eating a meal. I feel really bad.

练习 Exercises

■ 一、口语练习 Oral Practice

（一）回答问题 Answer the following questions

　　1. 环环的妈妈去王老师家做什么？

　　2. 王老师给环环妈妈看了一件什么东西？为什么给她看？

　　3. 王老师的爱人在信上为什么提起环环家的事？

　　4. 环环的妈妈有什么事瞒着环环？她为什么要这样做？

　　5. 王老师说："坦诚就是一剂良药。"这句话是什么意思？

　　6. 环环的妈妈把事情的真相告诉邻居们以后，邻居们对她和环环比以前
　　　更好了，还是没有以前好？请举例说明。

（二）讨论 Discussion

　　1. 大人做了错事应该不应该让孩子知道？

　　2. 如果你是环环的妈妈，你会不会把环环爸爸的事请告诉环环？为什么？

　　3. 中国有句俗话，"家丑不可外扬"，你认为这句话对不对？

（三）角色扮演 Role Play

　　两人一组对话，一方是王老师，建议把环环爸爸的事情告诉环环，另一方
　　是环环的妈妈，主张对环环隐瞒她爸爸的事情。两个人看谁能说服对方。
　　对话中要用下面的词语。

　　Make a dialogue in pairs. One party plays Wang Laoshi，who suggests for
　　Huanhuan to be told the truth about her father，and the other party plays
　　Huanhuan's mother who insists on hiding the truth from Huanhuan. Both
　　parties try to find good arguments to convince the other party. The dia-
　　logue should incorporate the items given below：

1. 不体面	2. 为难	3. 瞒不下去	4. 原原本本
5. 快乐地成长	6. 抬不起头来	7.（没）有勇气	8. 害了
9. 坦诚	10. 轻松	11. 后果	12. 希望
13. 诚实			

二、书写练习 Written Exercises

（一）选择题 Circle the answer which most reflects the meaning of the underlined part in the following sentences.

1. 甲：哎，你们两个人在说什么？

   乙：没说什么，都是些<u>家长里短</u>的事情，你不会感兴趣的。

   A. 家里人关心的事情

   B. 家庭矛盾

   C. 跟家庭有关的小事情

   D. 孩子的事情

2. 甲：小谢，你教我们唱一个英文歌吧！

   乙：你听听我的嗓子（sǎngzi 即 voice），我哪儿会唱歌啊！你们可别<u>为难我了</u>。

   A. 让我难过

   B. 让我觉得不好办

   C. 让我失望

   D. 让我害怕

3. 虽然张天华已经上大学了，可她的父母总把她当小孩子，每次打电话他们都<u>关照</u>她要早一点睡觉。

   A. 照顾

   B. 关心

   C. 再三告诉

   D. 担心

4. 小李说她找了两年的工作都没找到，觉得在别人面前<u>抬不起头来</u>。

   A. 很不高兴

   B. 很失望

   C. 很紧张

   D. 很没面子

5. 你不用做任何解释，只要把这件事<u>原原本本</u>告诉他就行了。

   A. 原来的情况

   B. 本来的情况

   C. 事实

   D. 从头到尾（从开始到最后）

6. 他能去北京读大学真不容易，一连考了三次大学，今年终于考上了，而且是北京大学。
  A. 考好了北京大学
  B. 考完了北京大学
  C. 考进了北京大学
  D. 考成了北京大学

（二）补语练习 Exercise on the verbal complements

选择适当的补语填空 Fill in the blanks with the appropriate verbal complement

A. 清楚	B. 不来	C. 会	D. 给	E. 死
F. 下	G. 到	H. 错	I. 下去	J. 住
K. 出来	L. 好	M. 饱	N. 暖	O. 坏
P. 走	Q. 起	R. 齐	S. 断	T. 透

1. 孩子做_____了事情，千万不能打骂，只有耐心教育才能解决问题。其实，很多孩子的问题是由于家长没有管教_____造成的。

2. 这件事已经有很多人知道了，瞒是瞒不_____的，最好的办法是主动说_____。

3. 环环的妈妈用一把大锁把她自己的心锁_____了。

4. 环环的妈妈辛辛苦苦地赚钱为了环环能吃_____穿_____，但是环环还是不满意。环环的妈妈怎么想也想不_____这是为什么。

5. 陈阿婆说那些日本的糖和点心她都吃_____，中国人还是习惯吃中国的东西。

6. 环环不但学习成绩下降，而且还学_____了骗人，这真让环环妈妈伤心_____了。

7. 环环的妈妈向环环保证，她一定把环环画的画儿带_____环环的爸爸。

8. 邮递员说这个信箱太小了，放不_____大包裹，我们得换一个大一点儿的信箱。

9. 他三年以前滑雪的时候不小心把腿摔（to fall）_____了，从那以后就很少再运动了。

10. 你明年要去南京啊？可别夏天去，那儿的夏天简直热_____人了。

11. 你说这事儿多奇怪啊！我几分钟以前刚把钱包放在客厅的桌子上，这会儿就怎么找都找不_____了！真是出鬼了！

12. 我看啊，现在的孩子学_____多半是因为家长没有花足够的时间教育孩子，而是把主要时间精力放在工作赚钱上了。

13. 环环看到陈阿婆家里没有人，就把桌子上的 70 块钱拿_____了。

14. 丈夫进了劳改农场以后，家里的生活水平急剧下降，大房子住不_____了，许淑芬只好带着女儿搬进了一个小公寓。

15. 环环说，他爸爸写信告诉她，等她明年过 10 岁生日的时候，一定帮她把最喜欢读的《灌篮高手》这套书买_____。

（三）这个故事对你有什么启发？写一篇 400 字左右的观后感。

What does this story tell you? Write a reflection of this story containing about 400 Chinese characters.

■ 三、文化方面的讨论 Culture Discussion

1. 在你们国家，一般人对罪犯家属的态度怎样？如果亲人犯了罪，人们会想办法隐瞒吗？

In your country, how do ordinary people treat family members of a criminal? If someone's family member is a criminal, will he/she feel bad enough as to hide the fact from others?

2. 如果丈夫或妻子犯了罪，另一方会向孩子隐瞒吗？

If a husband or wife committed a crime, would the spouse try to hide it from their child/children?

第六课 都市彩虹

Rainbow in the City Sky

导读：

随着国有企业改革的不断深入，一些职工不得不离开国企这个"铁饭碗"，重新去找工作。丢掉了"铁饭碗"的一部分人，开始"下海"经商。但并不是每个人一"下海"就能赚到大把的钞票，有的还要"呛（喝）几口水"。本剧的杨彩虹就是一个离开国企的下岗工人，骗子们看她没有经验，就利用她想发财的心理欺骗她，使她差一点倾家荡产。幸运的是，她遇到了一家大型国营企业的厂长，这位厂长为了维护工厂的荣誉，正在寻找假冒他们工厂品牌的羽绒服。杨彩虹买的羽绒服恰巧就是假冒这个工厂的牌子。羽绒服工厂向杨彩虹买回并销毁了假冒产品，使杨彩虹免受损失。有了一点经商经验的杨彩虹，开始帮助像她一样刚刚"下海"的姐妹。

本剧虽然主线是揭露商场中的骗子，但更侧重表现市场经济环境中的新生事物，展现人们之间的友爱互助精神，正是这样的新气象构成了都市中的一道美丽的彩虹。

Introduction:

As the economic reform accelerated, some government workers had to leave their jobs that used to be their "iron rice bowls" and looked for other jobs. Some of those workers started their own businesses (which is called "jumping into the ocean" in Chinese). However, not everyone who "jumped into the ocean" could make big money immediately. Some of them would have to "swallow some ocean water" before they started making any profits at all.

Yang Caihong, the main character of this story, is one of many who had such an experience. Caihong was a laid-off worker from a government-owned enterprise and had just started her own business of selling goose down coats. Inexperienced and eager to make money, Caihong was cheated by swindlers and almost went broke. Fortunately, she met the director of a big state-operated factory, who was trying to find all the fake products that were sold in their name brand in order to protect the reputation and credibility of the factory. The factory bought and destroyed all Caihong's fake goose down jackets that she had unwittingly bought from the swindlers. Caihong's business was saved. Caihong, now an experienced business woman, began to help other women just like her, who were beginners in business.

This story exposes business swindlers, but, more importantly, it shows the new and uplifting characteristics of the new market economy and demonstrates the compassion, friendship, and cooperation between people. It is this kind of spirit that has created a beautiful "rainbow" across the city sky.

主要人物（Main Characters）

杨彩虹	Yáng Cǎihóng	a middle-aged woman
张祥林	Zhāng Xiánglín	Yang Caihong's husband
刘 眉	Liú Méi	Yang Caihong's friend
李大兴（大头）	Lǐ Dàxīng（Dàtóu）	Yang Caihong's high school classmate
张茂林	Zhāng Màolín	Zhang Xianglin's younger brother
（张）茂林妻	（Zhāng）Màolín qī	Zhang Maolin's wife
张英子	Zhāng Yīngzi	Yang Caihong's daughter
旅馆服务员	lǚguǎn fúwùyuán	a hotel clerk

胖女人	pàng nǚrén	a fat woman
厂长	chǎngzhǎng	factory director
顾客一	gùkè yī	customer A
顾客二	gùkè èr	customer B
骗子	piànzi	a trickster
卖货者	mài huò zhě	a (warehouse) salesman
看电话人	kān diànhuà rén	a telephone keeper
众顾客	zhòng gùkè	customers
电视主持人	diànshì zhǔchírén	a TV anchorman
大嫂	dàsǎo	sister-in-law; (a polite form of address for a woman about one's own age)

字　幕：**彩虹**很美丽，但它只是在**瞬间**发生。每个人都在追求自己心中的彩
　　　　虹，但这要靠自己在现实中去**拼搏**，才能把美丽的**瞬间**变成心中的**永
　　　　恒**……

胖女人：啊，瞧一瞧，看一看啦，北京的**羽绒服**，羽绒服啊，来看一看。

顾客一：这质量行吗？

胖女人：可以可以，没问题。你看哪，你看看啊，北京的**原料**，外国的**技术**
　　　　啊，真正的中外技术**合作**的**产品**。哎，我的产品绝对**货真价实**，啊。

顾客二：给您钱。

胖女人：哎，您走好[N1]了啊。

顾客二：哎，好，好。

胖女人：啊，瞧一瞧，看一看啦，北京的羽绒服，国际流行色了，啊，来看一
　　　　看，快来买了啊。

杨彩虹：大姐。

胖女人：哎。

杨彩虹：您的羽绒服挺好卖的，挣不少吧？

胖女人：哎，**凑合**吧。我瞧你那声儿，刚**练摊**儿[N2]吧？

都市	dūshì	n.	big city; metropolis
彩虹	cǎihóng	n.	rainbow
拼搏	pīnbó	v.	struggle hard; exert one's utmost strength
瞬间	shùnjiān	adv.	in the twinkling of an eye; moment
永恒	yǒnghéng	adj.	eternal; perpetual
羽绒服	yǔróngfú	n.	down jacket
原料	yuánliào	n.	raw material; unprocessed material
技术	jìshù	n.	technology; technological
合作	hézuò	v.	cooperate
产品	chǎnpǐn	n.	product; manufactured goods
货真价实	huò zhēn jià shí		genuine goods at a fair price; the genuine item; true to the name
凑合	còuhe	v.	make do
练摊儿	liàn tānr	vo.	have a stand to sell merchandise

杨彩虹：嗯。

胖女人：是**下岗**的吧？

杨彩虹：啊，就算，**重新**就业吧。

胖女人：那你先生怎么不来帮你呢？

杨彩虹：啊，他，他忙。

胖女人：好啊，男人忙好啊，挣大钱啊，是不是？

杨彩虹：嗯。

胖女人：哟，坏了，哎呀，我还有点儿急事。大妹子，你帮我看会儿摊儿，成吗？

杨彩虹：我，我能行吗？啊？

胖女人：啊，哎。

杨彩虹：我，我能行吗？大姐，我……

胖女人：没问题，没问题。哎，我告诉你啊，你帮我看着点儿摊，我一会儿就回来，一会儿就回来啊。

杨彩虹：啊，不是……哎。瞧一瞧啊，买羽绒服啊，来晚了就买不着了。哎，哎，您……

骗　子：你这个羽绒服卖多少钱哪？

杨彩虹：690。

骗　子：这个**牌子**倒是**熟**。

杨彩虹：是。

骗　子：就是贵了点儿。

杨彩虹：不贵。你看，这是**纯鸭绒**的，用手摸一摸，不一样。

骗　子：我给你550。

杨彩虹：不行。

骗　子：我给你580。我说你这个人，你这个人做生意咋[N3]这么**死**呢？

杨彩虹：我实话跟您说了吧，这不是我的，我是替别人卖的。

下岗	xià gǎng	vo.	lay off
重新	chóngxīn	adv.	once again
牌子	páizi	n.	brand；trademark
熟	shú	adj.	familiar
纯	chún	adj.	pure；unmixed
鸭绒	yāróng	n.	down
死	sǐ	adj.	rigid；stubborn

骗　子：别说了，别说了，我懂，我明白。我看你这个人，倒是蛮实在的。

杨彩虹：是吗？

骗　子：我给你个价，不过你可就别**还价**了啊。600 块钱一件，我要 100 件。

杨彩虹：100 件？

骗　子：反正是**公家**的事儿呗，**年底**了，厂子里给**职工谋**点儿**福利**[N4]。**咋样**啊？
　　　　就这样吧。发票，发票给开 650 一件。

杨彩虹：这，这，能行吗？

骗　子：不**中**[N5]，就算了。

杨彩虹：哎，大哥，我没说不行哪，我也没说不行啊。不过，**我手头现在没有**
　　　　那么多现货。

骗　子：那没关系，反正我**后**儿个晚上的火车，明儿个把货送到不就中了么？
　　　　啊我住在**西城宾馆**415 房间。咱一手交钱一手交货[N6]。这是我的**名片**。
　　　　啊，哎，你把你的电话给我一个，咱们好联系。啊，嗯，你，你就写
　　　　到这上就中了。

杨彩虹：嗯，这是我家电话，有事儿打我家就行了，啊。

骗　子：这是 500 块钱，拿着，拿着，拿着，就算我交的**定金**。放心了吧？

杨彩虹：哎，啊，我怎么能先要你的钱呢？

还价	huán jià	vo.	bargain
公家	gōngjia	n.	the state organization or enterprise
年底	niándǐ		end of a year; year-end
职工	zhígōng	n.	staff and workers
谋	móu	v.	work for; seek
福利	fúlì	n.	material benefits
咋样	zǎyàng	pron.	(col.) 怎么样，How about that?
中	zhōng		(Northern dialect) 好，行，all right; fine
手头	shǒutóu	n.	on hand; at hand
现货	xiànhuò	n.	merchandise on hand; goods in stock
后儿个	hòurge	t.	(col.) 后天，the day after tomorrow
西城	xīchéng	n.	Western district (of a city)
宾馆	bīnguǎn	n.	旅馆，hotel
名片	míngpiàn	n.	name card; business card
定金	dìngjīn	n.	deposit

骗　子：你就别客气了。咳，你说，你，这个，算啥嘞。嘿，那就，别忘了开
　　　　发票啊。

杨彩虹：哎，哎。

杨彩虹：哎，我把咱那两万块钱给取出来了？我……

张祥林：什么？你把银行那两万块钱给取出来了？我不同意啊。

杨彩虹：你吵吵什么啊？

张祥林：那两万块钱是我用**粉笔末蘸**出来的，也是你一分钱分八半儿花[N7]省出
　　　　来了，万一[G1]有什么**闪失**[N8]，咱俩今后的日子该怎么过啊？哪有这天
　　　　上**掉馅儿饼**[N9]的事儿？**忒玄乎**[N10]。

杨彩虹：玄乎什么？**八辈子**也赶不上这一回，再说了，三万块钱这不就挣到手
　　　　了么？哎，我给你说啊，人家做大买卖的，打个电话，十万八万的都
　　　　挣来了，真没见过大**世面**！

张祥林：那，得得得，你见过。就是，你要进货，这两万块钱也不够啊。

杨彩虹：借钱！

张祥林：嗯？什么，你要借钱？这万一出个什么闪失，你怎么还哪？

杨彩虹：你别**咒**我行吗？又不是让你去借，有什么**差错**？再说了，人家住大宾
　　　　馆，是为职工谋福利。他又不是社会上的那个，那个，**闲杂盲流**[N11]。
　　　　我借钱怎么了？你以为大公司就不借钱啊？大公司也借钱，那叫**贷
　　　　款**，全都是一样的。生意做得越大啊，就越要大贷款。连这个你都不
　　　　懂，你还给学生讲什么**经济学**啊你？哼！

啥	shá	pron.	（col.）什么，what
粉笔末	fěnbǐ mò	n.	chalk powder
蘸	zhàn	v.	dip
闪失	shǎnshī	n.	accident; mishap
掉	diào	v.	fall; drop
馅儿饼	xiànrbǐng	n.	pancake with fillings
忒	tuī	adv.	（col.）太，too
玄乎	xuánhu	adj.	（col.）fantastic; inscrutable
八辈子	bā bèizi		（col.）in a million years; in a long time
世面	shìmiàn	n.	world; various aspects of society or world
咒	zhòu	v.	curse; put a curse on(sb.)
差错	chācuò	n.	mistake; error
闲杂盲流	xián zá mángliú		unemployed/unoccupied migrating peasants (as used in this story)
贷款	dài kuǎn	vo.	loan; borrow money from bank
经济学	jīngjìxué	n.	economics

张祥林：你才做了几天生意啊？

刘　眉：咳，谁跟谁啊[N12]？这是我们姐妹之间的事儿，你就拿着吧。

张祥林：那，我就替她收着。

刘　眉：啊哈，现在啊，就兴个相互帮助，谁有困难还得靠咱们姐妹儿。你看，彩虹刚**撂**电话，我立马[N13]就到。

李大兴：你大点儿声，谁啊？啊？噢，彩虹啊，你好你好，怎么有事儿？嗯，借钱？借多少？啊，你谈什么借啊，咱哥儿俩谁跟谁啊，就是割肉我也给你，啊，嘿嘿。这样吧，你啊，下午到我公司去，咱俩面谈，好不好？

兴	xīng	v.	encourage; promote
撂	liào	v	(col.) 放, put down
立马	lìmǎ	adv.	(col.) 马上, 立刻; immediately

注释 Notes

1. **"您走好"**：这是送客人走时的一句客气话。也可以说"（您）慢走。"
   This expression "您走好" is used when one sees off his/her guest(s). One can also say "（您）慢走。"

2. **"练摊ᵧ"**：意思是"摆摊卖东西"。
   "练摊" means to have a stand to sell stuff.

3. **"咋"**：意思是"怎么"，口语。
   "how come" or "how", colloquial expression.

4. **"给职工谋点ᵧ福利"**：这是指企业或事业单位在员工正常工资之外，设法让他们有一些额外的收益。
   "给职工谋点ᵧ福利" refers to enterprises，government organizations and institutions who give their employees extra money/benefits besides their regular salaries.

5. **"不中"**：意思是"不行"，北方方言。
   "不中" is an expression in Northern dialect. It means "it won't do"，similar to "不行".

6. **"一手交钱一手交货"**：这是做生意（多为小生意）时的一种规矩：买方给卖方钱，卖方给买方货。即一种现金交易。
   "一手交钱一手交货" is to get the product with cash. This expression is used to refer to one way of doing business（usually practiced by small businesses）—as the buyer gives the seller cash，the seller gives the buyer the product，a cash transaction.

7. **"一分钱分八半ᵧ花"**（pinch pennies）：把一分钱分成八份来花，意思是非常节省。
   This expression means to spend every single penny very carefully，or to spend money in a very stingy way.

8. **"闪失"**：是"意外的差错、损失"的意思，常用于没有发生的情况，比如假设句："万一有什么闪失，怎么办?"是口语的表达方式。
   "闪失"，as a colloquial expression，means unexpected mistake or loss. It is

commonly used in an unrealized situation. For example，in a hypothetical sentence，"万一有什么闪失，怎么办？"（What shall we do in case anything goes wrong?）

9. **"天上掉馅ㄦ饼"**：意思是：什么事都没做而意外得到了好处。遇到没有想到的好事，也可以说"这真是天上掉下来一个馅ㄦ饼。"

"天上掉馅ㄦ饼" is used to mean that good things happened to someone without his/her making any efforts（unexpectedly）. In this case，one can also say "这真是天上掉下来一个馅ㄦ饼。"（This is just pie in the sky.）

See more examples below：

（1）你姐姐的公司给你一个好工作？这真是天上掉下来一个馅ㄦ饼。

Your sister's company has offered you a good position? This is just pie in the sky.

（2）工作得你自己去找，人家不会来找你。世界上哪有天上掉馅ㄦ饼的好事？

You will have to find your own job，（since）employers will not come to you and give you a job. Where would you find money growing on trees?

10. **"忒玄乎"**："忒"的意思是"太"，北方口语，"玄乎"的意思是"玄虚不可捉摸"，"不合常理、不可思议"。

"忒" is a colloquial expression used around Beijing area，meaning "太". "玄乎" means to make（it）sound incredible，unbelievable，or unreasonable.

11. **"闲杂盲流"**："闲杂"是"闲杂人员"，指没有固定职业的人，"盲流"本指盲目流入某个城市的人，这里的意思是指没有固定工作、不可相信的人。

"闲杂" means persons without fixed duties. It originally refers to people unrelated to a certain matter. "盲流" originally refers to peasants migrating from country to city. "闲杂盲流" in this story refers to those who do not have long-term jobs，and some of them are not trust-worthy.

12. **"谁跟谁呀"**：见《风波》第一部分注释5。Refer to note 5 in part 1 of《风波》。

13. **"立马"**：意思是"立刻、马上"，北方口语。

"立马"，from Northern dialect，means right away or immediately.

语法 Grammar Notes

"**万一**"：副词。表示发生的可能性极小，一般用于不希望发生的事情。

"万一" is used when the possibility for a certain occurrence is very small, usually when the speaker does not wish for it to happen.

(1) 这万一出个什么闪失，你怎么还哪？

In case something goes wrong，how would you pay back（the money）?

(2) 明天我们安排老李大会发言，万一他不来怎么办？

We have arranged for Lao Li to give a speech at the meeting tomorrow. What if he does not show up?

(3) 我们下个月要买房子，万一利率调高了，怎么办？

We are going to buy a house next month. If the interest rate goes up, what are we going to do?

练习 Exercises

■ 一、口语练习 Oral Practice

（一）回答问题 Answer the following questions

1. 彩虹是做什么工作的？

2. 胖女人怎么知道彩虹刚刚开始"练摊儿"？

3. 那个男人说他为什么要买 100 件羽绒服？

4. 那个人给彩虹 580 块一件，彩虹为什么没有给他？

5. 男人告诉彩虹怎么跟他联系？

6. 彩虹回家以后跟丈夫商量什么事？

7. 彩虹需要钱做什么？她丈夫为什么不愿意她借钱？

8. 彩虹是怎样凑够钱的？

（二）讨论 Discussion

1. 谈谈彩虹的性格特点。你喜欢彩虹这样的人吗？为什么？

2. 彩虹的丈夫是做什么的？你同意他的看法吗？为什么？

（三）角色扮演 Role Play

两人一组对话。彩虹要从银行里取出两万块钱的存款来做生意（买羽绒服），她丈夫却不同意，怕她做生意赔钱。两人各自陈述自己的想法，努力要说服对方。对话中要用下列词语。

Caihong wants to withdraw twenty thousand Yuan from her family bank account to do business. Her husband doesn't agree because he is afraid that she would lose all the money. Both parties state their reasons in order to convince each other. The dialogue should incorporate the provided items below：

1. 一分钱分八半儿花	2. 一手交钱一手交货	3. 练摊
4. 贷款	5. （没）见过世面	6. 做买卖
7. 哪有天上掉馅饼的好事	8. 万一有个什么闪失	
9. 连……都不……，还……	10. 差错	

二、书写练习 Written Exercises

（一）选择适当的词语完成句子 Choose the most appropriate items to finish the sentences below

A. 一分钱分八半儿花	B. 一手交钱一手交货	C. 练摊
D. 闲杂盲流	E. 谁跟谁呀	
F. 哪有天上掉馅饼的好事	G. 万一有个什么闪失	

1. 老王看到他周围的不少朋友都到市场上去_____了，也想辞掉国营企业的工作自己干。

2. 天这么晚了，你一个女孩子自己走回家，_____，怎么办？还是我送你吧。

3. 他是个百万富翁，可是非常节俭，恨不得_____，但是对公众事业他可大方得很。上个月，他给艾滋病孤儿捐款，一次就捐了 30 万。

4. 昨天我刚到家就接到一个电话，说我得了大奖（prize），今年圣诞节可以带一个朋友免费去法国玩一个星期。我的女朋友不相信，她说，"_____？"

5. 一个美国学生买电脑跟他的中国好朋友借了 300 块钱，要写一个借条。他的中国朋友说："咱俩_____，还写什么借条！"

6. 在这个城市，走到哪儿都是人山人海。而且听说_____比任何一个大城市都多。

7. 在市场上买东西，都是_____，不用信用卡，也不用支票。

（二）选择题 Circle the answer which most reflects the meaning of the underlined part in the following sentences

1. 我的产品绝对<u>货真价实</u>。
   A. 价格绝对便宜
   B. 质量绝对好
   C. 绝对不是假冒，而且价格合理
   D. 绝对是热门货

2. 来，看一看了，北京的羽绒服，<u>国际流行色</u>。
   A. 这种颜色在北京很时兴
   B. 这种颜色在世界上很多地方都很时兴

C. 这种颜色在中国很多地方都很时兴

D. 这种颜色在北京年轻人中很时兴

3. 要是我们的工厂倒闭了，很多工人都会面临<u>重新就业</u>的问题。

　　A. 失业

　　B. 参加培训

　　C. 下岗

　　D. 失业后再次工作

4. 这是 500 块钱，就算是我的<u>定金</u>了。

　　A. 先交的一部分钱

　　B. 一次交清的所有的钱

　　C. 每个月交的钱

　　D. 借给你的钱

5. 生意做得越大，就越要<u>贷款</u>。

　　A. 给职工谋福利

　　B. 赚大钱

　　C. 向朋友借钱

　　D. 向银行借钱

6. 他呀，除了会教一点儿书本上的知识，<u>没见过什么世面</u>。

　　A. 没见过、不了解社会上各方面的情况

　　B. 没有面子

　　C. 没有到过世界上其他地方

　　D. 不知道世界上发生了什么事情

张祥林：我看，你就在这儿吃饭吧。

刘　眉：不了，不了。

张祥林：哎，啊。

张茂林：哥。

张祥林：哎嗬，来来。

刘　眉：那就先这样吧，我先走了啊。

张祥林：哎，好。

刘　眉：我走啦。

张祥林：我就不送啦。

张茂林：哎，哥。

张祥林：啊？

张茂林：我**嫂子**还没回来啊？

张祥林：没有。哎，你找她有事儿啊？

张茂林：啊，是这样，我呀，看上一家**门脸**儿[N1]，不过人家得先要定金。嗯，我那钱，还不够还……

张祥林：是啊，哎，是得先交定金。啊嗬，啊，这，你也不是不知道我的情况，就挣那点儿死钱。

张茂林：那嫂子不是做买卖了吗？

张祥林：啊呀，她也是刚做啊。喂？啊，啊，是啊，嗯？西城宾馆，找杨彩虹？哦，您是？张先生？什么？您明天晚上就要走？哦，哦好，好好好，我知道了，我知道了，回头我跟她说，啊，好嘞好嘞。

张茂林：哥，我到**别处**再去看看。

张祥林：哎，听你嫂子说，她最近有一批买卖，不过……

张茂林：你跟我嫂子说说，先救**救急**[N2]，我过两天给她。

嫂子	sǎozi	n.	elder brother's wife; elder sister-in-law
门脸儿	ménliǎnr	n.	store; shop(as used in this story)
别处	bié chù		别的地方,other place
救急	jiù jí	vo.	help to meet an urgent need

张祥林：哎，可你嫂子她现在还不知道找谁去救急了呢。

杨彩虹：哎，**办妥**了，全都办妥了。

张祥林：什么办妥了？

杨彩虹：钱呐。哎，**多亏**[G1]李大头啊。

张祥林：啊，你找李大头了？

杨彩虹：啊，老同学帮忙嘛。啊，**吃醋**了？哼，你看人家，大公司一坐，啪，**支票**一撕。啊，人家说啊割肉也帮我忙，还说啊，钱什么时候还都行。

张祥林：割肉？割什么肉？

杨彩虹：咳，你不懂，**股市**里的**行话**。英子，英子。

张英子：哎。

杨彩虹：哎哟，可把妈累死了。啊哈嘿。

张英子：哎，妈。

杨彩虹：英子啊，你不是最喜欢先帝**娃娃**么？等妈有了钱，给你买100个，啊。

张英子：嘿嘿。

杨彩虹：怎么样？啊？

张英子：妈，其实[G2]，我现在，也不想买什么先帝娃娃了。哎，您给我买个**随身听**吧。

杨彩虹：随身听？

张英子：嗯。

杨彩虹：那不就是BB机嘛。不，咱刚上**初中**，咱不要那个，影响不好，啊。

办妥	bàn tuǒ	vc.	handle sth. appropriately
多亏	duōkuī	v.	thanks to
吃醋	chī cù	vo.	envy; be jealous of
支票	zhīpiào	n.	(of bank) check
股市	gǔshì	n.	stock market
行话	hánghuà	n.	jargon
娃娃	wáwa	n.	doll
随身听	suíshēntīng	n.	walkman
初中	chūzhōng	n.	junior high school

张英子：哎呀，妈，您真**老外**[N3]，随身听啊，就是带在身上的**收录机**。我们班同学都有，听音乐、学外语，可方便哪。

杨彩虹：那得多少钱哪？

张英子：嗯，要 1000 来块钱吧。

杨彩虹：1000 块？

张英子：嗯。

杨彩虹：嗯，行。别人家孩子有的，咱英子也得有。

张英子：嘿嘿。

杨彩虹：行吗？

张英子：妈，您真**伟大**。

杨彩虹：哎，睡着了吗？

张祥林：没睡着。

杨彩虹：想什么呢？

张祥林：我这心里头不踏实[N4]啊。

杨彩虹：我也是。这前两天吧，这左**眼皮**就**一个劲**儿地[N5]跳。哎，你说是不是**应验**了？啊？嗯，我就想啊，你说，前两年吧，咱这苦日子过得**紧巴巴**的。现在有钱了吧，又不知道这钱该怎么花了，你说。

张英子：旅游啊，等夏天放假，咱们一家去**海边**。

杨彩虹：你这个孩子，你怎么还不睡觉啊？

张英子：一想到**大海**，我就睡不着了。

杨彩虹：啊，哈哈，好好好，带你去。快睡吧，啊，别跟着我们大人一块儿**掺和**[N6]。快睡吧。

张祥林：你说，这旅游一趟，得花千儿八百的吧？

老外	lǎowài	n.	layman; foreigner
收录机	shōulùjī	n.	radio-tape recorder
伟大	wěidà	adj.	great; awesome
眼皮	yǎnpí	n.	eyelid
一个劲（儿）	yígèjìn(r)	adv.	不停地，continuously; persistently
应验	yìngyàn	v.	turn out to be true
紧巴巴（的）	jǐn bābā (de)	adj.	tight (of budget)
海边	hǎibiān	n.	beach
大海	dàhǎi	n.	sea; ocean
掺和	chānhuo	v.	disturb; cause trouble (as used in this section)

杨彩虹：瞧你**抠抠唆唆**的样子。**千ル八百**？千ル八百块的钱现在能干什么呀？唉，咱们英子长这么大，连海是什么模样ル都没见过。我呢，也**下了海**[N7]了，也没见过海呀。哎，咱们啊，就**大大方方**地玩一趟，啊？

张祥林：我依你。其实，我也知道你的心思，花这么多钱，你比我还心疼。

杨彩虹：行了，别说这个了。哎，我问你，等有了钱啊，你想怎么花？

张祥林：我想拿出一部分帮帮**亲戚**朋友。

杨彩虹：什么亲戚朋友？不就是你们家的人嘛，你爸、你妈、你弟。

张祥林：剩下的钱把本钱留下，**继续**存银行，这样踏实。

杨彩虹：啊呀，要不咋说你这**傻脑瓜**跟不上**形势**呢，你看现在谁还把钱放在银行里啊？你没看报纸吗？现在的**利息**啊，又**下调**了。还说我不关心国家大事呢。哼！

张祥林：那么好，你说这钱怎么花？

杨彩虹：啊，**紧着点ル账**，**攒着点ル钱**，买点ル**股票**，做点ル小**投资**。从发展的眼光看，将来咱们也租个门脸ル，开个**服装店ル**，啊，怎么样？

张祥林：你想的还**挺**[G3]**全面**的？

抠抠唆唆	kōu kou suō suō	adj.	小气、吝啬，stingy；miserly
千ル八百	qiānr bā bǎi	num.	大约 800～1000，¥800～1,000
下海	xià hǎi	vo.	(relinquish one's old job and) go in for business；become a business person
大大方方	dà da fāng fāng	adj.	generous
亲戚	qīnqi	n.	relative(s)
继续	jìxù	v.	continue；go on with
傻	shǎ	adj.	stupid；foolish
脑瓜	nǎoguā	n.	brain
形势	xíngshì	n.	situation；circumstances
利息	lìxī	n.	interest
下调	xiàtiáo	v.	向下调整(降低)，readjust (interest or price) downwards
紧	jǐn	v.	tighten (budget)
账	zhàng	n.	account
紧着点ル账	jǐnzhe dianr zhàng		try to tighten the budget
攒钱	zǎn qián	vo.	save money
股票	gǔpiào	n.	share；stock
投资	tóu zī	vo.	invest (money)
服装店ル	fúzhuāngdiànr	n.	clothing shop
全面	quánmiàn	adj.	overall；all-sided

杨彩虹：哼，比你强多了。

张英子：啊嗬，妈妈，嘿嘿。

杨彩虹：这孩子，还没睡啊。

张英子：妈妈，明天下午啊，我爸爸去给我开家长会。你要是办完事早回家的话，就把厨房里咱们家的红辣椒啊，挂在**平台**上。让我和爸爸提前为您高兴。

张祥林：哎，我记得有部电影的名字叫"幸福的黄**手帕**"，这次啊，我们家要演"幸福的红辣椒"了，还挺**浪漫**的啊。

张英子：哈哈。

杨彩虹：嗬嗬，咱们哪，就得浪漫，得，英子——

张英子：嗯？

杨彩虹：就这么着了，妈听你的。

平台	píngtái	n.	terrace; flat roof
手帕	shǒupà	n.	手绢儿, handkerchief
浪漫	làngmàn	adj.	romantic

注释 Notes

1. **"门脸儿"**：即"铺面房"，指临街的商业用房，方言。

   "门脸儿"，used in a certain dialect，literally means store front. It is used here to refer to businesses/shops located on main streets.

2. **"救急"**：用人力、财力等帮助解决紧急的困难。

   Emergency rescue：use human and financial resources to help with the emergent situation.

3. **"老外"**："老外"常指外国人，在这里是"外行"的意思。"妈，这您可就老外了"：意思是"这您就不懂了（您是外行）。"

   Usually "老外" is a friendly term the Chinese use to refer to "foreigners"。However，it is used in this context to mean literally "outside of〔one's〕profession"。The sentence "这您可就老外了" means："Here is something you don't know anything about。"

4. **"心里不踏实"**："踏实"的意思是"安定、安稳"。见《项链》第四部分词语注释1。

   One's heart is not at ease；one feels troubled. "踏实" here refers to peace of mind. See note 1 in part 4 of 《项链》.

5. **"一个劲儿地"**：意思是"不停地"、"不断地"。中国有一句话是"左眼跳财，右眼跳祸（灾）"。意思是如果左眼皮跳，会有财来，右眼皮跳，会有祸事来。"这左眼皮就一个劲儿地跳"，意思是要发财了。

   "一个劲儿地" means constantly or incessantly. There is an old Chinese saying："左眼跳财，右眼跳祸（灾）"，meaning when one's left eyelid twitches，she/he is likely to make a good fortune；when one's right eyelid twitches，she/he is likely to have bad luck.

6. **"掺和"**：这里是"参与和自己无关的事"的意思，多指"搅乱、添乱、添麻烦"。

   "掺和" is to participate，to join. It often carries a negative connotation of "to interrupt；to bother；to get involved."

   （1）那件事跟你没有关系，你少掺和。

This matter has nothing to do with you, so don't interrupt.

（2）你们俩的事太复杂，我可不掺和。

This matter between you two is too complicated; I don't want to get involved.

（3）那个公司现在问题很多，你别掺和。

This company has a lot of problems right now, you don't want to get involved.

7. **"下海"**：可以指非艺人正式登台演出，这里指政府机关工作人员、学校的教师等放弃原来的工作，开始经商。

"下海" originally refers to amateur artists making formal appearances on stage.

Now this expression is frequently used to refer to government employees or educators who gave up their original jobs to start businesses.

语法 Grammar Notes

1. **"多亏"** （动词）：用"多亏"表示由于某种原因，避免了不如意的事情发生。如果是因为别人的帮助，说话人用"多亏"就有感激的意思。

   "多亏"，thanks to（verb.），is used to express that one avoided some kind of bad event，or accident due to some reason（s）. If it is due to someone's help，using "多亏" also entails some gratitude.

   （1）哎，多亏李大头啊 。

   　　　Oh，thanks to Li Datou（'s help）！

   （2）多亏你叫我，不然今天非迟到不可！

   　　　If it weren't for your waking me up，I would have been late today.

   （3）昨天我多亏没去看电影，听说那家电影院失火了。

   　　　I'm really thankful/lucky that I didn't go to see the movie yesterday—I heard that the movie theater had a fire.

2. **"其实"**：当对别人的说法、看法或上文有所修正或补充时，用"其实"引出说话人认为的真实情况：

   "其实"，"as a matte of fact；actually"，is used by the speaker to introduce information that she/he believes to be true，or to correct or add to what was said/assumed in the previous discourse.

   （1）其实，我也知道你的心思，花这么多钱，你比我还心疼。

   　　　Actually，I understand you perfectly.（It）cost so much money，you must feel more distressed than I do.

   （2）你们都以为我早就知道这件事，其实我也是刚刚才知道。

   　　　You all thought that I had known about this matter long before. As a matter of fact，I've just learned about it now.

   （3）别看她长那么高，其实还是一个孩子。

   　　　Don't just look at her height. Actually，she is still a kid.

3. **"挺"**：意思是"很"，北方口语。

   "挺" means "very；quite"，it belongs to Northern dialect.

   （1）今儿还挺忙的，啊。

Today is a quite busy day.

（2）甲：这个房间你住怎么样？

Would you like living in this room?

乙：挺好挺好。

Very good, very good.

（3）最近天气挺热，你要多注意身体。

It's been quite hot in the past few days; you need to take care of yourself.

练习 Exercises

■ 一、口语练习 Oral Practice

（一）回答问题 Answer the following questions

1. 刘眉为什么来彩虹家？

2. 张祥林（彩虹的丈夫）的弟弟张茂林为什么也来了？

3. 张茂林为什么跟他哥哥说"救救急"？

4. 张茂林为什么要找彩虹？

5. 李大头是谁？彩虹找他做什么？

6. 英子为什么说她妈妈是"老外"？

7. 彩虹为什么决定要给女儿买随身听？现在的孩子还买随身听吗？他们要买什么了？

8. 如果挣了大钱，彩虹打算做什么？

9. 如果挣了大钱，祥林打算做什么？

10. 彩虹和祥林那天晚上是什么心情？

（二）讨论 Discussion

谈谈祥林的性格特点。他跟彩虹的最大不同是什么？

（三）角色扮演 Role Play

两个人一组用所给的词语做一个彩虹和祥林之间的对话。内容是讲述第一次做生意时紧张而又兴奋的心情，并讨论赚大钱以后的计划。

Two people work in pair on a dialogue between Caihong and Xianglin. In the dialogue the couple needs to describe how nervous and excited they feel in anticipating the business opportunity，and what they are planning to do with the money they are going to make．Try to incorporate the items provided below.

1. 下海	2. 银行	3.（不）踏实	4. 利息	5. 随身听
6. 从发展的眼光看		7. 万一		8. 差错
9. 一个劲儿地 ＋ VP				

二、书写练习 Written Exercises

（一）选择题 Circle the right answer which most reflects the meaning of the underlined part in the following sentences

1. 在国营单位干，工作虽然比较稳定，但就挣<u>那点儿死钱</u>，永远也发不了大财。

    A. 很少的钱

    B. 很少的固定工资

    C. 很少的奖金

    D. 很少的政府的补助

2. 前两年，彩虹家的日子过得<u>紧巴巴</u>的，一家人连饭馆都很少去。

    A. 心情很紧张

    B. 时间很紧张

    C. 住房很紧张

    D. 钱很少

3. 好吧，好吧，<u>我依你</u>，明年夏天我们全家一起去海边度假。

    A. 我依靠你

    B. 我同意你的意见

    C. 我给你钱

    D. 我不想跟你吵架

4. 他遇到的这件事情很复杂，<u>你最好别掺和</u>。

    A. 你最好别跟他吵架

    B. 你最好别管

    C. 你最好别给添麻烦

    D. 你最好别跟他合作

5. 看他买东西时那种<u>抠抠唆唆</u>的样子，谁也想不到他居然是个百万富翁。

    A. 没有信心的样子

    B. 小气的样子

    C. 得意的样子

    D. 担心的样子

6. 人们都说，右眼皮跳说明要出事儿。自从我借了那三万块钱买了100件羽绒服以后，我的右眼皮就一个劲地跳，你说是不是<u>应验</u>了？

    A. 运气没有了

B. 好运气要来了

C. 生意出事了

D. 我们要发财了

（二）选择恰当词语填空 Choose the appropriate items to fill in the blank of the sentences below

| A. 办妥了 | B. 万一 | C. 其实 | D. 多亏 |
| E. 挺 | F. 心疼钱 | | |

1. 彩虹以为那个胖女人真的有急事要办，_____ 这个女人是有意想骗彩虹，因为她看彩虹刚开始做生意，什么都不懂。

2. 彩虹的丈夫不是_____，他只是担心 _____ 彩虹被人骗了，他们一家人的日子就没法过了。

3. _____ 王兰听了她丈夫的话，不再做生意了。要不然，他们两个人辛辛苦苦省出来的五万块钱一下子就没有了。

4. 表面上看，她做事好像_____ 有主意，但是实际上，她头脑还是比较简单，很容易受骗。

5. 你以为做生意容易吗？你以为贷了款，租了门脸儿就算都_____ ？麻烦事还多着呢！

（三）以彩虹的身份写一篇日记，日记中必须用下面所给的词语。

Write a diary entry from Caihong's perspective. The entry must incorporate the items provided below.

1. 下海	2. 银行	3.（不）踏实	4. 门脸儿
5. 随身听	6. 从发展的眼光看		7. 万一
8. 差错	9. 多亏	10. 其实	

杨彩虹：请问 415 房间有叫方正兴的吗？

服务员：没有，415 房间没住过姓方的。

杨彩虹：哎，什么？这是他的名片。

服务员：现在什么人哪，都能**印**名片。

杨彩虹：这么说他骗了我。

服务员：唉，不好说。

杨彩虹：同志，这货我能退了么？上午刚从这儿进的货。

卖货者：我们这儿没卖过羽绒服，您认错地方了吧？

杨彩虹：没错，就是你们这儿。哎，我这儿还有发票呢，哎，你们怎么能不**认账**了呢？

卖货者：我说你这位大嫂脑子有毛病吧？

张英子：妈，你就给我买个随身听吧。

杨彩虹：咱买，别人家孩子有的，咱英子也得有。

张英子：嘿嘿，妈，您真伟大。

杨彩虹：嘀嘀……

杨彩虹：啊！

张祥林：小虹，你告诉我，到底[G1]发生什么事了？

杨彩虹：你看着我干什么？

张祥林：看你怎么办，拿什么还钱？这下好了，财迷心窍[N1]！早知道……

杨彩虹：早知道什么？你说得对，我财迷心窍。可我为了谁啊？我还不是为了咱们这个家么？

张祥林：我不是**埋怨**你，我是说你啊，**头脑**太简单。

印	yìn	v.	print
认账	rèn zhàng	vo.	admit what one has said or done
埋怨	mányuàn	v.	blame；complain
头脑	tóunǎo	n.	brains；mind

杨彩虹：我是[G2]头脑简单，我傻，我被人骗了，可我还不是为了想把咱们的日子过得好一点儿吗？我让你安心工作；我还不是让咱们的英子，过得不比别人差吗？我一个女人，**成天东奔西跑**[N2]的，我求爷爷告奶奶[N3]，我为了什么啊我？我不让你下海，还不是为了咱们家体面一点儿吗？可是你倒好，我现在这个样子，你不劝我，也不**体谅**我，你反而**数落**[N4]我。还像个丈夫吗，你？

张祥林：这，你……

张英子：爸，妈，你们别吵了。妈，你们俩不要再吵了。妈，随身听我不想要了，妈，我再也不要什么随身听了。你把随身听退了吧，我真的不想要了。

张茂林：哎，哥，我呀。啊，对，哎，那事儿你跟我嫂子说了没有啊？

张祥林：好了好了，你还是到别处想办法吧。

张茂林：喂？喂？喂？喂？哼！

茂林妻：哎。

张茂林：叫我啊，到别的地方想办法去。哼，有了钱哪，连他兄弟都不认了。

茂林妻：可能嫂子也有难处。

张茂林：就这么怕老婆？这钱哪真不是好东西，哼！

电话亭：咳，说您哪，您还没交钱呢，您哪！

张祥林：哎，算了，都怪我，不该数落你。哎，人家广告里啊，都说啊，男人更需要**关怀**。

杨彩虹：嗯，我倒不是生你的气，我就是想，你说，那个男人为什么骗我？

张祥林：那羽绒服是厂家直销[N5]的吗？

杨彩虹：我也不知道，反正那女人在那儿**吆喝**着。我的货全都是从**批发部**进的，可我再去批发部的时候，就没人了。

成天	chéngtiān	adv.	all day long; all the time
东奔西跑	dōng bēn xī pǎo	v.	rush around (for work)
体谅	tǐliàng	v.	show understanding and consideration
数落	shǔluo	v.	(col.) scold; criticize (someone)
关怀	guānhuái	v.	care; concern; show care for
吆喝	yāohe	v.	shout out; loudly urge on
批发部	pīfābù	n.	wholesale (warehouse)

张祥林：这就对了，我琢磨着，那个骗子装外地人，还有那个胖女人，还有那个批发部都是**一伙**儿的，他们合起伙来骗人钱。

杨彩虹：哎，借钱总是要还的，咱不能不**守信用**吧？我招谁惹谁了[N6]？吃个哑巴亏[N7]吧。这下可好了，**自作自受**[N8]吧。

张祥林：没有过不去的**火焰山**[N9]，咱们**有难同当**，这么多年都过来了，我呀，也**豁出去**[N10]了。明天，我跟你一起上街，咱把羽绒服啊一件一件地都卖了。

杨彩虹：哎，小姐，你们俩试一下吧，脱了衣服试一下吧。

顾客们：有点儿**过时**了，我不想要了，我们不要了，走吧，咱们走吧。

杨彩虹：哎，小姐啊，哎。

厂　长：大嫂啊，这货是从哪儿进的？你有多少货？

杨彩虹：你要多少啊？反正我的货不是**蒙**来的[N11]。

厂　长：啊，100件。

杨彩虹：100件？什么？

厂　长：对，有多少要多少。大嫂，这是我的名片，给，大嫂，您就收着吧。啊。

杨彩虹：不卖了。

厂　长：啊，大嫂，您这是干什么啊？

杨彩虹：我不卖了。

厂　长：哎，大嫂，您别走啊，哎，大嫂，大嫂，哎呀，假的。

杨彩虹：我知道你是假的。

杨彩虹：我一看他就是假的，还装得跟真的似的。这回啊，我可不那么傻了。哎，多吃亏啊。

一伙儿	yìhuǒr		partnership; groups; crowds
守信用	shǒu xìnyòng	vo.	keep one's word
自作自受	zì zuò zì shòu		suffer from one's own actions
火焰山	Huǒyànshān	N.	name of a mountain in Xinjiang (Uygur A. R.)
有难同当	yǒu nàn tóng dāng		share the difficulties and hardships (of friends/loved ones)
豁出去	huō chuqu	vc.	risk anything; do sth. at any cost
过时	guòshí	adj.	old-fashioned; out of fashion
蒙	mēng	v.	cheat; deceive; swindle

刘　　眉：哎，**吃亏**长学问嘛。我说，彩虹，我看啊，你还是尽早地把那批货卖
　　　　　出去吧。

杨彩虹：哎，老张啊，你今天卖出几件啊？

张祥林：哪儿卖了几件啊，我总想往那**清静**地方跑，哪成想[N12]啊，哎，我这一
　　　　　上街啊，这两条腿啊就怎么也**不听使唤**了。

刘　　眉：张老师，你也**体验**体验彩虹吧，啊。

杨彩虹：也**难为**他了。

吃亏	chī kuī	vo.	suffer losses; be in an unfavorable situation
清静	qīngjìng	adj.	(of surroundings) quiet
不听使唤	bù tīng shǐhuan		(col.) hard to control
体验	tǐyàn	v.	learn through personal experience
难为	nánwei	v.	bring pressure on sb; make things difficult for sb.

注释 Notes

1. **"财迷心窍"**（be greedy for money；money-grubbing）：为了金钱而头脑不清楚（常常因此做出不应该做的事）。

   "财迷心窍" is used to refer to someone who is so greedy（for money）that she/he has totally lost his/her conscience，and has done something that she/he should not do.

2. **"东奔西跑"**：为了某事而到处奔走。

   "东奔西跑" means to rush around for a certain purpose.

3. **"求爷爷告奶奶"**：为了某事而请求很多人帮助。

   This expression indicates that someone seeks help from many people in order to reach his/her goal.

4. **"数落"**：批评。口语。

   "数落" is same as "批评"（to criticize），except that the former is more colloquial.

5. **"厂家直销"**：工厂直接卖给用户，通常价钱会便宜一些。

   "厂家直销" refer to factory direct sale. The factory sells its products directly to costumers. The price is usually lower than in stores.

6. **"我招谁惹谁了？"**：这是一个反问句，意思是我没有"招惹"任何人。"招惹"的意思是触犯、得罪。

   "我招谁惹谁了？" Who did I offend? This is a rhetorical question meaning "I didn't offend or hurt anyone."（the implied meaning：Why did I get all the bad luck!）"招惹" here means to offend or to bother（people）.

7. **"吃（个）哑巴亏"**：意思是"吃了亏"但是又不能说什么。

   "吃个哑巴亏" means one can't voice one's grievances. This sentence indicates that one suffered a loss，but could not complain or blame others for a certain reason.

8. **"自作自受"**：自己做的坏事，自己承受不好的结果。

   "自作自受" means to suffer from one's own action；or "as one sows, so shall one reap."

9. **"没有过不去的火焰山"**："火焰山"在新疆，是一个非常炎热、很难过去的地方，曾在《西游记》中提到过。"没有过不去的火焰山"这句话的意思是"什么困难、危机都可以过去"，常用来劝别人或安慰鼓励自己。

"火焰山" is located in Xin Jiang (Uygur A. R.), an extremely hot area that is supposed to be extremely difficult to cross. This place appeared in the well-known classic novel Journey to the West. The expression "There is no mountain that one cannot conquer" is used here to indicate that one can always overcome difficulties and get through a crisis no matter what. It is often used to comfort and encourage people or oneself in adversity.

10. **"豁出去了"**：意思是"不惜付出任何代价去（做某事）"，多用于遇到不利的情况时，表示的一种决心。口语。

This expression "豁出去了" means to risk anything at any cost (in order to reach a goal or to achieve something). It is commonly used to show one's determination or resolution in an adverse situation. It is a colloquial expression.

11. **"蒙来的"**："蒙"在这里是"骗"的意思。

"蒙" is similar to "骗" here, meaning to get something by cheating.

12. **"哪成想"**：意思是"没有想到"。

This expression, same as "没有想到", is used to indicate that one didn't expect ...

语法 Grammar Notes

1. **"到底"**（after all，actually，really）：这里的"到底"表示追问。

   This expression is commonly used in a question for emphasis or to push for an answer.

   (1) 小虹，你告诉我，到底发生什么事了？

   Xiao Hong, you tell me, what really has happened?

   (2) 你明天到底去不去见我们老板，你得给我一个明确的答复。

   Give me a definite answer—tomorrow are you going to meet our boss or not?

   (3) 她到底去哪儿了，你能告诉我吗？

   Where on earth did she go? Can you tell me?

2. **"是"**（表示肯定）："我是头脑简单"中的"是"表示肯定对方或某些人说的话或某种想法。"是"字重读。

   "是" in this sentence is used to confirm that what the addressee or someone else said or thought is true, as in "I AM simple-minded." "是" should be stressed in the sentence.

   (1) 张祥林：我不是埋怨你，我是说你啊，头脑太简单。

   Zhang Xianglin：I'm not blaming you. What I'm trying to say is that you are too simple-minded.

   杨彩虹：我是头脑简单，我傻，我被人骗了，可我还不是为了想把咱们的日子过得好一点儿么？

   Yang Caihong：I'm indeed simple-minded，foolish，and I've been cheated. But can't you see I did it all for our family to have a better life?

   (2) 大家都说北京夏天太热。不错，北京的夏天是很热，可是在家房间里有空调，出门汽车里、饭馆、商店都有空调，怕什么呀？

   Everyone says that Beijing's summer is too hot. Summer in Beijing is indeed hot，but you have air-conditioners at home，in the car，and in restaurants and stores. What does the hot weather matter to you?

   (3) 对，这个字我们是学过，你说得对。可是我忘了。

   Yes，we've learned this word indeed，you are right. But I forgot about it.

练习 Exercises

■ 一、口语练习 Oral Practice

（一）回答问题 Answer the following questions

1. 方正兴是谁？他住过 415 号房间吗？
2. 彩虹退货时是不是认错地方了？
3. 彩虹为什么生祥林的气？
4. 英子为什么不要随身听了？
5. 茂林为什么又给祥林打电话？他为什么说："这钱哪真不是好东西，哼！"
6. 为什么祥林决定上街卖羽绒服时，说"豁出去了"？
7. 为什么当一个男人要买 100 件羽绒服时彩虹不卖给他？
8. 祥林那天卖了几件羽绒服？为什么？

（二）讨论 Discussion

祥林是不是一个好丈夫？举例说明。如果你是祥林，你会怎么做？

（三）角色扮演 Role Play

两个人一组，用所给词语编一个彩虹和祥林之间的对话。祥林怪彩虹在这件事上头脑简单……；彩虹怪祥林不理解她一心为家庭的难处……。

Students work in pairs on a dialogue between Caihong and Xianglin. One side acts as Xianglin, blaming Caihong for her simple-mindedness; the other side acts as Caihong, complaining to Xianglin about his not being understanding about her difficult situation and not being appreciative of her efforts. The dialogue should incorporate the items provided below.

祥林可以用的词语：

1. 财迷心窍	2. 头脑简单	3. 吃哑巴亏	4. 自作自受
5. 辛辛苦苦	6. 哪成想	7. 反而	8. 不踏实
9. 万一	10. 差错		

彩虹可以用的词语：

1. 辛辛苦苦	2. 为了	3. 安心 V	4. 体面
5. 比	6. 数落	7.（不）劝	8.（不）体谅
9. 怪＋N	10. 东奔西跑	11. 求爷爷告奶奶	
12. 是＋VP，可是……		13. 反而	

■ **二、书写练习 Written Exercises**

（一）选择适当词语填空 Choose the appropriate phrase to fill in the blank in the following sentences

A. 吃哑巴亏	B. 守信用	C. 不认账	D. 厂家直销
E. 自作自受	F. 数落	G. 有难同当	H. 豁出去了

1. 我明明看见是他拿走了那本书，他怎么能_____呢?!

2. 他跟女朋友分手了，因为每当他遇到麻烦，他的女朋友不但不帮助他，反而总是_____他，他真受不了了。

3. 一个人想做好生意，最重要的一条就是_____。

4. 彩虹用借来的钱做生意，被骗了，而且找不到骗她的人，只好_____。

5. 这家商店卖的东西都是_____的，所以特别便宜。

6. 看着彩虹那个难过的样子，祥林不但不同情妻子，反而说她是_____。

7. 他们的婚姻很美满，这不是因为他们有钱、有地位，而是因为他们多少年来一直_____，他们常常说的一句话就是"没有过不去的火焰山。"

8. 第一次学游泳时，她很害怕，老师说："跳下去!"她只好把眼睛一闭，说："_____。"

（二）用所给词语改写下面的句子 Rewrite the following sentences with the items provided

1.（A：你没有经验，做什么生意!）

B：你说得对，我做生意没有经验。但是人都是从没有经验到有经验。要是一个人因为没有经验而不敢做事，那他就什么事都不能做了。（是）

2.（A：我想发大财，有什么错?）

B：你想赚大钱、发大财，这没有错，但是你不能去伤害别人。（是）

3. 厂家直销的产品倒便宜，但是有时会有一些质量问题。（是）

4. 彩虹很想搞清楚那个胖女人跟批发部有什么关系。（到底）

5. 明天的音乐会，你一会儿说去，一会儿又说不去，你能不能告诉我你去还是不去？（到底）

（三）作文 Composition

以彩虹或祥林的身份写一篇日记。内容是叙述那天发生的事情及其感受，至少要用下面词语中的 15 个。

Write a diary from either Caihong or Xianglin's perspective describing what happened that day and his/her feelings about the other party. The diary must involve at least 15 items out of those provided below.

1. 退货	2. 骗	3. 不认账
4. 批发部	5. 合（起）伙（来）	6. 数落
7. 财迷心窍	8. 有难同当	9. 没有过不去的火焰山
10. 豁出去	11. 反而	12. （不）体谅
13. 怪＋N	14. 辛辛苦苦	15. 为了
16. 安心 V	17. 体面	18. 比
19. 东奔西跑	20. 是 ＋ VP，可是……	

四

电　视：**观众**朋友们，我们记者在市场**管理部门**的协助下，**进行现场报道**。根据广大**消费者**的**举报**，在这条街上，**近来**有些**不法商贩**以[G1]**不正当**的方式**制造**、**推销假冒伪劣**[N1]商品，这极大地……

杨彩虹：就这两个骗子！看你往哪儿跑，我找他们去，我。

刘　眉：哎呀，你傻什么傻[N2]啊？你上哪儿找他们去？这又不是现场**直播**。回头啊，向有关部门**反映**一下，他们俩啊跑不了。

张祥林：你就是找到他们俩啊，他们俩也不会认账的。

杨彩虹：啊，我给气蒙了。

电　视：这就是不法商贩在**地下加工厂**制造出来的**伪劣**产品，以劣等的**鸭毛**和旧**棉花掺和**在一起，**欺骗**广大的消费者……

观众	guānzhòng	n.	audience
管理部门	guǎnlǐ bùmén		supervising/management department/division
进行	jìnxíng	v.	conduct; carry on
现场	xiànchǎng	n.	scene (of an event or incident); on the scene
报道	bàodào	n./v.	report (news)
消费者	xiāofèizhě	n.	consumer
举报	jǔbào	v.	report (sth.) to the authorities; inform against
近来	jìnlái	adv.	最近，recently
不法	bùfǎ	adj.	illegal; unlawful
商贩	shāngfàn	n.	small retailer; peddler
不正当	bú zhèngdāng	adj.	improper; illegal
制造	zhìzào	v.	make; manufacture; produce
推销	tuīxiāo	v.	promote the sales (of goods)
假冒伪劣	jiǎmào wěiliè		fake and bad
直播	zhíbō	n.	live broadcast (on TV, radio, etc.)
反映	fǎnyìng	v.	make known; report
气蒙了	qì mēng le	vc.	too angry to think straight
地下	dìxià	adj.	underground; (of activity) secret
加工厂	jiāgōngchǎng	n.	processing plant or manufacturer
伪劣	wěiliè	adj.	(of goods)fake or of low quality; false and inferior
鸭毛	yāmáo	n.	geese down
棉花	miánhua	n.	cotton; raw cotton
掺和	chānhuo	v.	mix together (as used in this section)
欺骗	qīpiàn	v./n.	cheat; deceive

杨彩虹：这不是跟咱卖的羽绒服一样的吗？找谁啊？

李大兴：我呀，李大头，我是你哥啊。

杨彩虹：哦，是你啊。

李大兴：你该我的那三万块钱什么时候还？

杨彩虹：还钱？

李大兴：我可是赔惨了，我求求你帮忙行吗？一个星期之内一定还我。好不好？好借好还[N3]嘛！

杨彩虹：好你个李大头啊，当初你可是**雪中送炭**，现在你不会是**雪上加霜**[N4]吧？你放心，钱我一定还，一分钱也不少你的。

张祥林：我早就说过，那个李大头不是什么好东西。

杨彩虹：我不管他什么东西了，我这东西怎么办？你说说？

张祥林：这几十件全是钱哪。

杨彩虹：这回该轮到我割肉了。

张祥林：这，这，这，我们到底该怎么办啊？

杨彩虹：反正我不能再卖了。

张祥林：那你拿什么还钱哪？

刘　眉：啊，先别急，再想想办法，啊。

张茂林：哎，哥。

张祥林：啊，茂林。

张茂林：嫂子在家吗？

张祥林：哎，茂林，茂林，我不是跟你说过了吗？你嫂子她没有钱。

张茂林：哎，哥，哎。

张祥林：回去吧，回去吧！

张茂林：哎，哥，我啊，不是找嫂子借钱来的，我是给嫂子来送钱来的啊。

杨彩虹：送钱？

张祥林：哎呀，茂林哪，你开什么玩笑啊？我们，我们家这都，都火上房了[N5]！哎，哎，你们回去吧，你们回去吧。

张茂林：哎，哥，哥，哥……

茂林妻：茂林，快把钱拿出来。

张茂林：哎。

惨	cǎn	adj.	miserable; serious
雪中送炭	xuě zhōng sòng tàn		give help in time of need
雪上加霜	xuě shàng jiā shuāng		one disaster after another

茂林妻：我们真的是给嫂子送钱来的。哎，嫂子，嫂子，您的事儿啊，我们都知道了，我们的门脸儿就先不租了。这是两万块钱，您先拿着，给您。

杨彩虹：哎哟，这可不行。

张祥林：来来来，茂林，来来。

茂林妻：哎呀，嫂子，您就拿着吧。

杨彩虹：这哪儿能行？啊，不行不行。

茂林妻：哎呀，嫂子，您客气什么啊，快拿着吧。

张茂林：拿着吧，嫂子。

张祥林：我看，你就把钱收下吧。

刘　眉：是啊，彩虹，你就拿着吧。

张茂林：拿着吧，拿着吧，

杨彩虹：不好意思啊，不好意思啊。

茂林妻：亲不亲一家人[N6]嘛。

刘　眉：你看事情解决了。

杨彩虹：给大家添麻烦了，不好意思。

张茂林：没事儿。

杨彩虹：今儿还挺忙的，啊。

厂　长：哎，大嫂，您好。

杨彩虹：哎，哎，你，你怎么跑家（里）来了，我不是说我不卖吗！

厂　长：哎呀，误会了。我呀，是羽绒服服装厂的厂长。今天哪，我看你卖的羽绒服是假货。我**观察**了半天，才知道，你不是不法商贩，**一准儿**[N7]啊，也是一个上当受骗的。我们啊，想把您的假货啊都买回去，把它**销毁**，这也是为了我们厂的**声誉**。这不，我把我们厂的**销售科长**请来了，由他来负责这件事儿，啊。

科　长：大嫂啊，给您添麻烦了，实在[G2]对不起啊。

杨彩虹：哎哟，谢谢，谢谢，进屋坐，进屋坐吧，哎，二位坐这儿，坐这儿，你看这事儿……

观察	guānchá	v./n.	observe carefully; observation
一准儿	yìzhǔnr	adv.	(col.)一定，certainly
销毁	xiāohuǐ	v.	destroy
声誉	shēngyù	n.	reputation; fame
销售	xiāoshòu	n.	sales
科长	kēzhǎng	n.	section chief

厂　　长：啊咳！

杨彩虹：快来买，快来看啊，真正的厂家直销，绝无假货啊，您看看这个。

顾客三：您衣服咋卖啊？

杨彩虹：看这个，我们这是厂家直销，**一流**的产品，价格合理。啊，您试试，
　　　　穿着看看，看看怎么样？

顾客们：给我拿一件啊。拿一下这件。

顾客三：行。

杨彩虹：怎么样？啊您穿着这件好看，太好看啦，您慢走啊。

顾客们：啊，再见。

杨彩虹：再见。

大　　嫂：大姐，有**开水**吗？

杨彩虹：有，给。

大　　嫂：那就谢谢了啊。

杨彩虹：哎，我看你有点儿**面生**，刚练摊儿的吧？

大　　嫂：两三天了，这不刚拉下脸来[N8]。

杨彩虹：哎咳，都这样，你这也是下岗的吧？

大　　嫂：啊，哎。

杨彩虹：有什么事儿啊，需要我帮忙你就说话。嘿，谁让你啊，**挨着**我这摊儿
　　　　呢，咱们哪，就是邻居了。刚出来都不适应，我以前啊，跟你一样。

大　　嫂：谢谢了。那我就过去了，啊。

杨彩虹：啊，好。哎，哎，我有点儿事，我求求你行么？哎，我想求你啊帮我
　　　　卖几件衣服，哎呀，这样吧，我也不能让你白卖。这样吧，你卖完以
　　　　后啊，把那个本钱归我，剩下的啊都给你，我不能让你白卖。

大　　嫂：哎，不，不，我不是这个意思，你听我说，哎呀，我行吗？

杨彩虹：没问题，哎，我问你，假如有人要买100件，你卖不卖？

大　　嫂：卖呀，不是能赚钱嘛。

杨彩虹：咳……你就听我的，啊。

一流	yīliú	adj.	of the best quality; first-class
开水	kāishuǐ	n.	boiled water
面生	miànshēng	adj.	unfamiliar
挨着	āi zhe	v.	be next to

大　嫂：啊，这**大妹子**真**逗**，怎么放着大钱不赚呢？

杨彩虹：哎，听我的没错，绝不吃亏。

大妹子	dàmèizi	v.	an affectionate term used to address a woman younger than the speaker
逗	dòu	adj.	interesting; funny

注释 Notes

1. **"假冒伪劣"**：都是指商品。"假冒"的意思是用假的冒充真的，"伪"的意思也是"假"，"劣"的意思是"次、不好（的)"。

"假冒" to claim something fake as real，or to pass off defective goods as ones of good quality；"伪" means fake or phony；"劣" means defective，of poor quality. "假冒伪劣" is used to refer to merchandise.

2. **"你傻什么傻啊？"**：就是"你为什么这么傻?"是反问句，所以意思是"你别这么傻"。

How come you are so silly?

It is a rhetorical sentence indicating "Don't be so silly."

（1）你别这么傻。Don't be so foolish.

3. **"好借好还嘛!"**：这句话重点在后边的"还"上，意思是"跟别人借了东西或钱，（如果）能按时还"，下面还有一句话是"再借不难"。

To return what one has borrowed on the terms promised. What is emphasized in this expression is to "return money or other things borrowed earlier on the terms promised." The second half of this phrase，which is usually omitted，is "再借不难"，meaning（then）one can always borrow again from that person.

4. **"雪中送炭"，"雪上加霜"**。"雪中送炭"的意思是在很困难的时候给予帮助。"雪上加霜"的意思是"在很困难的时候还给增加困难"。

This expression "雪中送炭" means to provide timely help，or to provide material help to others in need. "雪上加霜"，literally interpreted as "add frost to snow"，indicates to add more trouble or difficulties to an already difficult situation.

5. **"火上房了"**（house on fire）：字面意思是"火已经着到房顶上了"，比喻情况已经很紧急了。

This expression literally means that the fire has burned to the roof. It is usually used to indicate that the situation is pressing and urgent。

6. **"亲不亲一家人"**。意思"都是一家人，所以关系是很亲近的。"

After all，everyone is from the same family，so the relationship should be close (in spite of any disagreements/conflicts) .

7. "一准儿"：意思是"一定"，口语。

"一准儿" has the same meaning as "一定" (certainly, definitely) except that the former is a colloquial expression.

8. "拉下脸来"：意思是"不顾面子"或"打破情面"。有时形容不高兴的表情。

This expression indicates that one does something without fear of hurting other people's feelings，or does something without fear of losing face. It can be used to describe an unpleasant facial expression.

（2）这件衣服（的质量）实在（太糟糕）了。
　　Sorry, I _ _ really _ _ know _ about your difficult situation.
3. 你是一定要来的，我相信一定，请再提一个要求。
　　(Do you really _ _ _ _ books? I can _ _ get another copy.)

语法 Grammar Notes

1. **"以"（不正当的方式）**："以"是介词，意思是"用"，书面语。

"以不正当的方式" is a prepositional phrase meaning "in an inappropriate way", or "in an illegal way". "以" is very similar to "用" here, except that it is more formal.

（1）以劣等的鸭毛和旧棉花掺和在一起，欺骗广大消费者。

(They) mixed eider down of poor quality and old cotton to cheat customers.

（2）你们不能以伪劣产品冒充优质品。

You cannot pass off goods of bad quality as those of good quality.

（3）我以家长的名义向学校反映意见。

As a parent, I am going to inform the school authority of my opinion.

2. **实在**(indeed)：本课的"实在"有两个，一个是形容词，意思是"诚实、不虚假"。

"实在" in this text has two grammatical functions with two different meanings: the first one is adjective, meaning "honest; true; straightforward."
For example:

（1）我看你这个人，倒是蛮实在的。

I think you are quite honest.

（2）她挺实在的，不是跟你客气。

She really meant it; she's not just trying to be polite.

（3）我是一个实在的人。

I am a straightforward person.

另一个是副词，意思是"的确"、"真的"。

Another function of "实在" is adverb meaning "indeed", or "really".

（1）大嫂啊，给您添麻烦了，实在对不起啊。

Ma'am, (I'm) really sorry to bother you.

（2）对不起，我实在不知道你有困难。

Sorry，I really didn't know about your difficult situation.

（3）那本书实在找不到，就再买一本吧。

(If) you really cannot find the book，(you) can go and get another copy.

练习 Exercises

一、口语练习 Oral Practice

（一）回答问题 Answer the following questions

1. 电视新闻里说了些什么？
2. 杨彩虹为什么生李大头的气？
3. 为什么彩虹不想再卖那些羽绒服了？
4. 茂林来做什么？
5. 后来到彩虹家的两个人是谁？他们来做什么？
6. 彩虹现在卖的厂家直销产品怎么样？
7. 彩虹为什么不认识在她对面卖东西的妇女？
8. 彩虹为什么让这位妇女帮她卖几件衣服？

（二）讨论 Discussion

1. 作者通过这个故事想告诉我们什么？
2. 你认为杨彩虹追求的是什么？
3. 在传统的中国社会，做生意或经商的人受人尊重吗？你为什么得出这个结论？
4. 《都市彩虹》中的"彩虹"指的是什么？

二、书写练习 Written Exercises

（一）选择适当词语完成下列句子 Choose the appropriate phrase to fill in the blanks in the following sentences

A. 雪中送炭	B. 亲不亲一家人	C. 雪上加霜
D. 火上房	E. 假冒伪劣	F. 实在（adj）
G. 拉下脸来	H. 实在（adv）	

1. 有些不法商贩以不正当的方式制造、推销_____商品，扰乱了市场，损害了广大消费者（consumer）的利益。

2. 李大头在彩虹最需要钱的时候催她还钱，这对彩虹来说实在是_____。

3. 茂林要开一个饭馆，急需两万块钱当定金，这时哥哥和嫂子送来了一万块钱，真是_____。

4. 当哥哥有困难的时候，茂林急得要死，决定先不租门脸了，把自己仅有的两万块钱借给哥哥，哥哥很感动，说："真是_____啊！"

5. 要想学好外语，最重要的就是要能_____，敢说，多说，不怕出错。这样，就能学得快，学得好。

6. A：嗨，听说老张刚开了一家饭馆，今天晚上我带你去吃一顿，怎么样？

   B：这两天不行，我这儿都_____了，给老板写的报告还没完，太太又得了急病住院了，等过了这段时间再说吧。

7. 听说李大头这个人对人不_____，你最好别跟他做生意。

8. 茂林在他自己这么困难的时候，还想到去帮助别人，_____是难得。

（二）用所给词语改写下面的句子 Rewrite the following sentences with one of the items provided below

A. 以……的方式	B. 实在

1. 那些用非法手段做生意的人不会有好结果。

2. 尽管我们对这个问题看法不同，但还是可以通过协商的方式解决，没有必要吵架。

3. 彩虹完全没有想到李厂长会亲自来她家跟她说对不起。

4. 茂林在彩虹最困难的时候给她送来了两万块钱，这真的让彩虹感动得不知道说什么好。

5. 虽然张天明是在美国出生、在美国长大的，但是他父母却用中国的教育方式培养他。

（三）写一篇本剧故事观后感 Write a reflection of this movie

■ **三、讨论 General Discussion**

像本剧这样制造假货、贩卖假货的违法现象，你认为会随着中国经济发展有所改变吗？你觉得用什么办法可以使之改变？在你的国家有什么样的法律措施来制止这种情况？

As China is undergoing a transformation from a planned economy to a market economy, some illegal economic activities have emerged, such as those shown in this story. Do you think that this kind of situation can be changed? What do you think should be done to crush these illegal activities? In your society, what kind of judicial measures have be taken in order to prevent people from doing business illegally?

第七课 新来的钟点工

The New "Hourly Paid Worker"

导读：

　　城市里的年轻人越来越忙了，既要做好工作，照顾好家里的老人和孩子，还得在下班后为家务事操劳。为了减轻他们的负担，近些年来，许多城市出现了一种新兴职业：钟点工或小时工。所谓钟点工、小时工，就是请来帮忙做家务的人，以年轻女性居多，他们的工资通常按小时计费。有的家庭每天请两个小时的钟点工，也有的一个星期请几次。常年受雇于一个家庭，为人操持家务的人就称为保姆。钟点工或保姆大都来自安徽、四川等地农村。这些保姆如今在城市居民的生活中扮演着重要角色。每到春节他们一回家过年，大城市缺保姆就成了严重问题，政府有关部门不得不临时紧急招聘。

　　钟点工、小时工不是城市常住人口，没有固定的工作，所受的教育一般也不多。她们是一些什么样的人呢？本剧反映了城市人对钟点工的不同态度，也让我们走近钟点工，了解这些劳动在城市人身边的年轻女孩。

Introduction：

Life for young urban couples has become terribly busy. In addition to work and family, they also have to deal with endless housework on a daily basis which they find increasingly burdensome. This situation led to the birth of a new profession: Zhongdiangong (hourly paid workers). The people who work as "Zhongdiangong" are predominantly female. They are hired to help with housework and are paid by the hour. Some families hire a "Zhongdiangong" for two hours a day while others hire one a few times a week. They are different from "Baomu (housemaids)" who work full-time for one particular family on a year-round basis. Those "Zhongdiangong" and "Baomu" working in this city come mostly from the rural areas of Anhui and Sichuan provinces. They are now playing an important role in the life of the city and have become an integral part of the lives of the city people. Every year when the Spring Festival arrives, those people usually go home for the occasion, the lives of the city people are immediately disrupted as a consequence. The local government has to take some emergency measures to meet the challenge.

"Zhongdiangong" are obviously not permanent residents of the city. They have no job security and usually have very little education. What are they like? How are they treated by the city people?

This story provides us with a rare window to look into the interplay between the people and the world of "Zhongdiangong". It helps us understand those young girls who we see every day.

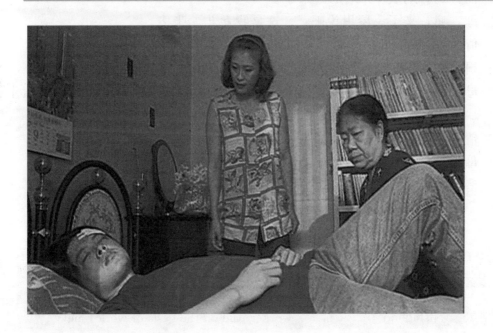

主要人物（Main Characters）

张楠	Zhāng Nán	a young sale's man
叶小娟	Yè Xiǎojuān	a "hourly worker"
张母	Zhāng mǔ	mother of Zhang Nan
张倩	Zhāng Qiàn	sister of Zhang Nan
娟姐	Juān jiě	cousin of Ye Xiaojuan

一

邮递员：38 号，拿信。

张　楠：你找谁呀？

叶小娟：啊，我叫叶小娟，是刘阿姨叫我来的。

张　楠：噢，新来的钟点工，是吧？

叶小娟：嗯。

张　楠：请进吧。

叶小娟：哎。

张　楠：妈，刘姨[N1]介绍的人来了。

张　母：噢，来了。屋里说吧[N2]。这是我女儿，张倩。

张　倩：哦，你好！

叶小娟：你好！哎，妈，叫人坐呀。

张　母：噢，对，坐吧。你之前呀，我们用过一个计时工，手脚不利索不说，也不干净。

张　倩：妈，您说这些干什么呀。

张　母：哦。

张　倩：喝水。

姨	yí	n.	aunt（maternal aunt，i. e. mother's sister）
钟点工	zhōngdiǎngōng	n.	hourly paid worker
刘姨	Liú yí	N.	Aunt Liu
计时工	jìshígōng	n.	worker paid on the basis of work time

张　母：哦，好，不说她了。你们**安徽**姑娘啊**勤快**，**手脚**也**利索**，我早有**耳闻**。

叶小娟：阿姨，我会认真做的。

张　母：那就好，那就好。其实我们家的活儿也不多，嗯，收拾收拾这屋子，买买菜。她在**魏公村**有个小家，不常在。平时呢，就我跟小楠两个。小楠，在公司搞**直销**，经常啊，到外头去跑，这衣服得**勤**洗着点儿。至于[G1]我的衣服嘛，你**顺手搓**一把就行了。啊，嗯，这个厨房，噢，对了，这个厨房的抽**油烟机**得经常擦着点儿，要不**油乎乎**的，怪[N3]不卫生的。这个，几个屋子的地啊，你来一回擦两遍就行了。就这么点儿活儿。每周来两次，二五的下午，嗯，每次两个**钟点**。至于**工钱**嘛……

安徽	Ānhuī	N.	(Anhui Province，P. R. China)
勤快	qínkuai	adj.	diligent；hard-working
手脚利索	shǒu jiǎo lìsuo		nimble；agile
早有耳闻	zǎo yǒu ěr wén		heard about (it) long ago
魏公村	Wèigōngcūn	N.	Weigongcun(name of a place in Beijing)
直销	zhíxiāo	v.	direct sale
勤	qín	adv.	frequently (as used in this story)
顺手	shùnshǒu	adv.	conveniently；easily；(do sth.) without extra efforts
搓	cuō	v.	rub with the hands；twist
油烟机	yóuyānjī	n.	exhaust fan
油乎乎	yóuhūhū	adj.	oily；greasy
钟点	zhōngdiǎn	n.	hour
工钱	gōng·qián	n.	wages；pay；charge for a service

张　母：他这是怎么了？**发什么神经**啊？

张　倩：**琳琳**来信，和小楠吹了，在美国找了个老头儿，马上要结婚了都[N4]。妈！

张　母：这是怎么话说的[N5]。小楠！小楠！都快吃饭了，上哪儿去？

张　倩：妈！妈！您别管他了，让他出去溜达溜达吧。

吃饭人等：来，来来，干杯。干杯！干杯！哎，好。

吃饭人1：**肖锋**不是会**划拳**吗？

吃饭人2：是这手吗？

吃饭人1：那你以为呢？让你不**服**！

吃饭人等：肖锋**加油**！

吃饭人1、2：**棒子**、棒子、**虫**⋯⋯

张　母：哎，那两个箱子小心点儿啊，那是张楠的**饭碗子**。大学毕业以后，他一直帮一家**高科技**公司推销这种**灯泡**，还挺**辛苦**的呢。

吃饭人3：哎哟喂这⋯⋯

吃饭人2：你们俩干吗呢？

吃饭人3：有什么不行的呀？

发神经	fā shénjīng	v.	go mad; crazy; fig. state contrary to reason or against common sense
琳琳	Línlin	N.	name of a female person
肖锋	Xiāo Fēng	N.	name of a male person
划拳	huá quán	vo.	play a drinking game
服	fú	v.	be convinced; submit (oneself to)
加油	jiāyóu	v.	(used to cheer sb. on) Go! Come on!
棒子	bàngzi	n.	stick; club; cudgel
虫	chóng	n.	insect; worm
饭碗子	fànwǎnzi	n.	job; bread and butter
高科技	gāokējì	n.	high tech, high technology
灯泡	dēngpào	n.	light bulb, electric bulb
辛苦	xīnkǔ	adj.	work hard

吃饭人2：OK，你**饶**了我吧。你算了，别让我妈打我。哎哎哎，干吗呢？**刺激**我呢？你饶了我。

吃饭人等：哎啊。你要玩儿自己找啊。刺激我？你。刺激我？对对。你喊什么呀？我受不了了！咱俩喝。甭管他。（有）毛病！你是个**怪物**，真是个怪物。笑累了……

张　　楠：朋友，我跟你说啊，别看现在她跟你起**腻**[N6]，这女人的心哪，跟小孩的脸似的，说变就她妈变。不知道哪天把你给**蹬**了你……

吃饭人等：你谁呀？喝高了[N7]吧？干吗呢？这不是找**瓶**[N8]吗？

张　　楠：……踹您跟**踹**个狗似的。

吃饭人等：哎呀，什么找瓶呀！啊……

叶　小　娟：阿姨再见！

张　　母：小楠这孩子哪儿去了？

张　　楠：朋……朋友，你要是相……相信我的话，咱们把这杯酒，咱干了，啊？

吃饭人1：那你喝高了吧？啊？

吃饭人3：您到底什么事？

吃饭人女：臭**德行**[N9]！

张　　楠：**老爷们儿**这儿没你什么事儿，一边儿待着去[N10]！

吃饭人4：你这呀是不是**有病**[N11]呀？你找死呀？找死啊你！

张　　楠：狗咬吕洞宾，你不识好人心[N12]哪你。

饶	ráo	v.	forgive; spare
刺激	cì·jī	v.	provoke; irritate
怪物	guàiwù	n.	monster, monstrosity, freak
腻	nì	adj.	sticky; greasy 起腻；(see note 5)
蹬	dēng	v.	pedal; treadle
踹	chuài	v.	kick; tread; stamp
德行	déxing	n.	(see note 8)
老爷们儿	lǎoyémenr	n.	adult man
有病	yǒu bìng		be (mentally) sick; crazy, (see note 10)
狗	gǒu	n.	dog
咬	yǎo	v.	bite
吕洞宾	Lǚ Dòngbīn	N.	One of the Eight Immortals in Taoist mythology known for his kindness.

吃饭人 4：我打你个吕洞宾。

吃饭人女：啊！

吃饭人 1：还**还手**？

吃饭人等：让你**多管闲事**。装他妈什么孙子^{N13}，去你的！

饭店老板：行，行，别打了，出去打去！

群众 1：哎，这人怎么了？

群众 2：不知道，好像喝多了。

群　众：打得**够呛**！

叶小娟：大哥，大哥，你咋了？

叶小娟：大哥，我就不送你了，你自己回去吧。路上小心啊。

张　楠：小娟，谢谢你。

叶小娟：不谢！

张　母：小楠，小楠，小楠！都睡了两天了，能坐起来就坐会儿，老躺着头**晕**，啊？

张　楠：妈，你让我安静一会儿。

张　母：小倩，你少看会儿书，去给小楠买点儿**营养品**。

张　倩：为了她，值得么？

张　母：你买的这是什么呀？

张　楠：妈，这您可就老外了。高级营养品！**美国货**！

张　母：他是**外伤**，这是**发物**^{N14}！

叶小娟：阿姨，我来了。

张　母：你先**打扫**打扫客厅。都快当妈的人了，这么点儿事儿都办不好。

还手	huán shǒu	vo.	fight back
多管闲事	duō guǎn xiánshì		mind other people's business
够呛	gòuqiàng	adj.	terrible; unbearable
晕	yūn	v.	dizzy
营养品	yíngyǎngpǐn	n.	nutritiousstuff (food)
美国货	měiguóhuò	n.	American merchandise or goods
外伤	wàishāng	n.	external injury or wound
发物	fāwù	n.	(see note 14)
打扫	dǎsǎo	v.	clean; sweep; bream; scavenge

张　倩：以后小楠要吃什么东西啊，让他**自个**儿买去，又不是什么起不来的病！**堂堂**一个**男子汉**，为了一个压根儿不值得的**小丫头片子**变成这样！整天在家什么事儿都不做不说，好好的工作放一边不管，出门就**惹是生非**[N15]，还跟**有功**了似的[G2]。

张　母：小倩！少说两句行不行？

张　倩：少说两句？瞧人家小娟，每天都跑好几家**干活**呢！就这样，抽时间去**裁剪**学校学习！可他呢？为了那小丫头片子！没出息！

张　母：还说，还说！

张　倩：**志熙**今天出差回来，我回去了。起来干儿点事儿啊，别光让妈伺候你！

张　母：小倩，小倩，小倩！小倩！

张　倩：我走了。

自个儿	zìgěr	pron.	自己，oneself; by oneself
堂堂	tángtáng	adj.	(of a man) impressive looking; dignified in appearance
男子汉	nánzǐhàn	n.	a real man, true man
小丫头片子	xiǎo yātou piànzi	n.	maiden; girl (derogative)
惹是生非	rě shì shēng fēi		stir up trouble; provoke a dispute
有功	yǒu gōng	vo.	having done a meritorious deed
干活	gàn huó	v.	work (manual, physical)
裁剪	cáijiǎn	v.	tailor; cut material according to a certain size and shape while making a garment
志熙	Zhìxī	N.	name of the husband of Zhang Nan's sister

注释 Notes

1. **刘姨/刘阿姨**：谈到与母亲同辈的女性，可以在其姓后加"姨"，比如"刘姨"、"王姨"，也可以在姓后加"阿姨"，如"刘阿姨"、"王阿姨"。

   The word "aunt（姨 or 阿姨）", followed by her surname，is a common way to address one's mother's similar-aged female friends or acquaintances. E. g.："Aunt Liu" or "Aunt Wang" may be called "刘姨"，"王姨" or "刘阿姨"，"王阿姨".

2. **"屋里说吧"**：来/去屋里说吧。Let's talk inside.

   （1）里边儿坐吧。Come and sit inside.

   （2）外边儿说吧。Let's talk outside.

3. **"怪"**：是"很"的意思，口语。

   "怪" is the same as "很" meaning "very，quite or rather" with an overtone of abhorrence or appreciation. It is mostly used to modify adjectives or descriptive phrases.

   （1）这个厨房的抽油烟机得经常擦着点儿，要不油乎乎的，怪不卫生的。

   The exhaust fan in the kitchen has to be cleaned often；otherwise，it becomes too greasy and not very hygienic.

   （2）喜欢是喜欢，但是怪贵的。

   I like it，sure，but it's rather expensive.

   （3）不是不会做，只是怪费时间的。

   It's not that I can't do it，it's just too time consuming.

4. **"马上要结婚了都"**，这个句子是一种"追加"现象，正常语序是"马上都要结婚了"。见《项链》第二部分语法注释1。

   The regular syntax structure for "马上要结婚了都"（You are just about to be married）should be "马上都要结婚了". See grammer note 1 of Part 2 in 《项链》.

5. **"这是怎么话说的。"** 意思是"事情怎么会这样"。见《门里门外》第四部分词语注释5。

   "What do you mean by saying this?" See note 5 of part 4 in 《门里门外》.

6. **"起腻"**：意思是"粘上"某个人，肢体跟某个人特别亲近，通常用于小孩子对父母、长辈，或男女朋友之间。口语。

"腻" means "sticky" or "greasy". "起腻" is a colloquial expression used here to describe a man and woman who openly display an indecently intimate or excessively sentimental behavior. This expression can also be used to describe the behavior of a child who acts spoiled, constantly cuddling or snuggling up to his/her parents or to other older family members.

7. **"喝高了"**：意思是酒喝多了。

"喝高了" means "had a lot to drink" or "being drunk".

8. **"找瓴"**：意思是"自己找挨打"。

"（He) brought the beating upon himself" or "（He) asked for it."

9. **"德行"**：对某人说"瞧你那德行"，意思是看不起某人的仪表、行为、作风等。女孩子喜欢用"德行"骂男人。有时跟自己比较亲近的人说"德行"时，不一定是真的骂他。

"德行" literally means "virtuous character and behavior". "瞧你那德行" is used to express a dislike feeling towards someone's behavior, conduct, manner, etc. However, "德行" is often used by a girl to scold a man as a mild disapprobation. In this story when "德行" is modified by "臭" it means "Disgusting！", "Puke！"

10. **"一边儿待着去"**：字面意思是"离开这里，到别的地方去"。实际上意思是"这里的事跟你没有关系，你不要说话，不要管"。这样说时，很不客气。

The literal meaning of "一边儿待着去" is "leave here, go somewhere else." It is used to mean "the matter has nothing to do with you; hence you should play no part in it since it is none of your business." Colloquially, it's the equivalent to the expression in English "Keep away from this！" or "Get out of here！"

11. **"有病"**："你这呀是不是有病呀？"这里"有病"的意思是"脑子有毛病，思维不正常。"

"有病（be sick）" means here to be "mentally sick", "crazy". The sentence simply means：Are you crazy?

12. **"狗咬吕洞宾，不识好人心"**：吕洞宾是传说中的"八仙（八位神仙）"之一。

"狗咬吕洞宾，不识好人心"是俗语，意思是"好心人被误解"。

吕洞宾 is one of the Eight Immortals in Taoist mythology known for his

kindness. The sentence means：What a fool you are for attacking the person who cares about you.

13. "装他妈什么孙子，去你的！""装孙子"的意思是"假装出一副可怜的样子"。

"孙子" means grandson. Since the position of a grandson in a Chinese family is the lowest, therefore the term is often used to mean a low person of little worth. "装孙子" used in this context means "act like a grandson (to invite sympathy)" or "to make one look pitiable". The whole sentence "装他妈什么孙子，去你的！" means："Don't feign this pathetic look, get the hell out here!"

14. "发物"：指可以使某些疾病、外伤更严重的食物，如羊肉、鱼虾等。

"发物" is a certain kind of food, such as lamb, fish or shrimp, which is thought to cause the worsening of wounds or certain diseases.

15. "惹是生非"：意思是"引起是非、麻烦"。

"惹是生非" means "to provoke a dispute" or "to stir up trouble".

语法 Grammar Notes

1. **"至于"**：用在句子或分句的开头，引起一个与上文有关的另一个话题。

   "至于" is "as for" or "as to". It always appears in the beginning of a sentence or a clause, and is used to introduce another topic on which comments or views are added in the following part. Its object can be any word, phrase or construction.

   (1) 小楠，在公司搞直销，经常啊，到外头去跑，这衣服得勤洗着点儿。至于我的衣服嘛，你顺手搓一把就行了。

   Xiao Nan is a salesman for his company; he is out meeting customers all the time, so his clothes need to be washed frequently, as for mine, it's a small addition to throw in.

   (2) 我只是觉得，她身上有什么东西吸引我，至于是什么，我也搞不清。（本剧第三部分）

   I just feel there is something about her that attracts me. As for what it is, I can't tell.

   (3) 最近几年，中国的经济发展很快，至于今后几年情况会怎样，人们的看法有些不同。

   The Chinese economy developed really fast in the last few years, as for how long this will be going on in the foreseeable future, people have different opinions.

   (4) 我已经通知你了，至于你去不去，我不管。

   I have informed you, as for your going or not, it's not my business.

   注意："至于"引出的话题后要有一个停顿，而且这个话题不是一个全新的信息。例如例（1），上半句谈到"衣服"，"至于"后谈的也是"衣服"。例（2），上半句说的是"她身上有什么东西吸引我"，"至于"后还是"什么东西吸引我"，只是略去了。例（3）"至于"前后谈的都是"经济发展情况"，例（4）上半句实际上是"我已经通知你（去做什么）了"，所以"至于"后才说"去不去（做）"。

   Note: The topic that "至于" introduces to is often followed by a pause, the topic is not a new one. For example, in pattern sentence (1), the topic is clothes in the first part of the sentence, the topic after "至于" is also about clothes. In pattern sentence (2), "what attracts me about her" is the topic in the former part of the sentence, the topic is still "what attracts me" for the latter part of the sentence, but it is habitually omitted. In pattern sentence (3), "economic development" is the topic before and after "至于". In pattern sentence (4), the first part of the sentence in fact is: "I've informed you to do something or to go some where", therefore, the latter part asks whether he is indeed to do or to go or not.

2. "（跟、像）……似的"：用在名词，代词或动词的后边，表示跟某种事物或情况相似。

"（跟、像）……似的" "be like……" or " as if" is used after a noun, pronoun and a verb to indicate similarity。

（1）你出门就惹是生非，还跟有功了似的。

You always get into trouble whenever you are out of the house, yet you look as if you've done us a great service!

（2）看他吃饭的样子，像8年没吃过饭似的.

Look at the way he eats, he looks as if he hadn't had food for a life time.

练习 Exercises

■ 一、口语练习 Oral Practice

（一）回答下列问题 Answer the following questions

1. 张家有几口人？他们都是谁？都做什么工作？
2. 叶小娟是哪儿的人？她为什么到张家来？
3. 张家以前用过记时工吗？她为什么走了？
4. 叶小娟每天都要来张家打工吗？
5. 张母要叶小娟每次来做哪些事情？
6. 为什么张楠的衣服得勤洗？
7. 家里要吃饭了，张楠为什么不吃饭就走了？
8. 张楠到哪儿去了？在那儿发生了什么事情？
9. 张倩对弟弟最近的表现很不满，我们是怎么知道的？
10. 张倩结婚了吗？有孩子了吗？

■ 二、书写练习 Written Exercises

（一）选择适当词语完成句子 Chose the most appropriate items to finish
the sentences

A. 没出息	B. 似的	C. 早有	D. 不说	E. 自个儿
F. 一边儿	G. 压根儿	H. 抽	I. 多管闲事	

1. 在你之前呀，我们用过一个计时工，手脚不利索＿＿＿＿＿，也不
干净。
2. 你们安徽姑娘啊勤快，手脚也利索，我＿＿＿＿＿耳闻。
3. 这女人的心哪，跟小孩的脸＿＿＿＿＿，说变就她妈变。
4. 老爷们这儿没你什么事儿，＿＿＿＿＿待着去！
5. 让你＿＿＿＿＿。装他妈什么孙子，去你的！
6. 以后小楠要吃什么东西啊，让他＿＿＿＿＿买去，又不是什么起不来
的病！

7. 堂堂一个男子汉，为了一个_____不值得的小丫头片子变成这样！

8. 瞧人家小娟，每天都跑好几家干活呢！就这样，还_____时间去裁剪学校学习！

9. 你也真是的，为了那小丫头片子！_____！

（二）选择题 Circle the answer which most reflects the meaning of the under-lined part in the following sentences

1. 张倩：琳琳来信，和小楠吹了，在美国找了个老头，马上要结婚了都。妈！

   张母：这是怎么话说的。
   A. 话怎么能这样说
   B. 怎么能这样说话
   C. 你说些什么我不懂
   D. 事情怎么会这样

2. 哎，那两个箱子小心点儿啊，那是张楠的饭碗子。
   A. 箱子里装的是张楠吃饭的碗
   B. 箱子很重要，没箱子就没饭吃
   C. 张楠用箱子当饭碗吃饭
   D. 张楠就靠箱子里的东西吃饭

3. 我受不了了！咱俩喝。甭管他。（有）毛病！
   A. 那个人有病
   B. 那个人有坏习惯
   C. 那个人神经不正常
   D. 那个人多管闲事

4. 这女人的心哪，说变就她妈变。不知道哪天把你给蹬了……
   A. 不知道哪天会把你打了……
   B. 不知道哪天会用脚踢你……
   C. 不知道哪天会不理你了……
   D. 不知道哪天会把你害了……

5. 臭德行！
   A. 没有道德
   B. 味道不好闻
   C. 样子不好看
   D. 让人讨厌

6. 可你呢？为了那小丫头片子！<u>没出息</u>！

  A. 没出去过

  B. 没休息过

  C. 没有用

  D. 没赚钱

（三）完成句子 Complete the following sentences with the words given

  1. 他的生日晚会我会去的，_____。（至于）

  2. 他下个月去日本，_____。（至于）

  3. 张母说他家里没什么事情做，_____。（其实）

  4. 他说是没时间，_____。（其实）

  5. 他这几天_____，下星期你再跟她谈吧。（怪）

  6. 张母这个人_____，我不爱听她说话。（怪）

  7. 这个孩子说话_____。（似的）

  8. 他跑得_____。（似的）

张　楠：哎，小娟啊，那天多亏^{N1}了你了！哎，你来北京多久了？

叶小娟：快三年了。

张　楠：你是边打工边上学啊？

叶小娟：嗯。

张　楠：想不想家？

叶小娟：想也没办法。大哥，你的书真多啊。

张　楠：我这些书啊，看着对你有用的，你**随便**拿。

叶小娟：那太好了。

张　楠：哎，你还有时间看书啊？

叶小娟：**抓**时间呗。等我毕业了，我也像你一样整天待家里，光看书，啥也不干。啊，对不起啊，我……

张　楠：没错，你说得对，我是应该出去走走。

（广　播：**听众**朋友们，《人生**热线**》节目今天就**播送**到这里，请您明天同一时间继续**收听**，再见。）

张　母：唉！

叶小娟：阿姨，我星期五再来。

张　母：哎，等等，小娟，这桌子是你收拾的？你没看见什么东西吗？

叶小娟：嗯，没有啊。

张　楠：妈，您跟那儿**啰唆**什么呢？她有别地儿要去呢。

叶小娟：那……

张　楠：那你先走吧。

打工	dǎ gōng	vo.	have a part-time or a temporary job (usually manual work)
随便	suíbiàn	adj.	do as one pleases
抓(时间)	zhuā(shíjiān)	v.	find (the time) to do sth.
听众	tīngzhòng	n.	audience; listeners
热线	rèxiàn	n.	hotline (communications link)
播送	bōsòng	v.	broadcast; transmit
收听	shōutīng	v.	listen to (the radio); tune in
啰唆	luōsuo	adj.	repetitive; loquacious; garrulous (of words)

叶小娟：我走了。

张　母：我明明^{G1}放在壶底下准备交**水电费**的。

张　楠：兴许您忘了放什么地儿了吧。小娟不是那种人哪。

张　母：你什么**眼神**^{N2}呀？看谁都是好人。要不怎么那**小蹄子**^{N3}在美国把你给扔了呢？

张　楠：**太过分**了你！

小娟友：这本书借我看，好么？

叶小娟：人家大哥挺^{N4}爱他书的。

小娟友：不是爱书，是爱人了吧？

叶小娟：乱说！

小娟友：看什么呢？

叶小娟：噢，没什么。

张　母：我告诉你啊，今天她来了，你不问我问。

张　楠：不可能！他不是那种人。您肯定是忘了。

张　母：你这**吃里爬外**^{N5}的小子，你妈还没老到那份儿**上**^{N6}呢。出来打工的，哪个不为钱？

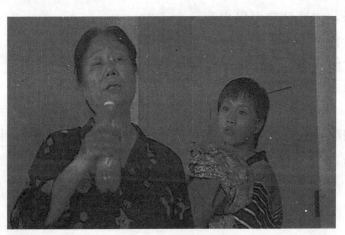

水电费	shuǐdiànfèi	n.	water and electricity bills
眼神	yǎnshén	n.	眼力, expression in one's eyes; look in one's eyes
小蹄子	xiǎotízi		bitch, (see note 3)
过分	guòfèn	adj.	excessive; beyond or over the limit
吃里爬外	chī lǐ pá wài		living off one person while working for another

张　楠：我都不信！小娟能干这事儿？

张　母：你不相信？不相信，不相信！前面那钟点工你也不相信？

张　楠：妈，你怎么了？前面那个你也没有证据啊。妈，这人与人之间能不能多点儿信任？

张　母：什么时候到的？

叶小娟：刚到。大哥怎么样了？

张　母：哼，伤倒不重，可**魂**儿丢了^{G2}。你劝了他几句，他出去一**趟**，还是你的面子大呀。

叶小娟：我给大哥买了个骨棒。

张　母：骨棒？

叶小娟：嗯，熬汤喝的。

张　母：哟，怎么好让你**破费**呢？

叶小娟：啊，不值几个钱，一点儿心意。

张　母：值不了几个钱？这还不得 100 块呀？小娟啊。

叶小娟：啊？

张　母：沙发上**沙发巾**该洗洗了啊。

叶小娟：哎，好嘞。吵着你了？

张　楠：噢，没有。

叶小娟：大哥，你这灯泡可以卖我一个不？

张　楠：咳，什么卖不卖的，随便拿去用吧。

叶小娟：名片给几张。

张　楠：想拿多少拿多少。

张　楠：大娘啊，您好！我是**金森利公司**的**推销员**，我向您介绍一种我们的新产品。

大　娘：噢，不要不要，走吧。

魂儿	húnr	n.	soul; spirit
破费	pòfèi	v.	spent (money) or time
（沙发）巾	（shāfā）jīn	n.	a piece of cloth (as used for a towel, scarf, kerchief, etc.), 沙发巾 sofa cover
金森利	Jīnsēnlì	N.	name of a company
推销员	tuīxiāoyuán	n.	salesperson

张　　楠：大娘您听我好好解释解释，好不好？

大　　娘：走吧，走吧，再不走我喊人了，走吧走吧。

张　　母：一个都没卖出去啊？

张　　楠：对。

张　　母：那你不会多跑几家？

张　　楠：没用，人家都把我当贼。

张　　母：哟，我儿子哪像贼呀？家里头倒**招来**个贼。

张　　楠：妈，人与人之间能不能多点儿信任啊？我就老是不被人信任，才懂得
　　　　　信任的**可贵**。

张　　母：哼，妈知道你的心思。我就不明白，我那100块钱是长了腿飞了？

张　　楠：又是您的100块钱！你有完没完哪？喂？啊，是我啊，噢，好好好。
　　　　　好嘞，我马上给您送过去啊。

张　　楠：大妈啊，这将来呀，您进进出出的，可就方便多了。

大　　妈：可不是嘛，小娟想得多周到。

张　　楠：您跟小娟挺熟的啊？

大　　妈：啊，熟啊，她在我家干了快三年了，还能不熟？

张　　楠：大爷，您是怎么知道我那**呼机号**的呀？

大　　爷：是小娟那**闺女**告诉我的。那姑娘，**仁义**着呢[G3]。上次啊，我发烧，在
　　　　　床上**足足**躺了一个礼拜，多亏了她跑前跑后地照顾我，要不我这把老
　　　　　骨头啊也就进**火葬场**了。

叶小娟：姐。

娟　　姐：哎，小娟来了呀？

叶小娟：忙么？

招来	zhāo lai	vc.	invite (thief, problems, disaster, etc.)
可贵	kěguì	adj.	treasured; valuable
呼机号	hūjīhào	n.	beeper number
闺女	guīnü	n.	(northern expression) girl; maiden; daughter
仁义	rényì	adj.	kind
足足	zúzú	adv.	fully; no less than
火葬场	huǒzàngchǎng		cremation center

娟姐的同事：忙，噢。

叶小娟：师傅，您要什么？呀，大哥，是你啊。

张　楠：啊。

叶小娟：来碗**豆腐脑**怎么样？我请客。

张　楠：成啊。哎，小娟啊，听说你最近在学裁剪，是吧？

叶小娟：嗯，我都可以做衣服了。

张　楠：是吗？这三年啊，真够难为你的了。

叶小娟：苦点儿，累点儿，倒没啥。我们到了城里来，不就是为了**见见世面**，
　　　　学点儿本事吗？就是……噢，不说它了。

张　楠：小娟啊，谢谢你！

叶小娟：谢我？嘿，我还得谢谢你呢！

张　楠：谢我什么呀？

叶小娟：谢你信任我！到北京三年了，我觉得信任比什么都重要。

张　楠：小娟，这 200 块钱是你应得的。

叶小娟：我？哎呀，大哥，我不是图钱。

张　楠：我知道。

叶小娟：我是不愿看你整天没魂儿似的。我也是**搂草**打**兔子**[N7]，顺手的事嘛。

张　楠：这钱啊，你一定要拿着，不然的话，我会心不安的。

叶小娟：得，那我就收下了。正好**派上用场**。

张　楠：小娟啊，我送你回去吧。

叶小娟：不了，大哥，你回吧。大哥。

张　楠：哎？

叶小娟：我祝你以后工作顺利，生活愉快！

张　楠：瞧你说得一本正经的，搞得跟**告别仪式**似的。

豆腐脑	dòufunǎo	n.	soft bean curd
见世面	jiàn shìmiàn	vo.	see the world；become experienced，become sophisticate
搂（草）	lōu(cǎo)	v.	gather up；rake together
兔子	tùzi	n.	rabbit
派上用场	pài shang yòngchǎng		(skill of sb. or things one has) found the use of
告别	gàobié	v.	farewell
仪式	yíshì	n.	ceremony

注释 Notes

1. **"多亏"**：见《都市彩虹》第二部分语法注释 1。
   See grammer note 1 of Part 2 in《都市彩虹》.

2. **"眼神"**：这里的意思是"眼力"，指分辨人或事物好坏的能力。
   "眼神"usually refers to "the expression in one's eyes" or "the look in one's eyes."
   But "眼神"used in this context means "眼力". It refers to one's ability to distinguish good from bad in people and things.

3. **"小蹄子"**：骂年轻的女人的话。现在较少用。
   "小蹄子" is the same as "bitch" in English. It is an old fashioned swear word for a young woman.

4. **"挺"**：见《都市彩虹》第二部分语法注释 3。
   See grammer note 3 of Part 2 in《都市彩虹》.

5. **"吃里爬外"**：做损害自己方面（人、单位）而对外人有好处的事，有贬义。
   "吃里爬外" literally means "Eating food inside while raking things to the outside"; it is used to means "hurting one's benefactor by helping someone else". In the context of the story here, it means "living on your family but siding with an outsider".

6. **"那份儿上"**："你妈还没老到那份儿上呢"，"份儿"在这里表示"程度"。这句话的意思是"你妈我还没有那么老（会糊涂到分不清好人坏人的程度）。"
   "那份儿上"means"程度"here. The sentence means "Your mother has not become so old (that she can't even tell a good person from a bad one).

7. **"搂草打兔子，顺手的事嘛"**：歇后语。意思是：做一件事的同时，顺便做了另一件事，没有另外花时间和精力。
   "搂草打兔子，顺手的事" is a "歇后语". "歇后语" is a two-part allegorical saying, of which the first part, always stated, is descriptive, while the second part, sometimes unstated, carries the message. This expression means：Caught a rabbit while removing the hay—gained something without extra effort.

语法 Grammar Notes

1. "**明明**(it's obvious that ...)"：副词，意思是"显然是这样"，后面常有表示疑问、反问或转折的句子。

   "**明明**" is an adverb, meaning obviously, plainly, undoubtedly. It is followed by a turn in meaning in the latter part of the context.

   (1) 那天她明明去了，却说没去，真奇怪。

   She went on that day and every one saw her, but she just says that she didn't. How strange!

   (2) 我明明告诉过你，你怎么说不知道？

   I undoubtedly told you, how could you say that you didn't know it?

   (3) 你明明知道，为什么还要问我？

   You obviously know it, why do you still have to ask me?

2. "**······倒······，可······**"：意思是：一件事比想象的要好，但是另一件不好的事出现了。用法与"虽然······但是······"近似。

   "**······倒······可······**" means "(One thing turned out to be) better than one would have expected, but something else (negative) unexpected happened. It is used similarly to 虽然······但是······".

   (1) 伤倒不重，可魂儿丢了。

   He's physically OK, but his mind is elsewhere.

   (2) 头倒不疼了，可老不想吃饭。

   The headache is gone, but I've lost my appetite.

   (3) 今天天气倒不错，可他又没空儿了。

   The weather turned up to be unexpectedly nice, but he happened to be busy today.

3. "**着呢**"：用在形容词或表示心理活动的动词后，表示程度高、程度深。口语。

   "**着呢**" is used after an adjective or a verb which is a colloquial expression meaning "really", "quite". E. g.：

   (1) 她唱歌唱得好着呢。

She sings really well.

（2）我家远着呢，走路走不到。

My home is quite far away, you can't walk there.

（3）叶小娟能干着呢，虽然是一个农村小女孩。

Xiao Juan is really capable although she's a country girl.

练习 Exercises

■ 一、口语练习 Oral Practice

（一）回答下列问题 Answer the following questions

1. 叶小娟在北京做什么？她来北京多久了？

2. 张家发生了什么事？

3. 张楠对叶小娟的信任让张母很反感。我们是怎么知道的？

4. 为什么张楠和叶小娟都认为人与人之间"信任"很重要？

5. 叶小娟爱上张楠了吗？

6. 张楠是不是爱上叶小娟了？

7. 张母说："哼，妈知道你的心思。"张母说这话是什么意思？

8. 张母对儿子张楠在交女朋友方面有什么看法？

（二）角色扮演 Role Play

两人一组用下列词语编一个对话，一个扮演叶小娟，一个扮演张楠。两人在一个小饭馆一边儿吃饭一边谈话。

Divide students into pairs. One plays 叶小娟 and the other plays 张楠. The two are eating in a small restaurant while chatting. The following words and phrases must be used in the conversation.

1. 来碗……怎么样？	2. 我请客	3. 听说	4. 最近
5. 难为	6. 不就是	7. 见世面	8. 学本事
9. 信任	10. 重要	11. 图钱	12. 没魂儿似的
13. 心不安	14. 派上用场	15. 一本正经	16. 工作顺利
17. 生活愉快			

■ 二、书写练习 Written Exercises

（一）选择题 Circle the answer which most reflects the meaning of the underlined part in the following sentences

1. 说这种话，<u>太过分了</u>你！

A. 让你太过分了

B. 别过分了

C. 对你太过分了

D. 你太过分了

2. 哟，怎么好让你破费呢？

A. 又破又费

B. 费用太多

C. 花钱

D. 打破费用

3. 值不了几个钱？这还不得 100 块呀？

A. 值几块钱

B. 很便宜

C. 不到几块钱

D. 几块钱足够了

4. 这三年啊，真够难为你的了。

A. 为难够多了

B. 让你为难了

C. 你很难

D. 够难的了

5. 苦点儿，累点儿，倒没啥。我们到了城里来，不就是为了见见世面，学点儿本事么？

A. 就是不为了

B. 只是为了

C. 还为了别的

D. 就不是为了

6. 这钱啊，你一定要拿着，不然的话，我会心不安的。

A. 不安心

B. 担心

C. 不放心

D. 心里过意不去

7. 瞧你说得一本正经的，搞得跟告别仪式似的。

A. 永远不再见面了

B. 很正式的告别会

C. 追悼会

D. 毕业典礼

（二）完成句子 Substitute the underlined parts with your own phrases or sentences

1. 伤倒不重，<u>可魂儿丢了</u>。

    （1）我忙倒不忙，可_____。

    （2）这个工作钱倒不少，可_____。

    （3）这个工作累倒不累，可_____。

    （4）他倒没发烧，可_____。

2. 那天她<u>明明</u>去了，却说没去，真奇怪。

    （1）_____，你怎么说不知道。

    （2）_____，为什么还要问我？

    （3）_____，怎么还说饿？

    （4）_____，怎么就不见了呢？

3. 她跳舞跳得<u>好着呢</u>。

    （1）_____，现在没时间接你的电话。

    （2）_____，天天给她打电话。

    （3）_____，得坐飞机去。

    （4）叶小娟_____，虽然是一个农村小女孩。

■ 三、用中文解释句中画线部分的意思

Explain in Chinese the meaning of the underlined parts in the following sentences

1. 我都不信！<u>小娟能干这事儿</u>？

2. 这人与人之间能不能多点儿<u>信任</u>？

3. 你这<u>吃里爬外</u>的小子，我还没老到<u>那份儿</u>上呢。

4. 你劝了他几句，他出去一趟，<u>还是你的面子大</u>呀。

张　母：回来了？

张　楠：嗯。

张　母：吃饭了吗？

张　楠：吃了。

张　母：和谁一块儿吃的？

张　楠：朋友。

张　母：朋友？男朋友还是女朋友啊？

张　楠：妈，什么时候您参加了小脚侦缉队[N1]了？问那么**详细**干吗呀？

张　母：咳，小楠，别跟我**打马虎眼**[N2]。告诉你，再**掉价**，也不能娶个钟点工！

张　楠：妈，你瞎说什么呢？

张　母：我瞎说？我都看见了。

张　倩：看见什么了？有话好好说呗。进屋说去，这儿呢……

张　母：这叶小娟，表面看上去挺老实，其实，**一肚子花花肠子**[N3]！

张　倩：妈！您看您……

张　母：我没说错吧？早就对你动心思了。想得倒美，再怎么着，张家的媳妇也轮不到她头上！

张　倩：妈！

张　楠：妈您别再说啊，再说我跟您急噢。

张　倩：小楠！

张　母：哼！你还有脸跟我急？**好歹**[G1]也是个大学生，什么样的对象找不着？**犯得着**[N4]跟一个钟点工**轧马路**吗？

张　倩：行了！

详细	xiángxì	adj.	detailed
打马虎眼	dǎ mǎhuyǎn		pretend to be ignorant of something,（see note 2）
掉价	diào jià		fall or drop in price（used here to mean lowering or losing one's social status）
肚子	dùzi	n.	stomach
花花肠子	huāhua chángzi		deceitful ideas or thoughts
好歹	hǎodǎi	adv.	无论如何，不管怎么样，good or bad; for better or worse; no matter what
轧马路	yà mǎlù	vo.	take a stroll（usually with a lover）

张　母：我这就给你刘姨打电话去！看她介绍的什么人哪？我给你说，从今以后，不许她再**踏进**这个门！

张　倩：哎呀，行了！别老跟人家小钟点工过不去，干吗呀？

张　楠：妈老怀疑人家小娟**手脚不干净**[N5]，每次人家一来，总是**旁敲侧击**[N6]，**指桑骂槐**[N7]的。

张　倩：妈，您又来了，您老是这么随便怀疑人可不好！

张　母：什么随便怀疑人？那天我明明把 100 块交水电费的钱压在壶底下了，没了！家里就这么几个人，不是她拿了谁拿了？

张　倩：100 块钱？

张　母：对！

张　倩：搁壶底下那张？

张　母：是！

张　倩：我拿的！不给您儿子买营养品了吗？

张　母：咦！

张　倩：您倒是问问呀。实事求是地告诉我，你们俩到底怎么回事ル？

张　楠：我只是觉得，她身上有什么东西吸引我，至于是什么，我也搞不清。

张　倩：那她呢？

踏进	tà jìn	vc.	step in; work in
手脚不干净	shǒujiǎo bù gānjìng		a pilferer，(see note 5)
旁敲侧击	páng qiāo cè jī		make oblique references，(see note 6)
指桑骂槐	zhǐ sāng mà huái		make oblique accusations，(see note 7)

张　楠：姐，我不知道。反正我觉得我们现在还谈不到爱不爱，倒是**彼此之间**
　　　　有一种**莫名其妙**[N8]的**信任感**。哼，我想也许是由于工作上的原因吧，
　　　　两个人对"信任"这两个字特别敏感。

张　倩：哎，那你想怎么办啊？

张　楠：不知道。下星期一是她 22 岁的生日，她说呀，她将会有一个重大的
　　　　人生决定。

张　倩：什么决定？

张　楠：她没说。不过，我想，在那天呀，送她一**束**花儿。

张　倩：臭德行！

张　母：请小娟来家过生日，我好给孩子做顿饭。

娟　姐：哎，你好！

张　楠：怎么是你啊？

娟　姐：你是张楠吧？

张　楠：啊。

娟　姐：我是叶小娟的**表姐**。

张　楠：那小娟呢？

娟　姐：嗯，她让我给你带封信。

小娟信：张楠大哥，当你看到这封信的时候，我已经离开北京回家了，因为那
　　　　里有个他在等着我。我们一起走过生活中的**风风雨雨**[N9]，用我们学到
　　　　的知识去**改变**家乡的**贫困面貌**。我很**怀念**在北京打工的日子，它使我
　　　　见了世面，懂得了许多**做人**的道理，也**有幸**[N10]**结识**[N11]了许许多多的
　　　　好人，当然，也包括你。用上次你付给我的劳务费，为你买了一把新
　　　　吉他。希望你永远快乐！

彼此之间	bǐcǐ zhī jiān		between each other
莫名其妙	mò míng qí miào		being baffled，(see note 8)
信任感	xìnrèn gǎn	n.	sense of responsibility
束	shù	m.	bundle; bunch
表姐	biǎojiě	n.	older female cousin with a different surname
风风雨雨	fēng fēng yǔ yǔ		(see note 9)
改变	gǎibiàn	v.	change; alter
贫困	pínkùn	adj.	impoverished
面貌	miànmào	n.	appearance
怀念	huáiniàn	v.	cherish the memory of; think of
做人	zuò rén	vo.	conduct oneself; behave
有幸	yǒuxìng	adv.	fortunate; lucky
结识	jiéshí	v.	get acquainted with sb.; get to know sb.
吉他	jí·tā	n.	guitar

张　母：小娟是个好姑娘！都**怨**我**错怪**了这个闺女。小倩，你赶快给"北京热
　　　　线"打个电话，我要与小娟和**所有的**打工妹说句话。不说一说，妈这
　　　　辈子都不**安生**。

广　　播：我们的一位听众家曾经**雇佣**了一个钟点工，因怀疑她偷走了自己的
　　　　100元钱而闹出了许多不愉快的事情。后来她发现自己错怪了这个钟
　　　　点工而**愧疚不已**。她给**本**台人生热线还打了个电话，想通过我们，向
　　　　那个**朴实**而**善良**的农村姑娘叶小娟表示**深深的歉意**。下面，我们就请
　　　　听众**刘秀珍**对叶小娟讲几句心里话。

张　母：小娟啊，你好吗？真的很对不起你！

怨	yuàn	v.	怪，blame；complain
怪	guài	v.	blame
所有的	suǒyǒu de		all
打工妹	dǎgōng mèi	n.	young female temporary worker
（一）辈子	(yí)bèizi	n.	all one's life，lifetime
安生	ān·shēng	adj.	living in peace；living peacefully
雇佣	gùyōng	v.	hire；employ
愧疚不已	kuìjiù bùyǐ		be very ashamed and remorseful
本	běn	pron.	this（used to modify a noun）
朴实	pǔshí	adj.	sincere and honest；simple；plain
善良	shànliáng	adj.	kind-hearted；good and honest
深深的	shēnshēn de		very sincere；profound
歉意	qiànyì	n.	apology；regret
刘秀珍	Liú Xiùzhēn	N.	name of a female

注释 Notes

1. **"小脚侦缉队"**：见《门里门外》第一部分词语注释1。

   See note 1 of part 1 in《门里门外》.

2. **"打马虎眼"**：故意装糊涂骗人。口语。

   "打马虎眼" means "Pretending to be ignorant of something (in order to gloss it over)" or "to act dumb". It is a colloquial expression.

   (1) 你总是给她打马虎眼，她明明没病你为什么说她病了？

       You always try to shield her. Why did you claim she was sick when she was not?

   (2) 你到底准备了没有？别跟我打马虎眼！

       Did you actually review〔the material〕or not？Don't you try to fool me！

3. **"花花肠子"**："花花肠子"比喻狡诈的心计，"一肚子花花肠子"的意思是说某人很狡诈，总是想算计别人。方言。

   "花花肠子" is a figure of speech meaning scheming，deceitful，crafty or cunning.

   "一肚子花花肠子" is used to describe a deceitful，sly and crafty person. It is an expression in Northern dialect.

   (1) 那个人看上去不错，可是一肚子花花肠子，小心着他点儿！

       That man appears to be a nice guy，but he is really deceitful and crafty. Be careful of him！

   (2) 他一肚子花花肠子，我不跟他来往。

       He is so crafty and untrustworthy that I decided to have nothing to do with him.

4. **"犯得着……吗？"**：意思是"不值得……"。

   "犯得着……吗?" means "不值得……"：unworthy；not worthwhile；not worth doing.

   (1) 犯得着跟一个钟点工轧马路么？

       这句话的意思是"不值得跟一个钟点工交朋友（而降低了自己）。"

       Is it worthwhile〔for a college graduate〕to date an hourly-paid worker？

（2）跟她生气，犯不着。

It's not worth the trouble of being angry with her.

5. **"手脚不干净"**：意思是"偷东西"。

It literally means "〔Someone's〕hands and feet are dirty", used to refer to a pilferer.

（1）不知为什么他落了个手脚不干净的名声。

I don't know how he got a reputation for being a pilferer.

（2）那个人手脚不太干净，你小心点儿。

Be careful, that guy is a petty thief.

6. **"旁敲侧击"**：成语。意思是说话或写文章时，不愿意或不便直接说出本意，而从侧面曲折地表达。

"旁敲侧击" is an idiom used to describe a speaker or a writer who doesn't want to say something directly, but chooses to make oblique references.

有什么想法直说，不用旁敲侧击。

There is no need to make oblique references, just say it frankly.

7. **"指桑骂槐"**：成语。字面的意思是"指着桑树骂槐树"，比喻一个人表面上说这个人，而实际上是在骂另一个人。

指桑骂槐 is an idiom. It literally means "pointing at the mulberry and abusing the locust". It is used here to mean "pointing at one while abusing another/ making oblique accusations."

（1）有意见就说，指桑骂槐的，真没有意思！

Speak out if you disagree, don't make oblique accusations!

8. **"莫名其妙"**：成语，形容非常奇特，无法说出其中的奥妙，使人无法理解。有时觉得一个人的言语行为很奇怪，自己不理解、不满意，也可以用这个成语。

"莫名其妙" is an idiom. It is used to describe a sense of "being baffled" or "being unable to make heads or tails of something". It is used when a person's behavior or sayings are incomprehensible to you.

（1）这个人真莫名其妙，昨天说好今天一定来，可是又不来了。

What's wrong with that guy; he said yesterday that he would certainly come, but changed his mind overnight.

（2）昨天晚上他喝了酒以后，说了很多莫名其妙的话。

He had a lot to say after some drinks last night, all was strange and incomprehensible.

9. "**风风雨雨**"：成语。比喻困难、阻碍。多用于描写在一段较长时期中经历了很多困难。

"风风雨雨" is a metaphor for all the difficulties, problems and obstacles one has to go through in a period of time.

(1) 他们一辈子经历了很多风风雨雨，晚年倒生活得很幸福。

The couple went through a lot in their younger years; fortunately they found peace and happiness in their old age.

(2) 多少年共同经历的风风雨雨，使他们结下了深厚的友谊。

They stood together through thick and thin for many years. This is what formed their deep friendship.

10. "**有幸**"：意思是"很幸运"。

"有幸" means "very lucky or fortunate."

11. "**结识**"：意思是"认识并与之来往"。

"结识" means "got to know and became friends. The sentence "有幸结识了许许多多的好人" means "They had the luck of meeting and knowing a lot of wonderful people." Or "They were fortunate to have met and known many wonderful people."

语法 Grammar Notes

"**好歹**"："好歹"有几个意思，本课中"好歹"的意思是"无论如何"、"不管怎样"。这样的句子中常隐含着"不好"等某种负面意思。是口语。

"好歹" has different meanings when used in different contexts. It literally means "good or bad", "for better or worse". It is a colloquial expression used largely in spoken Chinese.

However，"好歹" used in the context of this story, it means "no matter what". It implies something negative in the meaning of the sentence. For example，in the story when 张母 said to her son：

(1) 好歹也是个大学生，什么样的对象找不着，犯得着跟一个钟点工轧马路么？

这个句子的意思是"张楠无论情况多不好（比如没有好工作），但是他还是一个大学生，什么样的对象都能找到……"

She meant to say, no matter how unsatisfactory the situation 张楠 is in, such as not having a great job or some other aspect of his life that is not so great，张楠 is still a college graduate (this is something that will never change) which carries a certain social prestige，he can still have any girlfriend he wants to.

(2) 有儿子在身边（虽然工作很忙），好歹也能照顾一点老人的生活。

Having a son living nearby〔even though he is very busy〕，he would be some help to his parents.

(3) 好歹也是四星级宾馆，条件不会太差。

For better or worse，it is a four-star hotel；the conditions can't be too bad.

练习 Exercises

■ 一、口语练习 Oral Practice

（一）回答下列问题 Answer the following questions：

1. 张楠和母亲是无话不谈的朋友吗？你怎么知道的？

2. 张母看不起叶小娟，是不是因为她怀疑叶小娟手脚不干净？

3. 张母说叶小娟"一肚子花花肠子"是什么意思？

4. 张倩和张楠对母亲对叶小娟的态度有什么看法？你是怎么知道的？

5. 张母是不是一个坏人？请举例说明。

6. 张母是个什么样的人？在你的生活中遇到过这种人吗？

7. 要是小娟没有男朋友，还待在北京，她和张楠最终会结婚吗？

8. 要是你是张楠，你会娶小娟吗？

■ 二、书写练习 Written Exercises

（一）用下列词语完成句子 Fill in the blanks with the words given

A. 世面	B. 结识	C. 由于	D. 至于	E. 敏感
F. 道理	G. 通过	H. 表示	I. 错怪	J. 不已

1. 我只是觉得，她身上有什么东西吸引我，_____ 是什么，我也搞不清。

2. 我想也许是_____工作上的原因吧，两个人对"信任"这两个字特别_____。

3. 我很怀念在北京打工的日子，它使我见了_____，懂得了许多做人的_____，也有幸_____了许许多多的好人。

4. 张母发现自己_____了这个钟点工，愧疚_____。她想_____北京热线节目向那个朴实而善良的农村姑娘叶小娟_____深深的歉意。

（二）选择题 Circle the answer which most reflects the meaning of the under-lined part in the following sentences

1. 小楠，别跟我打马虎眼。告诉你，再掉价，也不能娶个钟点工！

    A. 价钱再低

    B. 价格又低了

    C. 地位无论降到多低

    D. 价钱掉了

2. 哼！你还有脸跟我<u>急</u>？一个大学生犯得着跟一个钟点工轧马路吗？

    A. 着急

    B. 紧急

    C. 发脾气

    D. 急忙

3. 您<u>倒是问问</u>呀。

    A. 你问倒了

    B. 你为什么不倒着问

    C. 你为什么不问（她）呢

    D. 问错了

4. 我要与小娟说句话。不说一说，妈这辈子都<u>不安生</u>。

    A. 身体不好

    B. 心不安

    C. 生活不安全

    D. 生活不安定

5. 哎呀，行了！别老跟人家小钟点工<u>过不去</u>，干吗呀？

    （1）为难钟点工

    （2）不让钟点工进来

    （3）跟钟点工生气

    （4）找钟点工的麻烦

（三）完成句子 Substitute the underlined parts with your own phrases or sentences

1. 想得倒美，再怎么着，<u>张家的媳妇也轮不到她头上</u>！

    （1）说得倒好听，再怎么着，_____！

    （2）想得倒美，她再找不到男朋友，_____！

2. <u>好歹</u>也是个大学生，什么样的对象找不着？犯得着<u>跟一个钟点工轧马路吗</u>？

    （1）好歹_____，_____？犯得着_____？

3. 我没说错吧？他早就<u>对你动心思了</u>。

（1）我没说错吧？他早就＿＿＿＿＿＿＿＿＿＿＿＿＿＿＿＿。

（四）填空 Fill in the blanks with the words given

A. 吃里爬外	B. 实事求是	C. 指桑骂槐
D. 风风雨雨	E. 莫名其妙	F. 旁敲侧击

1. 经过多年的＿＿＿＿＿＿＿，他们的友情已经牢不可破了。

2. 他从没结过婚，突然出现了几个孩子，搞得大家＿＿＿＿＿＿＿。

3. 你可以直接问我是不是同性恋，不必＿＿＿＿＿＿＿。

4. 你爸爸是个直性子的人，跟谁过不去他就会指名道姓地说出来，从来不会＿＿＿＿＿＿＿。

5. 我付他工资，他却一心帮别的公司赚钱，这种＿＿＿＿＿＿＿的人我还能要吗？

6. 张楠跟姐姐可以＿＿＿＿＿＿＿地谈他对小娟的感觉，但是跟妈妈却不行。

（五）作文 Composition

1. 根据本剧写一篇叙述文（400字左右）。

Write a narrative of at least four hundred words based on the story.

2. 你对社会地位、经济条件、教育水平与爱情的关系有什么看法。

Write an essay to express your view on the relationship between love and social position, financial status and educational level.

第八课 电梯上的故事

The Elevator Incident

导 读：

中国有这么两个成语："众口铄金"和"人言可畏"。意思是说，舆论是很可怕的，谎话说的人多了，人们就很难不相信了。本剧的故事起源于电梯里一个男青年对一个女青年的一个不经意的小动作，结果被夸大，被渲染，闹得满城风雨。最后，那位女青年的丈夫怀疑妻子怀的不是自己的孩子，使这个小家庭解体；那位男青年的恋人也经不住流言蜚语的困扰而与他分手。

在我们旁观者看来，这个故事似乎有点可笑，其中有的人物很可悲。可是生活中这种事不会发生吗？如果你真爱一个人，你就应该相信他（她）。话人人都会说，但做起来就没有那么容易了。你说是这样吗？

Introduction:

There is an old Chinese saying："public clamor can confound right and wrong", another one is "Rumors kill people". They all mean that public opinion can be terrifying. A rumor that is repeated many times becomes truth. Here is a story to that effect.

It began with a young man who casually touched the collar of a young woman in a crowded elevator. Such a trivial act somehow became a subject of hot gossip. The rumor was eventually blown out of proportion and became a well-known scandal overnight. This incident led the husband of the young woman to suspect the paternity of the child his wife was carrying. This in turn caused the disintegration of their marriage. During which time the girlfriend of the young man, unable to bear with this constant rumor, also left him.

The audience may find this supposed tragedy laughable. But could it happen to us in real life? If you truly love someone, you ought to trust him/her. It is something that's easy said than done. Do you think so?

主要人物（Main Characters）

小宋	Xiǎo Sòng	a young woman surnamed Song
小罗	Xiǎo Luó	a young man surnamed Luo
苗苗	Miáomiao	Xiao Song's husband
都都	dūdu	Xiao Luo's girl friend
老者	Lǎozhě	a elderly gentleman

一

老　者：虽说上了**岁数**[N1]了，可我特别喜欢跟年轻人**扎堆**儿[N2]。经常聊，就听了许多的故事。这大千世界，无奇不有[N3]啊。有的听了叫人**快活**，有的简直[G1]是让人**啼笑皆非**[N4]。这不，……**晚报社**里**新近**就**闹**出这么一段儿故事。唉，怎么说呢？这个故事啊……

男　一：这破电梯真够呛[N5]，开门儿慢，跑得更慢，赶着上下班儿人多的时候层层都停，真够烦啊。

老者	lǎozhě	n.	an old man; the aged; elderly people
上岁数	shàng suìshu		getting on in age
扎堆儿	zhā duīr	vo.	hang out with a group of people
快活	kuàihuo	adj.	happy; joyful; cheerful
啼笑皆非	tí xiào jiē fēi		not knowing whethers to laugh or cry; between tears and smiles
晚报社	wǎnbào shè	n.	evening newspaper publisher
新近	xīnjìn	adv.	最近，recently; lately
闹	nào	v.	instigate; create

女　一：听说要装修了，不是要**更换**新电梯吗？

男　一：明年啦。

女　二：小宋，小宋！

小　宋：哎？

女　二：你今天怎么**打扮**得这么**漂亮**啊？啊？

小　宋：今天是我爱人的生日，我们**约**好了下班儿以后到**玛格菲斯**餐厅去庆祝一下。

女　二：玛格菲斯算什么呀，应该到**峰顺**吃**海鲜**。你们家那口子这几年在**广告部**不是干得挺**火**[N6]的吗？还这么**抠门**儿[N7]啊？

更换	gēnghuàn	v.	换，replace；change
打扮	dǎban	v.	do up；dress up；make up
漂亮	piàoliang	adj.	pretty
约	yuē	v.	make an appointment；arrange
玛格菲斯	Mǎgéfēisī	N.	name of a restaurant
峰顺	Fēngshùn	N.	Name of a restaurant
海鲜	hǎixiān	n.	seafood
广告部	guǎnggàobù	n.	advertising department
火	huǒ	adj.	do a roaring business
抠门儿	kōuménr	adj.	小气，吝啬，stingy；miserly

小　宋：啊？我们家苗苗可是个好同志，平时在广告部拼命给报社**创收**[N8]，自己却两**袖**清风[N9]，特正[N10]。

女　二：哎呀，**嘻嘻**……

小　罗：什么书啊？

男　二：《**肮脏**的手》。

小　罗：**瞅**[N11]你肮脏的**胡子**吧，也不**刮**刮。可看[N12]！

男　二：也太辛苦了吧！这一**顿煎饼馃子**[N13]就算**早餐**啦？

小　罗：哈，有面，有蛋，有**葱花**儿，有**排叉**儿[N14]，**营养**可以。天天都是**奶昔**、**雀巢**、**麦当劳**、**炸薯条**儿，怎么攒钱呀？哎，都都今天晚上就跟我去看**家具**。

男　二：呵，什么时候请大家吃**喜糖**呀？

小　罗：**指日可待**[N15]。

男　二：呵呵，哎呀，我还[G2]真看不出来，这都都可是咱们单位人见人爱的大美女，她怎么就看上你了呢？

创收	chuàngshōu	vo.	earn extra income
袖	xiù	n.	sleeve，两袖清风，(see note 9)
嘻	xī	ono.	giggle; laugh; sound of merry laughter
肮脏	āngzāng	adj.	脏，dirty; filthy
胡子	húzi	n.	beard
刮	guā	v.	shave
顿	dùn	m.	for meals
煎饼	jiānbing	n.	pancake; griddle cake
馃子	guǒzi	n.	油条，deep fried doughnut; twisted fritters
早餐	zǎocān	n.	breakfast
葱花儿	cōnghuār	n.	chopped shallot/scallion
排叉儿	páichàr	n.	fried snack that is thin and crisp
营养	yíngyǎng	n.	nutrition
奶昔	nǎixī	n.	milkshake
雀巢	Què cháo	N.	Nescafe
麦当劳	Màidāngláo	N.	McDonald's
炸薯条儿	zhá shǔtiáor	n.	French fries
家具	jiājù	n.	furniture
喜糖	xǐtáng	n.	wedding candy
指日可待	zhǐ rì kě dài		(something) can be expected soon，(see note 15)

小　罗：**嘘**！我很**丑**，可是我很温柔。**关键**是咱[N16] 在**副刊**干得十分**出色**，**待人接物**[N17] **富有魅力**。咱**幽默**，是**标准**的**味精**！

男　二：走吧。

小　罗：哎，**挤**一**挤**、**挤**一**挤**……我**个子**大，**分量**重，我出来。我……我也不差。小宋，你这**领子**应该翻在外头啊，还是缩在里头啊？

小　宋：哎，请放下你的手。

男　二：肮脏的手。

众　人：哈哈哈……

女　二：肮脏的手？哈哈……

众　人：**头条**ル**新闻**。

女　一：别说了，那么缺德，你们这帮人。

男　一：好好，**打住**[N18] 了、打住了，上班ル了、上班ル了。

嘘	xū	interj.	sigh; hiss
丑	chǒu	adj.	ugly; unsightly; hideous
关键	guānjiàn	n.	decisive factor, the most crucial; key
副刊	fùkān	n.	supplement (of newspaper)
出色	chūsè	adj.	excellent; remarkable; outstanding
待人接物	dài rén jiē wù		manner of dealing with people
富有	fùyǒu	v.	be full of；be rich in
魅力	mèilì	n.	charm; captivation; fascination; enchantment
幽默	yōumò	adj.	humorous
标准	biāozhǔn	n.	standard
味精	wèijīng	n.	味素，monosodium glutamate（MSG）
挤	jǐ	v./adj.	push; squeeze
个子	gèzi	n.	(of a human being or animal) height; build
分量	fèn·liàng	n.	weight; heft
领子	lǐngzi	n.	collar
条ル	tiáor	m.	for news
新闻	xīnwén	n.	news

注释 Notes

1. **"上了岁数"**：意思是"年纪大了"。

   "上了岁数" means "to be getting on in age."

2. **"扎堆儿"**：很多人聚在一起，常用于很多人喜欢在一起做某事。

   "扎堆儿" is a colloquial expression meaning "hanging out with a group of people".

   (1) 这个班的学生不喜欢扎堆儿，下了课，各自回自己的宿舍。

   Students in this class don't hang out together; they all go back to their respective dormitory once a class is over.

   (2) 你们不要扎堆儿，自己做自己的事情。

   Don't hang out with others now; get on with your own business.

3. **"大千世界，无奇不有"**："大千世界"意思是"广大的世界"，"无奇不有"意思是"没有什么奇怪的事是不存在的，什么奇怪的事都有"。"大千世界，无奇不有"常常一起用。意思是"世界很大，什么奇怪的事都有。"

   "大千世界" means "the vast or boundless universe", "无奇不有" means "there is no lack of strange things. "大千世界，无奇不有" are often used together to mean "The world is so huge; anything can happen".

4. **"啼笑皆非"**：意思是"哭也不是，笑也不是，不知道应该怎么样。"

   啼笑皆非 is used to describe a situation in which one doesn't know whether one should laugh or cry; It's also used to describe the feeling of finding something that's both funny and annoying, e. g.

   天黑了才找到她，我们累得都说不出话来了。她却说："路上的风景不错吧?"真叫我们啼笑皆非。

   We didn't find her until it was dark. Everyone was so tired that no one wanted to say a word; then she said："Is the scenery great?" Should we laugh or cry?

5. **"够呛"**：口语。意思是"够受的"，"让人受不了"。

   "够呛" is a colloquial expression meaning "unbearable", "can't stand" and "intolerable".

(1) 你这个人真够呛！

You are simply unbearable!

(2) 她累得够呛。

She was terribly tired.

6. **"火"**：口语，形容生意很好或歌星、影星等很受欢迎。

"火" literally means "fire", used colloquially to mean business that's thriving and flourishing. It can be also used to describe someone or something (such as one's business) is hot and popular.

7. **"抠门ᵧₗ"**：口语，意思是"小气、吝啬"。

"抠门ᵧₗ" is a colloquial expression referring to someone being stingy, miserly or tight with money.

(1) 我爸真抠门ᵧₗ，出门矿泉水也舍不得买一瓶。

My father is really tight with money; he wouldn't buy a bottle of mineral water when we go out.

(2) 他抠门ᵧₗ是有名的，别指望他请你喝茶。

He's well known for being stingy; don't count on him to invite you to a cup of tea.

8. **"创收"**：学校、科研机关等非营利单位利用自身的条件创造收入，使单位及其工作人员增加收入。

"创收" is a term used to describe such activities as schools or research institutes using its own advantage to create extra income for its employees.

9. **"两袖清风"**：形容做官清廉。

This idiom is used to describe an official who remains uncorrupt. E. g.

(1) 现在两袖清风的官不少，是因为法律很严厉。

Strict laws have made a lot of uncorrupt officials now.

(2) 他做了 25 年的市长，两袖清风，自己连一套房子都没有！

Being the Mayor of the city for twenty five years, he didn't even have a house in his name!

10. **"特正"**：口语，"特"意思是"特别"；"正"是"正派"，就是不做不应该做的事，这里是指不拿不该拿的钱。

"特正" is a colloquial expression, **"特"** means **"特别"**; **"正"** means honest and upright. The expression is used to describe someone who does not do what he should not do. In the context here, it means 苗苗 would not take money he did not earn.

11. "瞅"：口语，意思是"看"。

"瞅" is a colloquial term for "看".

12. "可看"：意思是"值得看"。

"可看" means "worth reading".

13. "煎饼馃子"："煎饼"是一种多用小米面烙成的薄饼，"馃子"通称"油条"。

"煎饼" is a kind of thin pancake made of millet flour，"馃子" is deep-fried dough sticks.

14. "排叉儿"：北京的一种很薄很脆的油炸食品。

"排叉儿" is a Beijing specialty—a fried snack that's thin and crisp.

15. "指日可待"：不久就可以实现。

"指日可待" means something can be expected soon，or something is just around the corner. E. g.

战争快结束了，你儿子回家指日可待了。

The War is near end，the day your son will return home is just around the corner.

16. "咱"："关键是咱在副刊干得十分出色，待人接物富有魅力。咱幽默，是标准的味精！"这里"咱"的意思是"我"。

"咱" in this sentence means "我".

17. "待人接物"：指与他人交往相处。例如：

待人接物 refers to "（one's）manner of dealing with people". E. g.

他在待人接物方面一向周到热情。

He's a man of manners；he always treats people with thoughtfulness and warmth.

18. "打住"：口语，意思是"停住"，"别说了"。

"打住" is a colloquial expression meaning "stop talking"；it should be only used in very informal situation.

语法 Grammar Notes

1. **"简直"**（副词）：意思是"完全或差不多"，常用于"差不多如此，但是并不是真的如此"的意思，因而有夸张的语气。

"简直" is an adverb, an emphatic expression meaning "simply; at all". It is used usually to modify descriptive words and phrases, which may imply exaggeration to indicate a higher degree. E. g.：

（1）他说他放弃上大学了，我简直不敢相信。（事实上还是相信了）

He said that he had given up college education, I simply couldn't believe it. (He in fact had accepted such a fact)

（2）这个人太坏了，简直不是人！（他还是人）

The man is so vile, he is an animal! (He of course is a human being)

（3）今年天气太反常了，夏天简直把人热死了，冬天又冷得冻死人。

The weather this year is so unusual, we almost died of the heat in summer, and then the temperature in winter freezes you to death.

"简直"有时表示完全如此：

Sometimes "简直" is also used to describe a real situation. E. g.

（4）昨天他简直把我气坏了，我几乎一夜没睡觉。

He got me so worked up yesterday that I almost didn't sleep all night.

2. **"还"**：语气副词，说话人对某事或某种情况有些出乎意料，有时含有感叹的语气。

"还" is a modal adverb used to indicate a slight surprise because of something that's not apparent or unexpected. It harbors certain sense of admiration.

（1）我还真看不出来，这都都可是咱们单位人见人爱的大美女，她怎么就看上你了呢？

Well, what a surprise! 都都 is a beauty loved by everyone around her, how could she have fallen in love with you?

（2）还真让你猜对了，我今天本来不想来。

Surprising，but you got it right；I indeed didn't want to come in the first place.

（3）这么好的大学，你还真考上了，不简单！

How remarkable，you have been accepted by such a wonderful university！

练习 Exercises

■ 一、口语练习 Oral Practice

（一）回答问题 Answer the following questions

1. 此剧开始时老者说了些什么？

2. 这个大楼的电梯怎么样？

3. 小宋今天看上去跟平常有什么不一样？

4. 今天是什么日子，小宋有什么打算？

5. 苗苗在哪儿工作？他是不是不太喜欢他的工作？

6. 小宋对丈夫苗苗的看法如何？

7. 小罗早餐吃什么？他是不是快结婚了？

8. 在小罗看来，都都这个人见人爱的大美女为什么就看上他了呢？

■ 二、书写练习 Written Exercises

（一）完成句子 Complete the following sentences

1. 用"简直"完成下列句子 Complete the following sentences with "简直"

（1）他们认识一个星期就结婚了，_____。

（2）又要工作，又要赶写论文，我_____。

（3）都都这个大美女怎么就看上小罗了呢？我_____。

2. 用"还"完成下列句子 Complete the following sentences with "还"

（1）我_____你们公司现在办得这么火！

（2）我_____你是这儿的总经理！

（3）这么难的问题你_____。

（二）选择题 Circle the answer which most reflects the meaning of the under-
lined part in the following sentences

1. 虽说上了岁数了，可我特别喜欢跟年轻人扎堆儿。

A. 我喜欢跟年轻人一起工作

B. 我不喜欢跟没上岁数的人聊天

C. 我怕老，所以喜欢跟年轻人在一起

　D. 我喜欢聊天，尤其喜欢跟年轻人一起聊天

2. 这大千世界，无奇不有啊。

　　A. 这个世界没有什么事是奇怪的

　　B. 这个世界什么奇怪的事都有

　　C. 这个世界没有什么奇怪的事

　　D. 这个世界奇怪的事看多了就不奇怪了

3. 这破电梯真够呛！

　　A. 电梯实在太破了

　　B. 这个电梯慢得真让人受不了

　　C. 电梯破了，不修危险

　　D. 这个电梯破得让人看了就烦

4. 玛格菲斯算什么呀。应该到峰顺吃海鲜。

　　A. 玛格菲斯是什么饭馆？吃海鲜最好到峰顺

　　B. 玛格菲斯是太贵了，峰顺比玛格菲斯又好吃又便宜

　　C. 玛格菲斯不是最贵的饭馆，峰顺比玛格菲斯更贵

　　D. 玛格菲斯的菜不怎么样，你们应该到峰顺吃海鲜

5. 你们家那口子这几年在广告部不是干得挺火的吗？

　　A. 你们家那口子工作的广告部热得很

　　B. 你们家那口子在广告部常发脾气

　　C. 你们家那口子这几年在广告部工作干得很成功

　　D. 你们家那口子这几年在广告部干挺火的工作

（三）选择适当的语句完成下列对话 Fill in the blanks with appropriate expressions

A. 啼笑皆非	B. 扎堆儿	C. 够呛	D. 火
E. 抠门儿	F. 那口子	G. 特正	H. 还

1. 我不喜欢跟_____的人交往。

2. "电梯上的故事"真是让人_____。

3. 小罗是个爱热闹的人，就喜欢_____，哪儿人多去哪儿。

4. 去年北京热得_____。

5. 我_____真看不出来，你这么能干！

6. 他人_____，没人能说出他的不好。

7. 这个电影明星几年前_____得很，现在不行了。

8. 你们家＿＿＿＿＿＿＿＿接人待物没话说，非常周到。

（四）写作 Composition

此剧开始时的一段话借一老者之口说出，为什么不用一位年轻的姑娘呢？对此，你有什么看法？

The Introduction to the story is said by an elderly man，why not by a young woman. What's your opinion on this?

二

男　三：等苗苗呢？

小　宋：啊。

女　三：哎，小宋，今天穿这么漂亮啊？

男　四：等苗苗呢？

小　宋：啊。

女　二：哎，小宋，你今天打扮得真漂亮。

男　二：等苗苗呢？

小　宋：啊。

苗　苗：啊，哎、哎……好咧、好咧。东哥，再见啊，打电话联系。

小　宋：哎，走吧。

苗　苗：那肮脏的**手摸**你哪儿了？

小　宋：你说什么呀？

苗　苗：还我说什么^{G1}？报社都**传开了**，谁不知道啊。

小　宋：你……

苗　苗：行了行了……不至于紧张成这样啊。

小　宋：他只不过是摸了一下我的衬衣的领子。

苗　苗：哎，行了行了，我又^{G2}没说他摸你别的地方儿了。

小　宋：那……那咱们还去玛格菲斯餐厅吗？

苗　苗：去啊，干嘛不去啊？不能因为一个小罗，就**扫了**咱俩的**兴**^{N1}了。上车。我看，还是你点吧。来。

小　宋：哦，还是老**规矩**，你来点吧，我什么都行。

摸	mō	v.	touch; feel; stroke
传开（了）	chuán kāi（le）	vc.	spread out
扫兴	sǎo xìng	vo.	disappointing
规矩	guīju	n.	established practice; established standard，rule or habit

苗　苗：啊，**火腿沙拉**，**黄油鸡卷**ₙ，**奶油椰茸汤**，**咖喱牛里脊**，法式……**烤鱼**，德国土豆**甜饼**，还要两个**苹果派**，一个汤，一个水，一个**椰汁**。

服务生：好了，请您稍等。

苗　苗：听他们说，小罗是你同学，是吧？

小　宋：哎？怎么是我同学呀？我八八届，他九一届，差了好几届呢，而且又不是一个系的，我学**管理**，他学中文呀。

苗　苗：他们都说你们俩挺熟的。

小　宋：谁说的呀？我们俩在一个楼层里上班，有的时候见面就是**打个招呼**，而且小罗这个人，平时很随便，**嘻嘻哈哈**的。我本来就有点儿看不惯他。

苗　苗：呵呵，你干嘛这样啊？我就是趁着^G3 上菜没事ₙ，跟你随便说说，呵，你还大**贬人**一顿。不要**欲盖弥彰**^N2 嘛。

小　宋：你**胡说八道**些什么呀？

火腿	huǒtuǐ	n.	ham, salted leg of pork
沙拉	shālā	n.	salad
黄油	huángyóu	n.	butter
鸡卷ₙ	jījuǎnr	n.	chicken roll
奶油	nǎiyóu	n.	cream
椰茸汤	yēróngtāng	n.	coconut soup
咖喱	gā·lí	n.	curry
里脊	lǐji	n.	tenderloin〔lean meat taken from under the spinal column of a hog or a cow〕
烤鱼	kǎoyú	n.	baked fish
甜饼	tiánbǐng	n.	pie
苹果派	píngguǒpài	n.	apple pie
椰汁	yēzhī	n.	coconut juice
服务生	fúwùshēng	n.	waiter; server
届	jiè	m.	graduating classes
管理	guǎnlǐ	v.	manage; in charge of; run
打招呼	dǎ zhāohu	vo.	(by words or gestures) greet sb. say hello
嘻嘻哈哈	xīxi hāhā	adj.	not serious; laughing and joking; mirthful
贬人	biǎn rén	vo.	put someone down; belittle
欲盖弥彰	yù gài mí zhāng		try to cover up a misdeed only to make it more conspicuous
胡说八道	húshuō bā dào		talk nonsense or drivel; random talk; unsubstantial or irrational words; similar to 信口胡说

苗　苗：**大庭广众**^{N3}之下，他就**敢**摸你，呵，成何**体统**^{N4}啊？再说当时电梯里边儿，也不完全是你一个女的，他怎么不敢摸别人？是不是你**鼓励纵容**他了？

小　宋：你……我怎么鼓励他啦？我说了什么**挑逗**他的话了吗？你找个证人啊！

苗　苗：呵呵呵……其实有时候挑逗不完全**限于**语言，有时候一个眼神儿、一个小动作，更刺激人。

小　宋：你这是以小人之心度**君子之腹**^{N5}！

小　罗：这一款满意吗？**清凉**清凉！这就交订金。

（歌词：深深的海洋／你为何不平静？／不平静就像我爱人／那一颗**动摇**的心……）

都　都：你先回去吧，一会儿我去书店看看。

小　罗：买什么书？**时装**杂志还是**港台**小说？

都　都：原来我在你眼中就只会读这种书啊？我比不上你。我是个电大生，在报社里只是一个小小的打字员儿。**怪不得**你对我，**用情不专**^{N6}。

小　罗：这是从何说起？这、这是从何说起嘛？

都　都：你自己心里清楚。

小　罗：我清楚？好，我清楚。你说吧，想买什么书我陪你去。书名儿什么？

大庭广众	dà tíng guǎng zhòng		(before) a big crowd;（on）a public occasion
敢	gǎn	v.	dare; have the courage
体统	tǐtǒng	n.	decorum; propriety; decency
鼓励	gǔlì	v.	encourage
纵容	zòngróng	v.	connive; wink at
挑逗	tiǎodòu	v.	provoke; tease; flirt
限于	xiànyú	v.	be confined to; be limited to; be restricted at
君子	jūnzǐ	n.	gentleman; man of honor
腹	fù	n.	belly; abdomen; stomach
清凉	qīngliáng	adj.	cool and refreshing; cool and pleasant
动摇	dòngyáo	v.	turmoil; turbulent;（social or political）unrest
时装	shízhuāng	n.	fashion; vogue; latest fashion
港台	Gǎng Tái	n.	Hong Kong and Taiwan
怪不得	guài bu de	vc.	no wonder, that explains why; so that's why
用情不专	yòng qíng bù zhuān		(of a woman) of easy virtue; promiscuous;（of a man）skirt chaser,（see note 6）

都　都：《肮脏的手》。

小　罗：肮、肮……哎，都都，都都，是谁告诉你那件事儿的？

都　都：我是不会**出卖**朋友的。

小　罗：你不敢说，也说不出是谁。

都　都：这还用说吗？整个报社的人都知道了，传得**沸沸扬扬**[N7]的。

小　罗：哎，都都，你知道《肮脏的手》是一本儿什么书吗？

都　都：肮脏的手，**顾名思义**[N8]，就是说那些男男女女乌七八糟[N9]的事儿呗。

小　罗：呵，都都，你怎么能往那上想呢？怪不得，今天"深深的海洋"变得如此不平静。**人言可畏**[N10]呀！可恨，可气，可笑！我亲爱的都都，这个《肮脏的手》啊，是法国**存在主义**作家**萨特**写的，是写**政治斗争**的。

出卖	chūmài	v.	betray
沸沸扬扬	fèifèiyángyáng		a hubbub, noisy scene,（see note 7）
顾名思义	gù míng sī yì		just as its name implies,（see note 8）
乌七八糟	wū qī bā zāo		a horrible mess; a place in great disorder; things that are obscene, dirty and filthy,（see note 9）
人言可畏	rén yán kě wèi		rumor kills people,（see note 10）
存在主义	cúnzài zhǔyì		existentialism
萨特	Sàtè	N.	Sartre (Jean-Paul Sartre, French Existentialist)
政治	zhèngzhì	n.	politics
斗争	dòuzhēng	n.	struggle

都　都：真的呀？

小　罗：嗯。

都　都：那他们为什么把这个书名用在你的身上呀？

小　罗：开玩笑呗。咱报社的人都爱开玩笑。

都　都：可不管怎么说，你今天总是摸了小宋一下。你敢说不承认？

小　罗：承认。

都　都：你敢说不是？

小　罗：有！是！不过当时，她那两个领子吧，有点儿矛盾，特别不**协调**，挺**别扭**的。我也是**无意之间**碰了她一下。你不想想，当着那么多人的面儿，我神经有毛病呀？**众目睽睽**[N11]的，对人女同志动手动脚[N12]。就算我喜欢她，我也不能暗的不来来[N13]明的呀。

都　都：你不骗我？

小　罗：不骗。

都　都：那骗我是什么？

小　罗：小狗儿呗。

都　都：你都说了好几次了。

协调	xiétiáo	adj./v.	coordinate；balanced；harmonious；in turn
别扭	bièniu	adj.	awkward
无意之间	wúyì zhī jiān		not intend to；inadvertently
众目睽睽	zhòng mù kuíkuí		under the gaze of people；in the public eye；stared at by a lot of people，(see note 11)

注释 Notes

1. "扫……兴"：正在高兴的时候遇到不高兴的事，使兴致低落下来。

   "扫兴" mean literally to sweep away one's cheerful spirit. It is used here to mean "having one's spirit dampened" or "feeling disappointed".

   （1）这次聚会要是你不去就会扫大家的兴。

   Everyone would be disappointed if you were not there.

   （2）星期天我们刚到长城就下雨了，真扫兴！

   It started raining as soon as we arrived at the Great Wall. What a disappointment!

2. "欲盖弥彰"："欲"意思是"要"，"盖"意思是"掩盖"，"弥"意思是"更加"，"彰"意思是"明显"。"欲盖弥彰"的意思是"想要掩盖事实的真相，结果使真相更加明显。"

   "欲" means "wish or desire", "盖" means "to cover up", "弥" means "even more" and "彰" means "obvious". The idiom "欲盖弥彰" means "Try to cover up a misdeed only to make it more conspicuous".

   （1）我知道你喜欢她，何必还说她不好呢，这不是欲盖弥彰吗？

   I know you are very fond of her, Why do you have to bad-mouth her, it only proves that you're thinking of her all the time.

   （2）你犯下这么严重的罪行，还要诬蔑陷害别人，企图转移我们的视线，结果欲盖弥彰。

   You committed such a serious crime, but still try to incriminate others in order to distract our attention; it has only made you more conspicuous.

3. "大庭广众"：意思是"人很多的公开场合"。

   "大庭广众" refers to a public place with a lot of people.

   （1）这个小偷竟敢在大庭广众之下偷东西。

   This thief dared to steal in broad daylight.

   （2）他竟在大庭广众之下打他的太太。

   He dared to beat up his wife in public.

4. **"成何体统"**："何"意思是"什么"，"体统"意思是"体制、规矩"等。"成何体统"有反问的语气，意思是不成体统。

"何" means "什么"，"体统" means "decorum"，"propriety" or "decency". "成何体统" is used to express one's disapproval of things someone has said or done as most improper and downright outrageous.

(1) 男女未婚同居，成何体统！

It is downright outrageous to live together without being married!

(2) 家里的事，孩子说了算，成何体统！

It is outrageously improper to let children make all the decisions for the family!

5. **"以小人之心度君子之腹"**："以"意思是"用"，"小人"指"卑鄙的人"，"度"意思是"衡量"。"以小人之心度君子之腹"的意思是"用自己不好的想法去揣度别人的心思、想法。"

"以" means "using"，"小人" refers to "vile character；villain；mean man"，"度" means "to measure，to think". This expression means to "gauge a gentleman with one's own mean measure". Or "think negatively of others because of one's own mean-spiritedness."

(1) A：老高提升了，你不服气吧？

Mr. Gao got a promotion, you aren't very happy about it, are you?

B：他提升了我为他高兴。你别以小人之心度君子之腹！

I am happy for him. Don't you think negatively of me because of your own mean-spiritedness!

(2) 他自己用情不专，还以为别人跟他太太有什么特别的关系，这真是以小人之心度君子之腹！

He is a skirt chaser, but constantly suspects his wife of being unfaithful；it only confirms he is a mean spirited man.

6. **"用情不专"**：主要指对男女之间的感情不专一。

"用情不专" describes an unfaithful lover who is a philanderer or a flirt.

她明知丈夫用情不专，可是还一心一意地爱着他。

She knows for sure that her husband has been unfaithful，but she still loves him with all her passion.

7. **"沸沸扬扬"**：像沸腾的开水一样喧闹，多指议论纷纷。

"沸沸扬扬" describes a hubbub, noisy scene. It is often about something that is sensational or scandalous that everyone is talking about.

这部新电影出来以前，媒体就炒得沸沸扬扬了，现在看了，也并不怎么样。

There had been so much publicity in the press before the movie hit the theater, now we've seen it; it's merely another so-so movie.

8. **"顾名思义"**：意思是"看到名称就会想出它的含义。"

It literally means "see the name, know the meaning" or just as its name implies.

"鲁迅故居"，顾名思义是鲁迅以前住过的地方。

鲁迅故居 means the place 鲁迅 once lived as the name clearly implies.

9. **"乌七八糟"**：十分杂乱，乱七八糟，常用于描写人做不正当甚至下流的事情。

"乌七八糟" is used to describe a horrible mess, a place in great disorder. It is also often used to describe things that are illegal, obscene, dirty, and filthy.

(1) 公司才让他管理了半年多，就搞得乌七八糟了。

The company is now in a horrible mess after he took it over barely half a year ago.

(2) 他专写一些男男女女乌七八糟的书，还发财了！

Well, believed it or not, he's made a fortune writing pornographic books.

10. **"人言可畏"**："人言"意思是"人们说的话，指流言蜚语"，"畏"意思是"怕"。"人言可畏"的意思是"流言蜚语是很可怕的"。

"人言" means "what people say", but it usually means rumors or gossip. "畏" means "fear". "人言可畏" essentially means "Rumors kill people."

丈夫死了以后她从来不跟男人接触，怕人说闲话。她知道人言可畏。

Worried about being hurt by malicious rumors, she would not dare to have anything to do with a man.

11. **"众目睽睽"**：意思是"大家的眼睛都注视着。"用于在大家的注视下做不好的事。

"众目睽睽" means "stared at by a lot of people". It is used to describe a scene where an unlawful or a morally degenerated act is carried out in the public eye.

(1) 那个小偷胆儿真大，竟敢在众目睽睽之下把一个博物馆的花瓶装进包里拿走了！

That thief was really downright audacious; he put a museum vase in his bag while everyone was staring at him and run away with it from the museum!

（2）他俩才不管别人怎么想呢，他们常常在众目睽睽之下亲吻拥抱，旁若
无人。

They couldn't care less what other people think; they often kiss and hug in public.

12. **"动手动脚"**：多指男人对女人有骚扰的行为。

"动手动脚" is used often to describe improper behavior a man inflicts on a woman.

（1）听说他喜欢对一些年轻姑娘动手动脚。你要防着他。

I heard that he likes to take advantage of young women; you ought to be careful of him.

（2）他只是说说而已，从不敢动手动脚。

He only talks dirty, but never dared to act.

13. **"来"**：代替动词。

" 来" is a substitute for a particular verb in a sentence.

（1）就算我喜欢她，我也不能暗的不来来明的呀。

这句话的意思是："就算是我喜欢她，我也不会不在暗中做而当着众
人的面做呀。"

This sentence means: "Even if I had been fond of her, I wouldn't have showed it in public while doing nothing in private."

（2）蛋糕我做不好，你来吧。

I don't know how to bake a cake, why don't you do it.

语法 Grammar Notes

1. **"还"**："还（说）我说什么。报社都传开了，谁不知道啊。"见《风波》第一部分语法注释 3。

   See grammar note 3 of part 1 in《风波》.

2. **"又"**：副词，加强否定的语气。

   "又" is an adverb; it's used to emphasize the negation.

   (1) 哎，行了行了，我又没说他摸你别的地方儿了。

   Oh，enough! Did I say he actually touched another part of your body?

   (2) 别担心，老师又没说你今年毕不了业。

   Don't worry. The teacher didn't say that you couldn't graduate this year. Did he?

   (3) 你想去就去吧，我又没拦着你。

   Go if you insist; am I standing in your way?

3. **"趁着"**（介词）。

   "趁着" means "at an opportune moment" or "take an opportunity; take advantage of".

   (1) 趁着去北京开会的机会，我去看了几个朋友。

   I visited a couple of friends while attending the conference in Beijing.

   (2) 趁着老师没来，咱们再复习一下今天要考的生词吧。

   Since the teacher hasn't arrived，why don't we do some more review on the new words that will be tested today?

   (3) 我趁着太太没注意，从她钱包里拿了 100 块钱。

   I took ＄100 from my wife's purse while she wasn't looking.

练习 Exercises

■ 一、口语练习 Oral Practice

（一）回答问题 Answer the following questions

1. 为什么这么多人都跟小宋打招呼？
2. 小宋跟小罗是同班同学吗？
3. 小宋跟小罗是怎么认识的？她对小罗的印象如何？
4. 苗苗为什么说小宋欲盖弥彰？
5. 苗苗对这一传闻是怎么想的？
6. 小宋为什么说苗苗胡说八道？
7. 苗苗都说了些什么？
8. 小罗为什么说"人言可畏"？
9. 在都都看来，什么样的人看时装杂志？
10. 小罗到底为什么摸小宋的领子？

（二）学生分成组饰演小宋跟苗苗、小罗跟都都的对话。

Pair students up to act out the dialogue between "小宋和苗苗" and "小罗和都都"。

■ 二、书写练习 Written Exercises

（一）完成句子 Complete the following sentences

1. 上星期就说好了＿＿＿＿＿＿，没想到下雨了＿＿＿＿＿
＿＿＿＿＿（扫兴）。
2. ＿＿＿＿＿＿＿把家里的酒都喝了。（趁）
3. 输了球＿＿＿＿＿＿，你有病吧。（还）
4. ＿＿＿＿＿＿＿，你干吗不理人家呢？（又）
5. 我认为现在＿＿＿＿＿＿。（用情不专）
6. 这种＿＿＿＿＿＿她是不会看的。（乌七八糟）
7. ＿＿＿＿＿＿＿。（成何体统）

（二）用下列词语造句 Make sentences with the following expressions

    1. 欲盖弥彰

    2. 以小人之心度君子之腹

    3. 顾名思义

    4. 人言可畏

（三）用适当的成语填空 Fill in blanks with appropriate idiom

A. 人言可畏	B. 啼笑皆非	C. 欲盖弥彰
D. 两袖清风	E. 沸沸扬扬	F. 顾名思义

    1. 那个明星的一点私事_____地闹了两年。

    2. 这人一天到晚丢三落四，还总说自己工作最认真，真让人_____。

    3. 现在的干部 _____ 的有很多。

    4.《电梯上的故事》这个短剧真是让我觉得_____。

    5. "Bathroom"，_____ 是洗澡的屋子。

    6. 不要胡扯了，你都做了什么事，就老老实实地说了吧，免得_____。

（四）写作 Composition

    1. 苗苗为什么说小宋欲盖弥彰？他对这一传闻是怎么想的？

    Why did Miaomiao say that Xiao Song's explanation would only make her more conspicuous? What does Miaomiao think of the incident and the rumor?

    2. 小罗为什么说人言可畏？你对这一说法有什么看法？

    Why did Xiao Luo say "rumors kill people"? What's your opinion on such a saying?

小　宋：咳……

苗　苗：怎么？怎么了你？媳妇儿，你怎么一下子变得这么有用？你说咱俩结婚这么多年了，一直都想要孩子，可怎么折腾也折腾不出一个孩子来。看病，吃药，你怨我，我怨你……咱们俩都流了不少**眼泪**。

小　宋：就是。那时候，我们还商量着要去**抱养**一个孩子。还说，是到医院去**领**呢，还是到农村去找。

苗　苗：真是啊，有心**栽**花儿花儿不开，无心**插柳**柳成**荫**[N1]。送子娘娘[N2]跟咱们俩开玩笑呢。呵呵……

小　宋：哎，不许动。

苗　苗：我听听，有没有**动静**儿。

小　宋：哎呀，行啦。八字还没一**撇**儿[N3]呢。

苗　苗：哎呀，呵呵……

小　宋：哎哎……手洗洗。你这手摸这儿摸那儿的，脏不脏啊？酸吧？

苗　苗：你到底怎么**怀**上的呀？有没有什么特殊的感觉？

小　宋：问你自己。

苗　苗：是得问问。哎哟，是得问问哪。你说我……我就觉得没跟平常有什么不一样的。怎么就给怀上了呢？哎，媳妇儿，那个事儿，问得不对，别生气啊。

（画外音：肮脏的手。**哈哈哈**……）

眼泪	yǎnlèi	n.	tears
抱养	bàoyǎng	v.	领养，adopt
领（养）	lǐng (yǎng)	v.	adopt
栽	zāi	v.	plant; grow
插	chā	v.	transplant; insert
柳	liǔ	n.	willow (Salix)
荫	yīn	n.	(of a place) sheltered by green foliage of trees
动静	dòngjing	n.	sound; voice; movement; activity
撇儿	piěr	n.	left falling stroke (in Chinese calligraphy)
怀	huái	v.	become pregnant
哈哈哈	hā hā hā	ono.	sound of laughing

苗　　苗：这孩子……不是小罗的**种**吧？

小　　宋：你……

苗　　苗：哎哎哎……你看……你看你，我都说过了，我说错了，你也别生气。

小　　宋：你**竟然**这样想。

苗　　苗：你总得让我**实话实说**吧。你刚刚一说这手，我这心里边儿……我不说
我心里边儿**憋**得难受。

小　　宋：如果你真有**胆量**的话，就应该去找……

苗　　苗：好了好了，对不起，算我**信口胡说**。我可能是**大喜过望**了，我老不相
信这样儿的好事儿会落在我头上。

小　　宋：**呜呜**……

种	zhǒng	n.	seed, sperm
竟然	jìngrán	adv.	to one's surprise; unexpectedly
实话实说	shí huà shí shuō		speak the plain truth; speak frankly; talk straight
憋	biē	v.	suppress; hold back; hold (breath)
胆量	dǎnliàng	n.	courage; guts
信口胡说	xìn kǒu hú shuō		talk irresponsibly; wag one's tongue too freely
大喜过望	dà xǐ guò wàng		overjoyed
呜	wū	ono.	sound of weeping

都　都：说吧，我看你还有什么可解释的？那本《肮脏的手》我已经见到了。

小　罗：看完啦？

都　都：嗯，算是看完了。

小　罗：读后感如何呀？

都　都：没全看懂。可是和你上次跟我说的，有很大的出入。你**糊弄**我是吧？最关键的，哎，人为什么要把那个名字安在你的身上？

小　罗：我真想给你弄瓶**镇静剂灌**下去。

都　都：哼，好**狠**哪。

小　罗：这是幽默嘛。

都　都：幽默？幽默也不能赶走我的**屈辱**。

小　罗：哎哟，好了，都都，给我闭上你的小臭**嘴**。你什么时候才能成熟起来？

都　都：哎呀，我也希望我成熟一点儿，好看清你的肮脏**本质**。

小　罗：你这句话分量有多重……你知道不知道？

都　都：可我总觉得你跟她……反正我就觉得别扭。

小　罗：都都，你心里应该有**一杆秤**，一边是我真实的为人，另一边是别人的玩笑。那，就算是——谣言，**别有用心的恶毒攻击**，你还不清楚吗？

都　都：有人说要带我去享受**休闲生活**的。

小　罗：我不享受……

都　都：啊？

小　罗：还能是谁呀？走吧。

都　都：哎呀，你干吗呀，你？

糊弄	hùnong		fool; deceive
镇静剂	zhènjìngjì	n.	sedative; tranquilizer
灌	guàn	v.	drink by force; pour into
狠	hěn	adj.	ruthless; relentless
屈辱	qūrǔ	adj.	shame; humiliation; indignity
嘴	zuǐ	n.	mouth
本质	běnzhì	n.	nature
一杆秤	yì gǎn chèng		a steelyard
别有用心	bié yǒu yòng xīn		have an ulterior motive; have an axe to grind
恶毒	èdú	adj.	venomous; vicious; malicious
攻击	gōngjī	v.	attack
休闲生活	xiūxián shēnghuó		leisurely life

小　罗：以后不许跟我闹了啊。

都　都：我就闹。我就闹、我就闹……

小　罗：再闹我打你**屁股**……

都　都：哎呀，**救命**呀……

　　　　（画外音：肮脏的手……）

服务生：您要的酒。

苗　苗：哦，搁这儿。谢谢。

服务生：不客气。

小　宋：你不该这样**疑神疑鬼**[N4]的。弄得我怀了孩子好像犯了罪一样。

苗　苗：哎呀，最近不知道是怎么了。烦死了。可能得了**忧郁症**、得了**强迫症**了吧。我觉得我都快被**折磨疯**了。

小　宋：照你这么下去，等孩子生下来，说不定你会把他**掐**死。

苗　苗：会的，有这可能。我控制不住自己。**呸**、**呸**……我肯定能控制自己。我吃**西洋参**，我吃**镇定**药，我吃安定片儿……我……我借愁浇酒[N5]。

　　　　（画外音：肮脏的手……）

小　罗：都都，怎么啦？人家小朋友跟你说"阿姨好"呢。

都　都：小朋友好。

小　孩：阿姨再见。

小　罗：再见。

屁股	pìgu	n.	buttocks；backside；butt
救命	jiù mìng	vo.	Help! Somebody help!
疑神疑鬼	yí shén yí guǐ		be terribly suspicious
犯罪	fàn zuì	vo.	commit crime
忧郁症	yōuyùzhèng	n.	depression
强迫症	qiángpòzhèng		force；compel
折磨	zhé•mó	v.	torment；persecute；excruciate
疯	fēng	v.	mad；insane；crazy
掐	qiā	v.	pinch；clutch；strangle
呸	pēi	interj.	pah；bah；pooh；boo (expressing disdain, annoyance or disapproval)
西洋参	xīyángshēn	n.	American ginseng (Panax quinquefolium)
镇定	zhèndìng	adj.	calm，cool，composed

小　罗：吃点儿什么？服务员儿小姐。

苗　苗：肮脏的手。

小　宋：哎，苗苗。

苗　苗：怎么了你？心疼啦？

都　都：你说谁呢？

苗　苗：说谁你清楚啊，戴**眼镜**儿那个**伪君子**。

都　都：你别诬陷人。小罗，**教训**教训他，他也太狂了。

小　罗：苗苗，咱们都是同事，有什么话咱们以后好好谈。

苗　苗：**软弱**？心里有**鬼**[N6]，心虚了吧，你？

小　宋：哎呀，苗苗，不许你胡说八道。

苗　苗：哎哟，太能说明问题了。你终于敢出来替这个**不知廉耻**的**家伙维护**了？

老　板：要不要打 110 [N7]？

都　都：你？我终于明白了，你为什么不敢教训他。你心里有鬼，你心虚。

苗　苗：甭跟我**兜圈子**[N8]，其实你这么**袒护**那姓罗的，我是个男人，我可以再原谅你一次。这样，要不然我重新……要不然你把孩子给我打掉！

小　宋：世界上竟有你这么**狠心**的父亲，这么**冷酷**的丈夫！

苗　苗：你可以再生第二个，才能证明那孩子确实是我的！

小　宋：**卑鄙**！

小　罗：都都，都都，你听我说嘛。

眼镜	yǎnjìng	n.	eye glasses, spectacles
伪君子	wěijūnzǐ	n.	hypocrite; dissembler
教训	jiàoxun	v.	teach (sb. a lesson); lecture (sb.)
软弱	ruǎnruò	adj.	weak; feeble; flabby
鬼	guǐ	n.	ghost
不知廉耻	bù zhī liánchǐ		have no sense of shame
家伙	jiāhuo	n.	fellow; guy (derogatory)
维护	wéihù	v.	protect; uphold
兜圈子	dōu quānzi	vo.	beat around the bush
袒护	tǎnhù	v.	be partial to
狠心	hěnxīn	adj.	cruel-hearted; heartless
冷酷	lěngkù	adj.	callous; grim; merciless
卑鄙	bēibǐ	adj.	despicable; contemptible; mean

都　都：你**撒手**。

小　罗：你听我说，我完全可以把他**揍趴**下，但是我不能。他可以当众**侮辱**我，
　　　　我能像他那样吗？我能以其人之道还治其人之身[N9]吗？好了，都都，人
　　　　的一生他不可能把自己的每一个动作都设计得**完美无缺**[N10]呀！我……

外国人：Excuse me, how to go to the … market?

小　罗：呃，go to the straight.

外国人：OK.

小　罗：呃，right.

外国人：OK. Thank you very much.

小　罗：呃，Thank you. 他……他问我……那个……哎，**青鸟**商场在哪儿，我告
　　　　诉他往前走向右拐。好了，都都，让一切都过去吧。啊？咱们定的家具
　　　　马上就要送来了，咱们还得打报告、开**证明**、准备结婚呢，我的好
　　　　夫人。

都　都：你别开玩笑了，谁是你夫人？

小　罗：你、你是啊。你是我一定能**成熟**起来、**坚强**起来的好夫人哪。

都　都：我不想结婚了。

小　罗：三年的花前月下[N11]，**山盟海誓**[N12]，却**抵不过**别人的**蜚短流长**[N13]。如此
　　　　不堪一击[N14]的爱情……

都　都：我不知道，我真的不知道……可我现在不想结婚。

撒手	sā shǒu	vo.	放开手，let go；give up
揍	zòu	v.	打，beat；hit；strike
趴	pā	v.	lie face down；lie on one's stomach
侮辱	wǔrǔ	v.	insult
完美无缺	wánměi wú quē		perfect
青鸟	qīngniǎo	n.	bird (Blue jay)
证明	zhèngmíng	n.	prove
夫人	fū·rén	n.	madam；wife
成熟	chéngshú	adj.	mature
坚强	jiānqiáng	adj.	strong；firm；staunch
山盟海誓	shān méng hǎi shì		couple's pledge of love as long lasting as the mountains and the seas；a solemn vows and pledges of love
抵不过	dǐ bu guò	vc.	not able to resist
蜚短流长	fēi duǎn liú cháng		gossip
不堪一击	bù kān yī jī		collapse at the first blow

小　罗：你是不是还想再等等啊？等到有一天，我**原形毕露**[N15]，或者找到你更
　　　　中意的……

都　都：我**看不透**你，我真的看不透你。

小　罗：**缺乏幽默感**的女人实在是太**可悲**了。都都，我祝你幸福。

原形毕露	yuán xín bì lù		show one's true colors; be revealed for what one really is
中意	zhòng yì	adj.	be to someone's liking; catch one's fancy
看不透	kàn bu tòu	vc.	cannot see through
缺乏	quēfá	v.	lack; be short of
幽默感	yōumògǎn	n.	sense of humor
可悲	kěbēi	adj.	sad; lamentable; deplorable

注释 Notes

1. **"有心栽花花不开，无心插柳柳成荫"**：意思是"有意要做的事没有做成，无意之间做的事竟成功了。"

   This expression is similar to the expression "hit a mark by a fluke"; meaning one failed at what he had set up to do, but succeeded in something else unexpectedly.

   他原想通过翻译提高自己的英文水平以便找工作，没想到他的翻译工作越做越成功，翻译竟成了他的职业。这真是"有心栽花花不开，无心插柳柳成荫。"

   His original idea of doing some translation work is to improve his English in order to find a job more easily. Much to his surprise, however, his translation work became so successful that it eventually became his real profession. This is really "有心栽花花不开，无心插柳柳成荫。"

2. **"送子娘娘"**：能给人送来儿子的女神。

   "送子娘娘" is the goddess who brings people sons.

3. **"八字还没有一撇儿呢"**："八"字连第一笔（撇）都还没写，意思是"事情还没开始，更谈不上有结果。"

   "八字还没有一撇儿呢" literally means "The character "八" is still missing a stroke", used to mean "premature", "nothing has been achieved" or "the work hasn't started".

   他想办个广告公司，八字还没有一撇儿呢，就嚷嚷得全世界都知道了！

   He wants to set up an advertising company, nothing has been done yet but the whole world has all heard about it!

4. **"疑神疑鬼"**：形容一个人多疑。

   "疑神疑鬼" is used to describe an overly-suspicious person.

   (1) 你这个人一天到晚疑神疑鬼的，是不是有毛病？

   　　You are suspicious of everything around you all the time, are you sick?

   (2) 你别疑神疑鬼的，老板不会叫你离开公司！

   　　You wouldn't loose your job〔The boss wouldn't ask you to leave the company〕, don't be so overly suspicious.

5. **"借愁浇酒"**：正确的说法应该是"借酒浇愁"，即用喝酒的方法来缓解忧愁，后边通常有"愁更愁"，意思是"借酒浇愁不但不能缓解忧愁，而会更加忧愁。"

"借酒浇愁" means "To drink one's worries away". It is used to describe someone who takes refuge in alcohol to forget about one's problems or seeks refuge in alcohol as the solution to one's worries. This expression is often followed by "愁更愁" meaning drinking would not take away you worries，but only brings more worries hence worsens the situation.

(1) 想开一点儿。走，喝两杯，借酒浇愁嘛！

Don't take it to heart. Let's go have a couple of drinks；alcohol will take care of your problems.

(2) 公司的生意不好，你借酒浇愁是解决不了问题的。

The business of your company is in trouble，but taking refuge in alcohol would not solve your problems.

6. **"心里有鬼"**：因为做了不好的事而心虚。

The expression of "心里有鬼〔there is a ghost in your heart〕" is the same as "心虚" which is used to describe someone who has a guilty conscience，or has done something shady that he/she is worried about being found out.

(1) 她不让调查这件事是因为她心里有鬼！

The fact she wouldn't allow this matter to be investigated is because that she had something to hide！

(2) 我才不怕呢，我心里没鬼！

I'm not the least worried，I have nothing to hide.

7. **"要不要打110"**：110 是报警电话。

110 is the emergency telephone number.

8. **"兜圈子"**：指说话不直接说。

"兜圈子" means "beating around the bush".

有话直接说，别兜圈子。

Say what's in your mind，don't beat the bush！

9. **"以其人之道还治其人之身"**：用那个人用的办法，去对付那个人。

The expression means "treat him with a dose of his own medicine." It is used to mean that one takes the same measure that one's enemy had employed，to fight against the enemy.

（1）在昨天的决赛中，上半场我们的对手用不正当的办法赢了我们，下半场我本想以其人之道还治其人之身，但是我的队友制止了我，最后在大家的努力之下，我们取得了胜利。

In the Final Match yesterday, our opponent led us by using shady moves in the first half, I was going to do the same to them in the second half, but my teammates stopped me, we eventually won with proper hard work by our team.

（2）他们大量收购你的股票，想吃掉你的公司，你也以其人之道还治其人之身，反正你的公司比他们实力雄厚得多。

They're aggressively buying your stock in order to takeover your company, you should do exactly the same to them 〔there is no fear〕 since your company is bigger and more powerful than theirs.

10. "完美无缺"：非常完美，没有缺点。

The phrase means "Perfect".

（1）世界上没有一个人是完美无缺的。

No one in the whole world is perfect.

（2）谁都知道完美无缺的人是没有的，但是还希望自己的太太、丈夫、孩子能什么都好。

Everyone knows that no one in the world is perfect, but still one wishes one's husband, wife or children to be perfect.

11. "花前月下"：指情人约会的地方。

The phrase "花前月下" literally means "in front of the flowers and under the moon". It's used to refer to the spot where lovers meet. However, it can also been used to mean "dating" in general.

（1）三年的花前月下，山盟海誓，却抵不过别人的蜚短流长。

Gossip and Rumors have taken away the promises of love we made to each other during the three years.

（2）当年我们花前月下海誓山盟定终身，难道这些你都忘了吗？！

Have you forgotten all the promises of love we made to each other before our marriage?

12. "山盟海誓"：也说"海誓山盟"，"盟"意思是"盟约"，"誓"意思是"发誓"。用于男女之间发誓：爱情要像山海那样久远、坚定。

"誓" means "swear, vow or pledge", "盟" usually means "oath of alliance". "海誓山盟" refers to "a couple's pledge of love", or "to swear an oath of enduring fidelity. "

当年他俩海誓山盟，没想到居然是我们班第一对离婚的。

How many promises of love were made in our college days between the two, no one could have predicted that they would be the first couple in our class to divorce.

13. **"蜚短流长"**："短、长"意思是"是非、善恶"，"蜚、流"意思是"散布"。"蜚短流长"的意思是"散布流言蜚语，造谣中伤"。

"短长" means "right and wrong or good and bad", "蜚流" means "to spread". "蜚短流长" means "to gossip" or "to spread rumors".

(1) 他一天到晚无所事事，到处搬弄是非，蜚短流长。

Spreading fabricated stories and malicious gossip to stir thing up has become the idler's life.

(2) 正经事都忙不过来，哪有时间理那些蜚短流长？

Don't even have enough time to deal with my own business, how could I find time to join the gossip?

14. **"不堪一击"**："不堪"意思是"经不起"，"击"意思是"打击"。"不堪一击"的意思是"一下打击都经不起"。

"不堪" means "can't stand", "击" means "attack". "不堪一击" means "collapse at the first blow."

(1) 拳王以为他的对手会不堪一击，没想到最后以故意"咬对方的耳朵"而身败名裂。

The boxing legend had thought his opponent would collapse at his first blow , but he ended up having to bite his opponent's ear in his desperate attempt to win the match. Consequently he brought disgrace and ruin on himself.

(2) 国家男队不堪一击的表现令观众大失所望。

The audience was terribly disappointed by the pathetic performance of their national team.

15. **"原形毕露"**："原"的意思是"原来"，"毕"的意思是"完全"，"原形毕露"的意思是"本来的样子完全露出来了"，含有贬义。

"原" means "original", "毕" means "completely", "原形毕露" is a pejorative expression. It means "to show one's true colors" or "be revealed for what one really is".

(1) 当周围的人把事实真相搞清以后，他原形毕露，开车就跑。

Once the truth was out, he showed his true colors and sped away for life.

（2）他原形毕露以前，大家都以为他是个善良、和气的老人。

Before his true identity was revealed, everyone thought he was a kind and friendly old man.

练习 Exercises

■ 一、口语练习 Oral Practice

（一）回答问题 Answer the following questions

1. 小宋和苗苗结婚后想要孩子吗？你是怎么知道的？

2. 苗苗激动地想听听小宋的肚子里有没有动静儿，小宋说"八字还没一撇儿呢。"她说这句话的意思是什么？

3. 小宋怀孕以后为什么不是特别高兴，反而哭了？

4. 苗苗得知妻子怀孕后心情如何？苗苗为什么把"借酒浇愁"说成"借愁浇酒"？

5. 电梯上发生的事情对都都有什么影响？

6. 苗苗为什么说小罗心里有鬼，他说这话是什么意思？

7. 都都为什么也说小罗心里有鬼？

8. 请你描述一下四个人在饭馆遇见时，每人的心情和态度。

9. 小罗和都都最后为什么分手了？

（二）个人口语练习 Individual Oral Practice

1. 都都告诉她的好朋友他和小罗之间发生的事情。

   Play the part of 都都 who is recounting to a friend what has happened between her and 小罗.

2. 小宋告诉妈妈他和苗苗现在的情况。

   Play the part of 小宋 who is telling her mother what has happened between her and 苗苗.

■ 二、书写练习 Written Exercises

（一）填空 Fill in the blanks with the words given

A. 疯	B. 到底	C. 下	D. 竟然	E. 透
F. 可	G. 走	H. 清		

1. 你 _____ 怎么怀上的呀？有没有什么特殊的感觉？

2. 苗苗_____会认为我怀上的孩子也许是小罗的！

3. 说吧，我看你还有什么_____解释的？

4. 幽默？幽默也不能赶_____我的屈辱。

5. 我也希望我成熟一点，好看_____你的肮脏本质。

6. 我最近可能得了忧郁症、得了强迫症了吧。我觉得我都快被折磨_____了。

7. 你听我说，我完全可以把他揍趴_____，但是我不能。

8. 小罗，我真的看不_____你。

A. 兜圈子	B. 完美无缺	C. 原形毕露	D. 别有用心
E. 信口胡说	F. 疑神疑鬼	G. 胡说八道	H. 不知廉耻
I. 蜚短流长	J. 心里有鬼		

1. 好了好了，对不起，算我_____。我可能是大喜过望了，我老不相信这样的好事儿会落在我头上。

2. 我终于明白了，你为什么不敢教训他。你_____，你心虚。

3. 这是谣言，_____地恶毒攻击，你还不清楚吗？

4. 小宋，你不该这样_____的。弄得我怀了孩子好像犯了罪一样。

5. 苗苗，不许你_____。

6. 你终于敢出来替这个_____的家伙维护了？

7. 甭跟我_____，其实你是祖护那姓罗的，你以为我看不出来吗？

8. 人的一生他不可能把自己的每一个动作都设计得_____呀！

9. 三年的花前月下，山盟海誓，却抵不过别人的_____。

10. 你是不是还想再等等啊？等到有一天，我_____，或者找到你更中意的……

（二）用中文解释画线部分语句在剧中的具体意思 Explain the actual meaning of the underlined part in this play

1. 你说咱俩结婚这么多年了，一直都想要孩子，可怎么折腾也折腾不出一个孩子来。真是啊，<u>有心栽花儿花儿不开，无心插柳柳成荫</u>。送子娘娘跟咱们俩开玩笑呢！

2. 苗苗听说太太怀孕了，高兴得要听听有没有动静儿。小宋说：哎呀，行啦。<u>八字还没一撇儿</u>呢。

3. 小罗对都都说：你听我说，我完全可以把他揍趴下，但是我不能。他可以当众侮辱我，我能像他那样吗？我能<u>以其人之道还治其人之</u>

身吗？

4. 三年的花前月下，山盟海誓，却抵不过别人的<u>蜚短流长</u>。如此<u>不堪一击</u>的爱情……

5. 你是不是还想再等等啊？等到有一天，我<u>原形毕露</u>，或者找到你更中意的……

（三）写作 Composition

假设你是小宋，请你写一封信给你的一个好朋友，告诉她整个事情的经过，以及你的想法、感受等。

Write a letter as you were 小宋 to a close friend telling her the whole incident and your thoughts，feelings and etc.

四

小　罗：我……我赶写一篇**影评**，没想到……已经下班很久了。

小　宋：哦，我也是报社让我**接待**两位读者，所以**耽误**了。

小　罗：听说，你真的离婚了？

小　宋：上个月就办了。

小　罗：我……我真的很对不起你。

小　宋：偶然是**必然**的**触发剂**。有些东西只是藏在我们生活的**表象**下面，只不过是我们错在**疏忽罢了**。

小　罗：你上大三的时候，我才上大一。咱们同学一年，还有分到报社这么多年，咱们除了彼此见面ㄦ打个招呼、点点头，说的话加在一块ㄦ也没今天多。小宋……

小　宋：你真的不**在乎**啊？我比你大好几岁。而且，还有个孩子。

小　罗：我认真地想过了，咱们是**患难知己**[N1]。我想，年龄又不是爱情的**隔阂**。你……这么热爱孩子才使我更加地爱你。放心吧，我会做个好父亲的。慢点ㄦ。哎，你看那边ㄦ变化多大呀！

小　宋：嗯。

小　罗：这边ㄦ也是。

影评	yǐngpíng	n.	movie review
接待	jiēdài	v.	receive
耽误	dānwu	v.	delay; hold up
必然	bìrán	adj.	inevitable; certain
触发	chùfā	v.	trigger, detonate by contact; touch off; spark
触发剂	chùfā jì	n.	agent that cause something to happen
表象	biǎoxiàng	n.	appearance; image
疏忽	shūhu	v.	neglect; oversight
罢了	bàle		a modal particle indicating (that's all, only); let it pass, or be done with it, denoting tolerance or unwilling acceptance
在乎	zàihu	v.	care; mind
患难知己	huànnàn zhījǐ		friends in adversity; tested friends
隔阂	géhé	n.	(of feeling and thought)estrangement; misunderstanding

老　者：小伙子，看样子你媳妇儿**有喜**了吧？走路要**留点**儿**神**[N2]哪。

小　罗：谢谢老大爷。

老　者：哦哦，我不老，年轻着哪。

小　罗：对，您不老，年轻着哪。

老　者：呃，看你们这么幸福**美满**，真为你们高兴哪。

小　宋：幸福什么呀？其实我们心里都挺痛苦的。

小　罗：是啊，都挺痛苦的。

老　者：痛苦也不错嘛。没有痛苦就不知道什么叫不痛苦。其实呢，痛苦和幸福不是**对立**的，它的对立面嘛，是不痛苦，对不对？

小　罗：哎，大爷，您拿这个**望远镜**看什么哪？

老　者：看**景致**啊。

小　罗：看、看景致……

老　者：哦，看世界呀。看，这世界多好啊，多美呀！

有喜	yǒuxǐ	v.	怀孕，pregnant
留神	liúshén	v.	pay attention to; be careful
美满	měimǎn	adj.	happy; satisfactory; harmonious
对立	duìlì	adj.	oppose; be antagonistic to; contradiction; antagonism
望远镜	wàngyuǎnjìng	n.	telescope; binoculars
景致	jǐngzhì	n.	view; scenery; scene

注释 Notes

1. **"患难知己"**："知己"的意思是"彼此互相了解而且情谊深厚的人"，"患难知己"的意思是"在患难（遇到很大的困难时）中结交的好朋友"。

   "知己" refers to "someone you know well and have deep friendship with".

   "患难知己" refers to "the 知己 you made during extraordinarily difficult times." The term generally means "friends in adversity" or "tested friends."

   我跟你王阿姨是"文革"下放劳动时认识的，可以说是患难知己。

   I met your Auntie Wang in a labor camp during the Cultural Revolution; we are truly "friends in adversity."

2. **"留神"**：意思是"注意"。

   "留神" is a colloquial expression meaning "to pay attention to〔something〕"

   冰天雪地的，走路要留神呐。

   Make sure to mind yourself walking in the world of ice and snow.

练习 Exercises

■ 一、口语练习 Oral Practice

（一）回答问题 Answer the following questions

1. 小宋和小罗为什么都那么晚才下班？
2. 小宋离婚了，小罗为什么向她道歉？
3. 小宋说："偶然是必然的触发剂。"这句话是什么意思？
4. 小宋觉得他和小罗很合适吗？
5. 小罗对他与小宋的爱情的看法如何？
6. 小宋和小罗决定要结婚了，但是他们为什么心里都很痛苦？

（二）讨论 Discussion

1. "人言可畏"吗？请用实例说明你的看法？
2. 谈谈你对剧中小罗的看法。
3. "没有痛苦就不知道什么叫不痛苦。其实呢，痛苦和幸福不是对立的，它的对立面嘛是不痛苦"，举例说明这句话是什么意思。你同意这句话吗？
4. 在剧的最后，老人为什么说"这世界多好啊，多美呀！"

（三）角色扮演 Role Play

1. 把学生分成组表演小宋跟小罗的对话。

   Pair students up to act out the dialogue between 小宋 and 小罗.

2. 把学生分成小组，饰演小宋、小罗跟老者的对话。

   Divide the students into groups of three to act out the conversation between 小宋，小罗 and 老者。

■ 二、书写练习 Written Exercises

（一）选择题 Circle the answers which most reflects the meaning of the underlined part in the following Sentences

1. 偶然是必然的触发剂。

   A. 事情的发生是必然的

B. 事情的发生是偶然的

C. 偶然跟必然是密切相关的

D. 偶然跟必然没有关系

2. 我认真地想过了，咱们是<u>患难知己</u>。年龄不是爱情的隔阂，我们结婚吧。

　　A. 共同经历了很多困难后成为好朋友

　　B. 因有了困难而对自己更了解了

　　C. 生病住院时交的朋友

　　D. 因都离开自己的爱人而成了朋友

3. 小伙子，看样子你媳妇儿<u>有喜了吧</u>？

　　A. 有高兴的事

　　B. 有她喜欢的东西

　　C. 怀孕了

　　D. 因为有希望而高兴

4. 其实呢，<u>痛苦和幸福不是对立的</u>。

　　A. 痛苦和幸福可以同时存在

　　B. 痛苦和幸福不会同时存在

　　C. 经历过痛苦才能知道什么是幸福

　　D. 拥有过幸福才能知道什么是痛苦

（二）写作 Composition

1. 苗苗给小宋写的一封信：几年以后，苗苗知道了真情，也知道孩子是自己的。他给小宋写了一封信表示后悔和歉意。

A few years after their divorce，苗苗 now knows the fact about the much-talked about "elevator incident" and that 小宋 was wronged and the child is his. He is writing a letter to his ex-wife to offer his apology and express his regret.

2. 写一篇 300～400 字的观后感。

Write an essay of 300～400 words on your thoughts and reflections after studying the play.

■ 三、文化方面的讨论 Cultural Discussion

在你们国家，像这样的事情会发生吗？为什么？

Could incidents like the one described in this story happen in your own country? Why?

第九课 胜负攸关

A Matter of Victory and Defeat

导 读:

　　足球在中国一直是备受广大球迷欢迎的运动之一。但中国国家足球队在国际比赛中的屡屡失败又使得球迷们非常失望。本剧故事发生在中国国家足球队"冲出"亚洲前，描写某文化公司的一位职员，在亚洲杯足球赛期间，在渴望国家荣誉和获得金钱利益之间的复杂情感。也反映了他周围的人对中国足球运动的不同态度。

　　其后，中国足球队在2003年终于"冲出亚洲"，参加了在日本和韩国举行的世界杯赛，这给中国球迷带来了极大的欢乐。可惜中国足球队的这种战绩到目前为止还只是昙花一现。跟中国很多体育运动相比，中国足球要真正走向世界，仍有很长的路要走。

Introduction:

Soccer has been by far the most popular sport in China. But the less than mediocre performance of the Chinese National Soccer Team has been a great disappointment for Chinese soccer fans. This story tells a young man's emotional roller coaster experience during the Asian Games of 2003. While the focus of the story is on the young man's struggle between national pride and personal financial gain, it also displays the different attitudes people have towards this sport.

In the end, The Chinese National Team won the Asian Games, and eventually went on to compete in Korea and Japan for the World Cup. The victory brought the fans enormous joy and happiness.

Unfortunately, no victorious news followed. As Chinese athletes successfully compete internationally in many other sports, Chinese soccer is still facing a long, difficult and upward battle.

主要人物（Main Characters）

刘　成	liú Chéng	name of a man
宋秋玲	Sòng Qiūlíng	name of a woman, a driver
老　王	Lǎo Wáng	a co-worker of Liu Cheng's
宋　母	Sòng Mǔ	mother of Song Qiuling
李　子	Lǐzi	Little Li, a buddy of Liu Cheng's

刘　成：哎，老王，巴西和中国的**时差**是多少？

老　王：晚 11 个小时吧。

刘　成：11 个小时？

老　王：11 个小时，一个西一个东。

刘　成：哦，11 个。老王，这么着，我啊，先走。我巴西那哥们儿今儿肯定给我回一个**电传**。电传要是来了，您马上**呼**我一下，告诉我那巴西队能来北京的日期，好吧？

老　王：唔。这么大的事儿，自己不盯着？

刘　成：我和宋秋玲约好了，一会儿要去照**婚纱照**。

售票员：哎，上车上车了哎。啊，**果园**的，来来来来，有座啊有座，有座有座。三块，三块一位。走，来了，上车。哎果园的有没有啊，走不走？啊，走，哎，上了，走嘞。上车就走啊，啊，还有没有？

宋秋玲：哎？上后头去！

售票员：**兄弟**哎，后边儿，后边有座儿啊，后边，后边，后边儿。

乘　客：**德胜门**多少钱？

胜	shèng	n.	victory; success
负	fù	n.	defeat，failure
攸关	yōu guān		攸：所；关：关联，关系到。be of concern; affect; be closely related to；胜负攸关 a matter of victory and defeat
时差	shíchā	n.	time difference；jet lag
电传	diànchuán	n.	fax
呼	hū	v.	page
婚纱照	hūnshāzhào	n.	wedding photographs
售票员	shòupiàoyuán	n.	conductor; ticket seller; box-office clerk
果园	Guǒyuán	N.	orchard
兄弟	xiōngdi	n.	brother; a familiar form of addressing a man younger than oneself
乘客	chéngkè	n.	passenger
德胜门	Déshèng Mén	N.	Desheng Gate (name of a place in Beijing)

售票员：来来来，三块钱，哎，快上快上！

乘　客：两块行么？

售票员：两块钱？

乘　客：啊。

售票员：我们这可是公家的，不**砍价**啊。

乘　客：干吗呀，不砍价就这样！

刘　成：哎，哎，哎……

宋秋玲：快，快，快，快快……

售票员：嗬，等咱刘成兄弟呢，早说啊。

刘　成：真不好意思啊，晚了晚了晚了。

售票员：哎，哟，哟，快点儿。好嘞，走嘞！

刘　成：嘿嘿。

宋秋玲：干吗**美滋滋**的？啊？

刘　成：嗯？

宋秋玲：嗯？你是不是以为把我骗**到手**了，啊？

刘　成：啊？

宋秋玲：告诉你，**有的是**照了相还吹的[N1]。

刘　成：不能够。哎，我要告诉你一**特大喜讯**。哎，我怕你呀，**承受**不住，咱
　　　　们下班以后再说吧。

宋秋玲：你能有什么**喜事**啊？**莫不是**[N2]，你那小**破**公司分了你一间房？

刘　成：哼，哼！你注意**行人**！

砍价	kǎnjià	vo.	haggle; bargain
美滋滋	měi zīzī	adj.	happy and complacent; pleased (with oneself);
到手	dào shǒu	vo.	in one's hands; in one's possession
有的是	yǒu de shì		很多，plenty
特大	tè dà		特别大的，especially large; exceptionally large
喜讯	xǐxùn	n.	好消息，happy news; good news
承受	chéngshòu	v.	receive; bear; endure
喜事	xǐshì	n.	happy event; joyous occasion; wedding
莫不是	mòbúshì		might it be...
破	pò	adj.	broken; damaged；小破公司 a lousy little company
行人	xíngrén	n.	pedestrian; passerby

宋秋玲：哎——

刘　成：哎，过来，来。

宋秋玲：你等着我啊。

刘　成：哎。

宋秋玲：干吗呀？什么事啊？啊？

刘　成：来吧。

宋秋玲：哎呀呀，说吧说吧。什么事啊？

刘　成：秋玲。

宋秋玲：啊。

刘　成：我这回要**发财**了！

宋秋玲：又发财！你骗我可不**止**一回了。

刘　成：哎，秋玲，我，哎秋玲，这回可是真的，啊，真的。

宋秋玲：那你倒说说啊。

刘　成：秋玲啊，哎，你说你开着车满世界^{N3}跑，你说哪_儿的房子最好？

宋秋玲：那当然是二**环**^{N4}以里的。

刘　成：要是我们在二环以里买一个小**两居**^{N5}，得多少钱？

宋秋玲：怎么着^{N6}也得五六十万。

刘　成：要是 30 来万，能在哪_儿买房子？

宋秋玲：那就四环的边上呗。

刘　成：咱们哪，就在四环那_儿弄一套房子。

宋秋玲：嘀嘀，你别吓唬我，我胆_儿小^{N7}，啊？

刘　成：哎，秋玲_儿，你以为我骗你呢，我说的是真事_儿。这回啊，最少咱们也得**净赚**他个 30 来万！我给我们文化公司啊，联系成了一次足球**对抗赛**，巴西国家足球队。知道吗？那是世界**冠军**哪，国际**排名**第一呀。

发财	fācái	vo.	get rich, make a fortune
止	zhǐ	v.	stop；不止一回 more than once
二环	èrhuán	n.	the Second Ring; the Second Circular Highway
两居	liǎng jū		两个卧室（的），two bedroom apartment
净赚	jìng zhuàn		net profit
对抗赛	duìkàng sài		sport meet between two or among several
冠军	guànjūn	n.	championship
排名	páimíng		ranking

宋秋玲：哎呀，你说**正事**儿，正事儿。

刘　成：啊，正事正事。哎，**巴西队**和中国队踢球，那就**意味着罗马里奥、罗纳尔多**都来呀，那他们……哎，正事儿，正事儿，正事儿，说正事儿，上次有一个公司啊，请来了**马拉多纳**，**刨出去成本费**和**税收**，净挣也千儿八百万哪。这次我和我们那**老总**算了一下，啊，最少，啊，也**落**(lào) 个这个数！那，老总说了，给我提成 5％至 10％，少说也 30 来万哪。

宋秋玲：30 万都是咱们的？

刘　成：啊！

宋秋玲：真的？

刘　成：啊！

宋秋玲：你别骗我！

刘　成：哎哟，秋玲儿，我这回要是骗你，我是，我是你孙子[N8]。

宋秋玲：哈哈哈……

刘　成：啊哈哈……哎，等等，哎我的**发型**，发型！

宋秋玲：啊嘿嘿，走走走。

刘　成：走走走。

正事儿	zhèng shìr		one's proper business or duty
巴西	Bāxī	N.	Brazil
意味着	yìwèi zhe	v.	imply; mean
罗马里奥	Luómǎlǐ'ào	N.	Romario, Name of a soccer player
罗纳尔多	Luónàěrduō	N.	Ronaldo, Name of a soccer player
马拉多纳	Mǎlāduōnà	N.	Maradona, Name of a soccer player
刨出去	páo chuqu	vc.	excluding; not counting; minus
成本费	chéngběn fèi	n.	production cost
税收	shuìshōu	n.	tax revenue
老总	lǎozǒng	n.	head of a company; CEO
落	lào	v.	end up (with)
发型	fàxíng	n.	hair style; hairdo

注释 Notes

1. **"吹"**：意思是"分手"。"告诉你，有的是照了相还吹的"，意思是"有的人照了结婚相以后还吹了（分手了）"。

   "吹" means "break up." The sentence "告诉你，有的是照了相还吹的" means "Let me remind you that there are plenty of people who went separate ways after having wedding photos taken". 秋玲 here wants 刘成 to know that having wedding photos taken does not guarantee that an actual wedding will take place. The implied meaning is that she might change her mind and not marry him even after they have taken their wedding pictures.

2. **"莫不是（莫非）"**：难道是；couldn't it be that...；might it be that...

   你能有什么喜事啊？莫不是，你那小破公司分了你一间房？

   What great things could happen to you? Could it be that your lousy little company has given you an apartment?

3. **"满世界"**：意思是"到处"。"你开着车满世界跑"，"满世界"是"（去、在）很多地方的意思"。

   "满世界" is a colloquial expression meaning "going everywhere" or "having been to a lot of places." The sentence literally means "You drive everywhere." It is used here to mean that since Song qiuling's job is a driver; she is on the road all the time therefore, she must have been to a lot of places. Hence 刘成 thinks she should know where the best houses are in this city.

4. **"二环"**：指北京的环城公路（环路），现在已建成的有二环、三环、四环、五环。

   "环" means "ring", "环路" refers to the circular highways inside the city of Beijing. The one that is the closest to the heart of the city is called Er Huan (The Second Ring Road), the farthest is Wu Huan (the Fifth Ring Road). The sentence "那当然是二环以里的" means "Of course we would only consider an apartment within the Second Ring Road—i. e. close to the heart of the city.

5. **"小两居"**：意思是小的、有两个卧室的公寓楼单元房。

"小两居" refers to a small two-bedroom apartment in a residential building.

6. **"怎么着"**：意思是"怎么样"，这里包含有"无论怎么样"或"不管怎么样"的意思，口语。参见《项链》第三部分注释2。

"怎么着" literally means "怎么样". However in this context, this expression "怎么着" means "no matter how" or "in any case." This is a colloquial expression. Please refer to note 2 in part 3 of 《项链》.

(1) 刘　成：要是我们在二环以里买一个小两居，得多少钱？

If we were to buy a small two-bedroom apartment within the Second Ring Road, how much would it cost?

宋秋玲：怎么着也得五六十万。

It would (no matter how small the apartment might be or how reasonable the price was) cost at least ￥500～600 thousand.

意思是"无论多便宜，也得五六十万。"

No matter how cheap it might be the price couldn't be lower than five or six hundred thousand yuan.

(2) 回老家，怎么着也得看看父母。(无论多忙……)

Making a trip visiting (one's) hometown, there is absolutely no excuse not to go see one's parents no matter how busy one might be.

(3) 你的毕业论文什么时候能写完？

When will you be able to finish your dissertation?

怎么着五月也写完了。(不管有什么情况……)

It has to be finished by May, no matter what.

7. **"我胆儿小"**：在"嘀嘀，你别吓唬我，我胆儿小，啊？"这句话里，"我胆儿小"，意思是我很怕事（如：怕天黑，怕有坏人做坏事，等等）。人们在听到一件很难相信的好事时，也会说这句话，意思是："你别说大话，把我吓着。"常常有开玩笑的意味。

"我胆儿小" literally means "I'm timid" or "I'm unduly fearful", (for example, someone is scared of the dark, or is fearful of evil doers, etc.) The expression is also often used to describe someone being timid and overcautious, or to be afraid of getting into trouble. However, when one is overwhelmed by unbelievably wonderful news, the person could also use such an expression in a joking way meaning "Don't scare me with your boast."

8. **"我是你孙子"**：在"哎哟，秋玲儿，我这回要是骗你，我是，我是你孙子。"这句话里，"孙子"有骂自己的意思。在中国人看来，辈分是很重要的，如果故意说别人或自己辈分小，比如"儿子、孙子"就等于骂别人或骂自己。相反，故意提高自己或别人的辈分，如"老子、爸爸、爷爷"就有相反的作用。

"孙子" is "grandson." The term, used in the sentence "哎哟，秋玲儿，我这回要是骗你，我是，我是你孙子." is meant to call oneself (Liu Cheng himself) names. In the eyes of the Chinese, one's position in the family hierarchy is very important—if one ranks high as in "爸爸—father" or "爷爷—grandfather", this commands importance and respect, while grandson and son denote "low and worthless." Hence, a bully may refer to himself as "老子," which means 爸爸 or 爷爷, to insult his victim. In contrast, the two terms "儿子" and "孙子" have no seniority in the family and hence are used as swearwords referring to a low and worthless person.

练习 Exercises

■ 一、口语练习 Oral Practice

（一）回答下列问题 Answer the following questions

1. 刘成正在联系一件什么事？
2. 秋玲和刘成是什么关系？秋玲是做什么工作的？
3. 刘成和秋玲约好要去做什么？
4. 刘成有什么特大喜事？
5. 刘成和秋玲特别高兴，是不是因为一会儿就要去照婚纱照了？
6. 如果能赚 30 万，刘成和秋玲想用这笔钱做什么？
7. 为什么刘成对秋玲说，"我这回要是骗你，我是你孙子"？是不是秋玲想要个孙子？

■ 二、书写练习 Written Exercises

（一）填空 Fill in the blanks with the words given

A. 住	B. 到	C. 着	D. 好
E. 净	F. 成	G. 砍	H. 吹

1. 唔。这么大的事儿，自己不盯_____？
2. 你是不是以为把我骗_____手了，啊？
3. 我和宋秋玲约_____了，一会儿要去照婚纱照。
4. 这回啊，最少咱们也得_____赚它个三十来万。
5. 我给我们文化公司啊，联系_____了一次足球对抗赛。
6. 售票员：我们这可是公家的，不_____价啊。
7. 告诉你，有的是照了相还_____的。
8. 不能够，哎，我要告诉你一特大喜讯。哎，我怕你呀，承受不_____，咱们下班以后再说吧。

（二）选择题 Circle the answer which most reflects the meaning of the under-lined part in the following sentences

1. 宋秋玲：干吗<u>美滋滋</u>的？啊？

　　A. 看上去很好看

　　B. 看上去很得意

　　C. 看上去很骄傲

　　D. 看上去很乐观

2. 你能有什么喜事啊？莫不是，<u>你那小破公司分了你一间房</u>？

　　A. 公司是刘成的

　　B. 公司很小而且坏了

　　C. 公司不怎么样

　　D. 房子又破又小

3. <u>秋玲你开着车满世界跑</u>，你说哪儿的房子最好？

　　A. 秋玲开车去过世界很多国家

　　B. 秋玲去过世界很多国家开过车

　　C. 秋玲开着车到处跑

　　D. 秋玲开车开得太快

4. 这次我和我们那老总算了一下，刨出去成本费和税收，净挣也<u>千儿八百万</u>呐啊！

　A. 1000 万

　B. 1800 万

　C. 1000 万～1800 万

　D. 800 万～1000 万

二

卖报者：哎，哥们儿，这回**亚洲杯**，国家队他有戏吗^{N1}？

买报者：说什么呢^{N2}，甲 A **联赛**^{N3}都两年了。

刘　成：哎，有戏。

买报者：那是^{N4}。

刘　成：拿出踢**桑普多利亚**和**AC 米兰**那**劲头**来，就能**抢入四强**。

卖报者：哎，对了。

买报者：哎呀。

刘　成：**兴许**打入**决赛**呢。

宋秋玲：哎呀，你**烦**不烦^{N5}？说几句就没个完，来这儿干什么来的？

刘　成：哎，买报纸。

宋秋玲：买报，买报。

刘　成：您给我拿**份儿**《**精品购物**》。

宋秋玲：哎，对，还有那，购，《**购物导报**》。

刘　成：还有那《购物导报》，哎，哎，再给我来份儿《**足球**》。

亚洲杯	Yàzhōubēi	N.	Asian Cup (for soccer)
联赛	liánsài	n.	league tournament; league matches
桑普多利亚	Sāngpǔduōlìyà	N.	U. C. Sampdoria—Name of an Italian soccer team
AC 米兰	A. C. mǐlán	N.	Milan—Name of an Italian soccer team
劲头	jìntóu	n.	drive; zeal; spirit; vigor
抢	qiǎng	v.	vie for; fight to win sth. scramble for
四强	sì qiáng	n.	The four finalists
兴许	xīngxǔ	adv.	可能、也许，perhaps; maybe
决赛	juésài	n.	final match or final round of matches in a sport which decides the positions in a competition; shoot-off
烦	fán	adj.	annoy; 烦不烦啊？Isn't that annoy or what!
份儿	fènr	m.	measure word for newspapers
精品购物	Jīngpǐn Gòuwù	N.	一种刊登商品介绍和广告的杂志
购物导报	Gòuwù Dǎobào	N.	一种刊登商品介绍和广告的报纸
精品	jīngpǐn	n.	top quality article; quality goods
购物	gòuwù	vo.	go shopping, shopping
导报	dǎobào	n.	Guide (magazine)

宋秋玲：咱们得回去研究研究这买房的**信息**。

刘　　成：啊，好好，哎。走走走。

宋秋玲：走走走，钱给了吗？

刘　　成：啊，给给给，给您，好。

宋秋玲：哎，哎，这个不错哎，哎，你看啊，这个每**平米**3888元，嗯？哎呀，你看这个嘛。

刘　　成：哎，哎哎。

宋秋玲：你看，哎这个就算两室一厅，60平米，唔，也就是二十三四万，哎，怎么样？

刘　　成：3888，哎，好啊，好，呵呵。不过，好是好，就这地点吧，好像太远了点儿。

宋秋玲：谁说的？

刘　　成：啊，没关系，咱们30万呢，买了房，哎，剩下点儿钱呐，正好可以买个**国产面包车**，五六万，呵呵，正好。

宋秋玲：真的？

刘　　成：以后你就有自己的面包车开了。哎，不但挣钱，而且还可以**顺路**接我，哈哈，嘿嘿。

宋秋玲：嗯。美得你，嘿嘿。

宋　　母：嗬，刘成来了。

刘　　成：哎，阿姨。

宋　　母：呦，你们在这儿干什么呢？铺得满屋子报纸。

宋秋玲：啊。

刘　　成：啊嘿。

宋　　母：嗬嗬，哎，秋玲，快去做饭去，给刘成弄点儿好吃的。

刘　　成：啊。

宋秋玲：啊，不了。妈，我们俩已经吃过了，到**馆子**里吃的。

信息	xìnxī	n.	information
平米	píngmǐ	m.	square meter
国产	guóchǎn	adj.	domestically produced (used to modify nouns)
面包车	miànbāochē	n.	van
顺路	shùnlù	adv.	on the way (to somewhere else)
馆子	guǎnzi	n.	restaurant

宋　母：哎呀，动不动[N6]就去下馆子，你把刘成当**大款**了？

刘　成：嘿嘿。

宋秋玲：嗯，那可**不咋**[N7]**的**，别小看了我的刘成啊。

宋　母：啊，哎，哈哈，还"我的刘成"！大姑娘家家的[N8]。

刘　成：哎，这事儿别告诉你妈。

宋秋玲：哎，你什么意思啊？

刘　成：你看你，嗯……

宋秋玲：你是不是还没**谱**呢？

刘　成：哪能啊！我怕你妈知道这事儿啊，一高兴再乐得**背过气去**[N9]。哈哈！

宋秋玲：去你的[N10]！你妈才乐背过气去呢。

刘　成：闹着玩儿，你，呵呵。

宋秋玲：哎，说真的，哎，要是，咱们将来有了孩子，得叫我妈**看**。

刘　成：嗯。

宋秋玲：我妈这一辈子还没住过**楼房**呢。

刘　成：我说啊……

宋秋玲：嗯？

刘　成：扯远了点儿吧？

宋秋玲：嗬嗬，哎，你赶快跟那巴西队联系啊，这**夜长梦多**[N11]。

刘　成：啊，**这由不得**咱，人家巴西那是足球大国，国内外的球事火[N12]着呢，人家答应来那就不错了。什么时候来呀，得**就合**着人家的工夫[N13]。

大款	dàkuǎn	n.	big shot
不咋的	bùzǎdì		不怎么样，不好，often means "not so great", "not so hot", but used in this context, it implies "(the expenses of) going to restaurant is nothing for 刘成，don't you underestimate him (his wealth)"
小看	xiǎokàn	v.	轻视，underestimate; look down upon; belittle
谱	pǔ	n.	something to count on; a fair amount of confidence
背过气	bèi guo qì		lose one's breath; faint; pass out
看	kān	v.	look after; take care of
楼房	lóufáng	n.	storied building; tower
夜长梦多	yè cháng mèng duō		a long night is fraught with Dreams; a long delay means trouble; (see note 11)
由不得	yóubude	vc.	be not in control; not have freedom of choice
就合	jiùhe	v.	迁就，accommodate oneself to; yield to

宋秋玲：那，那敢情这还是**没影**儿的事呢！啊？

刘　成：谁说的？我，我，我不是正在联系吗？

宋秋玲：什么呀？

刘　成：我……来了！啊哈，巴西队下月 28 号至 31 号可来京三天。啊嘿嘿！

宋秋玲：啊哈哈，**太棒了**！哈哈！

刘　成：哎，等等。

宋秋玲：怎么了？

刘　成：我说，哎，哪儿有电话啊？

宋秋玲：哎，那个，**隔壁赵大爷**。

刘　成：走走走。

宋秋玲：走。这边这儿。赵大爷，我们打个电话。

赵大爷：哎，来吧。

刘　成：哎，大爷！

宋秋玲：你去打吧。

刘　成：哎，好嘞。

宋秋玲：太棒了，哎哟，妈妈呀，我来帮你摘。

宋　母：哎，什么呀？太棒了？

宋秋玲：刘成联系成了一笔买卖。

宋　母：真的？哎哟。

宋秋玲：能挣啊，30 万！

宋　母：啊？哈哈哈。哎哎？

宋秋玲：啊？

宋　母：那路正？

刘　成：哎，不是，老王，那个电传上有没有说那时间哎，也就是日期，有没

没影儿	méiyǐngr		literally means "not even a shadow (of sth.)" used here to mean "besides talk, nothing substantial is happening or has happened"
棒	bàng	adj.	身体好、能力强或水平高，terrific; wonderful
隔壁	gébì	n	next-door neighbor
赵大爷	Zhào Dàye	N.	Uncle Zhao (not related)
笔	bǐ	m.	for business deals or a sum of money 一笔买卖；一笔钱
正	zhèng	adj.	"正当" legitimate; proper, 那路正? Is that a legitimate way (of getting money)?

有商量的**余地**？啊？什么？没有啊，哎，我说老王。

宋秋玲：啊，妈啊。

宋　母：那**税**啊，得上明白了。

宋秋玲：哎呀，妈，算好的，这是净挣的。

宋　母：啊？哎，你看，我说咱刘成行了，啊，**蔫不出溜**[N14]的，哈，尽[N15]干大事儿。

宋秋玲：嘀嘀，唔，怎么了？是不是电传有**误**？

刘　成：不，啊，没有，那巴西队啊下个月还真能来。

宋秋玲：啊。

刘　成：可咱们不行啊，咱们国家队下个月要，要去踢亚洲杯啊。

宋秋玲：那，那。

宋　母：什么亚洲杯？不踢足球了？

宋秋玲：哎呀，妈，去折腾**大白菜**去啊。

宋　母：哎，哎，那亚洲杯？

宋秋玲：哎，**合着**[N16]这事儿就吹了？

刘　成：倒有**一线**[N17]可能。

宋秋玲：什么？

刘　成：咱们国家队呀，这月底要去**西亚**，我**预计**怎么也能进决赛，最次也闹一四强啊，那，那，那就得打到下个月底了。

宋秋玲：哎哟。

刘　成：不是，啊，要是，要，要是连小组都出不了线哪，那下月中就回来了。

宋秋玲：嗯，啊，什么叫小组出线？

刘　成：就是一个小组哇，分四个队，前两名呢那就叫小组出线，后两名那就叫小组出不了线。

余地	yúdì	n.	leeway; margin; room
上税	shàng shuì	vo.	pay taxes
蔫不出溜	niān bu chūliū		lackadaisical; sluggish; droopy;(see note 14)
误	wù	n.	错误,mistake; error
大白菜	dàbáicài	n.	Chinese（Napa）cabbage
合着	hézhe		turn out to be; so (similar to "这样说" or "这样看来")
一线	yí xiàn		一点点,a ray of; a gleam of
西亚	Xīyà	N.	West Asia
预计	yùjì	v.	estimate; calculate in advance

宋秋玲：嗨，那咱们就不出线了嘛。

刘　成：啊，对！

宋秋玲：啊哈，出不了线，出不了线，出不了线，出不了线……

刘　成：哎，说什么呢你？

宋秋玲：哎，出不了线，不就可以跟巴西队踢了吗？

刘　成：哎呀，打巴西队，那，那只不过是个**商业**比赛。

宋秋玲：哎，哎，可不就是为了挣钱吗？

刘　成：可是踢**亚洲杯**、踢**世界杯**，那是**为祖国而战**[N18]，你知道吗你[N19]？你**盼**点儿好[N20]，行不行呀你？

宋秋玲：哎哎，干吗去？那相还照不照了？

刘　成：**改日**吧，我得赶紧**拟**个电传回去。

宋秋玲：你！

宋　母：闺女，别急，我看，中国队出不了线。

宋秋玲：妈，烦不烦哪？

宋　母：你？

刘　成：哎，老王，这事儿难了。

老　王：嗯？

刘　成：你说那巴西**足协**大概是**料定**咱们中国队出不了线，所以，**回复**的口气挺肯定的。嗯？这事儿是我联系的，我总不能**一味地**强调肯定能出线，肯定出线，那么你……

老　王：那你希望怎么着？

商业	shāngyè	n.	commercial
世界杯	Shìjièbēi	N.	World Cup
为……而战	wèi……ér zhàn		fight for; struggle for
盼	pàn	v.	yearn for; long for
改日	gǎirì		换成另一天，another day; some other day
拟	nǐ	v.	draft; draw up
足协	zúxié	n.	Soccer Association
料定	liàodìng	v	know for sure; be certain
回复	huífù	v.	reply
一味地	yíwèi de	adv.	persistently

刘　成：当然是中国队出线了，入四强，打决赛，夺冠军啊。可是你，哎呀，你说怎么什么都赶到一块儿去了[N21]？

老　王：我说啊——

刘　成：嗯？

老　王：咱换个**思路**。赢了，那当然好，你这个**球迷**，精神上享受了；输了呢，你不就得 30 万了嘛，**物质**上的满足啊。

刘　成：哎！

思路	sīlù	n.	train of thought; thinking
球迷	qiúmí	n.	fan, ball game buff; fandom
物质	wùzhì	n.	material

注释 Notes

1. **"有戏"**：意思是"有希望"。"这回亚洲杯，国家队他有戏吗?""亚洲杯"指亚洲足球锦标赛。"有戏"在这里的意思是"能赢"。

   "有戏" means "hopeful", "is likely to win". "亚洲杯—The Asian Cup" refers to "the Asian Football Tournament". The sentence "这回亚洲杯，国家队他有戏吗?" means "Can the national team win the Asian Game this time?" 如果说"找工作"，"有戏"就是能找到，"没戏"就是找不到，没有找到。

   While used in the context of looking for a job，"有戏" means "one is likely to get that job" or "is a strong candidate for the position"，"没戏" means "won't get the job" and "（the job）has gone south".

2. **"说什么呢"**：等于"你说什么话呢"，是一个反问句，意思是"你不应该这样说"。

   "说什么呢" is the same as "你说什么话呢". It is a rhetoric question meaning "You shouldn't have said this".

3. **"甲 A 联赛**(都两年了)"：指的是中国足球甲级 A 组联赛。

   "甲 A 联赛" refers to "the Division A Tournament". The Chinese team competed in it two years ago.

4. **"那是"**：意思是"（你说得）对。"

   "那是" means "（What you said）is right" or "you are right."

5. **"烦"**："哎呀，你烦不烦? 说几句就没个完，来这儿干什么来的?"

   "烦" 在这里是"使别人烦"的意思。这个动词可以有以下用法：

   "烦" here means "to annoy or bother others." The sentence "哎呀，你烦不烦? 说几句就没个完，来这儿干什么来的" means "Look, aren't you annoying or what? A real jabberer, what did you come here for?

   This verb can be used in the following ways.

   (1) 今天遇到了不高兴的事，我很烦。

   　　A couple of things annoyed me today. I feel so vexed.

   (2) 你别去烦他，让他安静点儿。

   　　Don't bother him; he needs rest (or a quiet environment).

（3）你这个人真烦人！

　　How annoying you are!

6. "动不动（就）"：easily；frequently，at every turn。意思是很容易做出某种行为或发生某种情况（多是说话人不希望的）。

"动不动" is used to describe something happens too frequently for the speaker's liking.

（1）动不动就去下馆子，你把刘成当大款了？

　　Restaurants have become you regular dining place, has Liu Cheng become a millionaire?

（2）你怎么动不动就拿自杀吓唬人？

　　How many times have you threatened us with your attempt at suicide?

（3）他动不动就发脾气。

　　He has a short fuse.

（4）我动不动就感冒，真没办法。

　　I catch cold very easily. There is nothing I can do about it.

7. "咋"：意思是"怎么"。"那可不咋（怎么）的"是一个反问句，意思是"就是这样"。

"咋" means "怎么"。"那可不咋的" is a rhetoric question, meaning "it is indeed the case". Used in this context, the expression implies "Liu Cheng is indeed a big shot, the expenses of going to a restaurant is nothing for Liu Cheng, don't you under estimate him [his wealth]."

8. "大姑娘家家的"：过去常说"姑娘家的"，强调"是一个年轻女孩子"，这里含有"女孩子就应该有女孩子的样子"的意思。按照中国文化，没结婚的成年女性，无论多大年纪都还被称为姑娘。已经到了结婚年龄的女孩常被称为"大姑娘"。过去，女孩子是不好意思谈论自己结婚的事，也不好意思夸自己的未婚夫的。妈妈这里说"大姑娘家家的"，意思是说：秋玲是一个到了结婚年龄的大姑娘，这样夸自己的未婚夫，应该觉得不好意思。

The expression "大姑娘家家的", or "姑娘家的" is used to emphasize the fact that SHE is still a girl, therefore, she should behave the way a girl is expected to behave. According to Chinese culture, she is addressed as a GIRL as long as she is not married regardless how old she might be. There is a distinctive code of behavior for a married woman and a "GIRL." For example, a married woman can talk about her husband, but a girl is expected to shy away from any talk of her future husband or her impending marriage. "A girl ought to behave like a girl". Qiuling's mother used this expression to scold Qiuling for not behaving properly by bragging about her fiancé so openly.

9. **"背过气去"**：意思是"突然停止呼吸"。

"背过气去" means "lose one's breath"; "faint" or "pass out".

The sentence "我怕你妈知道这事儿啊，一高兴再乐得背过（气）去。" means "I'm afraid that this wonderful news would overwhelm your mother so much that she might pass out".

10. **"去你的"**：意思是"别乱说！"或"胡说！"。

"去你的!" is similar to "Shut up!", "Stop the nonsense!" or "You fool!"

11. **"夜长梦多"**：通常用来表示担心一件好事拖得时间久了会发生变化。

"A long night is fraught with dreams"; "a long delay means trouble". This idiom is often used to express one's worry over a delay in have something done that could bring unforeseen troubles to a plan.

12. **"火"**：意思是"兴旺、兴隆"，一般用于形容生意买卖。参见《电梯上的故事》第一部分注释6。

"火" literally means "fire", used colloquially to mean business that's thriving and flourishing. See note 6 in part 1 of《电梯上的故事》

(1) 人家巴西那是足球大国，国内外的球事火着呢。

Brazil is a football giant，you know，football business of all kinds，whether domestic or international，is on all the time.

(2) 北京这几年川菜一直很火。

Sichuan cuisine has become really hot in Beijing in the last few years.

(3) 那家公司现在生意火极了。

That company is cooking with gas now.

13. **"就合"**：意思是"迁就、凑合"，口语；"工夫"指"时间"。

"就合" is used in spoken Chinese, meaning "yield to" or "accommodate to". It is used to refer to a situation in which one has to accommodate the schedule of other's or to yield to the other's demand. "工夫" means "time" here. The sentence "什么时候来呀，得就合着人家的工夫" means "We have to go along with whatever time they plan to come—it's not a negotiable matter.

14. **"蔫不出溜的"**：意思是"不声不响的，没有声张的"，"蔫不出溜的" is usually used to describe the personality and appearance of someone who

seems lackadaisical; sluggish or droopy.

15. "尽"：意思是"全"。

"尽" means "all or completely". For example："不可信" means "not to be believed word by word" or "to be taken with a grain of salt."

The sentence "我说咱刘成行了，啊，蔫不出溜的，哈，尽干大事儿。" implies "Well, our Liu Cheng has eventually made it big. How remarkable he accomplished all the amazing things in such a low-key way without saying a word.

16. "合着"：表示通过思考以后明白了，口语。

"合着" is a colloquial expression meaning "so..." or "I gather...". The sentence "合着这事儿就吹了" means："So，I gather［looking at the way things are］the whole thing (i. e. the visit by Brazil's team and hence the purchasing of the two-bedroom apartment) has all fallen through.

17. "线"：量词，用于抽象事物。"一线"的意思是"一点点"，形容极其微小。如"一线希望"、"一线机会"、"一线光"、"一线生机"。

"线" is a measure word used only for abstract things to mean something very tiny or minute. For example： "一线希望"—a ray（or gleam）of hope；"一线机会"—a slim chance；"一线光明"—a gleam of light；"一线生机"—a slim chance of life.

18. "为……而……"："为……而战"常一起用。

"为……而……" means "to do［sth.］for..." "为……而战" is often used as a fixed phrase. The sentence "那是为祖国而战，你知道吗你？" means："Don't you know those guys are fighting for our Motherland?"

19. "你知道吗你？"：句末用一个"你"，有加强语气的作用。

The second "你" in "你知道吗你？" carries an emphasized mood.

20. "好"：这里的意思是"好事情，好情况"。"你盼点儿好，行不行呀你？"意思是"你盼点儿好事，行不行？"

"好" in this context means "good things or a better situation，etc." "盼" means "to yearn or long for［something to happen］". "盼点儿好" means literally "wish something good［to happen］". The sentence "你盼点儿好，行不行呀你？" means："Be a little more positive，can't you?" or "Have some faith in our team，couldn't you?"

21. "赶到"：这里的意思是"遇到、碰到"。"你说怎么什么都赶到一块儿去了？"的意思是"为什么（所有的）事情都同时发生了"。

"赶到" is the same as "遇到、碰到" meaning "all happened at the same time". The sentence "你说怎么什么都赶到一块儿去了？" means："How come all the things happened at exactly the same moment?"

练习 Exercises

■ 一、口语练习 Oral Practice

（一）回答下列问题 Answer the following questions

1. 刘成认为中国足球队踢亚洲杯有戏吗？

2. 秋玲和刘成看中了一套什么样的房子？那个房子多少钱？远不远？

3. 秋玲的妈妈说："还我的刘成！""大姑娘家家的"，是什么意思？

4. 刘成为什么不让秋玲把"赚 30 万"的事告诉她妈妈？

5. 巴西队同意什么时候来？

6. 在什么情况下巴西队就不能来中国了？

7. 刘成希望中国队出钱，还是希望巴西队来中国？

8. 老王说："咱换个思路，……"，是什么样的思路？

■ 二、书写练习 Written Exercises

（一）选择题 Circle the right answer which reflects the meaning of the under-lined part in the following sentences

1. 哎，哥们儿，这回亚洲杯，<u>国家队他有戏吗</u>？

   A. 他会赢国家队吗

   B. 国家队会赢他吗

   C. 国家队会赢吗

   D. 他会进国家队吗

2. 国家队这次<u>兴许</u>打入决赛呢。

   A. 有可能

   B. 高兴就有可能

   C. 也许被允许

   D. 打入决赛就会高兴

3. 刘　成：以后你就有自己的面包车开了。哎，不但挣钱，而且还可以
   顺路接我，哈哈，嘿嘿。

   宋秋玲：嗯。<u>美得你</u>，嘿嘿。

A. 我看你真美

B. 你更美了

C. 我看你的美

D. 你别想得太美了，我不会接你

4. 你们在这儿干什么呢？铺得满屋子报纸。

  A. 用报纸铺屋子

  B. 用报纸铺屋子的地

  C. 铺地弄得一屋子报纸

  D. 地上到处都是打开的报纸

5. 啊，哎，哈哈，还"我的刘成"！大姑娘家家的。

  A. 大姑娘就是这样说话

  B. 一个大姑娘还没结婚就说这样的话，好意思吗

  C. 刘成是大姑娘家的

  D. 大姑娘都知道刘成

6. 我怕你妈知道这事儿啊，一高兴再乐得背过气去。哈哈！

  A. 高兴一次就死了

  B. 高兴过分，呼吸都停止了

  C. 因为高兴所以背过身去

  D. 高兴得离开了

7. 什么时候来呀，得就合着人家的工夫。

  A. 跟人家的工夫合起来

  B. 跟人家的时间合起来

  C. 人家说什么时间合适就定在什么时间

  D. 人家说有工夫就有工夫

8. 踢亚洲杯、踢世界杯，那是为祖国而战，你知道吗你？你盼点儿好，行不行呀你？

  A. 希望发生好事情

  B. 希望有点儿好

  C. 一点儿希望也好

  D. 希望比原来好

9. 宋母：什么亚洲杯？不踢足球了？

  A. 宋母是足球迷

  B. 宋母对足球没兴趣

  C. 亚洲杯比足球重要

D. 宋母以为亚洲杯跟足球没有关系

（二）填空 Fill in the blanks with the words given

1. | A. 由不得他　　B. 夜长梦多　　C. 火着呢　　D. 就合着 |

　　　　宋秋玲要刘成赶快跟巴西队联系，她怕 _____。但是刘成认为这事 _____，巴西是足球大国，国内外的球事 _____，巴西队能答应来那就不错了。什么时候来得 _____ 人家的工夫。

2. | A. 一线　　B. 一笔　　C. 没影儿　　D. 蔫不出溜　　E. 大事儿 |

　　　　刘成说他联系成了 _____ 买卖。宋秋玲认为那个买卖还是 _____ 的事呢！也许有 _____ 可能。但是宋母却认为虽说刘成 _____ 的，但是尽干 _____。

3. | A. 强调　　B. 联系　　C. 料定　　D. 肯定　　E. 思路
F. 享受　　G. 满足 |

　　　　你说那巴西足协大概是 _____ 咱们中国队出不了线，所以，回复的口气挺 _____ 的。嗯？这事儿是我 _____ 的，我总不能一味地 _____ 肯定能出线。

　　　　咱换个 _____。赢了，那当然好，你这个球迷，精神上 _____ 了；输了呢，你不就得 30 万了嘛，物质上的 _____ 啊。

（一个月以后）

刘　成：哎呀，我说，我让你去的时候你不去，今ㄦ这亚洲杯开赛了，你非今天去，唉。

宋秋玲：上一次，都是因为你，**临阵逃脱**。能怨我吗？

刘　成：那，我，我当时有……啊哟，不是有重要事嘛，你说你，这都一个月了，你愣[N1]说也抽不出时间来。

宋秋玲：我，我忙嘛！

刘　成：哎，来不及了，来不及了，这中乌球赛马上就要开始了，哎，咱们看完球赛再去，啊。李子[N2]那是咱哥们ㄦ，什么时候去都行。走吧？啊？

宋秋玲：不行！

刘　成：为啥？

宋秋玲：我告诉你啊，你要是今天不跟我一块ㄦ去……

刘　成：咋了？

宋秋玲：你这辈子都别再想跟我照相了。

刘　成：走，咱们现在就走。哎呀，我的姑奶奶[N3]！

刘　成：哎哟喂！

宋秋玲：哎！

李　子：哎，你们刚来啊，啊，你……

刘　成：来了，哎，我说，李子，今ㄦ踢后腰的是谁呀？

李　子：**本家**[N4]啊，哎！

刘　成：咳，李铁！

李　子：哎咳！

刘　成：嗬，嘿，哎，那**小范**ㄦ的脚够硬的啊？

李　子：啊哈，哎，啧，哎哟！

临阵逃脱	lín zhèn táotuō		desert on the eve of battle; sneak away at a critical juncture
本家	běnjiā	n.	a member of the same clan; a distant relative with the same surname
小范ㄦ（范志毅）	Xiǎo Fànr(FànZhìyì)	N.	a surname of a player

宋秋玲：哎，你们俩先看着啊，我出去转一转，啊。

刘　成：啊，你去吧去吧。哎，早点儿回来。

宋秋玲：哎，知道！

李　子：哎？怎么走了？

刘　成：让她去吧，咱们踏踏实实[N5]看会儿球。

李　子：那行那行，看完了，我好好给你们照啊，等会儿。

刘　成：哎，往前带啊，啧！

李　子：怎么样？

刘　成：哎，往前**传**！

李　子：啧，又**悬**[N6]了。

售货员：小姐，你要点儿什么？

宋秋玲：啊，随便看看。

刘　成：啊呀，这**区储良**能不能不**嚼**那**泡泡糖**啊？他嚼得我心直慌跟着[N7]。

李　子：哎，你瞧瞧，**李卫清**又上去了，哎啊，回防的时候又回不来。

刘　成：啧，立起来，你立起来呀，咳呀！

宋秋玲：多少了？

观　众：1比0。

宋秋玲：谁赢了呢？

观　众：咳，**乌兹别克斯坦**，哎，传哪！

刘　成：快，给**郝海东**啊！

李　子：别别，别！**趟**！对，往上趟！立起来呀，啧！

传	chuán	v.	to pass (basketball, soccer, etc.)
悬	xuán	adj.	危险, tricky; unpredictable; (see note 6)
售货员	shòuhuòyuán	n.	salesperson; shop assistant; salesclerk
区储良	Ōu Chǔliáng	N.	name of the Chinese Team Coach
嚼	jiáo	v.	chew
泡泡糖	pàopaotáng	n.	chewing gum
李卫清	Lǐ Wèiqīng	N.	name of a player
乌兹别克斯坦	Wūzībiékèsītǎn	N.	Uzbekistan
郝海东	Hǎo Hǎidōng	N.	name of a player
趟	tāng	v.	足球用语, jargon used in soccer game

刘　成：哎呀！

宋秋玲：好球！没进吧？

李　子：大姐[N8]，你看走眼[N9]了吧？

宋秋玲：啊？

李　子：白的是咱们中国。

宋秋玲：我知道。

李　子：哎，别，哎哟！

刘　成：哎哟，哎呀，人家早就盯上咱那个左后卫了，该换人，他就是不换人。

宋秋玲：哈哈哈！

李　子：就是嘛。

宋秋玲：咳咳，中国队没戏了吧？没戏了吧？是不是啊？

李　子：哎，我说大姐啊，您盼什么呢？

宋秋玲：盼中国队被淘汰，早点儿回国呀。只要是……

刘　成：说什么呢你？！你给我出去，滚！

宋秋玲：你！

李　子：哎，别，别，胜败乃兵家常事[N10]。哎，别，别别，别价！

宋秋玲：我走！

李　子：哎，大姐，别走，哎，这事儿怪我，咱早点儿照相，哎，我说，这事儿怪我，哎这要不看球，咱这相就照了。

刘　成：哎呀，跟你没关系，哎呀，走走走，咱照！

李　子：这相怎么照啊？

刘　成：这，照单人的。

看走眼	kàn zǒu yǎn		mistaken for，misjudge
后卫	hòuwèi	n.	rear guard；defender；linebacker
淘汰	táotài	v.	eliminate through selection or competition
滚	gǔn	v	Get out！Get the hell out here！
乃	nǎi	v.	是，be（formal）
别价	biéjie		别，不要，Don't

注释 Notes

1. **"愣"**：意思是违反常理或常规，坚持做某事，如同"偏要"。

   "愣" means "to insist on doing sth. that is thought by others as utterly unreasonable".

   你愣说也抽不出时间来。

   You insisted that he had no time for it.

2. **"李子"**：是对姓李的人的一种亲切的称呼，对年轻的也可以叫"小李子"。

   "李子" is a kind and an affectionate form of address to people surnamed Li. A young person surnamed Li may be called **"小李子"**.

3. **"姑奶奶"**：见《项链》第二部分注释4。

   See note 4 in Part 2 of《项链》.

4. **"本家"**：本来指同一家族的人，这里指同一个姓的。

   "本家" originally refers to people of the same clan. It's used here to mean "people with the same surname."

5. **"踏踏实实"**：见《项链》第四部分注释1。

   See note 1 in part 4 of Necklace.

6. **"悬"**：意思是"危险"。

   "悬" is a colloquial expression meaning "tricky" and "unpredictable". **"又悬了"** used in this context to mean："（winning the game）is once more uncertain!" "The game's become tricky again!" or "Winner and loser are in the air!"

7. **"他嚼得我心直慌跟着"**：这是一种特殊的句子，句子中本来应该在前边的一个成分出现在句末，这种现象叫"追加"。**"他嚼得我心直慌跟着。"**原来的句子是**"他嚼得我心跟着直慌"**。参见《项链》第二部分语法注释1。

   The peculiarity of this kind of sentence structure is that a part of the sentence（**"跟着"** as in this case）usually appears before the verb（**"慌"** as in this case）appears at the end of the sentence. This linguistic phenomenon appears only in spoken language, it's called "add-on." The regular form for **"他嚼得我心直慌跟着。"** is **"他嚼得我心跟着直慌"**（His constant gum-chewing makes me nervous.）Also see grammar note 1 in part 2 of《项链》.

The same structure appears in this script are：

（1）看完了，我好好给你们照啊，等会儿。

The regular form is：等会儿看完了我好好给你们照啊。

Wait until the game is over，I'll take some wonderful pictures for you.

（2）你说怎么回事儿啊这是？

The regular form is：你说这是怎么回事儿啊？（本课第四节 See Part 4 of this script）Tell me what happened?

"追加"的成分通常是说话人认为不那么重要的，而把最想告诉对方的话先说出来。

The "add-on" element is often something that the speaker thinks is not an important part of the sentence. What's said first is more important.

8. "大姐"：在"大姐，你看走眼了吧？"这个句子中，"大姐"是对和自己年龄相仿的女性的一种称呼。现在服务人员、卖东西的人常常这样称呼顾客。称呼年龄相仿的男性为"大哥"。称呼年长的为"阿姨"、"叔叔"。一般不大称陌生人为"爷爷、奶奶"，除非是对八九十岁的老人。

"大姐—big sister" is a friendly and respectful term to address a women of one's similar age，even if she is in fact younger. These days，service people and vendors often use such a term to address their customers. The term "大哥—big brother" is used for men of one's similar age，while "阿姨—aunt" and "叔叔—uncle" are used for older people. One would not generally address a stranger "爷爷—grandpa" or "奶奶—grandma" unless he or she is over eight years old.

9. "走眼"：意思是"看错"了，一般用于品评一个人或一件较贵重物品。

"走眼" means "misjudge" or "mistaken for"，The expression is usually used to refer to people or relatively expensive items. The sentence "大姐，你看走眼了吧？" means："Big sister，I think you have really misjudged this item".

Here are more examples on the use of "走眼"：

（1）你看走眼了，这件衣服不是真的阿迪达斯，你买亏了。

You made a mistake；this piece of clothing is not an authentic Adidas. You got ripped off on this one.

（2）她已经换了好几个男朋友了，前几个都很好，这个她可看走眼了，是个小偷！

She's already dated quite a few guys. The previous ones were very nice，

this time, she made a mistake, the guy turned out to be a thief.

（3）买古董的商人如果看东西看走眼了，可会赔很多钱。

If an antique dealer made a misjudgment, it could cost him a lot of money.

10. **"胜败乃兵家常事"**：来源于《旧唐书》的一句话，也可以用于比赛、考试。意思是"打仗失败是常事，（不要气馁）"，用来安慰、鼓励对方。

This expression is from *Jiu Tang shu*. It means "Victory and defeat are part of a soldier's life". It's now often used to comfort and encourage people who have had some set back in some pursuit.

　　　　　　　　练习 Exercises

■ 一、口语练习 Oral Practice

（一）回答下列问题 Discuss the following questions

1. 宋秋玲说刘成"临阵逃脱"是什么意思？是不是说他在球赛开始前想逃跑，不敢参加比赛？

2. 刘成跟李子是什么关系？

3. 刘成非常想看这场中乌球赛，为什么还是跟宋秋玲照相去了？

4. 宋秋玲不想跟刘成和李子一起看足球赛，刘成是不是很不高兴？

5. 宋秋玲对足球赛有兴趣吗？她为什么对这场比赛也很关心呢？

6. 宋秋玲希望谁赢，为什么？刘成为什么发脾气？

7. 李子是怎么安慰刘成的？李子为什么说宋刘吵架要怪他？

8. 刘成真的要自己一个人照相吗？

■ 二、书写练习 Written Exercises

（一）选择题 Circle the answer which most reflects the meaning of the underlined part in the following sentences

1. 上一次，都是因为你，<u>临阵逃脱</u>。能怨我吗？

　　A. 比赛开始前走了

　　B. 宋秋玲开车先走了

　　C. 快要去照相时跑了

　　D. 看要吵架赶快离开了

2. <u>李子那是咱哥们儿</u>，什么时候去都行。

　　A. 李子是我哥

　　B. 李子是我哥的朋友

　　C. 李子我的好朋友

　　D. 李子在我哥那儿

3. 啧，<u>又悬了</u>。

　　A. 又错了

B. 又可能要输了

C. 又要赢了

D. 输赢又难说了

4. 大姐，你看走眼了吧？

  A. 去看眼睛了

  B. 看着你眼睛走了

  C. 看着路走吧

  D. 看错了

5. 哎，别，别，胜败乃兵家常事。哎，别，别别，别价！

  A. 别输

  B. 别打

  C. 别这样

  D. 别问价

6. 咳咳，中国队没戏了吧？是不是啊？

  A. 中国队的戏演完了

  B. 中国队赢不了了

  C. 中国队的球打完了

  D. 不演中国队的戏了

7. 哎呀，我的姑奶奶！

  A. 怎么了，姑奶奶

  B. 原来你是我的姑奶奶

  C. 你很厉害，我惹不起你

  D. 姑奶奶，你真让人烦

（二）完成句子 Complete the following Sentences with the words given

1. 这孩子牙不好，还 ＿＿＿＿＿＿＿＿＿＿，妈妈一点办法也没有。（非）

2. 你要是今天不跟我一块儿去，＿＿＿＿＿＿＿＿＿。（这辈子）

3. 别说了，＿＿＿＿＿＿＿＿＿。（心直慌）

4. 这人是不是有病，＿＿＿＿＿＿＿＿＿。（盯）

5. 上星期我说去看她父母，＿＿＿＿＿＿＿＿＿。（愣）

6. 我早就告诉你了，＿＿＿＿＿＿＿＿＿。（愣）

7. 工作没做完，＿＿＿＿＿＿＿＿＿。（踏踏实实）

8. ＿＿＿＿＿＿＿＿＿，别着急！（踏踏实实）

四

宋秋玲：妈，你干吗去？

宋　母：哎，买菜去，这火上坐着水呢，你看着点儿啊。

宋秋玲：哎。

宋　母：秋玲，秋玲，刚才我看门口打电话那个像刘成。他老**背着身**，我也看不清楚，你说怎么回事儿啊这是？

宋秋玲：哎呀，妈，买您的菜去，啊。

宋　母：这孩子，咳。

宋秋玲：嗬嗬，哎！

刘　成：好，好，好，哦哦，中国队必胜，中国队必胜，哦哦，哦踢叙利亚四**平**，踢他个四平。哎哎，传哪，传哪，传哪！

老　王：哎哟，我以为屋里有多少人呢，你一个人在吆喝什么呢？

刘　成：哟，老王，太棒了，3比0，太漂亮了，这连着把日本队打出去啊，那出线是**手拿把掐**[N1]。

老　王：哎咳，我看，照你这么说啊……

刘　成：哎呀，中国队必胜，中国队必胜！

老　王：那30万，啊，就**吹了**啊，嘿嘿。

刘　成：哎，哎呀，老王，你先让我高兴高兴，行不行？

老　王：哎，哎咳，我为什么不当球迷啊，就是当不起，因为当球迷不易。

刘　成：你又碰到什么难事儿了吧？

老　王：我说你呢，别跟自己**怄气**啊，赶快找人家姑娘道歉去。

刘　成：我，找她道歉？哼！

老　王：这**臭小子**。

背着身	bèi zhe shēn		with the back towards people
平	píng	adj.	be on the same level; equal
手拿把掐	shǒu ná bǎ qiā		hold firmly in hand, (see note 1)
吹了	chuī le		(been blown away; gone; failed; fell through
怄气	òu qì	vo.	sulk, have the sulks
臭小子	chòu xiǎozi		little rascal; you bustard

刘　成：哎。

老　王：嘿嘿。

售票员：哎，走了，让一让让一让，哎。

乘客1：哎，你觉得今晚跟日本这场有戏吗？

乘客2：哎呀，按说吧，日本队跟咱们胜负差不多，不过这几年是进步大了点儿。

乘客1：是，他们搞联赛比咱们早，而[G1]日本有钱啊。

乘客2：嗯，没错。

售票员：哎，宋儿[N2]，刘成可有日子没来了啊，忙什么呢？

宋秋玲：哎咳，这个时候，球迷能干吗呀？

售票员：哎，说**曹操**曹操到[N3]，这不，在等着呢。

宋秋玲：啊？

售票员：刘成，哟，给我们送花，还挺正经呢。

刘　成：哎，这是祝咱们中国队获胜啊，嘿。哎咳，秋玲儿。

宋秋玲：哎。

刘　成：啊嗬！

宋秋玲：你，不看电视了？

刘　成：啊，我，我，我啊，我这儿准备着呢，看。

售票员：哟嗬，啊，多少钱买的？

刘　成：这个啊，借的。

刘　成：**挺住**，啊，挺住！哎，回防，赶快回防！哎，把球**断**过来，断他，断他！哎，断他！挺住！快呀，快呀，挺住！你说刚才起什么脚啊你！哎，别往前上！回去，回防，赶快回防！哎呀，盯住他，盯住三号，那三号盯住他，盯住！

宋秋玲：哎，是不是日本队进球了，啊？啊？那中国队该回来了吧？该跟巴西队踢了吧？啊？

刘　成：哎呀，你起来！

宋秋玲：你！

曹操	Cáo Cāo	N.	Head of the Wei State (220-265BD) in the Three Kingdom Period
挺住	tǐng zhù	vc.	hold out
断	duàn	v.	break off；cut off；stop

刘　成：你知道什么啊你！啊？中国队容易吗？这球都踢到这份儿上了，这愣没出线！多少年了，老说冲出亚洲，冲出亚洲，你说，多好一个机会，又失去了！以前，**怪体力**，怪没有技术，**怪运气**，怪没有**经济实力**。现在都有了。啊？职业**甲级**联赛都搞了两年了，你说，怎么又是，还这样呢？那年，搞足球的福利**抽奖**[N4]，我一下就买了 500 多块钱的**奖券**，我连个牙刷都没抽到，我为什么呀？我愿意！

宋秋玲：刘成，刘成，啊，刘成！啊。

刘　成：这样也好，能赚到钱，谁不高兴？是吧？咱国家队真照顾咱们啊。秋玲，你说，附近，哪儿房子最好？哪怕是一小间呐，咱们也算有了自己的房子，我听你的。

人　群：哦，哦，哦……

刘　成：哎，停！

球迷1：啊，你听我说啊，中国队出线了！

刘　成：哎，不是输给日本了吗？

人　群：哎嗬嗬！

球迷1：**叙利亚**把**乌兹别克**给踢出去了！

球迷2：中国队曾经 3 比 0 赢了叙利亚，所以就第二名了！

刘　成：哦，啊，喔……

人　群：啊，喔，喔……

宋秋玲：刘成，让大家上车。

刘　成：哎，上车，上车。

人　群：哎，啊，喔。哦来欧，来欧来欧来，哦来欧，来欧来欧来，……

体力	tǐlì	n.	physical power；physical strength
运气	yùnqi	v.	luck；fortune
经济	jīngjì	n.	economy
实力	shílì	n.	strength
甲级	jiǎjí	n.	top level
抽奖	chōu jiǎng	vo.	draw a lottery or raffle，福利抽奖 Lottery for charity
奖券	jiǎngquàn	n.	lottery ticket
人群	rénqún	n.	throng；crowd
叙利亚	Xùlìyà	N.	Syria
乌兹别克	Wūzībiékè	N.	Uzbekistan

字　幕：中国队小组出线，但未进入四强，巴西国家队来华一事未能成行，剧
　　　　中小两口的购房计划落了空。此剧拍摄时，中国队在世界杯外围赛中
　　　　败在西亚人脚下，失去了本世纪冲出亚洲的最后一次机会……

小两口	xiǎo liǎngkǒu	n.	a young married couple
落空	luò kōng	vo.	come to nothing；fail；fall through
外围	wàiwéi	n.	periphery；peripheral
世纪	shìjì	n.	century

注释 Notes

1. **"手拿把掐"**：字面意思是"握在手里了，"比喻"（做好某事）有把握，没有问题"。

   "手拿把掐" literally means "held firmly in one's hand", referring to something, whether being a victory over a game or a business deal, is certain. For example："出线是手拿把掐" means "Winning the knock-out competition is an absolutely sure thing".

2. **"宋儿"**："宋儿"相当于"小宋"。称呼人时，有些姓可以儿化，用法跟"小某"一样。

   Adding "儿" to a surname is similar to addressing someone with "小" in front of a surname.

3. **"说曹操曹操到"**：如果正在说到某一个人时，那个人来了，就可以用这句话。

   Speaking of 曹操 and there he is. Or Speaking of the devil (and he appears).

4. **"足球的福利抽奖"**：中国一种足球彩票。

   A lottery designed to benefit football players and football-related activities in China.

语法 Grammar Notes

"**而**"："他们搞联赛比咱们早，而日本有钱啊"。"**而**"，连词，常用于书面语，有两种功能：表示补充与转折。

"而" is a conjunction used primarily in writing. It has basically two functions："complementary" and "contradictory"。

1. 表示补充关系，意思类似"而且"，连接两个词或短语，通常不能用"而且"替换"而"。

   When "而" is used to connect elements which are complementary，it means "also" or "as well as". It is similar to "而且"，but it can not be replaced by "而且"。

   (1) 她是一个美丽而可爱的女孩。

   She is a lovely (and) pretty girl.

   (2) 漂亮而便宜的衣服不多。

   There aren't a lot of clothes that are both elegant and inexpensive.

2. 表示转折关系，所连接的两个词语或分句意思不同，相对或相反，有对比的意味，但是没有"但是、可是"所表示的转折关系那么明显。例如：

   When "而" is used as a conjunction for two clauses with a contrastive meaning，it means "whereas"；"but" or "instead". It's used to express comparison or contradiction，but is not as emphatic as "但是、可是"。

   (1) 会说中文而看不懂中文的人不少。

   There are quite a lot of people who can speak Chinese，but are unable to write.

   (2) 他要孩子好好儿学习，而自己却从来不看书。

   He demands that his children must study hard，but he himself never read a book.

   (3) 姐姐喜欢唱歌，而妹妹喜欢运动。

   The older girl loves singing while the younger one loves sports.

   (4) 看中文电视对听中文有好处，而对看中文书没有多大帮助。

   Watching Chinese TV is great for one's listening skill，but not for enhancing reading ability.

练习 Exercises

■ 一、口语练习 Oral Practice

（一）回答下列问题 Answer the following questions

1. 妈妈是不是宋秋玲无话不谈的朋友？
2. 老王为什么说："当球迷不易"？
3. 刘成为什么跟自己怄气？
4. 老王为什么叫刘成赶快找宋秋玲道歉去。
5. 老王骂刘成"臭小子"，是不是他很不喜欢刘成？
6. 刘成最后为什么那么高兴？
7. 谈谈你对刘成的女朋友的看法。
8. 谈谈刘成"胜负攸关"的矛盾心理。

■ 二、书写练习 Written Exercises

（一）选择题 Circle the answer which most reflects the meaning of the under-lined part in the following sentences

1. <u>这火上坐着水呢</u>，你看着点儿啊。
   A. 这儿火上有水
   B. 这种火坐在水上
   C. 水坐在火上
   D. 水正在火上烧着

2. 哎呀，妈，<u>买您的菜去</u>，啊。
   A. 提醒妈妈该去买菜了
   B. 叫妈妈赶快去买菜，别晚了
   C. 告诉妈妈赶快去买菜，别忘了
   D. 叫妈妈走开，买菜去，别管他们的事

3. <u>出线是手拿把掐</u>。
   A. 能不能出线悬了
   B. 手拿把掐才能出线

    C. 出线是肯定的了

    D. 出线要手拿把掐

  4. 说曹操曹操到。

    A. 因为说曹操，他就到了

    B. 曹操到时大家正说他呢

    C. 正说他呢他就到了

    D. 他说到就到

（二）填空 Fill in the blanks with the words given

A. 差不多	B. 一下子	C. 这是	D. 背着	E. 那儿等着
F. 不起	G. 祝	H. 愣	I. 哪儿	J. 谁

  1. 秋玲，刚才我看门口打电话那个像刘成。他老_____身，我也看不清楚，你说怎么回事儿啊_____？

  2. 哎咳，我为什么不当球迷啊，就是当_____，因为当球迷不易。

  3. 按说吧，日本队跟咱们胜负_____，不过这几年是进步大了点儿。

  4. 哎，说曹操曹操到，这不，在_____呢。

  5. 哎，这是_____咱们中国队获胜啊，嘿。哎咳，秋玲儿。

  6. 你知道什么啊你，啊，中国队容易吗？这球都踢到这份儿上了，这_____没出线！那年搞足球的福利抽奖，我_____就买了500多块钱的奖券。

  7. 能赚到钱，_____不高兴？咱国家队真照顾咱们啊。

  8. 秋玲，你说，附近_____房子最好？

（三）完成句子 Complete the following sentences with the words given

  1. 好像有多少钱似的，_____。（动不动）

  2. 这个人怎么啦，_____。（动不动）

  3. _____，现在就剩下定个日子搬家了。（手拿把掐）

  4. 他学习特棒，_____。（手拿把掐）

  5. 这场足球赛_____。（有戏）

  6. 那笔生意_____。（没戏）

（四）写作 Composition

  把此剧改写成一篇400字左右的叙述文。

  Write a narrative of at least four hundred words based on this script.

■ 三、文化方面的讨论 Cultural Discussion

  1. 刘成告诉宋秋玲他们很快就有钱买房子了，秋玲不信，说是刘成骗她。

刘成说："哎哟，秋玲儿，我这回要是骗你，我是，我是你孙子。"中国人为什么用"孙子"、"儿子"骂人？这两个词在你们国家的语言文化里可以用来骂人吗？为什么？

Liu Cheng told Song Qiuling that they would soon have the money to buy a two bedroom apartment. Qiuling didn't believe him when he said that Liu Cheng was trying to fool her again. Liu Cheng then said："Come on，Qiuling，if I cheated you this time，I'd be your grandson." What does Liu Cheng mean by saying "I'd be your grandson"? Why do Chinese use "grandson" and "son" as swearing and cursing words? Do people in your culture use these terms in the same way as the Chinese do? Why?

2. 宋母知道女儿和刘成又去饭馆吃饭了，就说："哎呀，动不动就去下馆子，你把刘成当大款了？"宋秋玲回答说："嗯，那可不咋的，别小看了我的刘成啊。"秋玲的妈妈说："啊，哎，哈哈，还'我的刘成'！大姑娘家家的。"宋母为什么觉得秋玲说"我的刘成"不合适？"大姑娘家家的"又是什么意思？你们国家的文化也是这样的吗？

Upon hearing that Qiuling and Liu Cheng dined in a restaurant again，Qiuling's mother said："Well，restaurants have become your regular dining place，has Liu Cheng become a millionaire?" Qiuling replied："It is indeed the case，don't you underestimate [the wealth of] my Liu Cheng." The mother responded："My goodness，"my Liu Cheng"，大姑娘家家的." Why did Song Mu feel it was improper for Qiuling to use the term "my Liu Cheng"? What did Song Mu mean exactly when she said" "大姑娘家家的"? Would people in your culture react the same way?

第十课 良心问题

A matter of Conscience

导读：

　　像很多国家一样，中国的大学也有助教、讲师、副教授、教授（正教授）等学术职称，研究单位有助理研究员、副研究员、研究员等职称。要评职称，首先要自己申请，然后经过系里或研究所的学术委员会讨论，最终由投票决定。本剧表现了一个自知不如别人的申请者，虽然没想真的评上职称，但怕一票都得不到而丢面子，因此去游说学术委员。他想得到的只是一票，可是为了保险，在十一个委员中找了六位。结果发生了谁都没有想到的事。

　　在这个故事里，申请者和评审者都遇到了面子和良心的问题，也都经历了一次良心战胜面子的痛苦历程。

Introduction:

As with universities and research institutes in many other countries, university faculty in China consists of full professors, associate professors, assistant professors and lecturers, while research institute faculty are ranked as senior, associate and assistant researchers, respectively. For promotion, one has to firstly submit an application, then the case will be extensively discussed among members of the Academic Committee, and the final decision is made by the committee's majority vote.

This story describes a man, who was well aware of his professional inferiority and his poor prospects for promotion, but in spite of this, he went on a lobbing campaign out of fear of being embarrassed by not having one vote in his favor within the committee. All he wanted was to have one vote to save his face. However, in order to make sure of that one vote, he sought out six of the eleven committee members for help. The final result came as a total surprise to everybody.

This story is not about one man's promotion; it is about honor, pride and fairness. The incident taught both the applicant and the committee members an invaluable lesson.

主要人物（Main Characters）

樊 进	Fán Jìn	an associate professor at a university
李可仁	Lǐ Kěrén	a clothing designer, wife of Fan Jin
刘教授	Liú jiàoshòu	a professor at a University

樊　妻：哎，你咋[N1]还不睡啊？

樊　进：睡不着。

樊　妻：咋的了？为**职称**的事ᵣ啊？**评**不上就评不上呗，就一个**名额**。人家**赵华**的业务能力就是比你强，他**上**你不上，这也是**正常**的啊。你**愁**啥呀？

樊　进：我愁的不是他上我不上，我愁的是赵华**全票**通过，我樊进啊，**剃个大光头**[N2]。

樊　妻：**学术委员会**不是后天才**投票**的吗？你**未卜先知**[N3]？

樊　进：那不明摆着吗？他有三本**专著**，我只有三篇文章，我要是**评委**啊，我也得投他一票。

良心	liángxīn	n.	conscience
副教授	fùjiàoshòu	n.	associate professor
职称	zhíchēng	n.	title of a technical or professional post
评	píng	v.	evaluate；assess（评职称 evaluate professional titles）
上	shàng	v.	to be promoted
名额	míng'é	n.	quota of people；number of people allowed
赵华	Zhào Huá	N.	Fan jin's rival for promotion
正常	zhèngcháng	adj.	normal, regular
愁	chóu	v.	worry；be anxious
全票	quánpiào		unanimous vote
剃光头	tìguāngtóu	vo.	have one's head shaved (used here to mean "not receiving one vote, not winning one point)
学术	xuéshù	n.	academic；academics
委员会	wěiyuánhuì	n.	committee
投票	tóu piào	vo.	vote, cast a vote
未卜先知	wèi bǔ xiān zhī		foresee the future without divining the Eight Trigrams；(see note 3)
专著	zhuānzhù	n.	monograph, book on a special subject
评委	píngwěi	n.	committee member

樊　妻：那你就**彻底认输**呗。

樊　进：哎呀，我现在算知道了。什么是**困兽犹斗**[N4]。

樊　妻：你斗啥啊？为啥斗，你咋斗啊？

樊　进：为这个，面子。

樊　妻：拉张**选票**不剃光头，**留点儿面子**。

樊　进：还是妻子理解我。

樊　妻：咱家有本写**戏剧**的书，叫《老好人》，我找出来给你看看。

樊　进：看过了。可仁，这回咱俩儿又想到一块儿去了。

樊　妻：你们学术委员会里有老好人[N5]吗？

樊　进：伟大领袖毛主席**教导**我们说，**凡是**有人群的地方就有左中右[N6]。

樊　妻：别**贫嘴**[N7]了。

樊　进：哎，**笔杆子**[N8]我**不及**赵华，哎，**嘴巴子**[N9]我那是全所第一。明天，我就到老好人家去做工作。我就不信找不到一个**心肠软**得不行[N10]的学术委员。走，上床睡觉。哎，你又怎么了？

樊　妻：你说，这么拉选票，道德吗？

樊　进：这就跟**夫妻**睡觉似的，不**存在道德**问题。

彻底	chèdǐ	adv.	completely, downrightly, thoroughly
认输	rèn shū	vo.	acknowledge one's defeat
困兽犹斗	kùn shòu yóu dòu		cornered beasts will still put up a desperate fight; (see note 4)
选票	xuǎnpiào	n.	vote; ballot
留面子	liú miànzi	vo.	save one's face; not make someone feel embarrassed
戏剧	xìjù	n.	drama; play
教导	jiàodǎo	n./v.	teach; give guidance
凡是	fánshì	conj.	any; every; all
贫嘴	pínzuǐ		loquacious, garrulous (derogatory)
笔杆子	bǐgǎnzi	n.	effective writer
不及	bùjí	v.	不如，not as good as; inferior to
嘴巴子	zuǐbàzi	n.	嘴，mouth
心肠	xīncháng	n.	heart
软	ruǎn	adj.	soft; gentle
夫妻	fūqī	n.	husband and wife
存在	cúnzài	v.	exist
道德	dàodé	n.	morals; morality; ethics

樊　妻：啧，哎呀，你啊，就别折腾了。这几天你天天**失眠**，啊，明天，量量**血压**去，啊。你笑啥啊？

樊　进：你知道狗为什么不得高血压呀？

樊　妻：**无聊**。

樊　进：因为狗啊不评职称。

樊　进：我先到刘教授这位老好人家里去，我就不信找不到一位心肠软得不行的学术委员。

刘教授：这怎么说呢？这个职称的评定啊，是按**参评人**的业务水平和**成果**来决定**取舍**的。我呀，不怕你听了不高兴，**凭**你的业务水平，你是**明显地**

失眠	shīmián	v.	suffer from insomnia
血压	xuèyā	n.	blood pressure
无聊	wúliáo	adj.	boring; nonsense
参评人	cān píng rén		applicants
成果	chéngguǒ		academic achievement, such as publications of books and articles, etc.
取舍	qǔshě	v.	accept or reject; make one's choice; selection
凭	píng	v.	base on; go by; take as the basis
明显	míngxiǎn	adj.	clearly; obviously

不及赵华好。当然了，你的**潜力**也不小。如果名额有**多余**，那你的职称也不是不可以考虑。另外，你也知道，这次**申报研究员**的就有两个，而名额呢只有一个啊。

樊　进：我不要这个名额。

刘教授：什么？不要这个名额？咦？那，你找我什么意思？

樊　进：我就要您这一票。

刘教授：什么？我那一票也是**神圣**的一票，不是你要随便就能要到的。你看，这是**家父**[N11]**晚年**对我的**训示**：唯以公心自守，**毁誉**在所不升；**宁**受人毁，也不**徇人之私利**[N12]。你说，我能**违背**家父对我的谆谆教诲吗？

樊　进：您投我一票，绝不是徇人之私利。

刘教授：那，我倒要听听你的**高论**[N13]了。

樊　进：我，我有**自知之明**[N14]，我知道，我不是赵华的竞争对手。这唯一的研究员的名额**理应**归赵华。可是，如果我今天不来求您，那明天投票的结果肯定是 11 比 0。我不怕**名落孙山**[N15]，我就怕吃个**零蛋**[N16]，说实在

潜力	qiánlì	n.	potential; latent capacity
多余	duōyú	adj.	surplus
申报	shēnbào	v.	report to a higher body
研究员	yánjiūyuán	n.	research fellow; researcher
神圣	shénshèng	adj.	sacred; holy
家父	jiāfù	n.	我父亲，my father (formal)
晚年	wǎnnián	n.	old age; one's later years
训示	xùnshì	n.	allocution; instruction or order to younger members of a family from elders
唯	wéi	adv.	唯有，only; alone; solely
毁誉	huǐ yù		praise or blame; praise or condemn
宁	nìng	conj.	宁可，would rather
徇	xùn	v.	ask for; enquire
人之私利	rén zhī sī lì		personal gain; private interest
违背	wéibèi	v.	violate; go against
自知之明	zì zhī zhī míng		self-knowledge; know oneself
理应	lǐ yīng		按道理应该，ought to; should
名落孙山	míng luò sūn shān		fail in a competitive examination; (see note 15)
零蛋	língdàn	n.	零分，zero

的，我太需要您这一票了。您这一票，对于**全局**来说，没有任何的影响。赵华得**满票**，11 票，他也当研究员，少您这一票，他也照样当研究员。可是这一票，对于我来说，是**救生圈**，是**遮羞布**[N17]，是鼓励我不要**沉沦**，重新**振奋**的**动员令**。您投我一票，救我一命，**胜**造**七级浮屠**[N18]。

刘教授：哎，你为什么偏偏来找我呢？

樊　进：您**乐善好施**[N19]，**有口皆碑**[N20]。您有一篇文章，写**人道主义**的，**引用**了**孟子**的一句话："**恻隐**之心，人皆有之"[N21]。

刘教授：啊哈，那孟子还有一句话呢，"是非之心，人皆有之"。樊进啊樊进，你啊，今天是给老师来出难题了，你是来要面子的。**知识分子**爱面子这我能理解，不过，你不能跟任何人说，你来找过我，这是第一；第二，我也不能**担保**明天我就投你一票。

樊　进：您哪，千万别为难。我也做好了剃光头的思想准备。哎，我爱人虽然满口东北大**糙**子话[N22]，可是说起来，她妈妈还是您的同乡呢，是**浙江**

全局	quánjú	n.	overall situation; situation as a whole
满票	mǎn piào		same as 全票, unanimous vote
救生圈	jiùshēngquān	n.	life buoy
遮羞布	zhēxiūbù	n.	fig leaf; something used to cover one's embarrassment
沉沦	chénlún	v.	sink into (grief, sorrow, etc.); sink into degradation; hit bottom
振奋	zhènfèn	v.	be inspired with enthusiasm
动员令	dòngyuánlìng		mobilizing order
胜	shèng	v.	better than
七级浮屠	qī jí fútú		Buddhist pagoda
乐善好施	lè shàn hào shī		a materially and spiritually charitable person
有口皆碑	yǒu kǒu jiē bēi		win universal praise; be universally acclaimed
人道主义	réndào zhǔyì		humanitarianism
引用	yǐnyòng	v.	quote; cite
孟子	Mèngzǐ	N.	Mencius
恻隐	cèyǐn	v.	feel compassion for sb.'s suffering; latent compassion of one's heart; sympathy; sense of pity
知识分子	zhīshi fènzǐ		intellectual; intelligentsia
担保	dānbǎo	v.	assure; guarantee; vouch for
糙	chá	n.	coarsely ground maize or corn
浙江	Zhèjiāng	N.	a province in southeast of China

绍兴人，心细，昨天晚上把家里的安眠药都收起来。行了，我不打扰您了，我走了。

刘教授：樊进，我得纠正你一下，我不是绍兴人，我是江苏镇江人。

樊　进：哦，行，那也挺好。

樊　进：哎，刘教授怎么说来的？第一，叫我不要对别人说我找过她；第二，她不担保明天投我一票。嗯，有希望。

绍兴	Shàoxīng	N.	a place in Zhejiang Province
心细	xīnxì	adj.	careful；scrupulous
安眠药	ānmiányào	n.	sleeping pill；soporific
江苏	Jiāngsū	N.	a province in China
镇江	Zhènjiāng	N.	a place in Jiangsu Province

注释 Notes

1. **"咋"**：怎么。口语。见《都市彩虹》第一部分注释 3。

   "咋" means "why" or "how come". see note 3 in part 1 of《都市彩虹》.

2. **"剃光头"**：通常比喻在比赛、游戏中得了零分。

   "剃光头" literally means "to have one's head shaved". It is used usually to mean "not winning one point". In this context, it means "not receiving one vote".

3. **"未卜先知"**："卜"意思是"算卦"。"未卜先知"的字面意思是"不用算卦就知道（会怎么样）"，形容一个人对某件事有预见性。

   "卜" means "tell fortunes"; "divine". "未卜先知" literally means "foresee the future without divining the Eight Trigrams." It is generally used nowadays to describe someone who claims to know the outcome of a future event without any supernatural help.

   (1) 这场战争刚开始的时候，很多人就未卜先知，说不会有好结果。

   When the War first broke out, many people predicted nothing positive would come out of it.

   (2) 他以为自己聪明过人，万事未卜先知，可是去年买股票却赔光了。

   He always thinks he is smarter than everyone else, he can predict the outcome of anything, but he lost miserably on the stock market last year.

4. **"困兽犹斗"**："犹"的意思是"还、仍然"。"困兽犹斗"的字面意思是"陷于困境的野兽还在挣扎"，比喻陷于绝境的人还在抵抗、挣扎。多用于坏人。

   "犹" means "still". "困兽犹斗" literally means "cornered beasts will still put up a desperate fight". It is used to describe someone who is in a hopeless situation but still struggles and fights. It is a derogative phrase usually used for devilish people.

   在有些人看来，那个罪犯现在是困兽犹斗，而警务人员则胜利在望。

   In the eyes of some people, criminal are stranded beasts putting on one last struggle，the police，on the other hand，see victory in sight.

5. **"老好人"**：指脾气随和、不得罪人的人。常含有"做事没有原则"的意思。

"老好人" refers to someone who is mild tempered and uncontentious，who tries never to offend anybody. The term，however，also implies a lack of principle and fairness in the person's character.

（1）有些老好人是天生的，但也有些人做老好人是为了保护自己。

Some 老好人 are born that way，but some act that way in order to protect themselves.

（2）老好人是做不了我们公司的经理的，我们需要一个有原则性的人。

A "老好人" wouldn't be capable of managing our company. What we need is a person with a strong sense of principle and fairness.

6. **"凡是有人群的地方就有左中右"**：这句话原来的意思是说，凡是有很多人的地方，人的政治立场就会有左、右与中间的不同。本课的意思是说，只要一个地方有很多人，人们的看法态度就不会一样，是会有不同的。

The original meaning of the sentence is "As long as there is a crowd of people there are different political opinions—left，right and center". The sentence in this story means that there are bound to be different opinions as long as there are people.

7. **"贫嘴"**：指爱说废话或开玩笑。有一点贬义。见《门里门外》第一部分注释 10。

"贫嘴" is a derogatory term for a loquacious，garrulous person. See note 10 in part 1 of《门里门外》。

8. **"笔杆子"**：指很会写文章的人。

"笔杆子" refers to someone who is an effective writer.

（1）他是我们办公室的笔杆子，重要的文件都由他起草。

He is the "笔杆子" in our office；all important documents have to be written by him.

（2）他是个笔杆子，经过他润色的文章没有不能发表的。

He is a "笔杆子"；any article that has been polished by him would not be rejected by a publisher.

9. **"嘴巴子"**：这里的意思是说话的"嘴"。有时指脸颊，如：打了他一个嘴巴子。

嘴巴子 means "a talking mouth"，it is used sometimes to refer to "cheek" or "face" as in the sentence "（Someone）slapped him in the face."

10. **"（软得）不行"**：“不行”表示程度，是“很、非常”的意思。“软得不行”意思是“很软，非常软”。

    “不行" refers to a degree, similar to “very" or “extremely". “软得不行",used in this story, means “an extremely kind-hearted" person.

11. **"家父"**：意思是“我的父亲”，用于比较正式的口语。

    家父 means my father. It is used usually in a formal speech.

12. **"唯以公心自守，毁誉在所不升；宁受人毁，也不徇人之私利。"**

    这段话的大意是：自己做事要坚持用公心对待，别人无论说自己好还是不好都不会动摇；宁可忍受别人说自己不好，也不为任何人追逐私利。

    This sentence takes the form of literary Chinese. It means “ (One) should live by principles only, not to be influenced by either praises or slander; (One) would rather be defamed than to pursue private ends for anyone. "

13. **"高论"**：是一种敬辞，通常用来说别人的看法。

    A respectful term used generally to refer to other people's arguments or opinions. (It could also be used in a sarcastic way.)

    (1) 樊进：您投我一票，绝不是徇人之私利。

    Fan Jin：You vote for me, it is absolutely not for anyone's personal gain.

    (2) 刘教授：那，我倒要听听你的高论了。

    Professor Liu：Really? Share with me now your brilliant argument please.

14. **"自知之明"**：意思是一个人能正确地了解自己（的缺点）。一般用在“有”、“没有”的后边。

    自知之明 means “knowing one's own limitations". It is often used after “有" or “没有".

    (1) 他太骄傲了，没有一点自知之明，没人愿跟他交往。

    He thinks he's perfect. He is so arrogant that no one wants to associate with him.

    (2) 人贵有自知之明，一个人只有能正确地了解自己，才能成功。

    It's important to know one's own limitations. Success is based on first knowing oneself well.

15. **"名落孙山"**：意思是“应考不中”（没有考上）。本课的意思是：没有评上研究员。

    The idiom “名落孙山" literally means “fall behind Sun Shan (who was last on the list of successful candidates). It is generally used to mean "fail in a competitive examination". In the context of this story, it refers to his failure to gain promotion.

(1) 他本来对今年要去美国留学很有把握，没想到出国外语考试名落孙山，这对他打击很大。

He was quite sure at first that he would go to America to study this year, never expecting that he would fail the English test. It dealt him a heavy blow.

(2) 去年评高级工程师时，她名落孙山，从此话也说得少了。

She failed to be promoted to senior engineer last year; she became much quieter ever since.

16. "零蛋"：意思是"零分"，因为零的阿拉伯数字写法是一个圆圈，像鸭蛋。一个学生得了零分，也可以说他得了个大鸭蛋。

零蛋" is the Arabic numeral for zero which looks like an duck egg. A student gets a zero; one may say he gets a big duck egg.

17. "遮羞布"："遮羞布"本指系在腰间遮盖下身的布，这里比喻掩盖羞耻的事情。

遮羞布 is the Chinese term for "fig leaf". The term is used to refer to something that is used to cover up one's embarrassment or hush up a scandal.

18. "救人一命，胜造七级浮屠"："浮屠"的意思是"塔"。全句的意思是"救一个人的性命，胜过修七级佛塔。"

"浮屠" is a Buddhist pagoda. The expression means "saving one man's life is more significant than building the highest Buddhist pagoda.

19. "乐善好施"：喜欢做好事，爱施舍。

The expression is used to describe a materially and spiritually charitable person.

(1) 史密斯虽非巨富，但乐善好施，因此在这一带小有名气。

Mr. Smith is well-known in this area for his devotion to charitable work even though he is not an enormously rich man.

(2) 孩子好奇地问：和尚无钱无物，如何乐善好施呢？

The child asks curiously："the monks have neither money nor possessions, how could they be philanthropic?"

20. "有口皆碑"：意思是"人人都称赞"。

有口皆碑 means "win universal praise" or "be universally acclaimed".

21. "恻隐之心，人皆有之"：每个人都有怜悯、同情受苦难的人的心。
   This expression means "Every human has a sense of pity".
   (1) 恶魔难道也有恻隐之心吗？
      Could devil have had any sense of pity?
   (2) 樊进利用有些人的恻隐之心为自己拉选票。
      Fan Jin used other people's sense of pity to canvass votes for himself.
      还有一句"是非之心，人皆有之"，"是非"的意思是"判断对错"。
      "恻隐之心，人皆有之" is the first line of a couplet; the second line is "是非之心，人皆有之" which means "Every human has a sense of right and wrong". "是非" here means (to tell) right from wrong.

22. "东北大碴子话"："大碴子"是加工过的玉米，颗粒较大，过去东北人经常吃。因此把东北话说成大碴子话。
   "大碴子" is roughly grounded corn. People in the Northeast use it to make porridge that they always have . This leads to people outside of the northeast to refer to the kind of Mandarin spoken by people in this region as "大碴子话" which is not a compliment.

练习 Exercises

■ 一、口语练习 Oral Practice

（一）回答问题 Answer questions

1. 樊进为什么睡不着觉？是不是他觉得自己应该评上研究员？
2. 樊妻为什么要丈夫看《老好人》一书？她的目的是什么？
3. 樊进说自己是"困兽犹斗"，他为什么要继续斗？跟谁斗？他是为评上研究员而斗吗？
4. 樊进是怎么说服刘教授的？
5. 从课文里可以看出樊进是个什么样的人？
6. 刘教授是个什么样的人？

（二）讨论 Discussion

1. 谈谈樊进的性格特点。像樊进这样的人多不多？你喜欢樊进这样的人吗？为什么？
2. 谈谈刘教授的性格特点。
3. 樊进跟太太关系如何？请举例说明.

（三）角色扮演 Role Play

把学生分成对，用下列词语，饰演樊进与刘教授的对话。

Pair students up to act out the dialogue between 樊进 and 刘教授, the following words and expressions must be used.

1. 职称	2. 评定	3. 业务水平和成果
4. 决定取舍	5. 潜力	6. 申报
7. 神圣	8. 违背	9. 谆谆教诲
10. 徇人之私利	11. 高论	12. 自知之明
13. 吃零蛋	14. 救生圈	15. 遮羞布
16. 鼓励	17. 乐善好施	18. 有口皆碑
19. 理解	20. 为难	21. 剃光头
22. 思想准备		

二、书写练习 Written Exercises

（一）用指定的词语完成句子 Complete the following sentences with words or expression given

1. 虽然樊进知道赵华各方面都比自己强，但是_____。（彻底）

2. 研究员这个职称的评定是_____。（决定取舍）

3. 刘教授认为樊进_____。（潜力）

4. 刘教授说，如果投樊进一票是_____。（违背……教诲）

5. 赵华各方面都好，_____。（理应）

（二）用所给词语改写句子 Rewrite the sentences with the given items

1. 樊进连觉也睡不着，因为他怕学术委员会投票时所有的人都不投他的票。（吃零蛋）

2. 学术委员会还没投票，樊进说他已经知道结果了。（未卜先知）

3. 樊进明知跟赵华比差得太远，但他还不肯罢休，为了面子还要争一争。（困兽犹斗）

4. 要是刘教授不讲情面就不会投樊进一票了。（给……留面子）

5. 刘教授不愿看到别人难过伤心。（心肠软，老好人）

6. 樊进喜欢说废话，爱开玩笑，真拿他没办法！（耍贫嘴）

7. 我们公司的文件都是他写！（笔杆子）

8. 那个公司只招两个人，可是有 20 个人申请，结果没要我！（名落孙山）

9. 刘教授是个人人赞扬的学者。（学问……有口皆碑）

10. 她虽不富裕，但对公益事业总是尽可能多捐钱。（乐善好施）

11. 她总爱说："谁没有同情心呢？"（恻隐之心，人皆有之）

（三）写作 Composition

写一篇 100 字左右的短文，叙述樊进的烦恼和他的希望。

Write a short essay of 100 or so words describing what is troubling Fan Jin and explain what he now regards as the best scenario to save his face.

二

刘教授：喂，李先生，我是老刘啊。什么？樊进也找了您？

樊　妻：哎，怎么样啊？你咋不说话呀？**卖什么关子**^{N1}啊？

樊　进：6 比 5。

樊　妻：就差一票啊？**够有面子的**。

樊　进：就多一票，面子啊太大了，哈哈，哈哈……

樊　妻：**范进中举**^{N2}？

樊　进：夫人，你说对了，我得六票，赵华得了五票。我樊进也中举了，啊啊。

樊　妻：那怎么可能呢？哎，你不就跟刘老师一个人说了吗？

樊　进：夫人，我向你**坦白**。11 个评委我一共找了六位，**一通动**天地**泣鬼神**^{N3}的**台词**分别讲给了六个评委听。

樊　妻：樊进，你也太不**地道**^{N4}了。

樊　进：哎，**天地良心**^{N5}，我的**初衷**就是想要这一票。哎，你忘了，那不是你跟我说的吗？你说这事情的**概率**是 6 比 1，要想保一票就得同时找六个评委，我要同时找六个评委，我就不得不撒谎。就得跟每一个评委说，只找了你一位，其他的都是事实。包括那天晚上，你把咱们家的安眠药都收起来了。

卖关子	mài guānzi	vo.	(see note 1)
范进	Fàn jìn	N.	a character in the classic novel The Scholars；(see note 2)
中举	zhòng jǔ	vo.	(see note 2)
坦白	tǎnbái	v.	confess; make a confession
(一) 通	(yí) tòng	m.	measure word for action as in "一通话；打了三通"
动	dòng	v.	感动，move or touch (one's heart)
泣	qì	v.	哭，snivel; sob
鬼神	guǐshén	n.	gods and ghosts; spirits; supernatural beings
台词	táicí	n.	uttering of a stage character, including dialogue monologue and aside
地道	dìdào	adj.	genuine; pure; real
天地良心	tiāndì liángxīn		I swear, (see note 5)
初衷	chūzhōng	n.	original intention
概率	gàilǜ	n.	probability

樊　妻：你这人怎么这样啊？我是把安眠药收拾起来了，那不是打扫房间吗？就你樊进，十年不给你评职称，你还能**自杀**呀？那你说吧，你咋对待今天**评选**的结果？

樊　进：我准备接受评委这神圣一票。反正[N6]也不是什么坏事。

樊　妻：樊进啊，你没那么糊涂吧？剃光头你没面子，得一票你**挽回**点儿面子，两票，三票，四票，五票，你，你也小有面子了。哎，你听我说啊，你现在已经是六票了，你比人家赵华多了一票，你多的这一票比剃光头丢的面子要大多了。剃光头你丢的是做学问的面子，你这六票，你看……你丢的是做人的面子啊。

樊　进：可仁，咱们换个话题谈好不好？现在的问题啊，是如何对待天上掉下来馅儿饼[N7]的问题。

樊　妻：天下掉下来馅饼？那是**炸弹**！**避**之**犹恐不及**[N8]！

樊　进：哎，你别大声**嚷嚷**成吧？

樊　妻：我，可以小声地跟你说一句话，你啊，可以跟一个**心灵安宁**的服装**设计师**睡在一张床上。可是我，不能跟一个**假冒**的研究员生活在一个房子里。

樊　进：反正，现在要想重新投票，怕也不那么容易。

樊　妻：那，那你总该有个态度吧？你现在就写份报告，把**原委**说清楚，做个**检查**，**拒绝**不该属于你的职称。不就完了。

自杀	zìshā	v.	commit suicide; take one's own life
评选	píngxuǎn	v.	choose and appraise through comparison
挽回	wǎnhuí	vc.	reverse the unfavorable situation; turn the table
炸弹	zhàdàn	n.	bomb; bombshell; crump
避	bì	v.	躲避, avoid; keep away
犹	yóu	adv.	(Lit.) 还, still
恐	kǒng	v.	怕, be afraid
不及	bù jí		来不及
嚷嚷	rāngrang	v.	make a uproar; yak; shout; yell
心灵	xīnlíng	n.	(Lit.) heart
安宁	ānníng	adj.	calm; peaceful
设计师	shèjìshī	n.	designer
假冒	jiǎmào	v.	pose as; palm off (a fake as genuine)
原委	yuánwěi	n.	the whole story; all the details
检查	jiǎnchá	v.	self-criticism
拒绝	jùjué	v.	refuse

樊　进：行，我听你的。

樊　妻：不过这事儿吧，也怨我。你说我让你看《老好人》那本书干啥呀？

樊　进：啊，我自己也是找不到北^{N9}了。哎，你说我要是把十一个评委我都找了，弄不好我还能得满票呢。

樊　妻：那就是天字第一丑闻^{N10}了！

樊　进：嗯哼，你说这知识分子成堆的地方^{N11}，这好人怎么这么多呢？

樊　妻：坏人啊，就你一个。

樊　进：哎，这好人多了，也能办坏事儿，啊。

刘教授：哎，咱们是一世清名被玷污^{N12}了，也算是晚节不忠吧。可咱们是哑巴吃黄连^{N13}哪。当然，当然不能就这么算了。我已经打电话请他到我家来做做解释。哦，我们家有人来了。就这样吧，再见。

丑闻	chǒuwén	n.	scandal
成堆	chéng duī	vo.	pile up; heap up; stack
玷污	diànwū	v.	stain; tarnish
晚节不忠	wǎnjié bù zhōng		cannot maintain integrity in one's later years
黄连	huánglián	n.	Coptis Chinensis (it has an incredibly bitter taste)

注释 Notes

1. **"卖关子"**：比喻说话、做事在重要时刻故弄玄虚，使对方着急。

   "卖关子" is a kind of speech style in which the speaker purposefully turns simple things into mysteries，or mystifies something at a key point to make the listener anxious to hear the outcome.

2. **"范进中举"**：小说《儒林外史》中一个著名的故事。说的是范进参加科举考试，一直不中，直到老年才中举人。

   范进中举 is a famous episode from the novel *The Scholars*．It is about Fan Jin's experience in taking the civil service examinations．He does not pass the provincial examination until he becomes an old man.

3. **"动天地泣鬼神"**：使天地感动，使鬼神也感动得哭泣。

   This phrase is used to describe an extraordinarily emotional scene．Something (a speech or an event) was so emotionally moving that it shook (the heart of) the Heaven and the Earth and made all the gods and spirits cry.

4. **"不地道"**："地道"有一个意思是"实在"、"够标准"，常用否定形式。说人或做事"不地道"，意思是这个人人品不好，或"做了不应该做、不够标准、或缺乏道德的事"。

   "地道" here means "honest"，"morally right" or "up to standard"．If a person is said as "不地道"，it means he has done something that is shady and morally wrong".

5. **"天地良心"**：用"天地良心"几个字向别人表明自己说的是真话，没有说谎。

   "天地良心" means literally "Heaven and Earth and my conscience (know)"．It means the same as the expression "on my honor" or "I swear" in English.

6. **"反正"**：见《无端介入》第一部分语法注释4。

   See grammar notes 4 of part 1 in《无端介入》.

7. **"天上掉馅儿饼"**：比喻没有经过任何努力、意外地得到了很大的好处。

   "天上掉馅饼" is the same expression as "manna falling from heaven" and "good fortune falling in one's lap"．It is used here to mean something wonderful happened to someone who didn't expect it nor had to expend any effort to obtain it.

8. **"犹"**：意思是"还"，书面语。"避之犹恐不及"中"之"是代词，整句话的意思是：躲它还怕来不及呢。

"犹" is the written form of "还" (still). "之" in "避之犹恐不及" is a pronoun (In the context of this story here, "之" refers to "the involvement in this case"). The whole sentence means "(One) should worry that there isn't enough time to escape from it."

9. **"找不到北"**：本来的意思是迷失了方向，比喻"不知该怎么办才好"。

Originally "找不到北" means "lost for directions", it is used more often these days to describe someone who is so overwhelmed that she/he can't think straight. I. e.

他高兴得找不到北了。

He was so happy that he felt lost.

10. **"天字第一丑闻"**：最大的丑闻。

The biggest scandal ever.

11. **"知识分子成堆的地方"**：意思是"知识分子很多的地方"。

"成堆" means "piled up". The sentence "知识分子成堆的地方" refers to a place filled with intellectuals or crowded with intellectuals. E. g.

大专院校及研究所当然是知识分子成堆的地方。

Universities and research institutes are naturally filled with intellectuals.

12. **"一世清名被玷污了"**："一世"意思是"一生"，"清名"意思是"清白、没有污点的名声"，"玷污"意思是"弄脏了"。"一世清名被玷污了"意思是"一生清白（没有污点）的好名声被玷污（弄脏）了"。

"一世" means "one's whole life"; "清名" means "clean name"; "玷污" means "stained". The sentence means：(One's) life-long good reputation is permanently stained (by one incident).

13. **"哑巴吃黄连"**：歇后语。"黄连"是一种很苦的中药。这句话完整的表达是："哑巴吃黄连，有苦说不出"。

The chemical named "黄连" is Coptis Chinensis which is an ingredient in some Chinese Medicine. It has an incredibly bitter taste. The expression literally means "a mute person is unable to express the bitterness of 黄连". It is used generally to mean "being compelled to suffer in silence".

练习 Exercises

■ 一、口语练习 Oral Practice

（一）回答问题 Answer questions

1. 樊进以 6 比 5 胜赵华以后心情如何？他想接受这个结果吗？

2. 樊妻得知樊进得胜后，反应如何？

3. 樊进听了妻子的谈话以后，态度有什么转变？为什么？

4. 职称评审结果出来以后，刘教授心情如何？为什么？

5. 樊妻为什么说这个"天上掉下来的馅ㄦ饼"是避之犹恐不及的炸弹！

（二）讨论 Discussion

1. 樊进是个诚实的人吗？樊进是个坏人吗？请你举几例说明。

2. 樊进说："这好人多了，也能办坏事ㄦ"是什么意思？你有没有同感？

（三）角色扮演 Role Play

把学生分成对，用下列词语，饰演樊进与妻子的对话。

Pair students up to act out the dialogue between 樊进 and 妻子，the following words and expressions must be used.

1. 卖关子	2. 不地道	3. 初衷	4. 糊涂
5. 挽回	6. 炸弹	7. 假冒的	8. 态度
9. 原委	10. 检查	11. 拒绝	12. 属于
13. 动天地泣鬼神		14. 天上掉下来馅饼	
15. 避之犹恐不及		16. 天字第一丑闻	

■ 二、书写练习 Written Exercises

（一）用指定的词语完成句子 Complete the following sentences with words or expressions provided

1. 樊进跟六个评委一个一个地谈了他的处境与希望。（分别）

2. 你知道，我最初的希望就是得一票。没想到有这么个结局。（初衷）

3. 那不是你跟我说的吗？你说这事情的概率是 6 比 1。我要同时找六个

评委，就非撒谎不可。（不得不）

4. 樊进：啊，我自己也是不知怎么办好了。（找不到北）

5. 咱们的一世清名被玷污了。可咱们是有苦说不出啊。（哑巴吃黄连）

6. 樊进比赵华还多一票，他觉得这真是连想也没想过的好事。（天下掉下来馅饼）

7. 在樊妻看来，这个"天下掉下来的馅饼"，是一颗炸弹，躲还怕来不及呢！（避之犹恐不及）

（二）填空 Fill in blanks with appropriate words from the text

| A. 初衷 | B. 拒绝 | C. 一通 | D. 地道 |
| E. 接受 | F. 原委 | G. 反正 | H. 概率 |

　　樊进的_____是想要一票来保住面子。没想到他那_____动天地泣鬼神的台词把六个评委都感动了。樊进"中举"以后，他最初准备_____评委这神圣一票，认为_____也不是什么坏事。但他太太说他这样做太不_____了。他太太好像忘了，当初是她跟樊进说这事情的_____是 6 比 1，所以樊进同时去找了六个评委。樊妻建议樊进写份报告，把事情的_____说清楚，做个检查，_____不该属于自己的职称。

（三）写一篇 150 字左右的短文，叙述樊进"范进中举"·后的反应与跟妻子谈了以后的思想转变及感想。

Write a short essay of 150 or so words describing Fan Jin's immediate reaction to the voting result, and his change of attitude and reflections upon the incident after talking with his wife.

三

刘教授：来了，谁啊？哦，您是？

樊　妻：啊，我叫李可仁，是樊进的妻子。

刘教授："范进"？樊进吧？

樊　妻：啊，我是东北人，**普通话**讲不好，哈哈。

刘教授：**嗬嗬**，请坐请坐。

樊　妻：刘老师啊，他是**无地自容**[N1]了，只有我来代表他向您**负荆请罪**[N2]了。

刘教授：哼，他**大获全胜**，还负荆请什么罪啊？

樊　妻：啊，不，刘老师，这可是一次失败啊。

刘教授：失败在哪儿啊？

樊　妻：是预测的失败。樊进啊，真的，本来他就想得一票就行了，他是怕剃**秃头**没面子。

刘教授：可他分别找了六个评委，并对每一个评委都说，"我只需要您一票"。

樊　妻：那是因为我们太相信概率了。我们**天真地**，不，我们**世俗地**认为，啊，要一张选票，最少得找六个评委。没想到……

刘教授：哼，哪知六个评委都不**坚持原则**。

樊　妻：不，刘老师，哪知道六个评委都是善良的好人啊。

刘教授：你，这是**讽刺**。

普通话	pǔtōnghuà	n.	Mandarin Chinese
嗬	hē		used to express surprise
无地自容	wú dì zì róng		feel too ashamed to see anybody；(see note 1)
负荆请罪	fù jīng qǐng zuì		ask for the most severe punishment；(see note 2)
大获全胜	dà huò quán shèng		获得很大的、全部的胜利，an overwhelming victory
秃头	tūtóu	n.	(of a person) hairless; bold
天真地	tiānzhēn de	adv./adj.	naively; innocently
世俗地	shìsú de	adv.	conventionally (derogatory)
原则	yuánzé	n.	principle
讽刺	fěngcì	v.	satirize; ridicule

樊　妻：绝不是！您比方说啊，我们单位**评优**的时候，也得跟方方面面[N3]的评委**打交道**。有的人还**送礼**呢，礼也不轻啊，他们全收了，都说这一票没问题。结果，六个评委只有一个**履行**了**诺言**。而你们，我们也没送礼，也没请客吃饭，结果都投了他的票。凡是范……范……樊进**拜访**过的同志，啊。

刘教授：但樊进送来了一口啊早就**具有**的**伶牙俐齿**[N4]，一脸临时装出来的忠诚老实。

樊　妻：我很**惭愧**，虽然你们比我们年岁大好多，结果，你们却比我们**单纯**许多。

刘教授：那我顺便问一下，那安眠药是你收走的吗？**确有其事**？

樊　妻：这，这个确有其事。

刘教授：那，你要**开导**开导樊进，这职称问题**迟早**都可以解决的嘛。

樊　妻：樊进会正确对待的，他已经向所里打了报告，希望所里重新地评选，让应该得到职称的同志得到它。

刘教授：这就好，我相信，六个评委都会**相应地**做出**表态**。不管怎么说，良心问题要比面子问题要紧得多。

评优	píng yōu	vo.	select the best; vote for the most outstanding
打交道	dǎjiāodào	vo.	come into contact with; have dealings with
送礼	sòng lǐ	vo.	give sb. a present; present a gift to sb.
履行	lǚxíng	v.	fulfill; carry out; perform; implement
诺言	nuòyán	n.	promise; pledge
拜访	bàifǎng	v.	pay a visit; call on (formal)
具有	jùyǒu	v.	有, possess
伶牙俐齿	líng yá lì chǐ		good at words; a good talker; (see note 4)
临时	línshí		momentarily
装出来的	zhuāng chulai de		put on an act; feign an act, act out
忠诚	zhōngchéng		faithful; loyal
惭愧	cánkuì	adj.	be ashamed
单纯	dānchún	adj.	naive; pure
确有其事	què yǒu qí shì		真有那件事, it did happen; sth. truly took place
开导	kāidǎo	v.	enlighten; help sb. see the point
迟早	chízǎo	adv.	sooner or later
相应地	xiāngyìng de	adv.	accordingly
表态	biǎotài	vo.	make known one's position; declare where one stands

樊　妻：刘老师，真是给您添难了！

刘教授：每次评职称，作为评委，我没有一次不痛苦的。不瞒你说，**僧多粥少**[N5]，苦哇。唉，作为评委呀，我不见得比那些参加评比的人**感受**少，我为那些够条件而评不上的人**遗憾**。在评比的这一两个月里边，我在**走廊**里最怕碰见的就是那应该评上而没有评上的人，我都不敢**正眼**看他们一眼。得，唉，我也知道，他们呀，不会埋怨我的。

樊　妻：会是这样的。

刘教授：我们聪明地活着，有的时候真没办法，就把良心**抛**在了一边。

樊　妻：您是说，樊进？

刘教授：也说我自己。

樊　进：敬爱的领导，这么叫不合适，尊敬的老师们，不，不说尊敬，他们讨厌**虚称**，就说老师们。嗯，老师们，我樊进……

樊　进：哎，可仁，你知道，10比1的投票结果**宣布**之后，是一番什么**景象**！啊？十一个评委首先向**入选**者赵华表示祝贺，然后……哎，你听着没有。

樊　妻：听着呢。

樊　进：然后，向只得一票的**落选**者，我樊某，表示祝贺，哎，可是祝贺的方

添难	tiān nán	vo.	create more trouble; make it more difficult
僧多粥少	sēng duō zhōu shǎo		too many people compete for too few positions; (see note 5)
感受	gǎnshòu	n.	feeling
遗憾	yíhàn	v.	regret; pity
走廊	zǒuláng	n.	corridor; passageway
正眼	zhèngyǎn		look squarely; look (someone) in the eye
抛	pāo	v.	throw; toss; fling
虚称	xūchēng	n.	empty or boastful titles
宣布	xuānbù	v.	declare; proclaim; announce
景象	jǐngxiàng	n.	scene
入选	rùxuǎn	v.	be selected, be chosen
落选	luòxuǎn	v.	lose an election or competition

式不一样。和赵华只是一般般地握过手，和我，又是**拍肩**，又是**握手**，又是**拥抱**。刘教授甚至**老泪纵横**[N6]啊，说我是**好样儿的**。看那意思，好像我**拯救**了她的**灵魂**似的。那**场面**，绝对，我比赵华有面子。

樊　妻：我看啊，你挺像阿Q[N7]。

樊　进：哼，我这个事情啊，是从《**范进中举**》到《**阿Q正传**》全包括了。

樊　妻：还有个良心问题。那天，我到刘教授家去，她说了一句话我挺受感动的，她说，"人呐，聪明地活着，有时候呢，却把良心抛到一边儿去了"。

樊　进：哦，哎，她是不是批判我呀？

樊　妻：那倒不是，她，她也有点儿**自责**吧。

樊　进：哎呀，我们是得想想良心问题了。开始的时候呢，我们想解决面子问题，后来出现了良心问题，于是就解决良心问题，面子问题也就**迎刃而解**[N8]了。

樊　妻：行了，行了，你啊，别发表这类**哲学见解**了。你说你这一个星期啊，**绞尽脑汁**[N9]，啊，你费了多少**脑细胞**啊？你还是早点儿休息吧，啊。

拍肩	pāi jiān	vo.	拍肩膀，pat shoulder
握手	wò shǒu	vo.	shake hands
拥抱	yōngbào	v.	embrace; hug
老泪纵横	lǎo lèi zònghéng		(an old person) be in tears；(see note 6)
好样儿的	hǎoyàngrde		Good man! A person of integrity and courage
拯救	zhěngjiù	v.	救，save; rescue
灵魂	línghún	n.	soul; conscience; spirit
场面	chǎngmiàn	n.	scene
范进中举	Fàn Jìn zhòng jǔ		(see note 2 of part 2)
阿Q正传	A Q Zhèngzhuàn		(see note 7)
自责	zìzé	v.	blame oneself
迎刃而解	yíng rèn ér jiě		(of a problem) readily solved；(see note 8)
哲学	zhéxué	n.	philosophy
见解	jiànjiě	n.	view; opinion; understanding
绞尽脑汁	jiǎo jìn nǎozhī		rack, cudgel or tax one's brains
脑	nǎo	n.	brain
细胞	xìbāo	n.	cell

樊　进：哼。

樊　妻：哎，你这是怎么了？

樊　进：我在想一个问题。

樊　妻：你还想什么呀？

樊　进：我那一票，到底是谁投的呢？

樊　妻：你累不累呀？

樊　进：啊。

樊　进：过几天，所里又要分房子了，有职称高的，有岁数大的，有**年头**儿多
　　　　的，有贡献突出的，还有领导，也是个良心问题。

字　幕：根据研究所门厅前大黑板上的通知，这天下午二时三十分又开一个全
　　　　体学术委员参加的会议，也有几位行政领导坐在里面。会议内容不
　　　　详……

年头儿	niántóur	n.	number of years; long time
不详	bù xiáng		detail unknown

398

1. **"无地自容"**：意思是没有地方让自己躲藏起来，形容十分羞愧。

   "无地自容" literally means "one can find no place to hide oneself from shame". It's used to describe a situation in which one feels too ashamed to see anybody.

2. **"负荆请罪"**："负"的意思是"背着"，"荆"的意思是"荆条"，是古时打人的刑具。"负荆请罪"的意思是背着荆条请求责罚，表示主动承认错误、认罪。这个成语故事来自《史记·廉颇蔺相如列传》。

   "负" means "to carry on one's back"; "荆" means "荆条 (twigs of the chaste tree)", used as an instrument of torture in ancient China. "负荆请罪" means someone, upon recognition of making or committing a grave mistake or a crime, asks for the most severe punishment — proffer a birch and ask for flogging. The expression originates in "The story of Lian Po and Lin Xiangru"（廉颇与蔺相如）in "Records of History" written by the famous historian Sima Qian（司马迁）.

   一进门，樊进的妻子就对刘老师说，她是代表樊进向刘老师负荆请罪来了。

   Once she entered the room, the wife of Fan Jin told Professor Liu that she came to ask for punishment on behalf of her husband.

3. **"方方面面"**：意思是"各个方面"。

   Same as "各个方面" meaning "in every aspect".

4. **"伶牙俐齿"**：意思是"口齿伶俐，能说会道"。

   This expression is used to describe someone who is good at words, a good talker, have the gift of the gab.

   （1）这个姑娘伶牙俐齿，以后当律师准行！

   　　 This girl is good at words; she'll be an able lawyer!

   （2）她伶牙俐齿，黑的能说成白的，我不是她的对手。

   　　 She's a good talker; she can turn black into white. I'm no match for her.

5. **"僧多粥少"**：字面意思是"和尚多，粥少，不够吃"，比喻"人多，工作、

职位或东西少，不够分配。"

"僧多粥少" literally means "there are more monks than porridge", used here to mean "too many people compete for too few positions".

在美国，大学生工作很难找，因为僧多粥少，尤其是学文科的，找工作更难。

Because there are too many people competing for too few positions, faculty positions are very difficult to obtain in America, especially for people in the humanities.

6. **"老泪纵横"**：形容老年人非常感动流下眼泪的样子。

"老泪纵横" is used to describe old people being emotionally overwhelmed and moved to tears.

终于与失散了近50年的女儿相见了，那位80岁的老人激动得老泪纵横。

Reunited again with his daughter who had been lost for nearly 50 years, the old man's face became covered with tears.

7. **"阿Q"**：鲁迅小说《阿Q正传》的主人公，他是一个在农村靠打短工生活的农民，地位非常低，经常受人欺负。但是他有一种"精神胜利法"，使自己"转败为胜"，达到自我安慰的目的。比如有一次他被人打了，他就用自己的手打自己的脸，他想，打人的是自己，被打的是别人，这样他就"心满意足地得胜"了。这也叫"阿Q精神"。现在如果说某人是阿Q，就是说他有"阿Q精神"。

"Ah Q" is the main character in "The story of Ah Q" written by Luxun (鲁迅). Ah Q, a temporary rural worker who was constantly bullied by fellow villagers and eventually developed a method of "spiritual victory" which turns a defeat into a victory, and henceforth to make him feel victorious after a defeat. For example, once he was beaten up by a fellow homeless man, he naturally felt physical pain, anger and sadness. To make himself feel better, he started slapping his own face while thinking of punishing the man who had beaten him up. Such a practice is called "the Ah Q spirit". These days when someone is referred to be "Ah Q", it means that he has the "Ah Q spirit".

8. **"迎刃而解"**："刃"是"刀刃"，字面意思是：用刀劈竹子，劈开了一个口，下面的就随着刀口自然裂开了。比喻主要问题解决了，其他相关问题就可以自然解决了。

"刃" means "the edge of a knife", The original meaning of the phrase is "bamboo splits as it meets the edge of a knife". This is used to draw an analogy — once the principle problem is solved, the related problems can be readily solved.

(1) 大家认识统一了，问题就都迎刃而解了。

Once everyone had the same understanding, other problems were solved immediately.

(2) 我相信，只要我们能把主要问题解决了，其他问题就会迎刃而解。

It is my belief that once we found the main obstacle, other problems would be easily solved.

9. "绞尽脑汁"：意思是"费尽脑筋、很费思考"。

"绞尽脑汁" means "to rack, cudgel or tax one's brains".

(1) 开饭馆没有资金，父亲绞尽脑汁也想不出谁能借钱给我们。

There is no money to start a restaurant; father racked his brains thinking who could help us.

(2) 谁都知道，他一天到晚绞尽脑汁在想怎么能发财。

Everyone knows how to become a millionaire is what is constantly on his mind.

(3) 为了避免公司破产，他绞尽了脑汁，度过了多少个不眠之夜。

He racked his brain and went through countless sleepless nights in order to avoid the fate of bankruptcy of his company.

练习 Exercises

一、口语练习 Oral Practice

（一）回答下列问题 Answer the following questions

1. 樊进为什么让太太去刘教授家替他认错？
2. 樊妻是怎样向刘教授解释丈夫的所做所为的？
3. 刘教授现在对自己的老好人态度有什么新看法？
4. 老好人好不好？你想做个老好人吗？
5. 本剧似乎认为知识分子比别的人都单纯、善良。你同意吗？为什么？

（二）讨论 Discussion

1. 请你谈谈通过这件事，樊进学到了什么？他太太学到了什么？刘教授及另外五位教授又学到了什么？
2. 剧终樊进很有面子，大家跟他又是拍肩，又是握手，又是拥抱。刘教授甚至还感动地老泪纵横。为什么？

二、书写练习 Written Exercises

（一）用中文解释句中画线部分的意思 Explain in Chinese the meaning of the underlined part in the following sentences

1. 樊妻：刘老师啊，他是<u>无地自容</u>了，只有我来代表他向您<u>负荆请罪</u>了。
2. 刘教授：哼，他<u>大获全胜</u>，还负荆请什么罪啊？
3. 樊妻：刘老师啊这可是一次失败啊。是<u>预测的失败</u>。
4. 评委们收了礼后都说这一票没问题。结果，六个评委只有一个<u>履行了诺言</u>。
5. 樊妻：刘老师，真是<u>给您添难了</u>！
6. 刘教授：我在走廊里最怕碰见的就是那应该评上而没有评上的人，我都不敢<u>正眼看他们一眼</u>。
7. 樊进：刘教授甚至老泪纵横啊，说我<u>是好样儿的</u>。
8. 良心问题解决了，面子问题就<u>迎刃而解</u>了。

9. 樊妻：行了，别发表你的哲学见解了。你这一个星期啊，绞尽脑汁，你费了多少脑细胞啊？

（二）用成语填空 Fill in blanks with appropriate idioms

A. 绞尽脑汁	B. 伶牙俐齿	C. 无地自容
D. 大获全胜	E. 天地良心	F. 迎刃而解
G. 晚节不忠（保）	H. 一世清名	I. 负荆请罪
J. 动天地泣鬼神	K. 忠诚老实	L. 老泪纵横

1. 刘教授没有坚持原则，被樊进一通 ＿＿＿＿＿＿ 的台词说服了。投了樊进一票，后来她很后悔，认为自己 ＿＿＿＿＿＿ ，＿＿＿＿＿＿ 被玷污了。

2. 太太说他不地道，樊进着急地说："＿＿＿＿＿＿ ，我的初衷就是只想要一票，不剃秃头就行了。"

3. 认识到错误以后，樊进觉得 ＿＿＿＿＿＿ ，只有求太太去代表他向刘教授＿＿＿＿＿＿ 了。

4. 刘教授说樊进 ＿＿＿＿＿＿ ，求人时又装出 ＿＿＿＿＿＿ 的样子，所以他才把六位学术委员都骗了。

5. 樊进公开承认错误以后，刘教授激动得 ＿＿＿＿＿＿ ，说樊进是好样的。那场面让人看上去，樊进绝对比赵华有面子。

6. 良心问题解决了，面子问题也就 ＿＿＿＿＿＿ 了。

7. 樊进为了面子，为了不剃光头而 ＿＿＿＿＿＿ ，没想到却 ＿＿＿＿＿＿ ，比赵华还多了一票。

（三）联系此剧谈谈你对面子、良心、原则的看法。写一篇 200 字左右的感想。Write an essay of about 200 words, based on this story, to express your view on the concept of face and honor, pride and fairness, conscience and principle.

附录一：生词索引^① Vocabulary Index

---

① 专有名词略。

白领	báilǐng	adj.	white collar (worker)	(2.2)
白忙活	bái mánghuo		make efforts in vain	(4.2)
败家	bàijiā	adj.	spendthrift；wastrel	(1.4)
拜访	bàifǎng	v.	pay a visit；call on (formal)	(10.3)
搬家	bān jiā	vo.	move	(3.4)
板儿	bǎnr	n.	board	(1.3)
办手续	bàn shǒuxù	vo.	办离婚手续 (as used in the context)	(3.4)
办妥	bàn tuǒ	vc.	handle sth. appropriately	(6.2)
半步	bàn bù	n.	half a step	(3.1)
半死不活	bàn sǐ bù huó		half-dead；more dead than alive	(1.1)
帮	bāng	m.	gang；clique；a group of people (derogatory)	(2.2)
榜样	bǎngyàng	n.	example；role model	(5.4)
棒	bàng	adj.	身体好、能力强或水平高，terrific；wonderful	(9.2)
棒子	bàngzi	n.	stick；club；cudgel	(7.1)
包	bāo	n.	purse；bag	(2.1)
包括	bāokuò	v.	include；consist of	(2.1)
包装	bāozhuāng	n./v.	pack；packing；packaging	(5.2)
宝贝（儿）	bǎobèi(r)	n.	treasure；precious thing	(1.3)
保管	bǎoguǎn	v.	take care of；store；keep	(5.2)
保护	bǎohù	v.	care and protect from harm	(2.2)
保险	bǎoxiǎn	adj./n.	safe	(4.2)
保证	bǎozhèng	v.	guarantee	(5.1)
保重	bǎozhòng	v.	take care of oneself	(2.4)
报答	bàodá	v.	requite；repay with action	(1.3)
报道	bàodào	n./v.	report (news)	(6.4)
报费	bàofèi	n.	newspaper fee	(5.3)
报社	bàoshè	n.	news press，newspaper office	(4.3)

抱养	bàoyǎng	v.	领养，adopt	(8.3)
卑鄙	bēibǐ	adj.	despicable; contemptible; mean	(8.3)
背过气	bèi guo qì		lose one's breath; faint; pass out	(9.2)
背着身	bèi zhe shēn		with the back towards people	(9.4)
本	běn		this (used to modify a noun)	(7.3)
本儿	běnr	n.	本子，notebook	(4.1)
本家	běnjiā	n.	a member of the same clan; a distant relative with the same surname	(9.3)
本钱	běn·qián	n.	principal (used to gain or pursue profit, gamble, etc.)	(1.1)
本质	běnzhì	n.	nature	(8.3)
本子	běnzi	n.	notebook	(2.1)
甭	béng	adv.	(col.) 不用，need not; no need to（same as 别）	(3.1)
逼	bī	v.	force	(4.2)
彼此之间	bǐcǐ zhī jiān		between each other	(7.3)
笔	bǐ	m.	for business deals or a sum of money 一笔买卖；一笔钱	(9.2)
笔杆子	bǐgǎnzi	n.	effective writer	(10.1)
必然	bìrán	adj.	inevitable; certain	(8.4)
避	bì	v.	躲避，avoid; keep away	(10.2)
贬人	biǎn rén	vo.	put someone down; belittle	(8.2)
扁豆	biǎndòu	n.	green beans	(1.3)
辨认	biànrèn	v.	identify; recognize	(2.1)
标准	biāozhǔn	n.	standard	(8.1)
表姐	biǎojiě	n.	older female cousin with a different surname	(7.3)
表妹	biǎomèi	n.	female cousin (with a different surname)	(1.4)
表态	biǎotài	vo.	make known one's position; declare where one stands	(10.3)

表象	biǎoxiàng	n.	appearance; image	(8.4)
表扬	biǎoyáng	v.	praise	(1.1)
憋	biē	v.	suppress; hold back; hold (breath)	(8.3)
别处	bié chù		别的地方，other place	(6.2)
别价	biéjie		别，不要，Don't	(9.3)
别有用心	bié yǒu yòng xīn		have an ulterior motive; have an axe to grind	(8.3)
别开	biè kai	vc.	force open (a lock) with a stick	(3.1)
别扭	bièniu	adj.	awkward	(8.2)
宾馆	bīnguǎn	n.	旅馆，hotel	(6.1)
丙	bǐng	num.	the third; the third position	(2.1)
拨打	bōdǎ	v.	dial; call	(2.1)
播送	bōsòng	v.	broadcast; transmit	(7.2)
搏	bó	v.	struggle; fight	(3.1)
补课	bǔ kè	vo.	tutor; redo sth. not well done	(5.2)
（不）带劲	(bú) dàijìn	adj.	uninteresting not impressive	(3.2)
不得了	bù déliǎo	adj.	terrible; horrible; desperately serious	(5.1)
不法	bùfǎ	adj.	illegal; unlawful	(6.4)
不及	bùjí	v.	不如，not as good as; inferior to	(10.1)
不及	bù jí		same as 来不及	(10.2)
不见了	bú jiàn le		disappear	(2.3)
不讲道理	bù jiǎng dàolǐ		unreasonable	(3.4)
不堪一击	bù kān yī jī		collapse at the first blow	(8.3)
不听使唤	bù tīng shǐhuan		(col.) hard to control	(6.3)
不详	bù xiáng		detail unknown	(10.3)
不咋的	bù zǎ dì		不怎么样，不好，often means "not so great", "not so hot", but used in this context, it implies "（the expenses of）going to restaurant is nothing for 刘成，don't you underestimate him（his wealth）"	(9.2)

不正当	bú zhèngdang	adj.	improper; illegal	(6. 4)
不知廉耻	bù zhī liánchǐ		have no sense of shame	(8. 3)
不止	bùzhǐ	adv.	more than; not limited to	(1. 3)
不至于	bú zhìyú		cannot go so far; unlikely	(3. 4)
部队	bùduì	n.	army; troops	(4. 2)
部位	bùwèi	n.	position; place; location	(2. 1)
擦	cā	v.	wipe	(1. 4)
猜	cāi	v.	guess	(4. 2)
财迷心窍(儿)	cái mí xīnqiào(r)		mad about money; money grubber	(1. 4)
财迷样儿	cáimíyàngr	v.	greedy look	(1. 4)
裁剪	cáijiǎn	v.	tailor; cut material according to a certain size and shape while making a garment	(7. 1)
彩虹	cǎihóng	n.	rainbow	(6. 1)
菜场	càichǎng	n.	菜市场, supermarket	(5. 3)
参评人	cān píng rén		applicants	(10. 1)
惭愧	cánkuì	adj.	be ashamed	(10. 3)
惨	cǎn	adj.	miserable; serious	(6. 4)
操心	cāo xīn	vo.	worry; concerned	(3. 4)
糙	cāo	adj.	rough; coarse	(1. 3)
恻隐	cèyǐn	v.	feel compassion for sb.'s suffering; latent compassion of one's heart; sympathy; sense of pity	(10. 1)
噌	cēng	ono.	describes the sound of certain kind of sudden movement, such as the sudden start of a car or a flock of birds suddenly making flight.	(2. 1)
插	chā	v.	transplant; insert	(8. 3)
插销	chāxiāo	n.	socket	(3. 2)
查出来	chá chulai	vc.	find out	(4. 3)
楂	chá	n.	coarsely ground maize or corn	(10. 1)
差错	chācuò	n.	mistake; error	(6. 1)

差（一）点儿	chà (yì) diǎnr	adv.	almost	(1.3)
差远了	chà yuǎn le		差多了，much too inferior	(1.3)
掺和	chānhuo	v.	disturb; cause trouble (as used in this section)	(6.2)
掺和	chānhuo	v.	mix together (as used in this section)	(6.4)
缠	chán	v.	pester; trouble	(1.1)
产品	chǎnpǐn	n.	product; manufactured goods	(6.1)
厂家直销	chǎngjiā zhí xiāo		factory direct sale	(3.2)
场面	chǎngmiàn	n.	scene	(10.3)
场子	chǎngzi	n.	soccer field (as used in this story)	(3.2)
钞票	chāopiào	n.	钱，money	(5.1)
超市	chāoshì	n.	（超级市场）；abbreviation for supermarket	(1.1)
吵架	chǎo jià	vo.	quarrel; argue vehemently	(3.1)
车辆	chēliàng	n.	vehicle; automobile	(2.1)
车棚	chēpéng	n.	awning or shed for bicycles	(3.1)
车型	chēxíng	n.	design or model of vehicles	(2.4)
彻底	chèdǐ	adv.	completely, downrightly, thoroughly	(10.1)
沉沦	chénlún	v.	sink into (grief, sorrow, etc.); sink into degradation; hit bottom	(10.1)
沉重	chénzhòng	adj.	heavy	(5.4)
衬衣	chènyī	n.	underclothes; shirt	(2.1)
趁着	chènzhe	prep.	while; taking advantage of	(3.4)
盛	chéng	v.	fill (a bowl)	(1.4)
成本费	chéngběn fèi	n.	production cost	(9.1)
成堆	chéng duī	vo.	pile up; heap up; stack	(10.2)
成果	chéngguǒ	n.	academic achievement, such as publications of books and articles, etc.	(10.1)
成了	chéng le		(col.) (sb.) got it! succeed	(1.1)
成熟	chéngshú	adj.	mature	(8.3)

成天	chéngtiān	adv.	all day long; all the time	(6.3)
成心	chéngxīn	adv.	故意, intentionally; on purpose; deliberately	(3.1)
承受	chéngshòu	v.	receive; bear; endure	(9.1)
乘客	chéngkè	n.	passenger	(9.1)
程度	chéngdù	n.	level; degree	(2.1)
吃不来	chī bu lái	vc.	(col.) 吃不惯, not used to eating (sth.)	(5.2)
吃醋	chī cù	vo.	envy; be jealous of	(6.2)
吃亏	chī kuī	vo.	suffer losses; in an unfavorable situation	(6.3)
吃里爬外	chī lǐ pá wài		living off one person while working for another	(7.2)
迟早	chízǎo	adv.	sooner or later	(10.3)
冲	chōng	v.	flush	(1.4)
虫	chóng	v.	insect; worm	(7.1)
重新	chóngxīn	adv.	once again	(6.1)
抽	chōu	v.	(col.) 打, slap someone on his/her face	(3.2)
抽奖	chōu jiǎng	vo.	draw a lottery or raffle, 福利抽奖 Lottery for charity	(9.4)
抽烟	chōu yān	vo.	smoke (a cigarette)	(5.1)
愁	chóu	v.	worry; be anxious	(10.1)
丑	chǒu	adj.	ugly; unsightly; hideous	(8.1)
丑闻	chǒuwén	n.	scandal	(10.2)
瞅	chǒu	v.	(col.) 看, look (at); take a look (at)	(3.1)
臭	chòu	adj.	smelly; stinky	(4.3)
臭小子	chòu xiǎozi	n.	little rascal; you bustard	(9.4)
出差	chū chāi	vo.	go on a business trip	(3.1)
出产	chūchǎn	v.	produce; manufacture	(4.1)
出点儿什么事	chū diǎnr shénme shì		(col.) (if something) goes wrong	(1.3)

出鬼了	chū guǐ le		(col.) How strange!	(5.3)
出卖	chūmài	v.	betray	(8.2)
出门（儿）	chū mén(r)	vo.	go out；be away from home	(3.1)
出面	chūmiàn	v.	act as a mediator	(3.4)
出纳	chūnà	n.	(of an organization or enterprise) payment and receipt of cash or bills	(2.2)
出色	chūsè	adj.	excellent；remarkable；outstanding	(8.1)
出主意	chū zhǔyi	vo.	offer an idea or a solution	(1.1)
出租车	chūzūchē	n.	taxi	(2.1)
初中	chūzhōng	n.	junior high school	(6.2)
初衷	chūzhōng	n.	original intention	(10.2)
触发	chùfā	v.	trigger, detonate by contact；touch off；spark	(8.4)
触发剂	chùfā jì	n.	agent that cause something to happen	(8.4)
踹	chuài	v.	kick；tread；stamp	(7.1)
传	chuán	v.	pass	(3.2)
传	chuán	v.	to pass (basketball，soccer，etc.)	(9.3)
传播	chuánbō	v.	spread (information，news，etc.)	(4.3)
传出去	chuán chuqu	vc.	(word) get out	(3.2)
传家宝	chuánjiābǎo	n.	family heirloom	(1.4)
传开（了）	chuán kāi (le)	vc.	spread out	(8.2)
闯祸	chuǎng huò	vo.	cause a big trouble	(5.1)
创收	chuàngshōu	vo.	earn extra income	(8.1)
吹了	chuī le		been blown away；gone；failed；fell through	(9.4)
纯	chún	adj.	pure；unmixed	(6.1)
纯金	chúnjīn	n.	pure gold	(1.2)
伺候	cìhou	v.	wait upon sb.；serve	(1.1)
刺激	cì•jī	v.	provoke；irritate	(7.1)
从小儿	cóng xiǎor	adv.	从小的时候，from childhood；as a child	(1.2)

葱	cōng	n.	green onion; scallion	(5.3)
葱花ㄦ	cōnghuār	n.	chopped shallot/scallion	(8.1)
凑合	còuhe	v.	make do	(6.1)
存在	cúnzài	v.	exist	(10.1)
存在主义	cúnzài zhǔyì	n.	existentialism	(8.2)
搓	cuō	v.	rub with the hands; twist	(7.1)
搭把手	dā ba shǒu		to help by lending a hand (to carry or lift things)	(2.1)
答应	dāying	v.	agree; comply with	(1.1)
打扮	dǎban	v.	do up; dress up; make up	(8.1)
打对折	dǎ duìzhé	vo.	打五折, have 50% discount	(4.1)
打工	dǎ gōng	vo.	have a part-time or a temporary job (usually manual work)	(7.2)
打工妹	dǎgōng mèi	n.	young female temporary worker	(7.3)
打交道	dǎjiāodao	vo.	come into contact with; have dealings with	(10.3)
打搅	dǎjiǎo	v.	disturb; bother	(5.2)
打马虎眼	dǎ mǎhuyǎn		pretend to be ignorant of something, (see note 2)	(7.3)
打牌	dǎ pái	vo.	play mahjong or cards	(3.3)
打拳	dǎ quán	vo.	practice Taiji (quan)	(4.2)
打扫	dǎsǎo	v.	clean; sweep; bream; scavenge	(7.1)
打招呼	dǎ zhāohu	vo.	(by words or gestures) greet sb.; say hello	(8.2)
大白菜	dàbáicài	n.	Chinese (Napa) cabbage	(9.2)
大白天（ㄦ）	dà báitiān(r)		bright daylight	(3.1)
大大方方	dà da fāng fāng	adj.	generous	(6.2)
大海	dàhǎi	n.	sea; ocean	(6.2)
大获全胜	dà huò quán shèng		获得很大的、全部的胜利, an overwhelming victory	(10.3)
大家伙ㄦ	dàjiāhuǒr	n.	(col.) 大家, everyone	(3.4)

大款	dàkuǎn	n.	big shot	(9.2)
大妹子	dàmèizi	v.	an affectionate term used to address a woman younger than the speaker	(6.4)
大婶（儿）	dàshěn(r)	n.	aunt (affectionate address for woman about one's mother's age)	(3.3)
大庭广众	dà tíng guǎng zhòng		(before) a big crowd; (on) a public occasion	(8.2)
大喜过望	dà xǐ guò wàng		overjoyed	(8.3)
呆头呆脑	dāi tóu dāi nǎo		stupid-looking	(4.2)
待人接物	dài rén jiē wù		manner of dealing with people	(8.1)
贷款	dài kuǎn	vo.	loan; borrow money from bank	(6.1)
戴	dài	v.	put on (or wear) sth. on the head, face, arm, etc.	(1.1)
单	dān	adv.	separately	(1.2)
单纯	dānchún	adj.	naive; pure	(10.3)
单独	dāndú	adv.	individually; alone; solely	(5.1)
单身	dānshēn	adj.	unmarried or single person	(2.2)
单位	dānwèi	n.	unit; work place	(3.1)
单子	dānzi	n.	list (of items); bill; form	(4.1)
担保	dānbǎo	v.	assure; guarantee; vouch for	(10.1)
耽搁	dānge	v.	delay; procrastinate	(4.2)
耽误	dānwu	v.	delay; hold up	(8.4)
胆大	dǎn dà	adj.	bold	(3.1)
胆量	dǎnliàng	n.	courage; guts	(8.3)
胆子	dǎnzi	n.	guts; nerve	(5.3)
当初	dāngchū	adv.	in the beginning; at first	(4.2)
当（面）	dāng(miàn)		to sb's face; facing sb.; confronting in sb's presence; in front of (someone)	(2.4)
当心	dāngxīn	v.	注意，watch out; look out; careful	(5.1)
荡	dàng	v.	walk around (as used in this story); swing	(4.3)

叨叨	dāodao	v.	chatter	(4.3)
叨咕	dāogu	v.	（col.）小声（反复）说一件事，talk about; mention about	(3.4)
导报	dǎobào	n.	Guide (magazine)	(9.2)
倒	dào	v.	pour; dump	(1.1)
到处	dàochù	adv.	about; everywhere	(1.1)
到底	dàodǐ	adv.	after all	(4.2)
到时候	dào shíhou		later	(3.1)
到手	dào shǒu	vo.	in one's hands; in one's possession	(9.1)
道德	dàodé	n.	morals; morality; ethics	(10.1)
道歉	dào qiàn	vo.	apologize	(2.3)
得得得	dé dé dé		（col.）alright, alright, alright	(1.1)
得意	déyì	adj.	pleased with oneself; proud of oneself	(3.3)
德行	déxing		(see note 8)	(7.1)
灯泡	dēngpào	n.	light bulb, electric bulb	(7.1)
蹬	dēng	v.	pedal; treadle	(7.1)
抵不过	dǐ bu guò	vc.	not able to resist	(8.3)
地道	dìdào	adj.	genuine; pure; real	(10.2)
地儿	dìr	n.	（col.）地方, place	(3.2)
地雷	dìléi	n.	landmine	(3.2)
地下	dìxià	adj.	underground;（of activity）secret	(6.4)
地震	dìzhèn	n.	earthquake	(4.2)
电表	diànbiǎo	n.	meter for measuring electricity; watt-hour meter	(3.2)
电冰箱	diànbīngxiāng	n.	refrigerator; fridge	(4.1)
电传	diànchuán	n.	fax	(9.1)
电费	diànfèi	n.	cost of electricity; electricity fee	(4.1)
电扇	diànshàn	n.	electric fan	(1.2)
电子琴	diànzǐqín	n.	electronic keyboard	(4.2)

店员	diànyuán	n.	shop assistant	(1.2)
玷污	diànwū	v.	stain; tarnish	(10.2)
吊	diào	v.	hang	(1.1)
掉	diào	v.	fall; drop	(6.1)
掉价	diào jià		fall or drop in price (used here to mean lowering or losing one's social status)	(7.3)
掉头	diào tóu	vo.	turn around	(1.3)
盯	dīng	v.	keep a close watch on; tail	(2.2)
盯	dīng	v.	fix one's eyes on; stare at	(3.1)
钉	dìng	v.	hammer a nail into sth; fix sth. to a position	(1.3)
顶	dǐng	m.	(for hats, caps)	(4.2)
顶层	dǐngcéng	n.	top storey, top floor	(4.2)
顶得住	dǐng de zhù	vc.	able to sustain	(4.2)
顶多	dǐngduō	adv.	at most	(3.1)
定金	dìngjīn	n.	deposit	(6.1)
丢人	diū rén	vo.	lose face; disgraced	(1.2)
东奔西跑	dōng bēn xī pǎo	v.	rush around (for work)	(6.3)
咚	dōng	ono.	rub-a-dub, rat-a-tat; boom (of a drum)	(2.1)
懂事	dǒngshì	adj.	(usu. of a child) sensible; thoughtful	(5.2)
动	dòng	v.	感动, move or touch (one's heart)	(10.2)
动静	dòngjing	n.	sound; voice; movement; activity	(8.3)
动脑子	dòng nǎozi	vo.	think about it; use (your) head	(5.3)
动摇	dòngyáo		turmoil; turbulent; (social or political) unrest	(8.2)
动员令	dòngyuán lìng		mobilizing order	(10.1)
都市	dūshì	n.	big city; metropolis	(6.1)
兜圈子	dōu quānzi	vo.	beat around the bush	(8.3)
斗争	dòuzhēng	n.	struggle	(8.2)

豆腐脑	dòufunǎo	n.	soft bean curd	(7.2)
豆奶	dòunǎi	n.	豆浆，soy milk	(5.3)
逗	dòu	adj.	interesting; funny	(6.4)
督促	dūcù	v.	supervise and urge	(5.2)
肚子	dùzi	n.	stomach	(7.3)
镀金	dùjīn	adj.	gold-plating; gilding	(1.1)
断	duàn	v.	broken	(4.3)
断	duàn	v.	break off; cut off; stop	(9.4)
队员	duìyuán	n.	team member	(3.2)
对不住	duì bu zhù	vc.	(col.) 对不起，sorry (as used in this context)	(3.3)
对得起	duì de qǐ	vc.	be fair (to sb.) (as used in this story)	(1.1)
对得住	duì de zhù	vc.	对得起，live up to (one's expectation)	(1.3)
对付	duìfu	v.	得到，manage to make (profit) (as used in this context)	(1.3)
对抗赛	duìkàng sài		sport meet between two or among several	(9.1)
对立	duìlì	adj.	oppose; be antagonistic to; contradiction; antagonism	(8.4)
顿	dùn	m.	for meals	(8.1)
多才多艺	duō cái duō yì	adj.	versatile; talented	(3.3)
多管闲事	duō guǎn xiánshì		mind other people's business	(7.1)
多亏	duōkuī	v.	thanks to	(6.2)
多余	duōyú	adj.	surplus	(10.1)
躲	duǒ	v.	seek refuge from (disaster)	(4.2)
恶毒	èdú	adj.	venomous; vicious; malicious	(8.3)
儿媳妇（儿）	érxífu(r)	n.	daughter-in-law	(1.4)
耳环	ěrhuán	n.	earrings	(1.4)
耳茄子	ěrqiézi	n.	(col.) a slap in the face	(3.4)

二环	èrhuán	n.	the Second Ring; the Second Circular Highway	(9.1)
发财	fācái	vo.	get rich, make a fortune	(9.1)
发票	fāpiào	n.	receipt; invoice	(1.4)
发神经	fā shénjīng	v.	go mad; crazy; fig. state contrary to reason or against common sense	(7.1)
发生	fāshēng	v.	happen; take place	(4.2)
发誓	fā shì	vo.	swear; pledge, vow	(1.2)
发物	fāwù	n.	(see note 14)	(7.1)
发型	fàxíng	n.	hair style; hairdo	(9.1)
法院	fǎyuàn	n.	court of law; court house	(3.4)
翻	fān	v.	turn over; turn up	(3.3)
翻毛皮鞋	fānmáo píxié	n.	suede shoes	(3.3)
凡是	fánshì	conj.	any; every; all	(10.1)
烦	fán	adj.	annoy; 烦不烦啊？ Isn't that annoy or what!	(9.2)
反映	fǎnyìng	v.	make known; report	(6.4)
反正	fǎnzhèng	adv.	(see grammar notes 4)	(2.1)
犯病	fàn bìng	vo.	have a recurrence of an illness	(1.3)
犯法	fàn fǎ	vo.	break the law; violate the law	(3.1)
犯吧挣	fàn yìzheng	vo.	(col.) (see note 4)	(3.1)
犯罪	fàn zuì	vo.	commit crime	(8.3)
饭碗	fànwǎn	n.	(col.) job; means of livelihood; rice bowl	(1.1)
饭碗子	fànwǎnzi	n.	job; bread and butter	(7.1)
防盗	fángdào	vo.	防备强盗, guard against theft; theft-proof	(3.1)
防震	fángzhèn	adj.	earthquake-proof	(4.3)
房顶	fángdǐng	n.	roof	(4.2)
房钱	fángqián	n.	房租, rent (of house)	(1.3)
放风	fàng fēng	vo.	spread news or rumors	(4.3)

蜚短流长	fēi duǎn liú cháng		gossip	(8.3)
肥差儿	féichāir	n.	profitable post or job	(2.2)
沸沸扬扬	fèifèiyángyáng		a hubbub, noisy scene, (see note 7)	(8.2)
费电	fèi diàn	vo.	energy-consuming; waste electricity	(3.2)
费劲	fèi jìn	vo.	labored; with great effort	(3.1)
分量	fèn·liàng	n.	weight; heft	(8.1)
粉笔末	fěnbǐ mò	n.	chalk powder	(6.1)
份儿	fènr	m.	measure word for newspapers	(9.2)
风波	fēngbō	n.	disturbance; rumpus	(4.1)
风风雨雨	fēng fēng yǔ yǔ		(see note 9)	(7.3)
风凉话	fēngliánghuà	n.	sarcastic remarks	(1.1)
疯	fēng	v.	mad; insane; crazy	(8.3)
讽刺	fěngcì	v.	satirize; ridicule	(10.3)
夫妻	fūqī	n.	husband and wife	(10.1)
夫人	fū·rén	n.	madam; wife	(8.3)
服	fú	v.	be convinced; submit (oneself to)	(7.1)
服务生	fúwùshēng	n.	waiter; server	(8.2)
服装店儿	fúzhuāngdiànr	n.	clothing shop	(6.2)
福利	fúlì	n.	material benefits; welfare	(6.1)
福气	fúqi	n.	good luck	(5.1)
副	fù	m.	(it is often used for one's appearance, usually in a derogatory sense)	(4.2)
负	fù	n.	defeat, failure	(9.1)
负荆请罪	fù jīng qǐng zuì		ask for the most severe punishment; (see note 2)	(10.3)
复杂	fùzá	adj.	complicated	(3.2)
副教授	fùjiàoshòu	n.	associate professor	(10.1)
副刊	fùkān	n.	supplement (of newspaper)	(8.1)

富有	fùyǒu	v.	be full of；be rich in	(8.1)
富裕	fùyù	adj.	well-to-do；rich	(5.3)
腹	fù	n.	belly；abdomen；stomach	(8.2)
咖喱	gā·lí	n.	curry	(8.2)
改变	gǎibiàn	v.	change；alter	(7.3)
改日	gǎirì		换成另一天，another day；some other day	(9.2)
改造	gǎizào	v.	reform；remold	(5.4)
改锥	gǎizhuī	n.	螺丝刀，screwdriver	(3.1)
概率	gàilù	n.	probability	(10.2)
干脆	gāncuì	adv.	simply；just；altogether	(1.4)
干豆	gāndòu	n.	dried beans or peas	(5.3)
干活	gàn huó	v.	work (manual, physical)	(7.1)
干粮	gān·liáng	n.	staple food	(4.2)
泔水	gān·shuǐ	n.	slops；dishwater	(2.1)
赶紧	gǎnjǐn	adv.	same as 赶快	(2.4)
赶明儿	gǎnmíngr	adv.	(col.) 以后，将来 later；later on	(1.2)
赶上	gǎn shàng	vc.	be in time for (sth. or event)；run into (a situation)	(3.2)
敢	gǎn	v.	dare, have the courage	(8.2)
敢情	gǎnqíng	adv.	原来，it turns out that...	(3.1)
感受	gǎnshòu	n.	feeling	(10.3)
干吗	gànmá		(col.) 干什么，why	(1.1)
钢琴	gāngqín	n.	piano	(4.1)
高跟（儿）	gāogēn(r)	adj.	high-heeled (shoes)	(3.1)
高科技	gāokējì	n.	high tech, high technology	(7.1)
搞特殊	gǎo tèshū	vo.	ask for privileges	(5.1)
告别	gàobié	v.	farewell	(7.2)
哥们儿	gēmenr	n.	buddy；guy	(1.1)

割	gē	v.	slice with a knife	(4.1)
搁	gē	v.	放，put；place	(1.4)
隔壁	gébì	n.	next-door neighbor	(9.2)
隔阂	géhé	n.	(of feeling and thought) estrangement；misunderstanding；alienation；	(8.4)
隔（一）段时间	gé(yí) duàn shíjiān		once in a while	(1.1)
个子	gèzi	n.	(of a human being or animal) height；build	(8.1)
（给某人）添麻烦	(gěi mǒurén) tiān máfan	v.	trouble (sb.)；bother (sb.)	(3.1)
更换	gēnghuàn	v.	换，replace；change	(8.1)
工钱	gōng·qián	n.	wages；pay；charge for a service	(7.1)
工资	gōngzī	n.	wages；salary	(1.3)
公家	gōngjia	n.	the state organization or enterprise	(6.1)
公款	gōngkuǎn	n.	public money or fund	(2.4)
公用	gōngyòng	adj.	public；for public use	(5.1)
工夫	gōngfu	n.	时间，period of time	(5.3)
攻击	gōngjī	v.	attack	(8.3)
狗	gǒu	n.	dog	(7.1)
狗屁	gǒupì	n.	rubbish；nonsense	(1.4)
购物	gòuwù	vo.	go shopping，shopping	(9.2)
够呛	gòuqiàng		terrible；unbearable	(7.1)
姑奶奶	gūnǎinai	n.	a woman hard to please or to deal with (as used in this story)；sister of paternal grandfather	(1.2)
轱辘	gūlu	n.	wheel	(1.3)
股票	gǔpiào	n.	share；stock	(6.2)
股市	gǔshì	n.	stock market	(6.2)
骨头	gǔtou	n.	bone	(4.3)
鼓励	gǔlì	v.	encourage	(8.2)

故事	gùshi	n.	story	(1.1)
故意	gùyì	adv.	intentionally；deliberately；on purpose	(5.4)
顾名思义	gù míng sī yì		just as its name implies，(see note 8)	(8.2)
雇佣	gùyōng	v.	hire；employ	(7.3)
刮	guā	v.	shave	(8.1)
乖	guāi	adj.	(of a child) obedient；well-behaved	(1.1)
怪	guài	v.	blame	(7.3)
怪不得	guài bu de	vc.	no wonder，that explains why；so that's why	(8.2)
怪物	guàiwù	n.	monster，monstrosity，freak	(7.1)
关怀	guānhuái	v.	care；concern；show care for	(6.3)
关键	guānjiàn	n.	decisive factor，the most crucial；key	(8.1)
关照	guānzhào	v.	tell	(5.4)
观察	guānchá	v./n.	observe carefully；observation	(6.4)
观众	guānzhòng	n.	audience	(6.4)
冠军	guànjūn	n.	championship	(9.1)
馆子	guǎnzi	n.	restaurant	(9.2)
管	guǎn	v.	look after；can also mean interfere (as used in 3.4)	(1.3)
管理	guǎnlǐ	v.	manage；in charge of；run	(8.2)
管教	guǎn jiào	v.	discipline；control and teach	(5.4)
管理部门	guǎnlǐ bùmén		supervising/management department/division	(6.4)
管用	guǎnyòng	adj.	efficacious；helpful	(4.2)
惯	guàn	v.	spoil	(3.3)
灌	guàn	v.	drink by force；pour into	(8.3)
光	guāng	adv.	只，only；just	(3.1)
广告部	guǎnggàobù	n.	advertising department	(8.1)
归	guī	v.	be in sb.'s charge (as used in this context)	(3.4)

规定	guīdìng	n.	rules and regulations	(5.1)
规矩	guīju	n.	established practice; established standard, rule or habit	(8.2)
闺女	guīnü	n.	(northern expression) girl; maiden; daughter	(7.2)
鬼	guǐ	n.	ghost	(8.3)
鬼神	guǐshén	n.	gods and ghosts; spirits; supernatural beings	(10.2)
柜子	guìzi	n.	cupboard; cabinet	(5.1)
贵重	guìzhòng	adj.	valuable; precious	(1.4)
跪	guì	v.	knell	(5.3)
滚	gǔn	v.	Get out! Get the hell out here!	(9.3)
国产	guóchǎn	adj.	domestically produced (used to modify nouns)	(9.2)
果园	guǒyuán	n.	orchard	(9.1)
馃子	guǒzi	n.	油条, deep fried doughnut; twisted fritters	(8.1)
过分	guòfèn	adj.	excessive; beyond or over the limit	(7.2)
过时	guòshí	adj.	old-fashioned; out of fashion	(6.3)
过意不去	guò yì bú qù	vc.	feel very distressed	(1.4)
哈哈哈	hā hā hā	ono.	sound of laughing	(8.3)
还不成吗	hái bùchéng ma		还不行吗? Isn't it enough?	(3.1)
海边	hǎibiān	n.	beach	(6.2)
海鲜	hǎixiān	n.	seafood	(8.1)
害	hài	n.	harm, 意思是 "害处"	(2.3)
涵养	hányǎng	n.	self-restraint; ability to control oneself; virtue of patience	(5.1)
寒酸	hánsuān	adj.	shabby and miserable; too simple to be respectable	(1.3)
行话	hánghuà	n.	jargon	
好不容易	hǎo bu róngyì	adv.	with a lot of efforts or difficulty; after all the trouble	(4.3)

好歹	hǎodǎi	adv.	无论如何，不管怎么样，good or bad; for better or worse; no matter what	(7.3)
好端端	hǎo duānduān	adj.	in perfectly good condition	(3.4)
好受	hǎoshòu	adj.	feel comfortable	(1.4)
好心好意	hǎo xīn hǎo yì		with all good wishes	(3.4)
好样儿的	hǎoyàngrde		Good man! A person of integrity and courage	(10.3)
好面子	hàomiànzi	v.	care (too much) about how other people think of oneself	(1.2)
耗子	hàozi	n.	mouse; rat	(3.2)
嗬	hē		used to express surprise	(10.3)
合着	hézhe		turn out to be; so (similar to "这样说" or "这样看来")	(9.2)
合作	hézuò	v.	cooperate	(6.1)
和事佬	héshìlǎo	n.	peace maker, esp. one who is more concerned with stopping the bickering than setting the issue	(5.1)
狠	hěn	adj.	ruthless; relentless	(8.3)
狠心	hěnxīn	adj.	cruel-hearted; heartless	(8.3)
哄嘴	hǒng zuǐ	vo.	say sth. sweet; sweet talk	(1.1)
后儿个	hòurge	t.	(col.) 后天, the day after tomorrow	(6.1)
后果	hòuguǒ	n.	最后的结果（多用于不好的情况）, consequence; aftermath (usu. in a negative sense)	(4.3)
后卫	hòuwèi	n.	rear guard; defender; linebacker	(9.3)
呼	hū	v.	page	(9.1)
呼机号	hūjī hào	n.	beeper number	(7.2)
和	hú	v.	win (term used in Majiang)	(3.3)
胡编	hú biān	v.	create nonsense; spin yarns	(4.3)
胡萝卜	húluóbo	n.	carrot	(1.3)
胡闹	húnào	v.	cause trouble	(5.1)
胡说	húshuō	v./n.	talk nonsense; nonsense	(1.1)

胡说八道	hú shuō bā dào		talk nonsense or drivel; random talk; unsubstantial or irrational words; similar to 信口胡说	(8.2)
胡思乱想	hú sī luàn xiǎng		give way to foolish fancies	(3.1)
胡同	hútòng	n.	lane; alley	(1.2)
胡（问）	hú（wèn）	adv.	same as "乱（问）" or "瞎（问）"; (see part 1, note 4)	(2.2)
胡子	húzi	n.	beard	(8.1)
糊弄	hùnong		fool; deceive	(8.3)
糊涂	hútu	adj.	muddled; confused	(4.3)
花花肠子	huāhua chángzi		deceitful ideas or thoughts	(7.3)
滑	huá	v.	slide	(4.3)
化妆品	huàzhuāngpǐn	n.	makeup; cosmetics	(1.2)
画勾	huà gōu	vo.	tick off	(2.2)
划拳	huá quán	vo.	play a drinking game	(7.1)
画外音	huàwàiyīn		voice outside the picture (screen)	(1.3)
怀	huái	v.	become pregnant	(8.3)
怀念	huáiniàn	v.	cherish the memory of; think of	(7.3)
怀疑	huáiyí	v.	suspect; question	(3.1)
还价	huán jià	vo.	bargain	(6.1)
还手	huán shǒu	vo.	fight back	(7.1)
患难知己	huànnàn zhījǐ		friends in adversity; tested friends	(8.4)
慌张	huāngzhāng	adj.	flurried; helter-skelter	(4.3)
黄连	huánglián	n.	Coptis Chinensis (it has an incredibly bitter taste)	(10.2)
黄油	huángyóu	n.	butter	(8.2)
灰色	huīsè	n.	grey; grey color	(2.1)
回复	huífù	v.	reply	(9.2)
回头	huítóu	adv.	(col.) later	(3.3)
会议	huìyì	n.	meeting; conference	(4.3)

毁	huǐ	v.	ruin; defame	(2.4)
毁誉	huǐ yù		praise or blame; praise or condemn	(10.1)
婚纱照	hūnshāzhào	n.	wedding photographs	(9.1)
馄饨	húntun	n.	wonton (a kind of dumpling)	(5.1)
魂儿	húnr	n.	soul; spirit	(7.2)
豁出去	huō chuqu	vc.	risk anything; do sth. at any cost	(6.3)
活儿	huór	n.	(col.) craftsmanship; work	(1.3)
火	huǒ	adj.	do a roaring business	(8.1)
火腿	huǒtuǐ	n.	ham, salted leg of pork	(8.2)
火葬场	huǒzàngchǎng		cremation center	(7.2)
货真价实	huò zhēn jià shí		genuine goods at a fair price; the genuine item; true to the name	(6.1)
机器	jī·qì	n.	machine	(1.2)
鸡卷儿	jījuǎnr	n.	chicken roll	(8.2)
吉利	jílì	adj.	auspicious; lucky	(4.3)
吉他	jí·tā	n.	guitar	(7.3)
挤	jǐ	v./adj.	push; squeeze	(8.1)
荠菜	jìcài	n.	a kind of Chinese vegetable	(5.1)
计时工	jìshígōng	n.	worker paid on the basis of work time	(7.1)
记性	jìxing	n.	memory	(3.3)
技术	jìshù	n.	technology; technological	(6.1)
剂	jì	m.	dose (of medicine)	(5.4)
继续	jìxù	v.	continue; go on with	(6.2)
加班（儿）	jiā bān (r)	vo.	work overtime; work on extra shifts	(1.3)
加倍	jiābèi	adv.	double	(1.2)
加工厂	jiāgōngchǎng	n.	processing plant or manufacturer	(6.4)
加小心	jiā xiǎoxin	vo.	be careful; be cautious	(3.1)
加油	jiāyóu	vo.	(used to cheer sb. on) Go! Come on!	(7.1)

夹攻	jiāgōng	v.	be caught in a two-way squeeze; attack from both sides	(4.2)
夹住	jiā zhù	vc.	hold (with a clamp-like device)	(5.1)
家长	jiāzhǎng	n.	通常为学生的父母，或法定监护人，u-sually parent（s），or legal guardian	(5.4)
家长里短	jiā cháng lǐ duǎn	n.	domestic trivia	(5.4)
家父	jiāfù	n.	我父亲，my father (formal)	(10.1)
家伙	jiāhuo	n.	fellow; guy (derogatory)	(8.3)
家具	jiājù	n.	furniture	(8.1)
家属	jiāshǔ	n.	family members;（family）dependants	(2.4)
甲级	jiǎjí	n.	top level	(9.4)
价钱	jià·qián	n.	price	(1.1)
假（的）	jiǎ（de）	adj.	fake	(1.1)
假冒	jiǎmào	v.	pose as; palm off（a fake as genuine）	(10.2)
假冒伪劣	jiǎmào wěiliè		fake and bad	(6.4)
奸商	jiānshāng	n.	unscrupulous merchant	(1.1)
坚持	jiānchí	v.	sustain	(4.2)
坚强	jiānqiáng	adj.	strong; firm; staunch	(8.3)
兼	jiān	v.	do two or more jobs concurrently	(2.2)
煎饼	jiānbing	n.	pancake; griddle cake	(8.1)
捡	jiǎn	v.	find（something that sb. has lost）; pick up	(4.1)
检测	jiǎncè	v.	test; examine; check up	(1.2)
检查	jiǎnchá	v.	self-criticism	(10.2)
见解	jiànjiě	n.	view; opinion; understanding	(10.3)
见世面	jiàn shìmiàn	vo.	see the world; become experienced, be-come sophisticate	(7.2)
见外	jiànwài	v.	behave too polite（like a stranger）	(5.2)
讲述	jiǎngshù	v.	tell about; narrate	(2.1)
奖金	jiǎngjīn	n.	bonus; reward	(4.1)

奖券	jiǎngquàn	n.	lottery ticket	(9.4)
犟	jiàng	adj.	stubborn	(5.3)
交班儿	jiāobānr	vo.	switch shifts	(1.1)
交通	jiāotōng	n.	transportation; traffic	(2.1)
郊区	jiāoqū	n.	suburban district; outskirts	(4.2)
娇气	jiāo·qì	adj.	delicate; squeamish; fragile	(2.3)
浇	jiāo	v.	get rained on (as used in this context)	(1.4)
嚼	jiáo	v.	chew	(9.3)
绞尽脑汁	jiǎo jìn nǎozhī		rack, cudgel or tax one's brains	(10.3)
轿车	jiàochē	n.	小汽（卧）车，car	(4.2)
较劲	jiào jìn	vo.	(col.) compete	(1.1)
教导	jiàodǎo	n./v.	teach; give guidance	(10.1)
教导员	jiàodǎoyuán	n.	political instructor	(5.2)
教训	jiàoxun	v.	teach (sb. a lesson); lecture (sb.)	(8.3)
接待	jiēdài	v.	receive	(8.4)
揭	jiē	v.	remove; peel off	(2.4)
街道	jiēdào	n.	residential district; neighborhood	(3.1)
街里街坊	jiē li jiē fāng		(col.) neighbors	(3.1)
劫	jié	v.	rob; plunder	(3.1)
结识	jiéshí	v.	get acquainted with sb.; get to know sb.	(7.3)
结实	jiēshi	adj.	sturdy; durable	(4.2)
截	jié	v.	intercept; stop	(2.1)
姐妹	jiěmèi	n.	female co-workers (as used in this story); sisters	(1.1)
解决	jiějué	v.	finish off (as used in this context); solve	(3.1)
解铃还须系铃人	jiě líng hái xū jì líng rén		the one who tied it can untie it	(3.4)
解说	jiěshuō	v./n.	explain (orally); comment	(2.3)
介入	jièrù	v.	get involved; intervene	(2.1)

届	jiè	m.	graduating classes	(8. 2)
戒指	jièzhi	n.	ring	(1. 4)
今儿	jīnr	t.	(col.) 今天，today	(1. 3)
今儿个	jīnrge		(col.) 今天，today	(3. 4)
筋	jīn	n.	tendon; sinew	(4. 3)
紧	jǐn	v.	tighten (budget)	(6. 2)
紧巴巴（的）	jǐn bābā (de)	adj.	tight (of budget)	(6. 2)
紧接着	jǐnjiē zhe		immediately; right after	(2. 1)
紧着点儿账	jǐnzhe diǎnr zhàng		tighten the budget	(6. 2)
尽管	jǐnguǎn	adv.	unhesitatingly (as used in this story)	(5. 1)
尽快	jǐnkuài	adv.	as soon as possible; as quickly as one can	(2. 4)
劲头	jìntóu	n.	drive; zeal; spirit; vigor	(9. 2)
近来	jìnlái	adv.	最近，recently	(6. 4)
进口	jìnkǒu	v.	import	(4. 1)
进行	jìnxíng	v.	conduct; carry on	(6. 4)
进展	jìnzhǎn	n. /v.	new development; making progress	(2. 4)
经得住	jīng de zhù	vc.	able to tolerate; can put up with	(3. 4)
经济	jīngjì	n.	economy	(9. 4)
经济学	jīngjìxué	n.	economics	(6. 1)
精品	jīngpǐn	n.	top quality article; quality goods	(9. 2)
精致	jīngzhì	adj.	exquisite; delicate	(1. 2)
景象	jǐngxiàng	n.	scene	(10. 3)
景致	jǐngzhì	n.	view; scenery; scene	(8. 4)
警察	jǐngchá	n.	police; policeman; cop	(2. 1)
净赚	jìng zhuàn		net profit	(9. 1)
竟然	jìngrán	adv.	to one's surprise; unexpectedly	(8. 3)
救急	jiù jí	vo.	help to meet an urgent need	(6. 2)

救命	jiù mìng	vo.	Help! Somebody help!	(8.3)
救生圈	jiùshēngquān	n.	life buoy	(10.1)
就当	jiù dāng		就当做，just take it as...	(3.2)
就合	jiùhe	v.	迁就，accommodate oneself to; yield to	(9.2)
居然	jūrán	adv.	竟，unexpectedly; to one's surprise	(3.1)
局	jú	n.	bureau	(4.2)
局外人	júwàirén	n.	outsider	(2.4)
举报	jǔbào	v.	report (sth.) to the authorities; inform against	(6.4)
拒绝	jùjué	v.	refuse	(10.2)
具有	jùyǒu	v.	有，possess	(10.3)
聚	jù	v.	get together	(4.1)
决赛	juésài	n.	final match or final round of matches in a sport which decides the positions in a competition; shoot-off	(9.2)
绝对	juéduì	adv.	absolutely	(1.2)
军烈属	jūnlièshǔ	n.	军人家属和烈士家属 dependant of revolutionary martyr	(4.2)
君子	jūnzǐ	n.	gentleman; man of honor	(8.2)
均	jūn	adv.	都,(lit) all; without exception; (see grammar note 6)	(2.1)
开导	kāidǎo	v.	enlighten; help sb. see the point	(10.3)
开水	kāishuǐ	n.	boiled water	(6.4)
开玩笑	kāi wánxiào	vo.	make a joke; break a jest	(1.2)
开销	kāixiāo	n.	expenses; spending	(4.1)
开支	kāizhī	n.	expenses; spending	(1.3)
砍	kǎn	v.	cut or reduce (price)	(1.2)
砍价	kǎnjià	vo.	haggle; bargain	(9.1)
看	kān	v.	look after; take care of	(9.2)
看不透	kàn bu tòu	vc.	cannot see through	(8.3)

看上	kàn shang	vc.	be attracted to	(3.3)
看走眼	kàn zǒu yǎn		mistaken for, misjudge	(9.3)
烤鱼	kǎoyú	n.	baked fish	(8.2)
科长	kēzhǎng	n.	section chief	(6.4)
咳嗽	késou	v.	cough	(3.1)
可悲	kěbēi	adj.	sad; lamentable; deplorable	(8.3)
可不是	kě bu shì		(col.) That's true; can't agree (with you) more	(3.1)
可恶	kěwù	adj.	hateful; abominable; obnoxious	(4.3)
可贵	kěguì	adj.	treasured; valuable	(7.2)
可恨	kěhèn	adj.	hateful; abominable	(4.3)
客户	kèhù	n.	client; customer	(5.1)
肯定	kěndìng	adv.	definitely; undoubtedly	(2.1)
空调	kōngtiáo	n.	air-conditioner	(4.1)
空落落	kōngluòluò	adj.	(see note 5)	(1.4)
恐	kǒng	v.	怕，be afraid	(10.2)
抠抠唆唆	kōu kou suōsuō	adj.	小气、吝啬，stingy; miserly	(6.2)
抠门儿	kōuménr	adj.	小气，吝啬，stingy; miserly	(8.1)
口气	kǒu·qì	n.	manner of speaking; tone of voice	(1.4)
口琴	kǒuqín	n.	mouth organ; harmonica	(4.2)
苦胆	kǔdǎn	n.	gall bladder	(2.3)
苦过来	kǔ guo lai	vc.	struggle through difficulties and hardships	(1.4)
快活	kuàihuo	adj.	happy; joyful; cheerful	(8.1)
会计	kuài·jì	n.	accountant; bookkeeper	(2.2)
亏	kuī	v.	treat unfairly	(1.1)
愧疚不已	kuìjiù bùyǐ		be very ashamed and remorseful	(7.3)
困兽犹斗	kùn shòu yóu dòu		cornered beasts will still put up a desperate fight; (see note 4)	(10.1)

拉	lā	v.	pull；draw	(5.1)
拉扯	lāche	v.	bring up (a child/children)	(1.3)
垃圾	lā·jī	n.	garbage；trash	(3.1)
辣椒	làjiāo	n.	hot pepper；chili	(5.3)
赖	lài	v.	blame；accuse sb. (of doing sth.)	(3.4)
篮子	lánzi	n.	basket	(5.3)
揽茬儿	lǎn chár	vo.	take upon oneself	(1.1)
烂	làn	v.	broken；badly damaged；（脸烂了）	(2.4)
浪漫	làngmàn	adj.	romantic	(6.2)
劳改农场	láogǎi nóngchǎng		labor camp where criminals get re-formed through labor	(5.2)
劳务	láowù	n.	labor and service	(1.1)
唠唠叨叨	láo lao dāo dāo		talk about sth. constantly；chatter	(4.2)
老板	lǎobǎn	n.	boss；shopkeeper	(1.3)
老板娘	lǎobǎnniáng	n.	shopkeeper's wife	(1.4)
老伴儿	lǎobànr	n.	one's spouse, wife or husband (of an old married couple)	(3.3)
老泪纵横	lǎolèi zònghéng		(an old person) be in tears，(see note 6)	(10.3)
老婆	lǎopo	n.	wife；old woman	(1.1)
老人家	lǎorenjia	n.	(an respectful form of address for an old person)	(5.1)
老太婆	lǎotàipó	n.	(of old couples) husband's term of ad-dress for his wife；my old lady；old woman	(4.1)
老天爷	lǎotiānyé	n.	God；Heavens	(1.4)
老头子	lǎotóuzi	n.	(of old couples) wife's term of address for her husband；my old man；old man	(4.1)
老外	lǎowài	n.	layman；foreigner	(6.2)
老爷们儿	lǎoyémenr	n.	adult man	(7.1)
老者	lǎozhě	n.	an old man；the aged；elderly people	(8.1)

老总	lǎozǒng	n.	head of a company；CEO	(9.1)
乐了	lè le	v.	(col.) 笑了；不生气了, smile, stop being mad	(3.1)
乐善好施	lè shàn hào shī		a materially and spiritually charitable person	(10.1)
嘞	lei	ono.	indicate a positive and optimistic attitude as in 好嘞, 我就去！(All right, I'm going now)！or 雪停了, 回家嘞！(It stopped snowing, let's go home)！	(2.2)
冷静	lěngjìng	adj.	sober；cool-headed	(4.3)
冷酷	lěngkù	adj.	callous；grim；merciless	(8.3)
愣	lèng	adv.	(col.) surprisingly (as used in this story)	(3.1)
礼拜	lǐbài	n.	(col.) 星期, week	(3.3)
里脊	lǐji	n.	tenderloin [lean meat taken from under the spinal column of a hog or a cow]	(8.2)
理论	lǐlùn	v.	debate；argue	(3.2)
理应	lǐyīng		按道理应该, ought to；should	(10.1)
力气	lìqi	n.	physical strength	(4.1)
立马	lìmǎ	adv.	(col.) 马上、立刻, immediately	(6.1)
利息	lìxī	n.	interest	(6.2)
俩	liǎ		(col.) 两个, two	(1.3)
联赛	liánsài	n.	league tournament；league matches	(9.2)
联系	liánxì	v.	make connection with	(1.1)
练摊（儿）	liàn tān(r)	vo.	have a stand to sell merchandise	(6.1)
链子	liànzi	n.	chain	(1.4)
良心	liángxīn	n.	conscience	(10.1)
良药	liángyào	n.	effective drug	(5.4)
两居	liǎngjū	n.	两个卧室（的）, two bedroom apartment	(9.1)
两口儿	liǎngkǒur	n.	(col.) couple (husband and wife)	(3.4)
两头（儿）	liǎng tóu(r)	n.	both sides；both aspects	(3.3)

了不得	liǎo bu de		(col.) awful；terrible	(3.4)
料定	liàodìng	v.	know for sure；be certain	(9.2)
撂	liào	v.	(col.) 放，put down	(6.1)
临时	línshí		momentarily	(10.3)
临阵逃脱	lín zhèn táotuō		desert on the eve of battle；sneak away at acritical juncture	(9.3)
伶牙俐齿	líng yá lì chǐ		good at words；a good talker；(see note 4)	(10.3)
灵	líng	adj.	clever；sensitive	(3.1)
灵魂	línghún	n.	soul；conscience；spirit	(10.3)
零蛋	língdàn	n.	零分，zero	(10.1)
零食	língshí	n.	snacks	(5.2)
领（养）	lǐng（yǎng）	v.	adopt	(8.3)
领子	lǐngzi	n.	collar	(8.1)
溜达	liūda	v.	stroll；patrol	(3.1)
留面子	liú miànzi	v.	save one's face；not make someone feel embarrassed	(10.1)
留神	liúshén	v.	pay attention to；be careful	(8.4)
柳	liǔ	n.	willow (Salix)	(8.3)
聋子	lóngzi	n.	deaf person	(3.4)
聋子没治好治成哑巴了	lóngzi méi zhì hǎo zhì chéng yǎba le	ex.	(col.) create a new problem instead of solving the old one	(3.4)
楼道	lóudào	n.	corridor；hallway	(3.1)
楼房	lóufáng	n.	storied building；tower	(9.2)
搂（草）	lōu（cǎo）	v.	gather up；rake together	(7.2)
鲈鱼	lúyú	n.	perch	(5.3)
履行	lǚxíng	v.	fulfill；carry out；perform；implement	(10.3)
乱套	luàn tào	vo.	turn things upside down	(4.3)
乱子	luànzi	n.	trouble；disturbance	(3.4)
轮椅	lúnyǐ	n.	wheelchair	(1.1)

啰唆	luōsuo	adj.	repetitive; loquacious; garrulous (of words)	(7.2)
落	luò	v.	fall; toss	(2.1)
落	lào	v.	end up (with)	(9.1)
落空	luò kōng	vo.	come to nothing; fail; fall through	(9.4)
落实政策	luòshí zhèngcè	vo.	implement policy	(4.2)
落选	luòxuǎn	v.	lose an election or competition	(10.3)
麻利	máli	adj.	fast; quick; agile	(4.3)
马桶	mǎtǒng	n.	night stool; chamber pot	(2.4)
埋	mái	v.	bury; cover up with earth	(4.2)
埋怨	mányuàn	v.	blame; complain	(6.3)
迈进	mài jìn	vc.	get in; step in	(3.1)
卖关子	mài guānzi	vo.	(see note 1)	(10.2)
蛮	mán	adv.	(col.) 很, quite; very	(4.2)
瞒	mán	v.	hide the truth from; conceal from	(5.4)
满票	mǎn piào		same as 全票; unanimous vote	(10.1)
满足	mǎnzú	v.	satisfy	(5.3)
漫画	mànhuà	n.	cartoon; caricature	(5.2)
忙活	mánghuo	v.	(col.) busy doing sth.	(1.3)
毛病	máo·bìng	n.	trouble; problem (as used in this story)	(3.4)
毛贼	máozéi	n.	(col.) thief	(3.1)
矛盾	máodùn	n.	problems; conflicts	(2.2)
帽子	màozi	n.	hat; cap	(4.2)
没出息	méi chūxi	adj.	good-for-nothing	(5.2)
没错	méi cuò	adj.	对, that's right	(4.1)
没劲	méijìn	adj.	(col.) 没有意思, not interesting; boring	(3.2)
没事（儿）吧	méi shì(r) ba		(col.) Are you alright?	(1.2)
没意思	méi yìsi	adj.	senseless (as used in this story)	(3.4)

没影儿	méiyǐngr		"not even a shadow（of sth.）" used here to mean "besides talk; nothing substantial is happening or has happened"	(9.2)
没招儿	méi zhāor	vo.	(col.)没有办法，helpless	(3.1)
没准儿	méizhǔnr		(col.)说不定，perhaps; probably	(1.1)
美国货	měiguóhuò	n.	American merchandise or goods	(7.1)
美满	měimǎn	adj.	happy; satisfactory; harmonious	(8.4)
美人儿计	měirénr jì	n.	sex-trap; sexual entrapment	(1.1)
美滋滋	měi zīzī	adj.	happy and complacent; pleased（with oneself）	(9.1)
魅力	mèilì	n.	charm; captivation; fascination; enchantment	(8.1)
门脸儿	ménliǎnr	n.	store; shop（as used in this story）	(6.2)
门面房	ménmiànfáng	n.	a shop on the street（facing the street）	(1.1)
闷	mēn	adj.	stuffy	(1.4)
蒙	mēng	v.	make a wild guess; hit good luck	(3.3)
蒙	mēng	v.	cheat; deceive; swindle	(6.3)
棉花	miánhua	n.	cotton; raw cotton	(6.4)
面包车	miànbāochē	n.	van	(9.2)
面部	miànbù	n.	脸，face	(2.1)
面貌	miànmào	n.	appearance	(7.3)
面生	miànshēng	adj.	unfamiliar	(6.4)
敏感	mǐngǎn	adj.	sensitive; susceptible	(2.4)
名额	míng'é	n.	quota of people; number of people allowed	(10.1)
名落孙山	míng luò sūn shān		fail in a competitive examination;（see note 15）	(10.1)
名片	míngpiàn	n.	name card; business card	(6.1)
明摆着	míngbǎi zhe		evidently; obvious	(2.4)
明儿	míngr	t.	(col.)明天，tomorrow	(1.4)

明明	míngmíng	adv.	obviously; undoubtedly	(5.3)
明显	míngxiǎn	adj.	clearly; obviously	(10.1)
命大	mìngdà		extremely lucky (in a very dangerous situation)	(4.3)
命令	mìnglìng	n.	order	(4.3)
摸	mō	v.	touch; feel; stroke	(8.2)
模样	múyàng	n.	appearance; looks	(2.1)
莫不是	mò bú shì		might it be	(9.1)
莫名其妙	mò míng qí miào		being baffled, (see note 8)	(7.3)
谋	móu	v.	work for; seek	(6.1)
木料	mùliào	n.	timber; lumber	(4.2)
目击者	mùjīzhě	n.	eyewitness; witness	(2.1)
内部	nèibù	n.	internal	(4.2)
那口子	nà kǒuzi	n.	(col.) spouse	(3.1)
乃	nǎi	v.	是，be (formal)	(9.3)
奶昔	nǎixī	n.	milkshake	(8.1)
奶油	nǎiyóu	n.	cream	(8.2)
男性	nánxìng	n.	male; man	(2.1)
男子汉	nánzǐhàn	n.	a real man, true man	(7.1)
难处	nánchu	n.	difficulty	(5.1)
难受	nánshòu	v.	feel miserable; feel sad	(4.2)
难为	nánwei	v.	bring pressure on sb.; make things difficult for sb.	(6.3)
脑	nǎo	n.	brain	(10.3)
脑瓜	nǎoguā	n.	brain	(6.2)
脑子好使	nǎozi hǎoshǐ		(col.) smart; intelligent	(3.3)
闹	nào	v.	instigate; create	(8.1)
闹别扭	nào bièniu	vo.	have problem with relationship (as used in this story)	(3.3)

闹误会	nào wùhuì	vo.	cause misunderstanding	(3.2)
闹着玩（儿）	nào zhe wánr		joke around	(4.2)
嫩	nèn	adj.	inexperienced	(2.4)
拟	nǐ	v.	draft; draw up	(9.2)
腻	nì	adj.	sticky; greasy; 起腻 （see note 5）	(7.1)
蔫不出溜	niān bu chūliū		lackadaisical; sluggish; droopy; (see note 14)	(9.2)
年底	niándǐ		end of a year; year-end	(6.1)
年纪	niánjì	n.	age	(5.4)
年头儿	niántóur	n.	number of years; long time	(10.3)
念旧	niànjiù	adj.	nostalgic	(1.4)
娘儿俩	niángr liǎ		mother and child	(5.1)
尿	niào	v.	urinate; piss; pee	(2.3)
宁	nìng	conj.	宁可，would rather	(10.1)
弄	nòng	v.	get; manage to obtain	(1.3)
弄邪的	nòngxié de	vo.	(col.) do crazy things	(3.4)
挪用	nuóyòng	v.	divert（funds）; embezzle; line one's pocket with public funds	(2.4)
诺言	nuòyán	n.	promise; pledge	(10.3)
噢	ō	interj.	(of surprised understanding or awareness) Oh	(1.1)
偶然	ǒurán	adj.	accidentally; unexpectedly; occasionally	(5.4)
怄气	òu qì	vo.	sulk, have the sulks	(9.4)
趴	pā	v.	lie face down; lie on one's stomach	(8.3)
拍肩	pāi jiān	vo.	拍肩膀，pat shoulder	(10.3)
排叉儿	páichàr	n.	fried snack that is thin and crisp	(8.1)
排除	páichú	v.	eliminate; rule out; exclude	(2.1)
排名	páimíng		ranking	(9.1)
牌子	páizi	n.	brand; trademark	(6.1)

派出所	pàichūsuǒ	n.	local police station	(2. 2)
派上用场	pài shang yòngchǎng		(skill of sb. or things one has) found the use of	(7. 2)
盼	pàn	v.	yearn for; long for	(9. 2)
旁敲侧击	páng qiāo cè jī		make oblique references，(see note 6)	(7. 3)
抛	pāo	v.	throw; toss; fling	(10. 3)
刨	páo	v.	excavate; unearth	(4. 2)
刨出去	páo chuqu	vc.	excluding; not counting; minus	(9. 1)
刨掉	páo diào	vc.	减去，扣掉，exclude; subtract	(1. 3)
泡泡糖	pàopaotáng	n.	chewing gum	(9. 3)
呸	pēi	interj.	pah; bah; pooh; boo（expressing disdain, annoyance or disapproval）	(8. 3)
陪伴	péibàn	v.	accompany	(4. 2)
赔	péi	v.	compensate	(4. 3)
赔不起	péi bu qǐ	vc.	cannot afford to lose money	(1. 1)
赔不是	péi búshì	vo.	(col.) apologize（＝道歉）	(3. 1)
赔偿	péicháng	v.	compensate; pay for indemnity	(1. 2)
赔礼	péi lǐ	vo.	apologize	(5. 4)
配	pèi	v.	match; go together (nicely)	(1. 2)
配套	pèi tào	vo.	make a complete set	(1. 2)
盆（儿）	pén(r)	n.	basin; pot	(3. 1)
批发部	pīfābù	n.	wholesale (warehouse)	(6. 3)
皮鞋	píxié	n.	leather shoes	(3. 3)
屁股	pìgu	n.	buttocks; backside; butt	(8. 3)
偏方	piānfāng	n.	folk prescription	(2. 3)
便宜	piányi	adj.	(col.) be too lenient with sb. let sb. off too easily	(4. 3)
骗	piàn	v.	deceive; fool	(1. 4)
骗人	piàn rén	vo.	deceive people; defraud others	(5. 2)

漂亮	piàoliang	adj.	pretty	(8.1)
撇儿	piěr	n.	left falling stroke (in Chinese calligraphy)	(8.3)
拼搏	pīnbó	v.	struggle hard; exert one's utmost strength	(6.1)
贫	pín	adj.	talkative in a witty way	(3.1)
贫困	pínkùn	adj	impoverished	(7.3)
贫嘴	pínzuǐ		loquacious，garrulous (derogatory)	(10.1)
平	píng	adj.	be on the same level; equal	(9.4)
平米	píngmǐ	m.	square meter	(9.2)
平台	píngtái	n.	terrace; flat roof	(6.2)
平稳	píngwěn	adj.	stable; smooth; calm	(2.2)
评	píng	v.	evaluate; assess（评职称 evaluate professional titles）	(10.1)
评委	píngwěi	n.	committee member	(10.1)
评选	píngxuǎn	v.	choose and appraise through comparison	(10.2)
评优	píng yōu	vo.	select the best; vote for the most outstanding	(10.3)
凭	píng	v.	base on; go by; take as the basis	(10.1)
苹果派	píngguǒpài	n.	apple pie	(8.2)
破	pò	adj.	broken; damaged; 小破公司 a lousy little company	(9.1)
破案	pò àn	vo.	solve; crack a criminal case; find out the truth of a criminal case	(2.1)
破费	pòfèi	v.	spent (money) or time	(7.2)
朴实	pǔshí	adj.	sincere and honest; simple; plain	(7.3)
普通话	pǔtōnghuà	n.	Mandarin Chinese	(10.3)
谱	pǔ	n.	something to count on; a fair amount of confidence	(9.2)
七级浮屠	qī jí fútú		Buddhist pagoda	(10.1)
欺骗	qīpiàn	v./n.	cheat; deceive	(6.4)

齐	qí	adj.	complete (of a set of books, furniture, etc.)	(5.3)
起哄	qǐ hòng	vo.	stir up trouble	(3.4)
起早贪黑	qǐ zǎo tān hēi		work from dawn to dusk	(5.2)
气蒙了	qì mēng le	vc.	too angry to think straight	(6.4)
泣	qì	v.	哭，snivel；sob	(10.2)
掐	qiā	v.	pinch；clutch；strangle	(8.3)
卡住	qiǎ zhù	vc.	be blocked；be held back；be stuck	(5.1)
千儿八百	qiānr bā bǎi	num.	大约 800～1000，￥800～1,000	(6.2)
牵	qiān	v.	involve；pull into；implicate	(2.3)
牵肠挂肚	qiān cháng guà dù		feel deep anxiety about	(5.1)
牵扯	qiānchě	v.	involve；implicate；drag in	(2.2)
铅笔盒	qiānbǐ hé	n.	pencil box	(5.2)
前科	qiánkē	n.	previous criminal record	(2.2)
钱包	qiánbāo	n.	purse；wallet	(4.1)
潜力	qiánlì	n.	potential；latent capacity	(10.1)
欠	qiàn	v.	owe	(2.4)
歉意	qiànyì	n.	apology；regret	(7.3)
枪毙	qiāngbì	v.	execute a death sentence；execute by shooting	(4.3)
强	qiáng	adj.	better (than)；superior (to)	(1.2)
强迫症	qiángpòzhèng		force；compel	(8.3)
墙脚（儿）	qiángjiǎo(r)	n.	corrner	(3.3)
抢	qiǎng	v.	vie for；fight to win sth.；scramble for	(9.2)
抢功	qiǎng gōng	v.	steal (other's) credit	(1.1)
抢险	qiǎng xiǎn	vo.	rush to rescue；rush to an emergency	(4.2)
敲门（儿）	qiāo mén(r)	vo.	knock at door	(3.3)
瞧	qiáo	v.	(col.) 看，look at	(3.1)

撬开	qiào kai	vc.	pry open; force open (with a metal stick)	(3.1)
亲戚	qīnqi	n.	relative (s)	(6.2)
勤	qín	adv.	frequently (as used in this story)	(7.1)
勤快	qínkuai	adj.	diligent; hard-working	(7.1)
青鸟	qīng niǎo	n.	bird (Blue jay)	(8.3)
清静	qīngjìng	adj.	(of surroundings) quiet	(6.3)
清凉	qīngliáng	adj.	cool and refreshing; cool and pleasant	(8.2)
清清楚楚	qīng qīng chu chu	adj.	crystal clear	(5.3)
情况	qíngkuàng	n.	information; development	(2.1)
请假	qǐng jià	vo.	ask for leave	(5.2)
穷	qióng	adj.	poor	(1.4)
穷搜搜	qióng sōusōu	adj.	poor, shabby	(4.2)
球迷	qiúmí	n.	fan, ball game buff; fandom	(9.1)
屈辱	qūrǔ	adj.	shame; humiliation; indignity	(8.3)
取舍	qǔshě	v.	accept or reject; make one's choice; selection	(10.1)
娶	qǔ	v.	marry (a woman); take (a wife)	(1.1)
娶了媳妇儿忘了娘	qǔle xífur wàngle niáng		sons tend to forget their mothers once they get married	(1.3)
全局	quánjú	n.	overall situation; situation as a whole	(10.1)
全面	quánmiàn	adj.	overall; all-sided	(6.2)
全票	quán piào		unanimous vote	(10.1)
劝	quàn	v.	persuade; advise; urge	(5.2)
缺德	quē dé	vo.	mean; wicked	(4.3)
缺乏	quēfá	v.	lack; be short of	(8.3)
确定	quèdìng	v.	sure; certain; definite	(2.1)
确实	quèshí	adv.	truly; indeed	(1.4)

确有其事	què yǒu qí shì		真有那件事，it did happen；sth. truly took place	(10.3)
嚷	rǎng	v.	talk aloud, shout and scream	(4.3)
嚷嚷	rāngrang	v.	make a uproar；yak；shout；yell	(10.2)
让	ràng	v.	yield	(2.1)
饶	ráo	v.	forgive；spare	(7.1)
绕回来	rào huílái	vc.	turn back to the original place	(3.2)
惹出	rě chu	vc.	cause (sth. bad) to happen	(3.4)
惹是生非	rě shì shēng fēi		stir up trouble；provoke a dispute	(7.1)
热乎	rèhu	adj.	intimate；close (in a relationship)	(3.4)
热线	rèxiàn	n.	hotline (communications link)	(7.2)
人道主义	réndào zhǔyì		humanitarianism	(10.1)
人家	rénjia	pron.	(here refers to 王娜)	(3.3)
人群	rénqún	n.	throng；crowd	(9.4)
人言可畏	rén yán kě wèi		rumor kills people，(see note 10)	(8.2)
人之私利	rén zhī sī lì		personal gain；private interest	(10.1)
仁义	rényì	adj.	kind	(7.2)
认输	rèn shū	vo.	acknowledge one's defeat	(10.1)
认账	rèn zhàng	vo.	admit what one has said or done	(6.3)
日常	rìcháng	adj.	daily；day-to-day	(4.1)
揉	róu	v.	rub	(3.2)
肉	ròu	n.	flesh	(4.1)
肉饼子	ròubǐngzi	n.	肉饼，meat pie	(4.2)
入选	rùxuǎn	v.	be selected，be chosen	(10.3)
软	ruǎn	adj.	soft；gentle	(10.1)
软弱	ruǎnruò	adj.	weak；feeble；flabby	(8.3)
撒（谎）	sā (huǎng)	v.	说（谎），说（假话）tell a lie；lie	(2.3)
撒谎	sā huǎng	vo.	tell lies	(5.2)

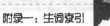

撒手	sā shǒu	vo.	放开手，let go；give up	(8.3)
塞	sāi	v.	stuff in	(5.2)
散	sàn	v.	fall apart	(3.4)
散装	sǎnzhuāng	adj.	unpackaged	(4.1)
扫兴	sǎo xìng	vo.	disappointing	(8.2)
嫂子	sǎozi	n.	elder brother's wife；elder sister-in-law	(6.2)
僧多粥少	sēng duō zhōu shǎo		too many people compete for too few positions，(see note 5)	(10.3)
（沙发）巾	(shāfā) jīn	n.	a piece of cloth（as used for a towel, scarf，kerchief，etc.），沙发巾 sofa cover	(7.2)
沙拉	shālā	n.	salad	(8.2)
沙子	shāzi	n.	sand	(3.2)
傻	shǎ	adj.	stupid；foolish	(6.2)
傻瓜	shǎguā	n.	fool	(1.4)
啥	shá	pron.	（col.）什么，what	(6.1)
山盟海誓	shān méng hǎi shì		couple's pledge of love as long lasting as the mountains and the seas；a solemn vows and pledges of love	(8.3)
闪失	shǎnshī	n.	accident；mishap	(6.1)
善后	shànhòu	n.	funeral arrangements；deal with the aftermath	(2.4)
善良	shànliáng	adj.	kind-hearted；good and honest	(7.3)
伤害	shānghài	v./n.	injure/injury；damage	(2.1)
伤心	shāng xīn	adj.	sad；grieved	(4.1)
商贩	shāngfàn	n.	small retailer；peddler	(6.4)
商业	shāngyè	n.	commercial	(9.2)
上	shàng	v.	to be promoted	(10.1)
上档次	shàng dàngcì		high-quality	(1.2)
上等	shàngděng	adj.	superior；of first-class	(4.2)
上税	shàng shuì	vo.	pay taxes	(9.2)

上岁数	shàng suìshu		getting on in age	(8.1)
少来这套	shǎo lái zhè tào		(col.) stop doing this; drop the act	(1.1)
哨子	shàozi	n.	哨儿，whistle	(4.2)
舍不得	shě bu de	vc.	grudge (money); hate to spend (money)	(1.1)
设计师	shèjìshī	n.	designer	(10.2)
射门	shè mén	vo.	shoot (at the goal) in soccer, football, etc.	(2.3)
申报	shēnbào	v.	report to a higher body	(10.1)
身份	shēnfen	n.	identity; status	(2.1)
身份证	shēnfènzhèng	n.	identification card (I.D.)	(2.1)
身子骨	shēnzigǔ	n.	身体，health	(4.2)
深刻	shēnkè	adj.	profound	(1.4)
深深的	shēnshēn de		very sincere; profound	(7.3)
神经病	shénjīngbìng	n.	(You're) crazy! lunatic	(4.2)
神圣	shénshèng	adj.	sacred; holy	(10.1)
婶（儿）	shěn(r)	n.	本来称叔叔的妻子，也可以称父辈的人的妻子，aunt (uncle's wife); a respectful form of address for an woman of one's parents' age	(3.1)
升值	shēngzhí	v.	rise in value	(1.4)
生意	shēngyi	n.	买卖，business	(1.4)
声誉	shēngyù	n.	reputation; fame	(6.4)
胜	shèng	n.	victory; success	(9.1)
胜	shèng	v.	better than	(10.1)
绳儿	shéngr	n.	rope	(5.1)
绳子	shéngzi	n.	rope	(4.3)
省得	shěngde	conj.	免得，avoid (extra efforts/trouble); save (trouble)	(5.1)
失眠	shīmián	v.	suffer from insomnia	(10.1)
失意	shīyì	adj.	frustrated; disappointed	(3.3)

10 万	shíwàn	num.	one-hundred thousand	(4. 3)
时差	shíchā	n.	time difference; jet lag	(9. 1)
时装	shízhuāng	n.	fashion; vogue; latest fashion	(8. 2)
实话	shíhuà	n.	honest words; truth	(2. 3)
实话实说	shí huà shí shuō		speak the plain truth; speak frankly; talk straight	(8. 3)
实力	shílì	n.	strength	(9. 4)
食客	shíkè	n.	restaurant customer	(1. 4)
世纪	shìjì	n.	century	(9. 4)
世面	shìmiàn	n.	world; various aspects of society or world	(6. 1)
世俗地	shìsú de	adv.	conventionally (derogatory)	(10. 3)
事故	shìgù	n.	accident; mishap	(2. 1)
势力	shì·lì	n.	power; influence	(4. 3)
收	shōu	v.	collect	(4. 1)
收回来	shōu hui lai	vc.	take back	(3. 2)
收录机	shōulùjī	n.	radio-tape recorder	(6. 2)
收入	shōurù	n.	income; earnings	(4. 1)
收听	shōutīng	v.	listen to (the radio); tune in	(7. 2)
手脚不干净	shǒujiǎo bù gānjìng		a pilferer, (see note 5)	(7. 3)
手脚利索	shǒu jiǎo lìsuo		nimble; agile	(7. 1)
手拿把掐	shǒu ná bǎ qiā		hold firmly in hand, (see note 1)	(9. 4)
手帕	shǒupà	n.	手绢儿, handkerchief	(6. 2)
手头	shǒutóu	n.	on hand; at hand	(6. 1)
守信用	shǒu xìnyòng	vo.	keep one's word	(6. 3)
首饰	shǒu·shì	n.	jewelry	(1. 1)
首饰盒	shǒushì hé	n.	jewelry box	(1. 2)
受害者	shòuhàizhě	n.	victim(s)	(4. 3)

受骗	shòu piàn	vo.	be cheated; be deceived	(4.1)
受气	shòu qì	vo.	be bullied; suffer wrong	(1.1)
售货员	shòuhuòyuán	n.	salesperson; shop assistant; salesclerk	(9.3)
售票员	shòupiàoyuán	n.	conductor; ticket seller; box-office clerk	(9.1)
疏忽	shūhu	v.	neglect; oversight	(8.4)
熟	shú	adj.	familiar	(6.1)
熟人	shúrén	n.	acquaintance; friend	(2.2)
束	shù	m.	bundle; bunch	(7.3)
数落	shǔluo	v.	(col.) scold; criticize (someone)	(6.3)
刷牙	shuā yá	vo.	brush teeth	(1.1)
摔	shuāi	v.	break	(3.1)
甩	shuǎi	v.	toss out (comments)	(1.1)
双休日	shuāngxiūrì	n.	two-day weekend	(5.3)
水电费	shuǐdiànfèi	n.	water and electricity bills	(7.2)
水钱	shuǐqián	n.	water fee	(1.3)
税收	shuìshōu	n.	tax revenue	(9.1)
顺路	shùnlù	adv.	on the way (to somewhere else)	(9.2)
顺手	shùnshǒu	adv.	conveniently; easily; (do sth.) without extra efforts	(7.1)
瞬间	shùnjiān	adv.	in the twinkling of an eye; moment	(6.1)
说不准	shuō bu zhǔn	vc.	(col.) unsure; uncertain	(1.2)
说到底	shuō dào dǐ		(col.) the bottom-line is...	(3.4)
说明	shuōmíng	v.	show; demonstrate	(1.4)
司机	sījī	n.	driver (of transportation vehicles such as train, automobile, trolley, etc.)	(2.1)
思路	sīlù	n.	train of thought; thinking	(9.2)
死	sǐ	adj.	rigid; stubborn	(6.1)
死钱	sǐ qián	n.	money that you cannot use for other purpose	(1.1)

死心眼（儿）	sǐxīnyǎn(r)	adj.	stubborn	(1.4)
死者	sǐzhě	n.	the dead；the deceased	(2.1)
四季	sìjì	n.	four seasons	(5.1)
四强	sì qiáng	n.	The four finalists	(9.2)
伺候	cìhou	v.	wait upon sb；serve；take care	(1.1)
送礼	sòng lǐ	vo.	give sb. a present；present a gift to sb.	(10.3)
俗了吧唧的	sú le bājī de		(see grammar note 4)	(1.1)
俗气	súqi	adj.	tacky	(1.1)
算谁的	suàn shuí de		（col.）谁负责？是谁的责任？Who is to blame?	(3.1)
随便	suíbiàn	adj.	do as one pleases	(7.2)
随口	suíkǒu	adv.	(speak) thoughtlessly；blurt out (whatever comes into one's head)	(1.1)
随礼	suílǐ	n/vo.	别人办婚事丧事等等时送礼，present given at a wedding or funeral	(1.4)
随身听	suíshēntīng	n.	walkman	(6.2)
随手	suíshǒu	adv.	conveniently；without extra trouble	(5.3)
岁数	suìshu	n.	年龄，(year of) age	(3.3)
孙子	sūnzi	n.	grandson	(1.1)
所长	suǒzhǎng	n.	head of an institute (head of 派出所 as in this script)	(2.2)
所有的	suǒyǒu de		all	(7.3)
索性	suǒxìng	adv.	might as well；simply；just	(3.1)
锁	suǒ	n./v.	lock	(5.4)
锁好	suǒ hǎo	vc.	lock up safely	(1.3)
锁上	suǒ shang	vc.	lock up	(1.3)
锁住	suǒzhù	vc.	lock up	(5.4)
他妈（的）	tā mā(de)	interj.	（骂人的话）Damn it!	(4.2)
塌	tā	v.	crumple；fall down；cave in	(4.2)
塌下来	tā xialai	vc.	collapse	

踏踏实实	tā ta shī shī	adj.	having peace of mind; free from anxiety	(1. 4)
踏进	tà jìn	vc .	step in; work in	(7. 3)
台词	táicí	n.	uttering of a stage character, including dialogue monologue and aside	(10. 2)
台风	táifēng	n.	typhoon	(4. 2)
坛坛罐罐	tán tán guàn guàn		jars & pots; kitchenware	(5. 1)
坦白	tǎnbái	v.	confess; make a confession	(10. 2)
坦诚	tǎnchéng	adj.	frank and sincere	(5. 4)
袒护	tǎnhù	v.	be partial to	(8. 3)
堂堂	tángtáng	adj.	(of a man) impressive looking; dignified in appearance	(7. 1)
趟	tāng	v.	足球用语，jargon used in soccer game	(9. 3)
趟	tàng	m.	a time; a trip	(3. 1)
掏出	tāo chu	vc.	draw out; pull out	(2. 1)
逃避	táobì	v.	run away from; escape	(2. 4)
逃逸	táoyì	v.	逃跑，escape; run away; abscond (formal)	(2. 1)
淘汰	táotài	v.	eliminate through selection or competition	(9. 3)
套装	tàozhuāng	n.	suit	(1. 2)
忒	tuī	adv.	(col.) 太，too	(6. 1)
特大	tè dà		特别大的，especially large; exceptionally large	(9. 1)
特意	tèyì	adv.	特别，especially; for a special purpose	(5. 2)
啼笑皆非	tí xiào jiē fēi		not knowing whether to laugh or cry; between tears and smiles	(8. 1)
提供	tígōng	v.	provide; supply	(2. 1)
提醒	tíxǐng	v.	remind; warn	(1. 1)
体会不到	tǐhuìbúdao	vc.	can not realize or comprehend	(1. 3)
体力	tǐlì	n.	physical power; physical strength	(9. 4)

体谅	tǐliàng	v.	show understanding and consideration	(6.3)
体面	tǐmiàn	adj.	decent; respectable	(5.4)
体统	tǐtǒng	n.	decorum; propriety; decency	(8.2)
体验	tǐyàn	v.	learn through personal experience	(6.3)
剃光头	tì guāngtóu	vo.	have one's head shaved (used here to mean "not receiving one vote, not winning one point)	(10.1)
天地良心	tiāndì liángxīn		I swear, (see note 5)	(10.2)
天体	tiāntǐ	n.	celestial body	(2.2)
天意	tiānyì	n	God's will; will of Heaven	(1.4)
天真地	tiānzhēn de	adv./adj.	naively; innocently	(10.3)
添乱	tiān luàn	vo.	add trouble to an already chaotic situation	(4.2)
添难	tiān nán	vo.	create more trouble; make it more difficult	(10.3)
甜饼	tiánbǐng	n.	pie	(8.2)
挑逗	tiǎodòu	v.	provoke; tease; flirt	(8.2)
挑剔	tiāo•tī	v.	nitpick; hypercritical	(3.3)
条	tiáo	m.	for news	(8.1)
条儿	tiáor	n.	note; written message	(2.4)
贴着	tiē zhe		posted	(3.1)
听众	tīngzhòng	n.	audience; listeners	(7.2)
挺住	tǐng zhù	vc.	hold out	(9.4)
同事	tóngshì		colleague; co-worker	(2.3)
同志	tóngzhì	n.	comrade (a customary title used between people in China)	(2.1)
痛苦	tòngkǔ	adj.	pain; suffering; agony	(2.4)
痛痛快快	tòng tong kuài kuài	adv.	joyfully; delightedly	(1.1)
偷走	tōu zǒu	vc.	steal	(5.3)
头脑	tóunǎo	n.	brains; mind	(6.3)

投案	tóu àn	vo.	give oneself up or surrender oneself to the police	(2.4)
投票	tóu piào	vo.	vote, cast a vote	(10.1)
投资	tóu zī	vo.	invest (money)	(6.2)
秃头	tūtóu	n.	(of a person) hairless; bold	(10.3)
土	tǔ	adj.	rustic; unenlightened	(4.1)
土地爷	tǔdìyé	n.	The Earth God	(4.3)
兔子	tùzi	n.	rabbit	(7.2)
推	tuī	v.	push	(1.1)
推销	tuīxiāo	v.	promote the sales (of goods)	(6.4)
推销员	tuīxiāoyuán	n.	salesperson	(7.2)
退	tuì	v.	return; send back	(1.2)
退货	tuì huò	vo.	return merchandize	(4.3)
托人	tuō rén	vo.	ask someone (to do sth.)	(5.2)
拖累	tuōlěi	v.	burden; be a burden (to sb.)	(1.1)
脱不开身	tuō bu kāi shēn		too busy to leave	(3.3)
娃娃	wáwa	n.	doll	(6.2)
挖	wā	v.	dig	(4.2)
瓦	wǎ	m.	watt	(3.2)
外国货	wàiguóhuò	n.	foreign products	(5.2)
外伤	wàishāng	n.	external injury or wound	(7.1)
外围	wàiwéi	n.	periphery; peripheral	(9.4)
外行	wàiháng	n.	layman; one that has no knowledge or experience for certain work	(4.2)
完美无缺	wánměi wú quē		perfect	(8.3)
玩儿命	wánrmìng		(col.) exert one's utmost strength	(3.2)
玩具	wánjù	n.	toy	(5.1)
玩意儿	wányìr	n.	(col.) thing	(1.1)

挽回	wǎnhuí	vc.	reverse the unfavorable situation; turn the table	(10.2)
晚报社	wǎnbào shè	n.	evening newspaper publisher	(8.1)
晚节不忠	wǎnjié bù zhōng		cannot maintain integrity in one's later years	(10.1)
晚年	wǎnnián	n.	old age; one's later years	(10.2)
万一	wànyī	adv.	in case; if by any chance	(4.2)
往后	wǎnghòu	t.	以后，from now on; later on	(5.4)
望远镜	wàngyuǎnjìng	n.	telescope; binoculars	(8.4)
微波炉	wēibōlú	n.	microwave	(4.1)
为……而战	wèi……ér zhàn		fight for; struggle for	(9.2)
为难	wéinán	v./adj.	make sb. feel embarrassed; make things difficult for sb.	(5.4)
违背	wéibèi	v.	violate; go against	(10.1)
唯	wéi	adv.	唯有，only; alone; solely	(10.1)
维持	wéichí	v.	maintain; support	(4.1)
维护	wéihù	v.	protect; uphold	(8.3)
伟大	wěidà	adj.	great; awesome	(6.2)
伪君子	wěijūnzǐ	n.	hypocrite; dissembler	(8.3)
伪劣	wěiliè	adj.	(of goods) fake or of low quality; false and inferior	(6.4)
委员会	wěiyuánhuì	n.	committee	(10.1)
卫士	wèishì	n.	guard	(3.1)
未卜先知	wèi bǔ xiān zhī		foresee the future without divining the Eight Trigrams; (see note 2)	(10.1)
味精	wèijīng	n.	味素，monosodium glutamate (MSG)	(8.1)
温柔	wēnróu	adj.	gentle; tender; feminie	(1.1)
文明	wénmíng	adj.	civilized	(5.1)
闻	wén	v.	smell	(4.1)
闻出来	wén chulai	vc.	figure out by smelling; smell out	(3.1)

窝囊废	wōnangfèi	n.	(a person) good for nothing	(4.2)
握手	wò shǒu	vo.	shake hands	(10.3)
污七八糟	wū qī bā zāo		a horrible mess; a place in great disorder; things that are obscene, dirty and filthy, (see note 9)	(8.2)
呜	wū	ono.	sound of weeping	(8.3)
诬陷	wūxiàn	v.	frame a case against; frame someone	(1.1)
无地自容	wú dì zì róng		feel too ashamed to see anybody, (see note 1)	(10.3)
无端	wúduān	adv.	unwarranted; for no reason at all	(2.1)
无风不起浪	wú fēng bù qǐ làng		there is no smoke without fire	(4.3)
无聊	wúliáo	adj.	boring; nonsense	(10.1)
无情	wúqíng	adj.	merciless; ruthless	(4.2)
无所谓	wúsuǒwèi		It doesn't matter; it is not important	(2.4)
无意之间	wúyì zhī jiān		not intend to; inadvertently	(8.2)
武器	wǔqì	n.	weapon	(4.3)
侮辱	wǔrǔ	v.	insult	(8.3)
物美价廉	wù měi jià lián		excellent (goods) at modest prices	(1.1)
物质	wùzhì	n.	material	(9.2)
误	wù	n.	错误，mistake; error	(9.2)
西城	xīchéng	n.	Western District (of city)	(6.1)
西洋参	xīyángshēn	n.	American ginseng (Panax quinquefolium)	(8.3)
息怒	xīnù	v.	停止发怒、别生气，stop being angry (formal)	(3.1)
嘻	xī	ono.	giggle; laugh; sound of merry laughter	(8.1)
嘻嘻哈哈	xīxī hāhā	adj.	not serious; laughing and joking; mirthful	(8.2)
媳妇（儿）	xífu (r)	n.	(col.) wife; young married woman	(1.2)
喜事	xǐshì	n.	happy event; joyous occasion; wedding	(9.1)
喜糖	xǐtáng	n.	wedding candy	(8.1)

喜讯	xǐxùn	n.	好消息，happy news；good news	(9.1)
戏剧	xìjù	n.	drama；play	(10.1)
细胞	xìbāo	n.	cell	(10.3)
瞎	xiā	adv.	aimlessly	(1.3)
瞎	xiā	adj.	(col.) be ruined	(3.1)
瞎编	xiā biān		make up (wild stories)	(4.3)
瞎（说）	xiā (shuō)	adv.	(see note 4)	(2.1)
下调	xiàtiáo	v.	向下调整（降低），readjust (interest or price) downwards	(6.2)
下岗	xià gǎng	vo.	lay off	(6.1)
下馆子	xià guǎnzi	vo.	go to a restaurant	(4.1)
下海	xià hǎi	vo.	(relinquish one's old job and) go in for business；become a business person	(6.2)
下坡路	xiàpō lù		downhill path；downhill journey	(2.3)
下水道	xiàshuǐdào	n.	sewer	(1.4)
吓唬	xiàhu	v.	吓，frighten；intimidate	(3.4)
吓(了)一跳	xià (le) yí tiào	v.	be taken aback	(3.1)
闲事（儿）	xiánshì(r)	n.	matter that does not concern one；other people's business	(3.4)
闲杂盲流	xián zá mángliú		unemployed/unoccupied migrating peasants (as used in this story)	(6.1)
嫌	xián	v.	(col.) 觉得 (as used in this story)	(1.1)
显得	xiǎnde	v.	appear (to be)，seem	(4.2)
显眼	xiǎnyǎn	adj.	conspicuous, showy；eye-catching	(1.2)
现场	xiànchǎng	n.	scene (of an event or incident)；on the scene	(6.4)
现货	xiànhuò	n.	merchandise on hand；goods in stock	(6.1)
现眼	xiànyǎn	v.	lose face；make a fool of oneself	(1.1)
线索	xiànsuǒ	n.	clue；thread；trail	(2.1)
限于	xiànyú	v.	be confined to；be limited to；be restricted at	(8.2)

馅（儿）饼	xiàn(r)bǐng	n.	pancake with fillings	(6.1)
羡慕	xiànmù	v.	admire; envy	(5.2)
相应地	xiāngyìng de	adv.	accordingly	(10.3)
香味（儿）	xiāngwèi(r)	n.	delicious smell	(4.1)
详细	xiángxì	adj.	detailed	(7.3)
享受	xiǎngshòu	v./n.	enjoy (life, rights, benefits, etc.)	(4.1)
响动	xiǎngdong	n.	sound of movement	(4.2)
想不开	xiǎng bu kāi	vc.	take things too seriously; not able to think through sth.	(4.1)
项链（儿）	xiàngliàn(r)	n.	necklace	(1.1)
消费	xiāofèi	v.	consume; expend	(4.1)
消费者	xiāofèizhě	n.	consumer	(6.4)
消气	xiāo qì	vo.	cool off (one's anger)	(5.2)
销毁	xiāohuǐ	v.	destroy	(6.4)
销售	xiāoshòu	n.	sales	(6.4)
小吃店（儿）	xiǎochīdiàn(r)	n.	small restaurant	(1.3)
小贩	xiǎofàn	n.	peddler; street vendor	(1.3)
小工	xiǎogōng	n.	(temporary) worker/helper	(1.3)
小脚	xiǎojiǎo	n.	bound feet (of women in the old days)	(3.1)
小金库	xiǎo jīnkù	n.	money secretly put away (as used in this story)	(1.2)
小看	xiǎokàn	v.	轻视, underestimate; look down upon; belittle	(9.2)
小两口	xiǎo liǎngkǒu	n.	a young married couple	(9.4)
小气鬼	xiǎoqìguǐ	n.	miser	(5.3)
小区	xiǎoqū	n.	residential area; subdivision	(3.1)
小人儿书	xiǎorénrshū	n.	picture books (for children)	(1.1)
小食店（儿）	xiǎoshídiàn(r)	n.	small shop to sell snacks and drinks	(1.3)
小题大做	xiǎo tí dà zuò		make a fuss over a trifle	(3.2)

小蹄子	xiǎotízi		bitch，(see note 3)	(7.2)
小偷（儿）	xiǎotōu(r)	n.	petty thief；sneak	(3.2)
小丫头片子	xiǎo yātóu piànzi	n.	maiden；girl（derogative）	(7.1)
小子	xiǎozi	n.	brat；chap	(3.1)
校服	xiàofú	n.	school uniform	(1.2)
歇	xiē	v.	(col.)休息，have a rest；take a break	(1.3)
协调	xiétiáo	adj./v.	coordinate；balanced；harmonious；in turn	(8.2)
协议	xiéyì	v./n.	reach agreement；agreement	(3.4)
协助	xiézhù	n./v.	assist；help	(2.1)
心肠	xīncháng	n.	heart	(10.1)
心灵	xīnlíng	n.	(Lit.) heart	(10.2)
心思	xīnsi	n.	thought；thinking	(1.4)
心疼	xīnténg	v.	distressed；love dearly	(1.4)
心细	xīnxì	adj.	careful；scrupulous	(10.1)
心虚	xīnxū	adj.	lack in self-confidence；have a guilty conscience	(1.1)
心意	xīnyì	n.	kindly feelings；regard	(5.2)
辛苦	xīnkǔ	adj.	work hard	(7.1)
新近	xīnjìn	adv.	最近，recently；lately	(8.1)
新品种	xīn pǐnzhǒng		new product	(4.1)
新闻	xīnwén	n.	news	(8.1)
新型	xīnxíng	adj.	new type；new kind	(4.3)
信	xìn	v.	believe	(1.4)
信号	xìnhào	n.	signal；sign given by light, electric wave, sound, gesture, etc. to convey information or a command.	(2.4)
信口胡说	xìn kǒu hú shuō		talk irresponsibly；wag one's tongue too freely	(8.3)
信任	xìnrèn	n./v.	trust	(3.4)

信任感	xìnrèn gǎn	n.	sense of responsibility	(7.3)
信息	xìnxī	n.	information	(9.2)
信箱	xìnxiāng	n.	mailbox	(5.1)
兴	xīng	v.	encourage; promote	(6.1)
兴许	xīngxǔ	adv.	可能、也许，perhaps；maybe	(9.2)
行人	xíngrén	n.	pedestrian; passerby	(9.1)
形容词	xíngróngcí	n.	adjective	(5.3)
形势	xíngshì	n.	situation; circumstances	(6.2)
幸亏	xìngkuī	adv.	thanks to (that …)	(3.1)
性命	xìngmìng	n.	life (of person)	(4.2)
性质	xìngzhì	n.	nature; character	(2.1)
兄弟	xiōngdì	n.	brother; a familiar form of addressing a man younger than oneself	(9.1)
休闲生活	xiūxián shēnghuó		leisurely life	(8.3)
休想	xiū xiǎng	v.	不要妄想，don't imagine that it's possible	(3.1)
袖	xiù	n.	sleeve，两袖清风，(see note 9)	(8.1)
虚称	xūchēng	n.	empty or boastful titles	(10.3)
嘘	xū	interj.	sigh; hiss	(8.1)
叙述	xùshù	v.	narrate; recount	(2.1)
宣布	xuānbù	v.	declare; proclaim; announce	(10.3)
宣传	xuānchuán	v.	publicize; promote	(3.1)
玄乎	xuánhu	adj.	(col.) fantastic; inscrutable	(6.1)
悬	xuán	adj.	危险，tricky; unpredictable; (see note 6)	(9.3)
选票	xuǎnpiào	n.	vote; ballot	(10.1)
学术	xuéshù	n.	academic; academics	(10.1)
雪上加霜	xuě shàng jiā shuāng		one disaster after another	(6.4)

雪中送炭	xuě zhōng sòng tàn		give help in time of need	(6. 4)
血口喷人	xuè kǒu pēn rén		make unfounded and malicious attacks upon sb. ; slander	(1. 1)
血压	xuèyā	n.	blood pressure	(10. 1)
训示	xùnshì	n.	allocution; instruction or order to younger members of a family from elders	(10. 1)
徇	xùn	v.	ask for; enquire	(10. 1)
压坏	yā huài	vc.	crash	(4. 2)
轧马路	yà mǎlù	vo.	take a stroll (usually with a lover)	(7. 3)
押金	yājīn	n.	deposit	(1. 3)
鸭毛	yāmáo	n.	geese down	(6. 4)
鸭绒	yāróng	n.	down	(6. 1)
哑巴	yǎba	n. /a.	silent; mute; a mute;	(3. 4)
压根儿	yàgēnr	adv.	(col.) 从来，根本，at all; simply	(3. 4)
严重	yánzhòng	adj.	serious; critical	(2. 1)
研究员	yánjiūyuán	n.	research fellow; researcher	(10. 1)
眼（睛）不花	yǎn (jing) bù huā		not presbyopic	(3. 3)
眼睛里不揉沙子	yǎnjing lǐ bù róu shāzi	ex.	(refer to note 5)	(3. 2)
眼镜	yǎnjìng	n.	eye glasses, spectacles	(8. 3)
眼泪	yǎnlèi	n.	tears	(8. 3)
眼皮	yǎnpí	n.	eyelid	(6. 2)
眼神	yǎnshén	n.	眼力，expression in one's eyes; look in one's eyes	(7. 2)
眼下	yǎnxià	t.	现在，right now; currently	(4. 3)
洋房	yángfáng	n.	foreign-style house; Western-style house	(4. 2)
洋酒	yángjiǔ	n.	foreign wine or liquor	(4. 1)
吆喝	yāohe	v.	cry out; loudly urge on	(6. 3)
吆五喝六	yāo wǔ hè liù	vo.	shout aloud	(3. 3)

腰部	yāobù	n.	腰，waist	(2.1)
谣言	yáoyán	n.	rumor	(4.3)
咬	yǎo	v.	bite	(7.1)
要不是	yàobúshi	conj.	（如果不是），if it were not for	(1.4)
要财不要命	yào cái bú yào mìng		risk (one's) life for money	(4.2)
钥匙	yàoshi	n.	key	(3.1)
椰茸汤	yēróngtāng	n.	coconut soup	(8.2)
椰汁	yēzhī	n.	coconut juice	(8.2)
噎	yē	v.	choke; choke sb. off	(3.3)
爷	yé	n.	老太爷，master; ancestor	(1.1)
咦	yí	interj.		(5.3)
夜长梦多	yè cháng mèng duō		a long night is fraught with Dreams; a long delay means trouble; (see note 11)	(9.2)
夜游	yèyóu	v.	a person who is up and about at night	(4.3)
（一）辈子	yí bèizi	n.	all one's life, lifetime	(7.3)
一本正经	yì běn zhèng jīng		in all seriousness; in dead earnest	(3.2)
一杆秤	yì gǎn chèng		a steelyard	(8.3)
一个劲（儿）	yígèjìn(r)	adv.	不停地，continuously; persistently	(6.2)
一伙儿	yīhuǒr		partnership; groups; crowds	(6.3)
一流	yīliú	adj.	of the best quality; first-class	(6.4)
一宿	yì xiǔ		（col.）一夜，one whole night	(1.2)
（一）通	(yí) tòng	m.	measure word for action as in "一通话；打了三通"	(10.2)
一味地	yíwèi de	adv.	persistently	(9.2)
一线	yí xiàn		一点点，a ray of; a gleam of	(9.2)
一早	yì zǎo		early in the morning	(5.3)
一眨眼	yì zhǎ yǎn		（col.）非常短的时间内，in the blink of an eye; in a very short time	(5.3)
一准儿	yìzhǔnr	adv.	（col.）一定，certainly	(6.4)

仪式	yíshì	n.	ceremony	(7.2)
姨	yí	n.	aunt（maternal aunt，i. e. mother's sister）	(7.1)
遗憾	yíhàn	v.	regret；pity	(10.3)
疑神疑鬼	yí shén yí guǐ		be terribly suspicious	(8.3)
意味着	yìwèi zhe	v.	imply；mean	(9.1)
荫	yīn	n.	(of a place) sheltered by green foliage of trees	(8.3)
引用	yǐnyòng	v.	quote；cite	(10.1)
饮料	yǐnliào	n.	beverage；drink	(4.2)
隐瞒	yǐnmán	v.	conceal；hide；cover up；hold back the facts from revealing	(2.4)
印	yìn	v.	print	(6.3)
应验	yìngyàn	v.	turn out to be true	(6.2)
迎刃而解	yíng rèn ér jiě		(of a problem) readily solved, (see note 8)	(10.3)
营养	yíngyǎng	n.	nutrition	(8.1)
营养品	yíngyǎngpǐn	n.	nutritious stuff (food)	(7.1)
影评	yǐngpíng	n.	movie review	(8.4)
硬币	yìngbì	n.	coin (of money)	(5.3)
哟	yō	interj.		(5.1)
拥抱	yōngbào	v.	embrace；hug	(10.3)
永恒	yǒnghéng	adj.	eternal；perpetual	(6.1)
勇气	yǒngqì	n.	courage	(5.4)
用不着	yòng bu zháo		there is no need	(2.3)
用得着	yòng de zháo		需要，有用；necessary	(5.1)
用情不专	yòng qíng bù zhuān		(of a woman) of easy virtue；promiscuous；(of a man) skirt chaser, (see note 6)	(8.2)
忧郁症	yōuyùzhèng	n.	depression	(8.3)

攸关	yōu guān		攸：所；关：关联、关系到。be of concern; affect; be closely related to; 胜负攸关 a matter of victory and defeat	(9.1)
幽默	yōumò	adj.	humorous	(8.1)
幽默感	yōumògǎn	n.	sense of humor	(8.3)
尤其	yóuqí	adv.	especially; particularly	(2.1)
由……做主	yóu……zuòzhǔ		decided by someone; someone has the final say	(5.1)
由不得	yóubude	vc.	be not in control; not have freedom of choice	(9.2)
犹	yóu	adv.	(Lit.) 还，still	(10.2)
邮递员	yóudìyuán	n.	mail carrier; postman	(5.2)
油乎乎	yóuhūhū	adj.	oily; greasy	(7.1)
油烟机	yóuyānjī	n.	exhaust fan	(7.1)
游戏机	yóuxìjī	n.	video game player	(4.1)
有病	yǒu bìng		be (mentally) sick; crazy, (see note 10)	(7.1)
有的是	yǒu de shì		很多，plenty	(9.1)
有福	yǒufú	adj.	lucky	(1.4)
有功	yǒu gōng	vo.	having done a meritorious deed	(7.1)
有看头	yǒu kàntour	vo.	值得看，interesting or exciting to watch	(3.2)
有口皆碑	yǒu kǒu jiē bēi		win universal praise; be universally acclaimed	(10.1)
有毛病	yǒu máobing		(of a person) crazy; have problems	(1.3)
有难同当	yǒu nàn tóng dāng		share the difficulties and hardships (of friends/loved ones)	(6.3)
(有钱) 有势	(yǒu qián) yǒu shì		(people) with (money and) power	(4.3)
有数	yǒushù	adj.	certain; knowing how things stand	(4.2)
有喜	yǒuxǐ	v.	怀孕，pregnant	(8.4)
有戏	yǒu xì	vo.	(col.) 有希望，hopeful (as used in this story)	(4.2)
有幸	yǒuxìng	adv.	fortunate; lucky	(7.3)

诱供	yòu gòng	vo.	trap a person into confession	(1.1)
余地	yúdì	n.	leeway; margin; room	(9.2)
羽绒服	yǔróngfú	n.	down jacket	(6.1)
预备	yùbèi	v.	prepare; make ready	(3.1)
预计	yùjì	v.	estimate; calculate in advance	(9.2)
欲盖弥彰	yù gài mí zhāng		try to cover up a misdeed only to make it more conspicuous	(8.2)
冤枉	yuānwang	v.	treat (someone) unfairly; wrong (someone)	(1.2)
原话	yuán huà	n.	original words	(4.2)
原谅	yuánliàng	v.	forgive; pardon	(5.3)
原料	yuánliào	n.	raw material; unprocessed material	(6.1)
原委	yuánwěi	n.	the whole story; all the details	(10.2)
原先	yuánxiān	adv.	从前，former; previous	(5.1)
原形毕露	yuán xíng bì lù		show one's true colors; be revealed for what one really is	(8.3)
原原本本	yuán yuán běn běn	adv.	exactly as it is	(5.4)
原则	yuánzé	n.	principle	(10.3)
怨	yuàn	v.	怪，blame; complain	(7.3)
约	yuē	v.	make an appointment; arrange	(8.1)
运气	yùnqi	v.	luck; fortune	(9.4)
晕	yūn	v.	dizzy	(7.1)
砸	zá	v.	smash; pound	(4.2)
栽	zāi	v.	plant; grow	(8.3)
在场	zàichǎng	v.	be on the scene; be present	(2.1)
在乎	zàihu	v.	care; mind	(8.4)
在意	zàiyì	v.	take notice of; mind; take to heart	(3.2)
咱俩	zán liǎ		(col.) 咱们两个，two of us	(1.3)
攒钱	zǎn qián	vo.	save money	(6.2)

暂且	zànqiě	adv.	for the moment；temporarily；for the time being	(2.2)
糟蹋	zāo•tà	v.	waste；ruin	(1.4)
早餐	zǎocān	n.	breakfast	(8.1)
早点	zǎodiǎn	n.	breakfast；morning snack	(1.1)
早有耳闻	zǎo yǒu ěr wén		heard about (it) long ago	(7.1)
造谣	zào yáo	vo.	cook up a story；spread a rumor	(4.3)
贼	zéi	n.	thief	(3.1)
怎么回事	zěnme huí shì		What's the matter? What's happened?	(5.3)
怎么了	zěnme le		Why did you say this? What's up?	(4.1)
怎么着	zěnme zhe		(col.) 不管怎么样，no matter what	(1.3)
咋	zǎ	pron.	(col.) 怎么，为什么，how, why	(5.2)
咋样	zǎyàng	pron.	(col.) 怎么样，How about that?	(6.1)
扎得慌	zhā de huang	vc.	prickly	(3.1)
扎堆儿	zhā duīr	vo.	hang out with a group of people	(8.1)
炸弹	zhàdàn	n.	bomb；bombshell；crump	(10.2)
炸薯条儿	zhá shǔtiáor	n.	french fries	(8.1)
蘸	zhàn	v.	dip	(6.1)
占	zhàn	v.	occupy；take	(3.3)
张口	zhāng kǒu	vo.	talk；open one's mouth	(3.3)
账	zhàng	n.	account	(6.2)
招	zhāo	v.	provoke sb.	(1.1)
招	zhāo	v.	beckon；invite	(3.4)
招来	zhāo lai	vc.	invite (thief, problems, disaster, etc.)	(7.2)
着火	zháohuǒ	v.	生气，get angry (as used in this context)	(4.2)
召开	zhàokāi	v.	be in session (of a meeting)；convene	(4.3)
照看	zhàokàn	v.	look after；attend to	(5.3)
照样	zhàoyàng	adv.	as before；in the same way；all the same	(4.2)

照应	zhàoying	v.	look after; take care of	(5.1)
肇事	zhàoshì	v.	cause trouble; create a disturbance	(2.1)
遮羞布	zhēxiūbù	n.	fig leaf; something used to cover one's embarrassment	(10.1)
折磨	zhé•mó	v.	torment; persecute; excruciate	(8.3)
折腾	zhēteng	v.	(col.) spend freely; take financial risks (as used in this context)	(1.1)
折腾	zhēteng	v.	(col.) do sth. repeatedly; toss from side to side	(1.2)
哲学	zhéxué	n.	philosophy	(10.3)
这片（儿）	zhè piànr		this area (= this neighborhood)	(1.1)
侦缉	zhēnjī	v.	detective	(3.1)
振奋	zhènfèn	v.	be inspired with enthusiasm	(10.1)
镇定	zhèndìng	adj.	calm, cool, composed	(8.3)
镇静剂	zhènjìngjì	n.	sedative; tranquilizer	(8.3)
震	zhèn	v.	quake; shake	(4.3)
挣开	zhèng kāi	vc.	struggle to get free	(2.4)
拯救	zhěngjiù	v.	救, save; rescue	(10.3)
整	zhěng	adv.	exactly; no less no more (of money)	(4.3)
整天	zhěng tiān	adv.	all day long; all the time	(1.1)
正	zhèng	adj.	"正当" legitimate; proper, 那路正? Is that a legitimate way (of getting money)?	(9.2)
正常	zhèngcháng	adj.	normal, regular	(10.1)
正经	zhèngjing	adj.	serious (work-related)	(2.2)
正事儿	zhèng shìr		one's proper business or duty	(9.1)
正眼	zhèngyǎn		look squarely; look (someone) in the eye	(10.3)
正宗	zhèngzōng	adj.	genuine; orthodox	(4.1)
证件	zhèngjiàn	n.	credentials; papers	(2.1)
证据	zhèngjù	n.	evidence; proof	(1.1)

证明	zhèngmíng	n.	prove	(8.3)
证人	zhèng·rén	n.	witness	(2.2)
政治	zhèngzhì	n.	politics	(8.2)
枝	zhī	m.	(for flower)	(1.2)
支票	zhīpiào	n.	(of bank) check	(6.2)
知识分子	zhīshi fènzǐ	n.	intellectual; intelligentsia	(10.1)
直播	zhíbō	n.	live broadcast (on TV, radio, etc.)	(6.4)
直销	zhíxiāo	v.	direct sale	(7.1)
值班	zhí bān	vo.	be on duty (in turn)	(2.2)
值钱	zhíqián	adj.	costly; valuable	(1.4)
职称	zhíchēng	n.	title of a technical or professional post	(10.1)
职工	zhígōng	n.	staff and workers	(6.1)
止	zhǐ	v.	stop; 不止一回 more than once	(9.1)
指日可待	zhǐ rì kě dài		(something) can be expected soon, (see note 15)	(8.1)
指桑骂槐	zhǐ sāng mà huái		make oblique accusations, see note 7	(7.3)
制造	zhìzào	v.	make; manufacture; produce	(6.4)
治病	zhì bìng	vo.	treat illness	(1.2)
中	zhōng		(Northern dialect) 好，行，all right; fine	(6.1)
中举	zhòng jǔ	vo.	(see note 2)	(10.2)
中意	zhòng yì	adj.	be to someone's liking; catch one's fancy	(8.3)
忠诚	zhōngchéng		faithful; loyal	(10.3)
钟点	zhōngdiǎn	n.	hour	(7.1)
钟点工	zhōngdiǎngōng	n.	hourly paid worker	(7.1)
种	zhǒng	n.	seed, sperm	(8.3)
众目睽睽	zhòng mù kuíkuí		under the gaze of people; in the public eye; stared at by a lot of people, (see note 11)	(8.2)

重点学校	zhòngdiǎn xuéxiào		key school	(5.2)
周到	zhōudào	adj.	thoughtful; considerate	(4.2)
咒	zhòu	v.	curse; put a curse on (sb.)	(6.1)
抓起来	zhuā qilai	vc.	arrest	(4.3)
抓（时间）	zhuā (shíjiān)	v.	find (the time) (to do sth.)	(7.2)
专著	zhuānzhù	n.	monograph, book on a special subject	(10.1)
转	zhuàn	v.	move around	(1.1)
装	zhuāng	v.	install	(1.3)
装出来的	zhuāng chulai de		put on an act; feign an act, act out	(10.3)
装修	zhuāngxiū	v.	fix up; remodel	(4.2)
撞	zhuàng	v.	strike; run into; bump into	(2.1)
撞上	zhuàng shang	vc.	locked up; 锁上	(3.1)
追	zhuī	v.	chase (run) after; pursuing	(2.4)
准	zhǔn	adv.	(col.) definitely; certainly	(1.4)
准许	zhǔnxǔ	av.	permit; allow	(5.2)
着地	zháo dì	vo.	land; touch down	(4.3)
姿势	zīshì	n.	posture; gesture (of the body)	(3.2)
自个儿	zìgěr	pron.	自己, oneself; by oneself	(7.1)
自杀	zìshā	v.	commit suicide; take one's own life	(10.2)
自首	zìshǒu	v.	(of a criminal) voluntarily surrender oneself; give oneself up	(2.4)
自我表扬	zìwǒ biǎoyáng		自己表扬自己, self-praise	(1.1)
自责	zìzé	v	blame oneself	(10.3)
自知之明	zì zhī zhī míng		self-knowledge; know oneself	(10.1)
自尊心	zìzūnxīn	n.	self-respect; self-esteem	(3.4)
自作自受	zì zuò zì shòu		suffer from one's own actions	(6.3)
总闸	zǒng zhá	n.	main switch	(3.2)
纵容	zòngróng	v.	connive; wink at	(8.2)

走廊	zǒuláng	n.	corridor; passageway	(10.3)
揍	zòu	v.	打，beat; hit; strike	(8.3)
足协	zúxié	n.	Soccer Association	(9.2)
足足	zúzú	adv.	fully; no less than	(7.2)
嘴	zuǐ	n.	mouth	(8.3)
嘴巴子	zuǐbàzi	n.	嘴，mouth	(10.1)
罪	zuì	n.	crime; guilt	(1.1)
昨儿	zuór	t.	(col.) 昨天，yesterday	(1.2)
左邻右舍	zuǒ lín yòu shè	n.	neighbor（same as "邻居"）	(5.4)
琢磨	zuómo	v.	想，ponder; think over	(1.3)
作证	zuò zhèng	vo.	testify; give evidence; bear witness	(2.4)
做人	zuò rén	vo.	conduct oneself; behave	(7.3)
作证	zuò zhèng	vo.	testify; give evidence; bear witness	(2.4)

附录二：注释索引 Notes Index

阿 Q	(10.3)
巴不得	(4.2)
八字还没有一撇儿呢	(8.3)
把门的	(3.4)
半死不活的	(1.1)
背过气去	(9.2)
本家	(9.3)
笔杆子	(10.1)
便宜他了	(4.3)
别冻着了	(2.3)
别开	(3.1)
搏	(3.1)
不地道	(10.2)
不堪一击	(8.3)
（软得）不行	(10.1)
不中	(6.1)
财迷心窍	(6.3)
财迷样儿啊	(1.4)
恻隐之心，人皆有之	(10.1)
掺和	(6.2)
厂家直销	(6.3)
成何体统	(8.2)
成心	(3.1)
吃（个）哑巴亏	(6.3)
吃里爬外	(7.2)
抽你	(3.2)
瞅	(8.1)

反正	(10.2)
犯得着……吗？	(7.3)
犯吃挣	(3.1)
范进中举	(10.2)
方方面面	(10.3)
放盆儿里	(3.1)
蜚短流长	(8.3)
沸沸扬扬	(8.2)
费劲巴拉的	(4.3)
风风雨雨	(7.3)
负荆请罪	(10.3)
干吗	(2.2)，(2.3)
赶到	(9.2)
敢情	(3.1)
高论	(10.1)
搁	(3.1)
搁（gé）	(3.3)
给职工谋点福利	(6.1)
狗眼看人低	(1.1)
狗咬吕洞宾，不识好人心	(7.1)
够呛	(8.1)
姑奶奶	(1.2)，(9.3)
顾名思义	(8.2)
怪	(3.1)，(7.1)
光	(2.3)
好	(9.2)
好（了五年）	(2.3)
好借好还嘛！	(6.4)

好面子	（1.2）
喝高了	（7.1）
合着	（9.2）
和事佬	（5.1）
花花肠子	（7.3）
花前月下	（8.3）
花心思	（1.4）
环路	（9.1）
患难知己	（8.4）
豁出去了	（6.3）
火	（8.1），（9.2）
火上房了	（6.4）
家长里短	（5.4）
家父	（10.1）
甲 A 联赛	（9.2）
假冒伪劣	（6.4）
煎饼馃子	（8.1）
见不得人	（2.4）
见外	（5.2）
绞尽脑汁	（10.3）
街里街坊的	（3.1）
结识	（7.3）
解铃还须系铃人	（3.4）
借愁浇酒	（8.3）
今儿	（2.2）
尽	（9.2）
救急	（6.2）
救人一命，胜造七级浮屠	（10.1）

留神	(8.4)
刘姨/刘阿姨	(7.1)
搂草打兔子，顺手的事嘛	(7.2)
马上要结婚了都	(7.1)
卖关子	(10.2)
蛮好	(5.1)
满世界	(9.1)
没本事	(2.4)
没错儿	(2.2)
没大注意	(2.1)
没劲	(3.2)
没前科	(2.2)
没有过不去的火焰山	(6.3)
门脸儿	(6.2)
蒙	(3.3)
蒙来的	(6.3)
名落孙山	(10.1)
明摆着	(2.4)
莫不是（莫非）	(9.1)
莫名其妙	(7.3)
哪成想	(6.3)
那份儿上	(7.2)
那是	(9.2)
闹出大天去	(3.4)
嫩	(2.4)
你傻什么傻呀？	(6.4)
你知道吗你？	(9.2)
蔫不出溜的	(9.2)

念旧	(1.4)
您走好	(6.1)
排叉儿	(8.1)
旁敲侧击	(7.3)
刨掉	(1.3)
赔不是	(3.1)
便宜他了	(4.3)
贫	(3.1)
贫嘴	(10.1)
起腻	(7.1)
起早贪黑	(5.2)
牵肠挂肚	(5.1)
前脚……后脚……	(3.2)
欠……情	(5.2)
强	(2.3)
亲不亲一家人	(6.4)
求爷爷告奶奶	(6.3)
情场失意，赌场得意	(3.3)
去你的	(9.2)
惹是生非	(7.1)
人言可畏	(8.2)
三缺一	(3.3)
扫……兴	(8.2)
僧多粥少	(10.3)
山盟海誓	(8.3)
闪失	(6.1)
伤筋动骨一百天	(4.3)
上档次	(1.2)

上了岁数	(8.1)
稍（副词）	(2.3)
胜败乃兵家常事	(9.3)
什么浪费不浪费的	(4.1)
手背	(3.3)
手脚不干净	(7.3)
手拿把掐	(9.4)
售票员	(9.4)
数落	(6.3)
谁跟谁呀	(4.1)，(6.1)
说什么呢	(9.2)
说曹操曹操到	(9.4)
送子娘娘	(8.3)
宋儿	(9.4)
他嚼得我心直慌跟着。	(1.2)，(9.3)
踏踏实实	(1.1)，(9.3)
抬不起头来	(5.4)
特正	(8.1)
啼笑皆非	(8.1)
剃光头	(10.1)
天地良心	(10.2)
天上掉馅儿饼	(6.1)，(10.2)
天字第一丑闻	(10.2)
添乱	(4.2)
挺	(7.2)
头几年	(2.2)
土地爷	(4.3)
忒玄乎	(6.1)

完美无缺	(8.3)
玩意儿	(3.1)
为……而……	(9.2)
唯以公心自守，毁誉在所不升；宁受人毁，也不徇人之私利。	(10.1)
未卜先知	(10.1)
我胆儿小	(9.1)
我是你孙子	(9.1)
我招谁惹谁了？	(6.3)
乌七八糟	(8.2)
屋里说吧	(7.1)
无地自容	(10.3)
无风不起浪	(4.3)
无所谓	(2.4)
洗东西呀？（打招呼）	(4.1)
瞎	(3.1)
瞎说	(2.1)
下海	(6.2)
闲杂盲流	(6.1)
线	(9.2)
向……提供（帮助、援助、情报、线索）	(2.2)
小脚侦缉队	(3.1)，(7.3)
小金库	(1.2)
小两居	(9.1)
小蹄子	(7.2)
小意思	(5.2)
心里不踏实	(6.2)
心里有鬼	(8.3)

悬	(9.3)
雪中送炭，雪上加霜	(6.4)
压根儿	(3.4)
哑巴吃黄连	(10.2)
眼睛里不揉沙子	(3.2)
眼神	(7.2)
吆五喝六	(3.3)
要不要打110	(8.3)
要不一分价钱一分货	(4.1)
噎	(3.3)
也就是	(2.1)
夜长梦多	(9.2)
一边儿待着去	(7.1)
一分钱分八半花	(6.1)
一个劲儿地	(6.2)
一世清名被玷污了	(10.2)
一手交钱一手交货	(6.1)
一准儿	(6.4)
疑神疑鬼	(8.3)
以其人之道还治其人之身	(8.3)
以小人之心度君子之腹	(8.2)
迎刃而解	(10.3)
用情不专	(8.2)
犹	(10.2)
有病	(7.1)
有口皆碑	(10.1)
有什么好的？	(2.2)
有数（心里有数）	(4.2)

有戏	（9.2）
有心栽花花不开，无心插柳柳成荫	（8.3）
有幸	（7.3）
欲盖弥彰	（8.2）
原形毕露	（8.3）
咋	（6.1），（9.2），（10.1）
在家呢（问候）	（2.2）
怎么啦？	（2.3）
怎么着	（9.1）
咱	（8.1）
扎堆儿	（8.1）
找瓶	（7.1）
找不到北	（10.2）
遮羞布	（10.1）
折腾	（1.2）
这叫（是）怎么话说的？	（3.4），（7.1）
这么着	（2.2）
这年头	（4.1）
知识分子成堆的地方	（10.2）
指日可待	（8.1）
指桑骂槐	（7.3）
众目睽睽	（8.2）
住一段	（2.4）
庄	（3.3）
装他妈什么孙子，去你的！	（7.1）
着火	（4.2）
自知之明	（10.1）
自作自受	（6.3）

走眼	(9.3)
足球的福利抽奖	(9.4)
嘴巴子	(10.1)
琢磨	(6.3)

附录三：语法索引　Grammar Notes Index

帮（量词）	(2.2)
本来	(2.3)
本来……倒……	(2.3)
（V）不起	(1.1)
补语（想不开、管得起）	(4.1)
补语：死、下、出、起、着、坏、走、好、全、断、饱、暖、清楚、给、透、下去、住、不来、说不定、过意不去	(5.4)
趁着	(8.2)
纯金的，这是	(1.2)
当＋Noun	(2.1)
倒……可……	(7.2)
倒	(5.1)
到底	(6.3)
……的	(4.1)，(5.3)
多亏（动词）	(6.2)
而	(9.4)
反问句	(3.1)
反正	(2.1)
够……的了	(1.1)
好	(5.1)
好歹	(7.3)
还	(8.1)
还	(8.2)
"还"用于反问	(4.1)
换什么换	(1.2)
回（量词）	(2.2)
基本（上）	(2.4)

简直	(8.1)
尽快（早）	(2.4)
就	(5.1)
均	(2.1)
忙着做饭	(5.3)
没什么钱	(1.1)
明明	(7.2)
其实	(6.2)
声（动量词）	(2.1)
实在	(6.4)
是（表示肯定）	(6.3)
（像）……似的	(7.1)
俗了吧唧的	(1.1)
索性	(3.1)
挺	(6.2)
桶（量词）	(2.1)
万一	(6.2)
为（wéi）	(2.4)
无害	(2.3)
一下	(2.4)
以	(6.4)
又	(8.2)
再 adj，……还/也……	(4.1)
者	(2.1)
至于	(7.1)
中文口语句子常常不用连词	(2.3)
着呢	(7.2)